Research Methods in Education

Research Methods in Education

Dr. Radha Mohan
former *Reader* in Education (Physical Science)
Stella Matutina College of Education
Chennai.
Principal
Rajalakshmi College of Education
Thandalam.

Foreword

Prof. E.G. Parameswaran
Former Dean
Faculties of Psychology, Management & Education
Osmania University
Hyderabad.

NEELKAMAL PUBLICATIONS PVT. LTD.
EDUCATIONAL PUBLISHERS
(EXPORTERS & IMPORTERS)
NEW DELHI HYDERABAD

RESEARCH METHODS IN EDUCATION

Dr. Radha Mohan

Foreword

Prof. E.G. Parameswaran

Edition : 2017
(Hardback)

ISBN : 978-81-8316-217-3

NEELKAMAL PUBLICATIONS PVT. LTD.
Sultan Bazar, Hyderabad - 500 095.
✆ 24757140, 24757197, 24757951, +91 80199-18182

Delhi Office:
4764/1, 23, Ansari Road, Daryaganj, New Delhi-110 002,
✆ 011-23244237, +91 98118-28953
e-mail : neelkamalbooks@gmail.com
website : www.neelkamalbooks.com

Published by ***Suresh Chandra Sharma*** for
Neelkamal Publications Pvt.Ltd., New Delhi, Hyderabad
and printed at ***Sri Vinayaka Art Printers***, Hyderabad, India.

Prof. E.G. Parameswaran
Former Dean
Faculties of Psychology, Management & Education
Osmania University
Hyderabad.

Foreword

Today's society is very often referred to as a knowledge-based society. This does not mean that earlier societies were not guided by knowledge. They were mostly guided by knowledge acquired reactively, incidentally or intuitively. Yet another source was knowledge, based on the vision and testimony of a few. As against this the emphasis today is on knowledge obtained through deliberate, well-planned and well-designed scientific investigation and very often this knowledge is proactive.

It is no wonder, therefore, that research is assuming increasing importance. While, research-based knowledge has been a part of the study and pursuit in the exact sciences and natural sciences, it is only more recently that social sciences, including education, have begun to be guided by such scientific research. This is more true of education where thought and practice for a long time remained dominated by the views of a few educationalists. Today, developments in education as a field of knowledge and practice rely on scientific empirical research and this trend is bound to grow. Such a situation has led to increasing importance that is being attached to providing sound training both conceptual and practical, including analytical skills to researchers in education. This, of course, necessitates well-written books. While there have been a number of books on research methods in the fields of social and behavioural sciences, there have been very few in the field of education. In this context Dr.Radha Mohan's attempt to bring out this volume is timely and welcome.

The volume is comprehensive in its coverage and provides adequate introduction and grounding both on the conceptual planning side of research and also the practical aspects of data collection and analysis. The adoption of the modular approach is something distinct. The sequencing of the chapters is in a logical order and follows the track which students will have to follow in their journey through their researches.

Indication of professionalism and scientific temper in educational research has become not only an absolute must but an urgent necessity. This book is a positive effort in that direction. Dr. Radha Mohan has my appreciation as well as good wishes.

– *Prof. E.G. Parameswaran*

Preface to the Second Edition

This second edition has been written keeping in mind rapid changes in today's world. It includes new sections within chapters besides:

- Better illustrations of the Scientific Approach in Chapter I.
- Clearer explanations for problem definition and statement of Research Questions (Chapter 2).
- Several examples with exhibits to make clear basic concepts in Chapter 3 on Hypotheses.
- A more comprehensive chapter on Review of Related Literature given the expanding use of Internet.

Extensive use of flowcharts have been made right through the book to help the reader understand the key concepts at a glance besides making it easy for relating various stages of the research process to one another.

I trust these changes have improved the textbook. I look forward to feedback from you.

Preface

The main purpose of writing this PRIMER on "Research Methods in Education" is to meet the felt need for a practitioner's guide for students of research in education. Therefore the objective of this book is to provide a framework for student researchers:

i. to understand and appreciate earlier attempts and outcomes and more importantly

ii. to plan and conduct research on their own with optimum effort and confidence.

The integral Modular Presentation of 5Ps (Purpose, Platform, Process, Pathway and Pronounce) – covering 12 Chapters sets forth the necessary basic course plan to potential researchers as follows:

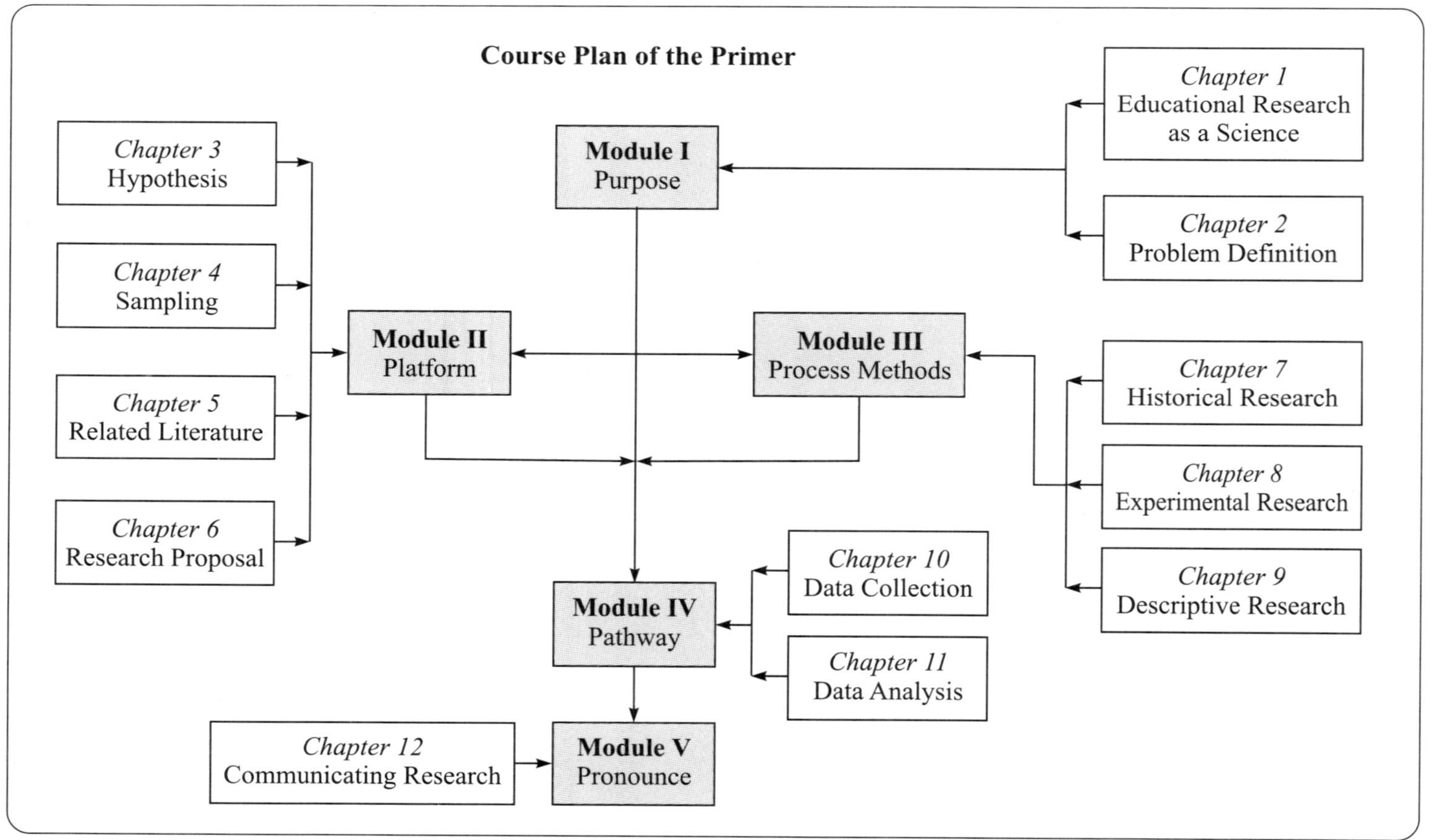
Course Plan of the Primer
Chapter 3
Hypothesis
Chapter 4
Sampling
Chapter 5
Related Literature
Chapter 6
Research Proposal
Module I
Purpose
Module II
Platform
Module III
Process Methods
Chapter 1
Educational Research as a Science
Chapter 2
Problem Definition
Chapter 7
Historical Research
Chapter 8
Experimental Research
Chapter 9
Descriptive Research
Chapter 10
Data Collection
Chapter 11
Data Analysis
Module IV
Pathway
Chapter 12
Communicating Research
Module V
Pronounce

The purpose of this primer would be met if it could motivate and facilitate students of research, particularly in the challenging field of Education, to adopt and adapt a structured approach in selection of all aspects of Research Design, Methods and Measurements, an informed choice which best fits their "Research Problem" on hand. Therefore the essential need for an approach necessary for balancing the aspects of accuracy, and correlation on the one hand with inputs (data collection analysis) and expected outcome on the other, is brought out in this process.

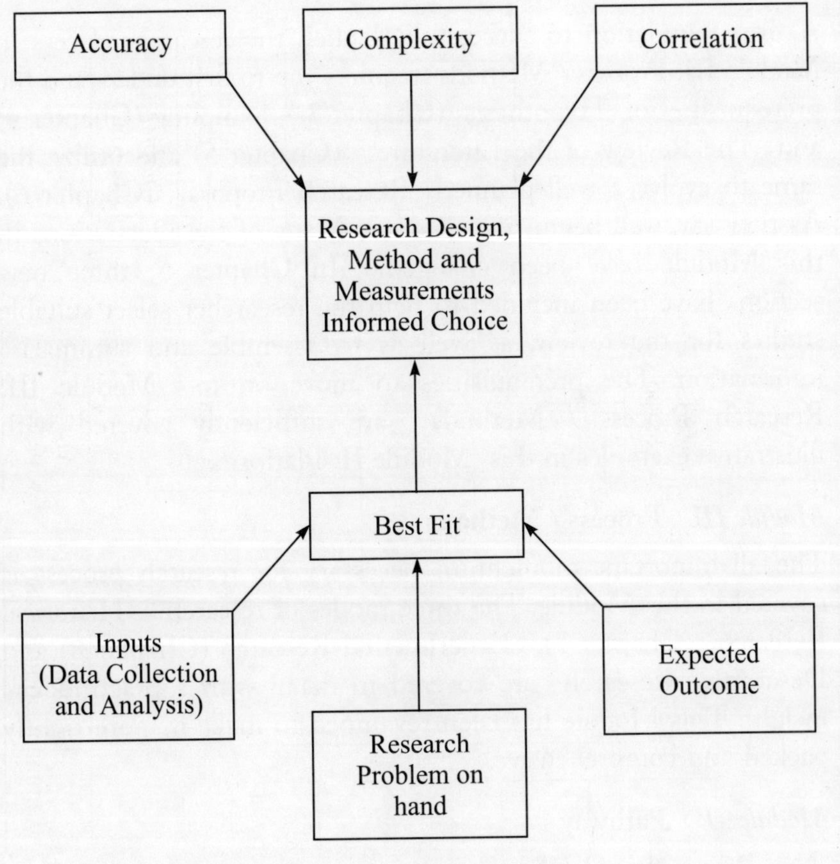

The balanced approach necessary for the above aspects is emphasised and brought out in this Primer.

The Five modules are set forth as follows:

Module I **Purpose**

Chapter 1 on "Educational Research: Its Nature and Characteristics "provides the background to move on to Chapter 2 on "Problem Definition". The ethical considerations necessary for carrying out educational research has been included in Chapter 1 of this edition. Then the necessary launch pad to start your research journey is provided in Module II: Platform.

Module II **Platform**

A firm foundation to successfully launch the research process in Module III: Process / Methods requires you to first understand the prerequisities of Hypothesis (Chapter 3), Sampling (Chapter 4) and The Review of the Literature (Chapter 5) and utilize the same to evolve a well-planned Research Proposal (Chapter 6). As they say, well begun is half done. Many of the illustrations in this Module have been changed. In Chapter 5, three new sections have been included to help the researcher select suitable studies for the review, as well as to assemble and summarise information. The prerequisities to move on to Module III: Research Process / Methods are sufficiently covered with illustrative examples in this Module II: Platform.

Module III **Process / Methods**

The all-important momentum necessary for research process is covered in this Module. The three modes of research - Historical Research (Chapter 7), Experimental Research (Chapter 8) and Descriptive Research are covered in detail with a practitioner's insight. This Module has been revamped to make it more tightly packed and comprehensive.

Module IV **Pathway**

"No Pain, No Gain". The painstaking pathway of Data Collection (Chapter 10) and Data Analysis (Chapter 11) is effectively chartered out for you in this Module. This should guide you securely and provide sufficient impetus through the most difficult part of your research efforts, in an economical, efficient and effective manner. A section on SPSS has been included to develop awareness of the ease of doing one's own statistical analysis.

You have to necessarily put in efforts to climb the mount and reach the peak since nothing ventured is nothing gained.

Module V **Pronounce**

Finally Module V provides useful tips for pronouncing and communicating your research finding succinctly (Chapter 12).

Thus the 5 Ps of Purpose, Platform, Process, Pathway and Pronounce provide the basic framework of the above Integral Modular Presentation in this Primer, within which the 12 chapters are coherently interwoven, guiding students of research embarking on their research journey.

Sufficient stress has also been laid on the theoretical / conceptual aspects necessary to understand the subject. Thus the book serves the dual purpose of serving both as the text-book for the students, and initiating them to effortlessly practise research thereafter.

All Chapters have been updated with latest references and web addresses given. Several illustrations, examples, graphs have also been changed.

According to Alvin Toffler:

"The illiterate of the 21st Century will not be those who cannot read and write, but those who cannot learn, unlearn and relearn".

Acknowledgements

I would like to acknowledge with gratitude:

- Colleagues from widely diversified academic disciplines in colleges and universities who volunteered valuable suggestions and critiques for incorporation in this revised edition.
- My mentor, the esteemed retired Professor and Head, University of Madras, Dr. P.S. Balasubramaniam for constantly updating me and forcing me to keep reading.
- My doctoral students who with their myriad questions have helped me think more clearly on several topics in research methods.
- My husband, Shri S. Mohan Kumar, who has over the years encouraged me to read, read and read … by borrowing and buying me excellent and rare books.
- My publisher, Shri Suresh Chandra Sharma, Managing Director, Neelkamal Publications Pvt. Ltd. for encouraging me to update and revise the first edition.

Thank you!! Without you, this revision would not have been possible.

– *Radha Mohan*

Research Methods in Education

Contents

❖ ❖ ❖

List of Exhibits

List of Tables

Educational Research Its Nature and Characteristics

1.0 Introduction

Human beings always studied their world but have often seemed to study distant things like astronomy before they studied their own society. A crucial question in social science is what constitutes the proper understanding of society, and how that understanding can be achieved. Krathwohl (1985) deals with those issues in depth. Among the points he emphasizes are the ways in which one's orientation to knowledge affects the research methods used and the different criteria utilized by researchers with different orientations.

Wilhelm Dilthey, a nineteenth century sociologist, espoused one of the most extreme positions. He believed that humans had free will, and thus no one can predict their actions and generalize about them. In its extreme form, this view would allow only for the study of unique events and not for explanation and prediction. Thus social science, as it is generally conceived today (as an explanatory science), would be precluded.

Emile Durkheim espoused essentially the opposite view. He said that social phenomena are orderly and can be generalized, His viewpoint was based on the assumption that phenomena adhere to underlying social laws just as physical phenomena follow physical laws. In Durkheim's view, then, there was little difference between physical and natural science, and social science except for the subject matter. The logic of inquiry was essentially the same. This strict scientific view is often labeled positivism. According to Durkheim, sociologists could use the methods of natural science, such as experimentation, to study and explain social phenomena just as others used them to study physical phenomena.

Max Weber, took an intermediate approach between the two extremes proposed by Dilthey and Durkheim. According to Weber, social phenomena were not merely determined by social laws but were the product of human volitional action. Thus, the use of the methods of natural science plays a role in social research, though not an exclusive role. He advocated the use of scientific methods when they seem legitimate, followed by direct qualitative understanding of the phenomena.

1.1 The Scientific Method

A discussion of the scientific method logically begins with the foundations of rational thought processes. These include conceptualization, definition and inference. Concepts, clearly defined, are used in the inference process for building propositions, hypotheses models, theories, principles, laws and so forth. The use of concepts and definitions for the development of propositions involves a building and testing process that Dewey has referred to as "the double movement of reflective thinking". While these ideas are associated with all types of reflective thought, they are more narrowly considered here as the critical building blocks in the method of science.

The scientific method is the use of techniques or procedures to analyze empirical evidence in an attempt to confirm or disprove prior conceptions.

Empirical means that something is verifiable by observation, experimentation or experience.

Scientific method is a structured approach to solving problems. Only in this synthesis does the scientific method exist. It must be that general model which is used in different ways as a structure of inquiry for solving different types of scientific problems. Dewey's five stages for the act of problem solving, in his analysis of reflective thinking, have been widely used as a basis for steps in the scientific method. By 1933 the five aspects of reflective thought that were mentioned earlier had developed into (1) suggestion (2) intellectualization (3) the guiding idea, hypothesis (4) reasoning (in the narrower sense) and (5) testing the hypothesis by action.

The primary goal of science is to understand – to understand all of the problems that perplex humans. The scientific method may be reduced to a set of rules, accepted by scholars, that is used to explain phenomena through systematic pursuit of knowledge. It provides a vehicle to extend and test what common sense provides as explanation to problems.

1.2 A Scientific Approach – Seven Steps

Moving from the general model to a specific example, a scientific approach to solving problems could be structured in seven steps:

1. A felt difficulty
2. Problem identification
3. Information
4. Hypothesis
5. Experimentation and / or observation
6. Conclusions
7. Replication

Let us now turn our attention to each one of these parts in isolation.

- **A felt difficulty.** The process is set in motion by a doubt, barrier, or an experience that causes bewilderment. The way to an end or goal may be blocked. An unexpected or unexplained event may result in a perplexity.

- **Problem identification.** This phase focusses the difficulty under study so that the problem is clearly recognized. It is limited so that the expanse of the study is brought into focus for the investigator and others interested in the same area. The problem is usually phrased in the form of a question. The answer to that question becomes the subject of the study.
- **Information.** The first search for the answer should be made within present knowledge. If the answer is found to the satisfaction of the investigator, of course, this is the terminal phase of the process. If the answer is not found in present knowledge, closely related information gives a background for further study and development of hypothesis.
- **Hypothesis.** If the answer is not found in present knowledge the most logically developed proposed answer is stated as a hypothesis. The hypothesis is stated in a declarative sentence and serves as an explanation to be tested by vigorous investigation. The hypothesis is formed inductively as a generalization. It serves as a major premise to be deductively tested by empirical means.
- **Experimentation and / or observation.** A well-developed design is produced to collect, organize, and analyze data pertinent to the question under study. The results will be organized as information to reach a decision about the tenability of the research hypothesis.
- **Conclusions.** The results are used as bases for the conclusions of the study. The researcher interprets the meaning of the results as it relates to the problem under study. This phase will (1) verify and support the hypothesis and, in turn, any theory that it is linked to, (2) cause the researcher to reject the hypothesis as untenable, or (3) bring about a modification of the hypothesis to be tested with new data.
- **Replication.** The hypothesis should be retested using new data gathered from the same design. Retesting a hypothesis under different conditions of time, location, and / or other factors will strengthen the value of the original results if the same outcome is observed. If a different outcome is found it may indicate (1) a

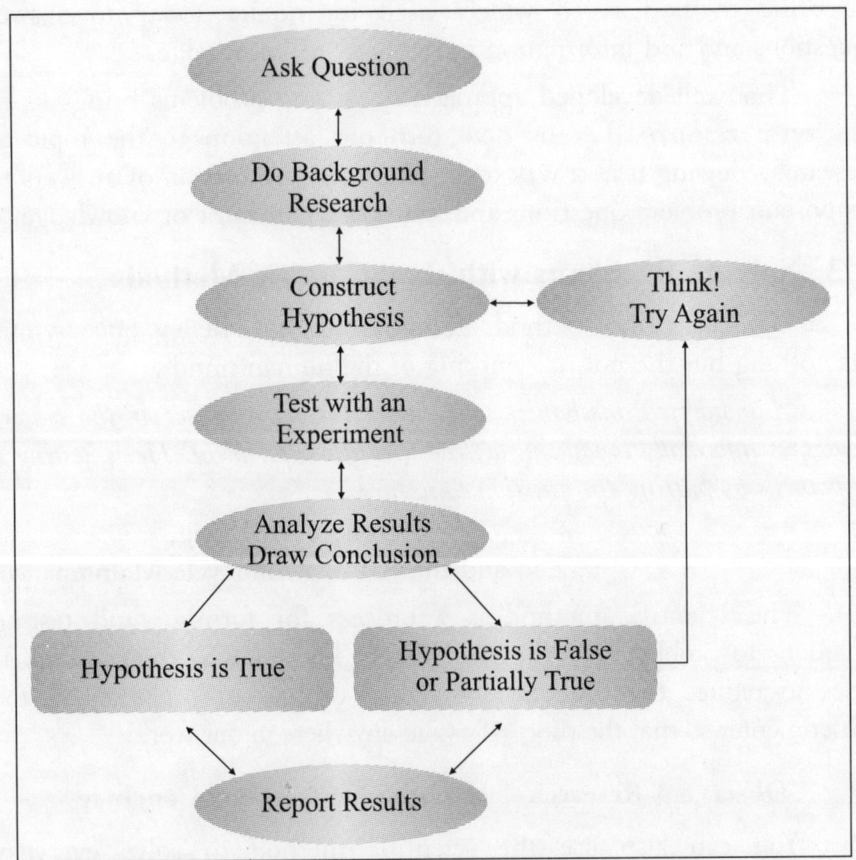

Exhibit 1.1: Research process

previous wrong decision. (2) the hypothesis does not hold under different conditions, or (3) the hypothesis is now invalid. The pooling of the results of many studies will provide data that is reliable. If the same study is conducted fifty different times with different subjects and the same outcome is found forty-seven times, it is likely that the supported outcome would be difficult to debate. The tendency to let one study stand alone as testimony causes this phase to be often overlooked.

The scientific method depends on a problem to make it work. Without the problem, there is no scientific method. The use of the hypothesis allows the researcher to develop a clear idea of a possible answer to his or her questions, and permits him or her to exclude part of the problem – solving activities (Exhibit 1.1). This is why the scientific method is so widely used in inquiry today to answer questions and add information to the body of knowledge.

This well-developed approach to solving problems brings us to the term ***research***. Let us now turn our attention to the topic of research, viewing it as a way to structure the production of answers to important problem questions and, thus, as a generator of knowledge.

1.3 Solving Problems with the Scientific Method

"The scientific method," Thomas Henry Huxley once wrote, "is nothing but the normal working of the human mind".

"A motorcycle mechanic, who honks the horn to see if the battery works, is informally conducting a true scientific experiment. He is testing a hypothesis by putting the question to nature."

Robert M. Pirsig,
Zen and the Art of Motorcycle Maintenance

The scientific method is a process for forming and testing solutions to problems, or theorizing about how or why things work. It tries to reduce the influence of "faith" or bias or prejudice of the experimenter so that the process is valid anywhere in our world.

Observe * Research * Hypothesize * Test * Conclude

You can also use the scientific method to solve everyday problems! If the lights go out in your residence, you can guess many reasons for it: you didn't pay your electricity bill, there was a storm that knocked out power, the toaster, the air conditioner, microwave overloaded a circuit, etc.

1. Look for the options or possibilities (research),
2. Select the best explanation (form a hypothesis),
3. Test it, and
4. Form a conclusion or theory.

If you think the toaster, the air conditioner, and the microwave were the answer, you can repeat this condition, and predict the outcome (experiment or test your theory). If paying your bill was the problem, you can repeat that also, but it can be expensive.

The basic framework for the scientific method envisages that you state the problem and observe conditions (Exhibit 1.2).

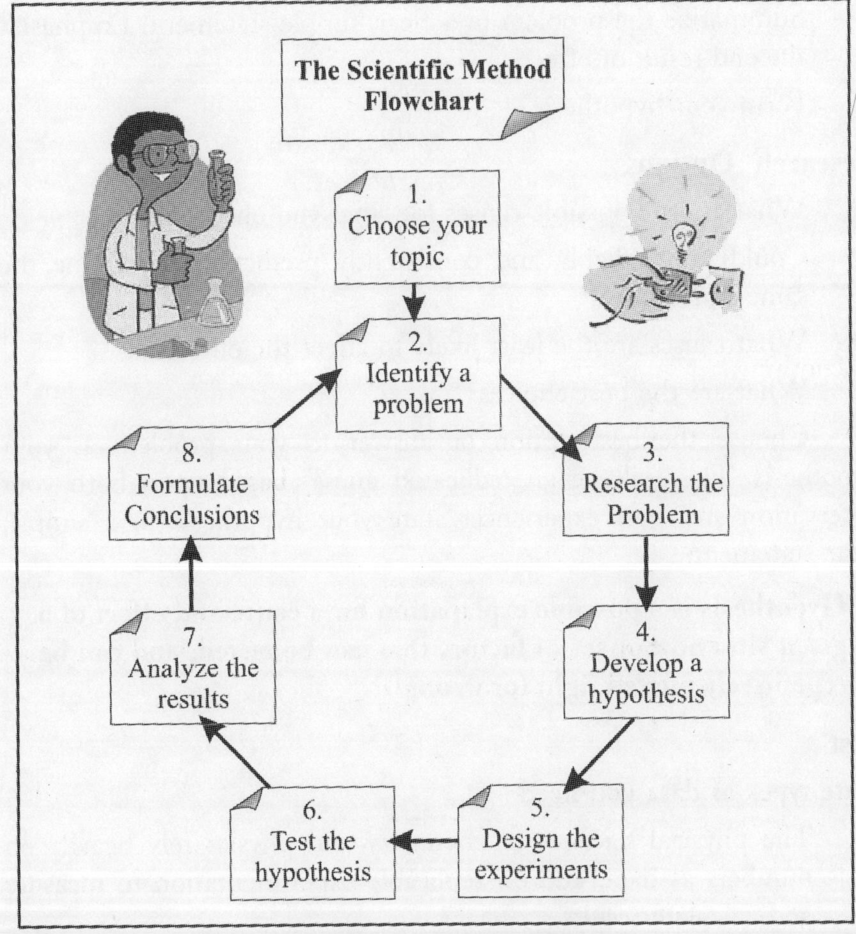

Exhibit 1.2: Scientific method

You observe or wonder about something in your world, or in your class, and wonder **how, why, when**, something occurs or does not occur.

— Create a short, meaningful title of your project
— Write a statement of purpose that describes what you want to do
— Make a careful, step-by-step notation of your observations.
— Be objective! Do not guess why something is happening. That takes place later.
— Gather information on similar research. This is a literature review.
— Identify significant conditions or factors of the situation.

— Summarize the problem in a clear, simple statement. Emphasize the end result or effect.

— Form your hypothesis

Research Options

- What are the possible causes for what you observed?
- Could they reliably and consistently predict or determine the same outcome?
- What causes are the least likely to affect the outcome?
- What are the best choices?

Choose the best option or answer to your problem as your hypothesis. This will be an "educated guess" based upon both your observation and past experiences.State your hypothesis in a simple, clear statement.

Hypothesis is a possible explanation for a cause and effect of a given situation or set of factors that can be tested, and can be repetitively proved right (or wrong!)

Test

State types of data you need

- The physical sciences of chemistry and physics rely heavily on numbers as data, and on replicable experimentation to measure and calculate results.
- Sciences such as sociology rely on interviews and observation due to limitations on experimentation with human subjects, and use descriptions and inferences to arrive at results.

Design an experiment to test your hypothesis

- Make a step-by-step procedure with each step's purpose
- List and obtain materials and equipment you will need
- Identify two groups in the test:
  The control group is your reference point; no variables are changed. The experimental group is the focus of changes to affect the outcome. Rely on your past experience to identify variables, but consult with a knowledgeable person for a second opinion.

Run a Series of Experiments

- Change only one variable in each experiment in order to isolate effects reliably
- Make and record accurate measurements
- Repeat the test as often as necessary with the experimental group to verify your results. Always change only one thing, or variable, in each test
- Repeat successful tests with other groups to verify your findings.

Draw Conclusions

- Summarize your results and conclusions
- Use graphs and tables to illustrate these.
- Refer back to your observations, data, and hypothesis for consistency.
- Note difficulties and problems, items for further research, or what you would do differently if you could.

If you did not prove your hypothesis, you have succeeded in another sense!

Unsuccessful Experiments

- Provide information that can lead to answers by eliminating options.
- Spare someone the trouble of repeating your experiments
- Suggest other ways of solving similar problems.

Common Mistakes

- The hypothesis is assumed to be the answer and is not supported with testing.
- Data that does not support your outcome is ignored
- Beliefs/bias blind you to major flaws in the testing phase
- Systematic errors are not noticed and are repeated within each experiment. These bias the outcome's standard deviation.
- Equipment or conditions are not adequate.

Websites for scientific method

http://en.wikipedia.org/wiki/Scientific_method

http://www.scientificmethod.com/

1.4 What Research Is

The taxonomy associates the "need to know" with inquiry procedures (research) that have as their major purpose the creation of generally applicable knowledge. There is agreement on contemporary definitions of research that research procedures are problem – solving methodologies designed to add to present knowledge.

Research is the systematic process of collecting and analyzing information to increase our understanding of the phenomenon under study. It is the function of the researcher to contribute to the understanding of the phenomenon and to communicate that understanding to others.

Paul Leedy defines *research as the manner in which we solve knotty problems in our attempt to push back the frontiers of human ignorance.*

McGrath says *research is a process (tool) which has utility only to the extent that the class of inquiry employed as the research activity vehicle is capable of adding knowledge, of stimulating progress and of helping society and man relate more efficiently and effectively to the problems that society and man perpetuate and create.*

In summary then, an operationally useful (though not rationally perfect) definition of research can be given: Research is the activity of solving problems which leads to new knowledge using methods of inquiry which are currently accepted as adequate by scholars in the field.

Kerlinger reluctantly "attempts" a definition of scientific research as *systematic, controlled, empirical, and critical investigation of hypothetical propositions about the presumed relations among natural phenomena.*

The following synthesis of current views of research provides the definition of research used in this book:

Research is structured inquiry that (1) utilizes acceptable scientific methodology to solve problems, and (2) creates new generally applicable knowledge.

The taxonomy in Exhibit 1.3 is designed to show the relationships among problem-solving strategies and, at the same time, to point out the differences. Readers will find it helpful to study

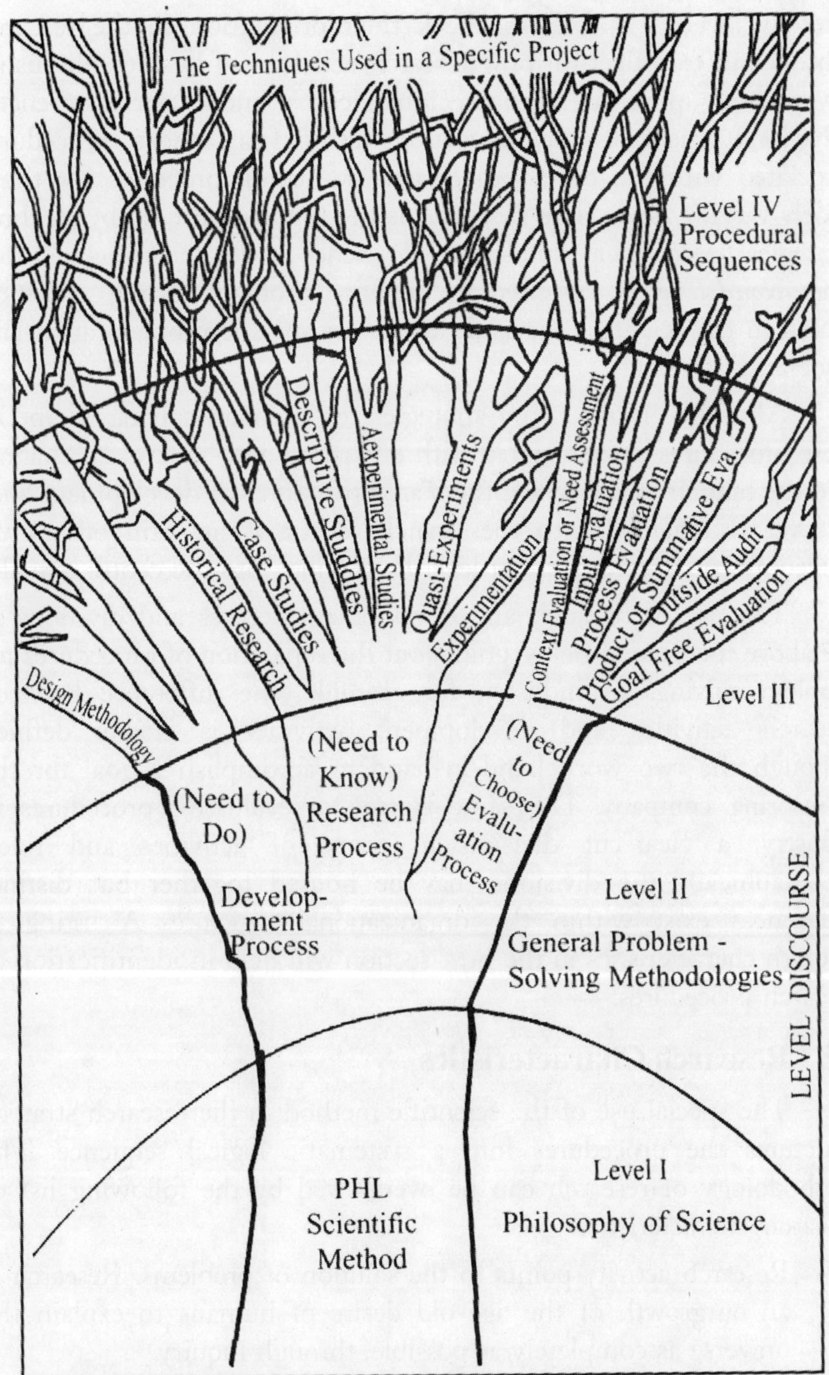

Exhibit 1.3: Taxonomy of problem-solving strategies

carefully levels I and II to check their orientation to the research process and to reflect on how research activities of business, industry, government, physical sciences, biological sciences, social sciences, behavioral sciences, and education differ from those procedures associated with the development and evaluation processes for those widely varying fields. The ***first level*** is the foundation used by all three strategies based on a philosophy of science – the scientific method. The ***second level*** is designed to organize problem-solving activities, rooted in the scientific method, into more specific problem areas and associated strategies.

All fields utilize many strategies for problem-solving. Some of these procedures are associated with evaluation and, at level II, channel into the branch to the left. Others are procedures of development and, at level II, channel into the branch to the right, Still others are procedures of research and, at level II, channel into the centre branch.

The use of research and development centres and divisions in the above mentioned fields' points out the separation of procedures for problem solving. In industry, for example, the difference between research activities and development activities is clearly defined although the two work hand-in-hand to accomplish a goal for the sponsoring company. The same is true of evaluative procedures in industry: a clear-cut division in terms of activities and roles. Geographically the divisions may be housed together but distinct differences exist within the organizational structure. A listing of research characteristics in the next section will help in identification of research procedures.

1.5 Research Characteristics

The special use of the scientific method in the research strategy structures the procedures into a systematic logical sequence. The methodology of research can be overviewed by the following list of research characteristics.

- Research activity points to the solution of problems. Research is an outgrowth of the age-old desire of humans to explain the universe as completely as possible, through inquiry.
- Research is conducted only after all other sources of answers have been exhaustively examined. There is no need to engage in

it if the proposed question has been answered to the satisfaction of the questioner, and is currently available in present knowledge.

— The research process is directed to problems based on a "need to know." The research role does not include problems based in formative or summative evaluation or problems based on development of tools, programmes and procedures.

— Research deals with the main problem through suitable sub-problems.

— Research processes study presumed relations among natural phenomena. Studies are designed to either (1) establish relationships and/or (2) study observed relationships for the cause-effect direction between or among variables.

— Research is used to test hypotheses – the more important of which are tied to a general theory. The hypothesis is used to bridge the gap between the generalizations proposed by inductive investigation and the testing of the generalization by the deductive process.

— Research findings add to knowledge by providing new knowledge. Communicating already existing knowledge is not to be considered as a research activity.

— Research is an orderly investigation that provides outcomes that withstand criticism of persons in the field. Findings should be free of legitimate attack by knowledgeable colleagues. The procedures are reported in detail so that the findings are subject to the reactions as a check against the investigator consciously or unconsciously committing human errors. All parts of the research activities connected to the inquiry are open to scrutiny by experts.

— Research can be thought of as a chain of reasoning, starting at problem formulation through investigation to finding. The total process from problem isolation to the addition of new knowledge is a logically structured inquiry into some well-defined problem.

— Research is circular. Research always gives rise to further unexplored questions. As Leedy states, "Every researcher soon learns that he creates more problems than he resolves."

1.6 Criteria for Good Research

1. ***The purpose of the research, or the problem involved, should be clearly defined and sharply delineated in terms as unambiguous as possible.***

The statement of the research problem should include analysis into its simplest elements, its scope and limitations, and precise specifications of the meanings of all words significant to the research. Failure of the researcher to do this adequately may raise legitimate doubts in the minds of readers as to whether the researcher has sufficient understanding of the problem to make a sound attack upon it.

2. ***The research procedures used should be described in sufficient detail to permit another researcher to repeat the research.***

Excepting when secrecy is imposed in the national interest, research reports should reveal with candour the sources of data and the means by which they were obtained. Omission of significant procedural details makes it difficult or impossible to estimate the validity and reliability of the data and justifiably weakens the confidence of the reader in research.

3. ***The procedural design of the research should be carefully planned to yield results that are as objective as possible.***

When a sampling of a population is involved, the report should include evidence concerning the degree of representativeness of the sample. A questionnaire ought not to be used when more reliable evidence is available from documentary sources or by direct observation. Bibliographic searches should be as thorough and complete as possible. Experiments should have satisfactory controls. Direct observation should be recorded in writing as soon as possible after the event. Efforts should be made to minimize the influence of personal bias in selecting and recording data.

4. ***The researcher should report, with complete frankness, flaws in procedural design and estimate their effect upon the findings.***

There are very few perfect research designs. Some of the imperfections may have a little effect upon the validity and reliability of the data: Others may invalidate them entirely. A competent researcher should be sensitive to the effects of imperfect design and his experience in analyzing the data should give him a basis for estimating their influence.

5. ***Analysis of the data should be adequate to reveal its significance: and the methods of analysis used should be appropriate.***

The extent to which this criterion is met is frequently a good measure of the competence of the researcher. Analysis of the data is the most difficult phase of research for the novice.

The validity and reliability of data should be checked carefully. The data should be classified in ways that assist the researcher to reach pertinent conditions. When statistical methods are used, the probability of error should be estimated and the criteria of statistical significance applied.

6. ***Conclusions should be confined to those justified by the data of the research and limited to those for which the data provides an adequate basis.***

Researchers are often tempted to broaden the basis of inductions by including personal experiences not subject to the controls under which the research data was gathered. This tends to decrease the objectivity of the research and weakens confidence in the findings.

Equally undesirable is the all-too-frequent practice of drawing conclusions from study of a limited population and applying them universally. Good researchers specify the conditions under which their conclusions seem to be valid. Failure to do so justifiably weakens confidence in the research.

7. ***Greater confidence in the research is warranted if the researcher is experienced, has a good reputation in research, and is a person of integrity.***

Were it possible for the reader of a research report to obtain sufficient information about the researcher, this criterion perhaps would be one of the best bases for judging the degree of confidence a piece of research warrants. For this reason, the research report should be accompanied by more information about the qualification of the researcher than is the usual practice.

Some evidence pertinent to estimates of the competence and integrity of the researcher may be found in the report itself. Language that is restrained, clear, and precise, assertions that are carefully drawn and hedged with appropriate reservations and an apparent effort to achieve maximum objectivity tend to leave a favorable impression of the researcher. On the other hand, generalizations that outrun the evidence upon which they are based, exaggerations, and unnecessary verbiage tend to leave an unfavorable impression.

1.7 Representations of the Research Process

There are a wide variety of views as to what research consists of, and great differences in actual practices as to what people research and how. A number of representations of the research process have been presented for study.

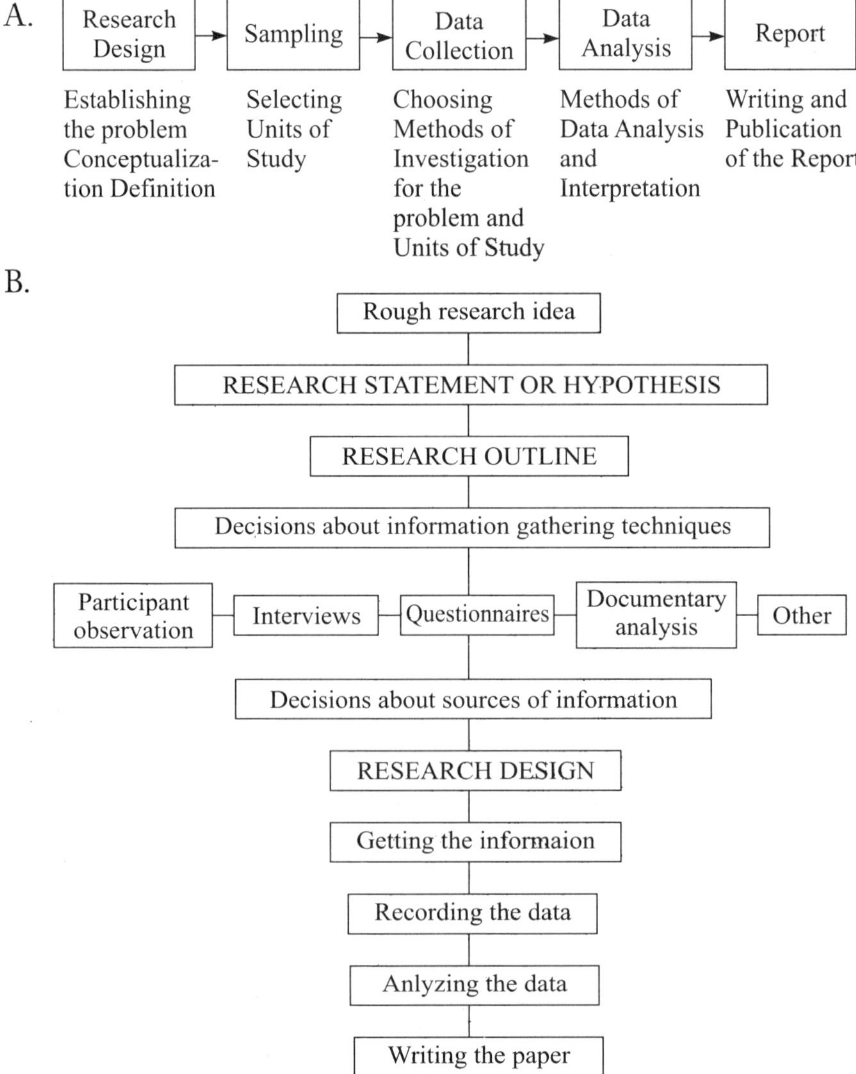

1.8 The Research Spiral

The nature of the cycle varies between research designs (Exhibit 1.4). For example, in most quantitative research, decisions about analysis have to be taken before any fieldwork or data collection is undertaken. This is because the types of statistical techniques that are possible vary with the types of data collected. Thus research from this viewpoint is a spiral. The key features of the research process in this case are:

Research

- is cyclical
- can be entered at almost any point
- is a never ending process
- will lead to reflective thinking
- will return you to a different starting place.

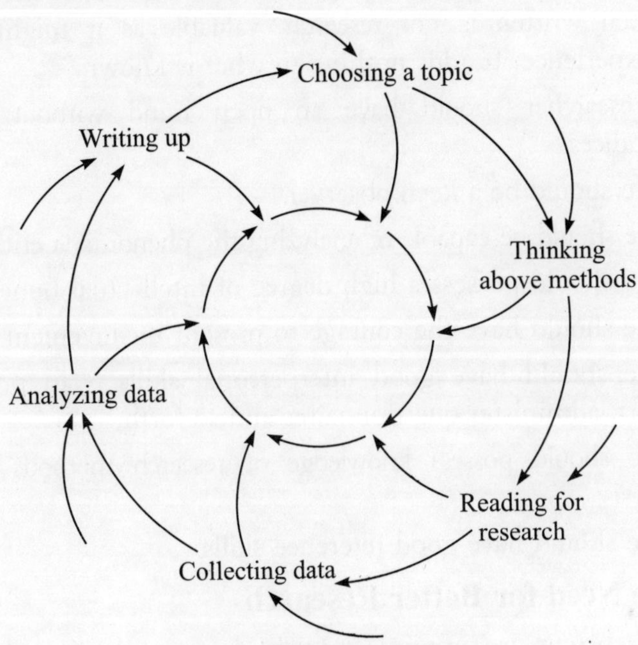

Exhibit 1.4: Research spiral

1.9 Qualities of a Researcher

Research is not going to the library or other sources of present knowledge to find the answer to a question that either a teacher has asked or is in the mind of an individual. This does not preclude historical research as a producer and synthesizer of knowledge. Use of present knowledge and knowledge of the past to answer the next question is indeed to be considered as scientific research, assuming acceptable procedures are used.

To read widely about a subject and write a review of the writing or the finding of an already known answer will not be considered as research here, although the teaching-learning process may find this to be an effective pedagogical procedure.

Best says, "Teachers frequently assign a so-called 'research project' that involves writing a paper dealing with the life of a prominent person. The students are expected to read a number of encyclopedias, books, or periodical references and synthesize the information in a written report. This is not research, for the data are not new. Merely recognizing or restating what is already known and what has already been written is not research, valuable as it might be as a learning experience. It adds nothing to what is known."

- A researcher should have an open mind without bias and prejudices.
- S/He should be a keen observer.
- S/He should be capable of analyzing the phenomena critically.
- S/He should possess a high degree of intellectual honesty.
- S/He should have the courage to present inconvenient truths.
- S/He should have good interpersonal skills – to present the report, administer questionnaires and so forth,
- S/He should possess knowledge of research methods and data analysis.
- S/He should have good reference skills.

1.10 The Need for Better Research

The current is running towards more sophisticated research applications in the entire field of education; but the developments to date are mixed. No amount of quantification or speed of data processing can overcome fundamental deficiencies of conceptualization and inference.

Educational research will improve when both administrators and teachers learn:

- to recognize that inquiry is a major part of decision-making and is too often neglected or undertaken poorly.
- to understand and conform to the requirements of the scientific method in applied research
- to understand and use the methods and techniques of research which are most appropriate to the posed problem.

SUGGESTED REFERENCES

- Best, John W. and James V. Kahn. Research in Education. 9th Edition. Prentice Hall of India Private Ltd., New Delhi. 2005.
- Cogan, Robert. Critical Thinking. University Press of America. April 1998.
- Dewey, John. How We Think. Boston: D.C. Heath. 1933.
- Fiebleman, J.K. Scientific Method. Netherlands: Martinus Nijhoff. The Hague. Netherlands. 1972.
- Fox, James Harold. "Criteria of Good Research." Phi Beta Kappa No.1. 39 (March 1958).
- Gophart, William J. et al in the Research and Evaluation Processes (Bloomington, In. Phi: Delta Kappa. 19-31, P 40.
- Kerlinger, Fred N. and Lee, H.B. Foundations of Behavioral Research. 4th Ed. New York: Holt, Rinehart and Winston. 1999.
- Krathwohl, D. Methods of Educational and Social Science Research: An integrated approach. New York: Longman. 1993.
- Mouly, George J. Science of Educational Research. New York. Van Nostrand Reinhold Co. 1971.
- Popper, Karl R. The Logic of Scientific Discovery. New York. Basic Books. 1959.
- Walton, Douglas N. Informal Logic: A Handbook For Critical Argument. Cambridge University Press. 1989.
- Wiersma, William and Stephen G. Jurs. Research Methods in Education. Allyn & Bacon; 8 edition (July 22, 2004)

WEB RESOURCES

- Basic Methods of Research
  http://www.siu.edu/departments/coe/ras1/504/Research_methods.htm
- Educational Research Course SDSU
  http://edweb.sdsu.edu/Courses/Ed690DR/690course.ht

❖ ❖ ❖

Problem Definition

2.0 Introduction

Students often wish to conduct a research project that is new, different, and vitally important. However, though this is a commendable goal, it often leads nowhere!! Several factors influence the selection of the problems for study. This chapter helps the research novice through the maze of educational research, highlighting the activities in the research process leading to the statement of problems definition.

2.1 Decision-Making

Formally defined, ***decision-making is the process of resolving a problem or choosing from alternative opportunities.*** The key to decision making is to recognize the nature of the problems/ opportunity, to identify how much information is available, and to recognize what information is needed. Every problem or decision-making situation can be classified on a continuum ranging from complete to absolute ambiguity. To facilitate discussion, the scale in Exhibit 2.1 shows three categories: certainty, uncertainty, and ambiguity.

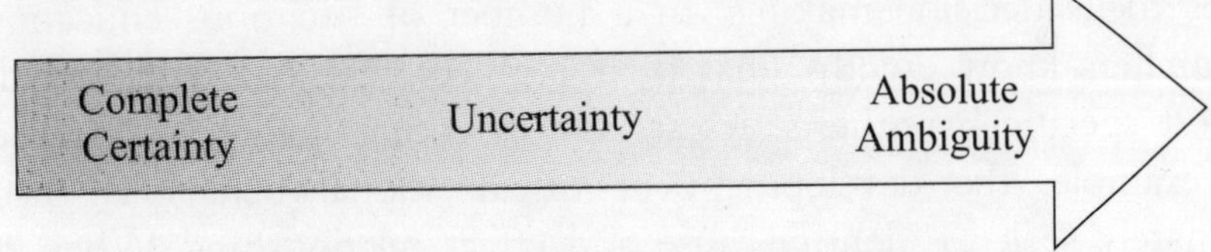

Exhibit 2.1: A continuum of decision-making

Certainty

Complete certainty means that the decision maker has all the information that he or she needs. The decision maker knows the exact nature of the problems or opportunity. For example, a school may need to know the demographic characteristics of its students. The school knows exactly what information it needs and where to find it. If a school manager is so completely certain about both the problem/ opportunity and future outcomes, then research may not be needed at all. However, perfect certainty, especially about the future, is rare.

Uncertainty

Uncertainty means that researchers grasp the general nature of the objectives they wish to achieve, but the information about alternatives is incomplete. Predictions about the forces that will shape future events are educated guesses. Under conditions of uncertainty, effective researchers recognize potential value in spending additional time gathering information to clarify the nature of the decision.

Ambiguity

Ambiguity means that the nature of the problem to be solved is unclear. The objectives are vague and the alternatives are difficult to define. This is by far the most difficult decision situation.

Researchers face a variety of decision-making situations. Under conditions of complete certainty when future outcomes are predictable, research may be a waste of time. However, under conditions of uncertainty or ambiguity, research becomes more attractive to the decision-maker. As the situation moves further along the scale towards ambiguity, the need to spend additional time on educational research becomes more compelling.

2.2 Types of Educational Research

Educational research produces information to reduce uncertainty. It helps focus decision-making. In a number of situations educational researchers know exactly what their problems are and design studies to test specific hypothesis. Most basic scientific studies in education, for example, the development of organizational behaviour theory ultimately seek to identify cause and effect relationships. When one thinks of science, one often associates it with experiments. Thus to predict a relationship between say, absenteeism and achievement in science, causal studies often create statistical experimental controls to establish "contrast groups". A number of experiments are conducted by both theory developers and pragmatic administrators.

2.2.1 Influence of Uncertainty on Type of Research

The uncertainty of the research problem is related to the type of research project. Exhibit 2.2 illustrates that exploratory research is conducted during the early stages of decision making when the decision situation

	Exploratory Research (Ambiguous Problem)	**Descriptive Research (Aware of Problem)**	**Causal Research (Clearly Defined Problem)**
Possible situation	Absenteeism in classis increasing and we do not know why.	What kind of student is prone to absenteeism?	Which of the two remedial measures- programmed instruction and supervised study- is more effective?

Exhibit 2.2: Types of educational research

is ambiguous and the researcher is very uncertain about the nature of the problem. When the researcher is aware of the problem but not completely knowledgeable about the situation, descriptive research is usually conducted. Causal studies require sharply defined problems even though there is uncertainty about future outcomes exists.

2.3 Activities of the Research Process

Educational research can take many forms, but systematic inquiry is a common thread. Systematic inquiry requires careful planning in an orderly investigation. Educational research, like other forms of scientific inquiry, is a sequence of highly inter-related activities. The activities in the research process overlap and it is somewhat of an oversimplification to state that every research project follows a neat and ordered sequence of activities. Nevertheless, educational research follows a generalized pattern.

The activities are

1. defining the problem
2. planning a research design
3. planning a sample
4. collecting data
5. analyzing the data and
6. formulating the conclusions and preparing the report.

These activities are portrayed in Exhibit 2.3 as a sequential process.

In practice, the activities overlap chronologically and are functionally interrelated. Sometimes the later stages are completed before the earlier ones. The terms ***forward*** and ***backward linkage*** are associated with the interrelatedness of the various stages. The term forward linkage implies that the earlier stages of research will influence the design of the later stages. Thus the objectives of the research outlined in the problem definition will have an impact on the selection of the sample and the way in which the data will be collected. The decision concerning who will be sampled will affect the wording of questionnaire items. For example, if the research concentrates on respondents who have low educational levels, the wording of the questionnaire will be simpler than the language used when the respondents are college graduates. The notion of backward linkage

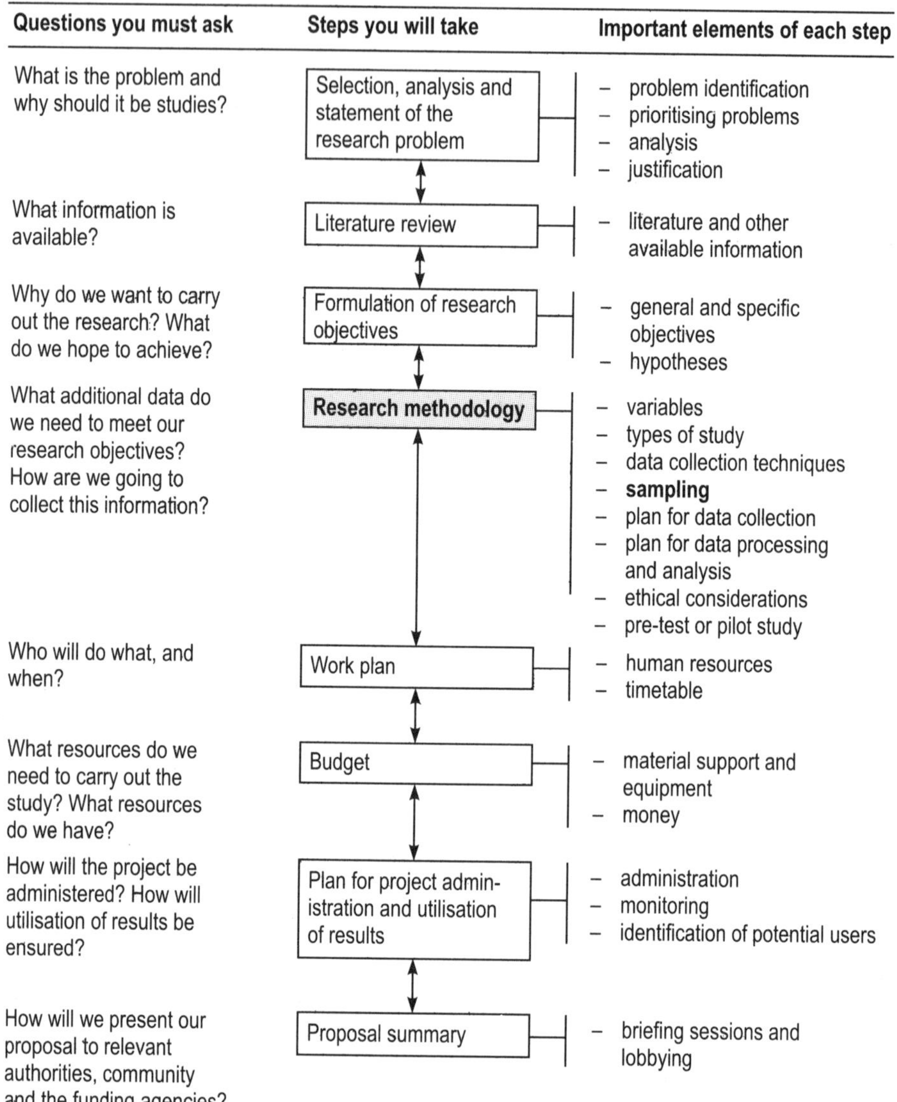

Exhibit 2.3: Sequential patterns of general activities in conducting a research study

implies that the later steps have an influence on the earlier stages in the research process. If it is known that the data will be analyzed by computer, then computer coding requirements are included in the questionnaire design. Perhaps the most important backward linkage is the knowledge that the examiners who read the research report need certain information. The professional researcher anticipates the reviewer's need for information in the planning process and considers this need during the analysis and tabulation stages.

Forward linkage is a term implying that the early stages of the research process influence the design of the later stages.

Backward linkage is a term implying that the late stages of the research process will have an influence on the early stages.

2.4 Decision Alternatives in the Research Process

A number of alternatives are available to the researcher during each of the stages of the research process. The research process can be compared with a guide or a map. On a map some paths are better charted than others. Some are difficult to travel, and some are more interesting and scenic than others. Rewarding experience may be gained during the journey. It is important to remember that there is no right path or best path for all journeys. The road one takes depends on where one wants to go and the resources (money, time, labour, and so on) one has available for the trip. The map analogy is useful for the educational researcher because in each of the stages of the research process there are several paths to follow. In some instances the quickest path will be the appropriate means of research because of certain time constraints. In other circumstances when money and human resources are plentiful, the path the research takes may be quite different. Exploration of the various paths of educational research decisions is our primary purpose.

Each of the stages in the research process is briefly described. Exhibit 2.4 shows the decision that researches must make in each stage of the research process. Discussion of the research process brings with it problems discovery and definition because most research projects, albeit at an earlier moment in time, are initiated because of some uncertainty about some aspect of the environment.

2.5 Problem Discovery and Definition

In Exhibits 2.4 and 2.5 the research process begins with problems discovery and identifying the problems is the first step towards its solution. The word problems, in general usage, suggest something has gone wrong. Unfortunately, the term problem does not connote, say, the need for evaluation of an existing programme, such as satisfaction of lecturers with the professional development

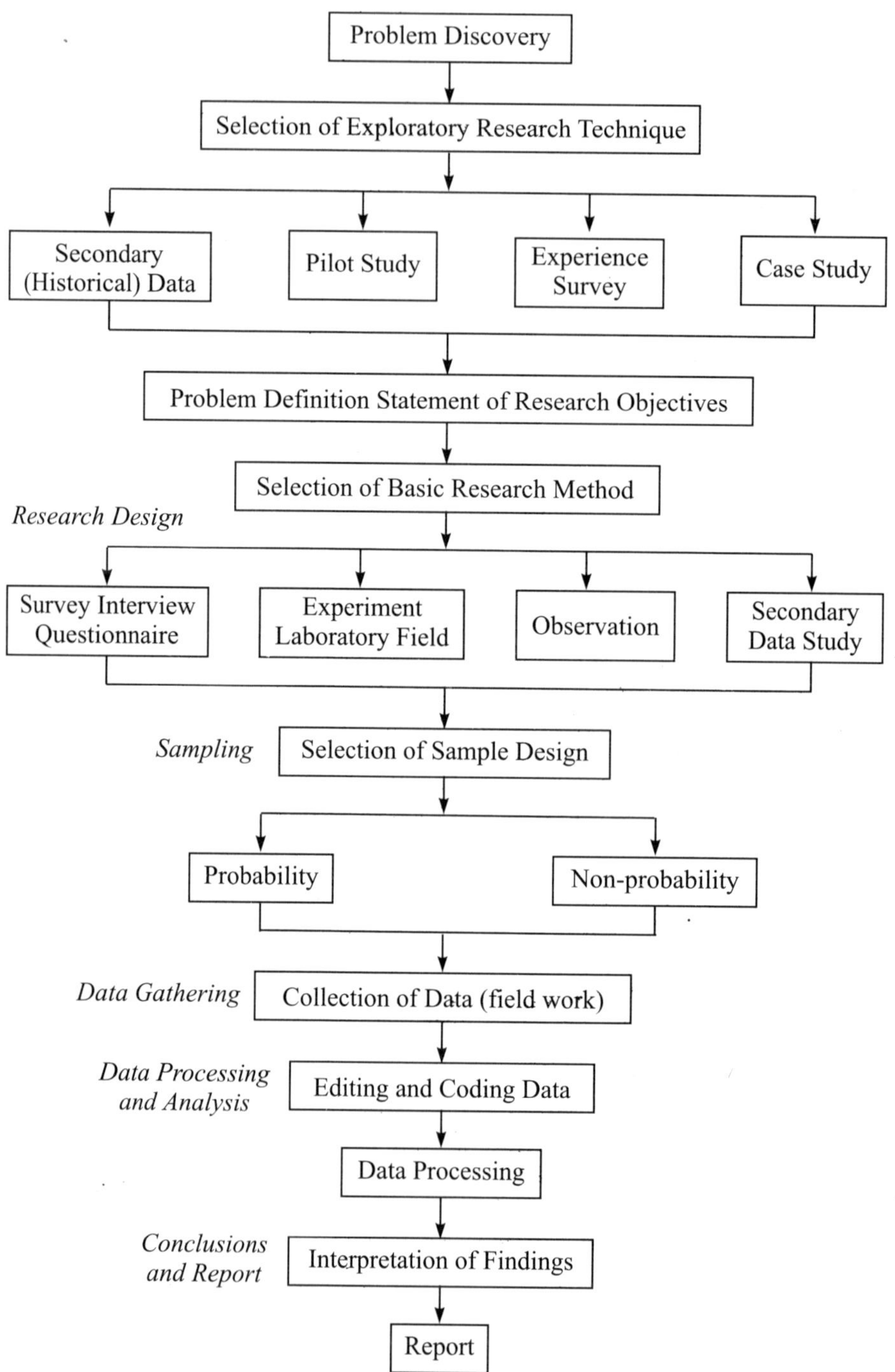

Exhibit 2.4: Flowchart of the research process

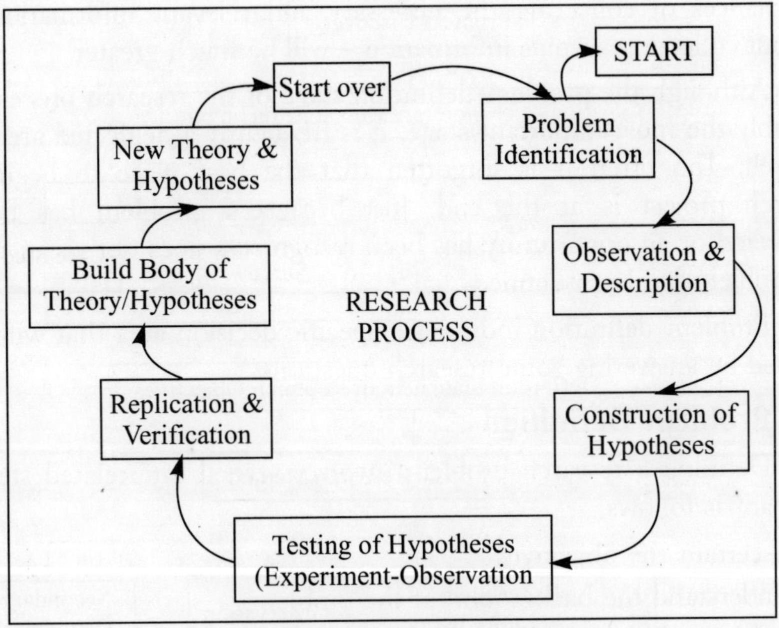

Exhibit 2.5: Research process

programmes. Actually, the research task may be to clarify a problem, to evaluate a programme, or to define an opportunity, and problem-discovery and definition will be used in this broader context. It should be noted that the initial stage is problem-discovery, rather than definition. The researcher may not have a clear cut statement of the problems at the outset of the research process. Often, only symptoms are apparent to begin with.

It was Albert Einstein who noted that "the formulation of a problem is often more essential than its solution". This is good advice. Too often researchers focus on finding the right answer than asking the right question. Many do not realize that defining a problem may be more difficult than solving it. In educational research, if the data is collected before the nature of the problem is carefully thought out, the data probably will not help solve the problem.

The adage "a problem well defined is a problem half solved" is worth remembering. This adage emphasizes that an orderly definition of the research problem gives a sense of direction to the investigation. Careful attention to problem-definition allows the researcher to set the proper research objective. If the purpose of the research is clear, the chances of collecting the necessary and relevant information – without collecting surplus information – will be much greater.

Although the problem-definition stage of the research process is probably the most important stage, it is frequently a neglected area of research. Too often it is forgotten that the best place to begin a research project is at the end. Just because a problem has been discovered or an opportunity has been recognized, does not mean that the problem has been defined.

Problem-definition indicates a specific decision area that will be clarified by answering some research questions.

2.6 Problem Definition

Defining a research problem involves several interrelated steps. They are as follows.

1. Ascertain the objective.
2. Understand the background of the problem.
3. Isolate and identify the problem rather than its symptoms.
4. Determine the unit of analysis.
5. Determine the relevant variable.
6. State the research questions (hypotheses) and research objectives.

Web link

Check list for evaluating the research problem
http://wps.prenhall.com/wps/media/objects/1532/1569569/checklists/chap03a.pdf

2.7 Statement of Research Questions

Initially a decision must be made as to precisely what should be researched. After identifying and clarifying the problem, with or without exploratory research, the researchers should make a formal statement of the problem and the research objectives. This delineates the type of information that should be collected and provides a framework for the scope of the study or the research project.

Selection of a research problem does not necessarily mean that it is adequately stated. Generally, the problem will need a lot of rewording and editing backed with systematic review of literature before it is feasible.

Research problems may be stated in question form or in statement form. The question form helps the researcher to focus on the problem on hand, and helps in forming sub problems. ***The best expression of a research problem is a well-formed, testable research hypothesis, and a hypothesis is a statement that can be refuted or supported by empirical data.***

Example

Problem area: Emotional maturity of students and stress

Restatement: A study of the relationship between the emotional maturity and examination stress level of eighth, ninth and tenth standard students in selected high schools of Kanchipuram

Question form: What factors of emotional maturity are related to the examination stress experienced by eighth, ninth and tenth standard students in selected high schools of Kanchipuram ?

A good statement of the problem should provide the researcher with direction in pursuing the research. The statement should indicate the general focus and the educational context of the problem. Key factors should be identified along with a general framework for reporting results.

In the example given, the word relationship implies certain procedures and certain types of results. Other questions which raise their head are:

— How do you measure emotional maturity?

— What are the factors of emotional maturity selected for this study?

— What kind of stress does the researcher mean?

— How do you quantify examination stress?

The three standard levels limit and define the population in the study.

"The selection of a problem involves reading, discussing, and conceptualizing. Typically, the process is one of successive approximations to the problem as factors related to the problem are concerned."

Wiersma and Jurs (2005)

Exhibit 2.6 lists the characteristics of a good research question, adapted from clinical research.

- **Feasible**
  Adequate # subjects and
  Expertise
  Time and money available
  Manageable
  Data to answer
- **Interesting**
  To the investigator
- **Novel**
  Confirms or refutes previous findings
  Extends previous findings
  Provides new findings
- **Ethical**
  Multiple levels including investigator conviction
- **Relevant**
  To scientific knowledge
  To clinical and health policy
  To future research directions

Exhibit 2.6: Characteristics of a good research question—FINER
Adapted from Designing Clinical Research by S. Hulley & S Cummings

2.8 Sources of Problems

The choice of a suitable problem is always difficult. The beginning researcher would do well to consider research topics in which s/he has a personal interest. With refinement, topics can be formed upto research problems. Education abounds with topics calling for research.

Some Good Sources of Research Topics

2.8.1 Topics for Teachers

Teaching has more good-questions that are practically begging to be researched-than do all other areas of education combined. Here are but a few aspects of teaching that abound in good topics.

- **Classroom environment**: Consider the numerous aspects of the physical and psychosocial environment of the classroom. What impact do they have on students' learning, behavior, attitudes, interest, assumption of responsibility, and interaction with teachers? How do they affect efficiency of instruction, movement, use of materials, and use of time?

- **Instructional materials**: Consider the uses of various media and specific equipment in promoting student attention, interest, achievement, creativity, enjoyment, and self-direction.
- **Classroom management**: Consider improvements that teachers can make in managing student behaviour, keeping records, establishing routines, and setting up communication networks, as a means of improving learning and attitudes, while reducing teacher stress.
- **Instruction:** We have just begun to explore the effects that a huge array of teaching behaviour have on student achievement, attitudes, and behaviour; there is great need for further research into
  - — factors that motivate and hold attention
  - — effective ways of giving directions, cues, and signals
  - — the best ways of teaching the different methods to achieve different objectives and goals
  - — effective teaching strategies, their timing and delivery
  - — ways of giving effective oral and written feedback in response to student efforts
- **The relation of human growth patterns to education:** While much basic information is available on human intellectual, social, physical, and emotional growth and development, relatively little has been done to develop teaching strategies that best match or promote
  - — individual interests and learning preferences
  - — individual rates of learning
  - — concerned, responsible behaviour; self-discipline
  - — natural student attention and teachable moments
  - — prime psychological "tasks" that strongly influence students' lives at different ages
  - — classroom esprit de corps, joy and pride in learning
- **Evaluation:** More information is needed about the effects that grades, grading systems, and evaluative feedback have on student motivation, stress, attitude, and learning.
- **Counselling:** Research is needed on how to maximize the value, and improve the efficiency, of teacher interaction with students and parents.

2.8.2 Topics for Administrators

Administrators have many of the same concerns as do teachers. In addition, they need reliable information and procedures for some of the following things.

- **Effective Communication**: The purposes, styles, and linkages with teachers, students, parents, other administrators, and the community need to be explored.
- **Effective Supervision**: What is the most effective way to motivate, guide, assist, and support quality teaching in faculties with diverse personalities and competencies?
- **Effective Public Relations**: What are the most effective strategies for ensuring the support of, and high regard from parents and community?
- **Effective Leadership Style**: What is the best way to model for, organize, direct, encourage, support, and otherwise get the best from teachers and students in the school?

The most likely sources to which one may go for a suitable problem are

- The classroom, the school and the community with which the researcher is familiar.
- Technological Innovation – e-learning, new techniques and procedures, flexi-timing, team teaching and so forth, provide rich sources of new problems.
- Review of the Literature – dissertations, journals reports, reading assignment provide a rich source for beginning researchers, by indicating the lacunae prevalent in current topics of research.

2.9 Criteria for Selecting a Problem

Possible topics for research are assessed in terms of certain considerations and cautions, some of which are given here.

— You should have a personal interest in the topic you select if the experience is to be adequately rewarding. Such interest may exist because the topic intrigues you, or is one in which you have had many pleasant experiences, or is one that has caused you unpleasant concern. Any topic that repeatedly suggests itself to you should be strongly considered.

— The topic you select should be important – not just because you are interested in it but because you believe it makes a true difference in education. You might have a keen personal interest in handwriting but unless you can convince yourself that handwriting makes a significant difference in education (and perhaps it does!), you should not select it as a topic for research.

— Basic research is done without regard for whether or not its findings have any practical use. However, your efforts will bring you much more satisfaction if you believe that the findings from your investigations have a good chance of being useful in education. While you might be personally intrigued with conditioning students to respond to bells, lights, and sounds, findings from such studies would probably not have practical use, and would be considered inconsequential.

— The newness of a research topic may stimulate your enthusiasm and satisfaction. Old does not mean bad – there is value in repeating previous research in order to validate its methods and findings and to see if they hold true over time. However, you may find it much more exciting to explore new topics, where you can bring information to light for the first time.

— In selecting research topics, you must always give attention to time. Compare the amount of time that a topic will require against what you have to invest. Other things being equal (which they seldom are), you do better to select research topics that can be completed in a relatively short time. It would be valuable, indeed, to do fifteen-year case studies of the individual development of literary taste, studies that might make a real difference in language curriculum and instruction. But few people are prepared to devote fifteen years to such a study. Or suppose you must research a topic as a requirement for earning an advanced degree, and you have one year in which to complete the project. It would be foolish to select a topic that could not be comfortably completed in the time available.

— Reflect also on the difficulty of researching the topic in which you might be interested. Many extremely interesting topics are difficult or impossible to research for a number of reasons. Select research topics that are interesting but feasible.

— Consider the expenses or costs associated with investigating your topic. Suppose, for example, you wanted to explore the familiar notion that "going to school is the student's job, just as working at home is the mother's job." To test the idea, you consider setting up an experiment in which you will pay 1,000 randomly selected high school students a minimum wage for attending school five hours a day for a period of a year. You do not manipulate any other variable. At the end of the year, you intend to compare their scores in science and mathematics, as well as their attitude towards school, against those of a randomly selected group of high school seniors not paid for going to school. You might be very interested in doing the study, and the results might turn out to be valuable. But you would have a hard time getting the money to pay the students.

2.10 Refining the Topic

After a good topic has been selected, it must be refined before it can be researched satisfactorily. Topics can be refined by:

- ***Limiting the subject***: Narrowing it down to a focus that is manageable in terms of time and effort. Most beginner researchers have difficulty in making their research topic small enough.
- ***Clarifying the problem:*** Stating precisely what you want to find out and wording your concerns so that they can be answered from the information that can be obtained.

REFERENCES

- Best, John W. and Kahn, James V. Research in Education. 9th Edition. Prentice Hall of India Pvt. Ltd. New Delhi. 2005.
- Fox, David J. The Research Process in Education. New York: Holt, Rinehart and Winston. 1969.
- Travers, R.M.W. Handbook of Research on Teaching. 2nd ed. Chicago: Rand McNally & Co. 1973.
- Wiersma, William and Jurs, Stephen G. Methods in Education: An Introduction (8th Edition). Allyn and Bacon. 2005.

Hypothesis

3.1 Meaning of Theory

Theory development is essentially a process of describing phenomena at increasingly higher level of abstraction. Things that we observe can be described as ideas or concepts. A concept is a generalised idea about a class of objects, attributes, occurrences, or processes that has been given a name.

Concepts abstract reality. Concepts however, may vary in degree of abstraction. The basic or scientific educational researcher operates at two levels: the abstract level of concepts and propositions and the empirical level of variables (and hypotheses). At the empirical level, we 'experience' reality that is, we observe or manipulate objects or events.

When we think of theories, we are at the highest level of abstraction because we are investigating the relationship between propositions. Theories are a network of propositions. (Exhibit 3.1)

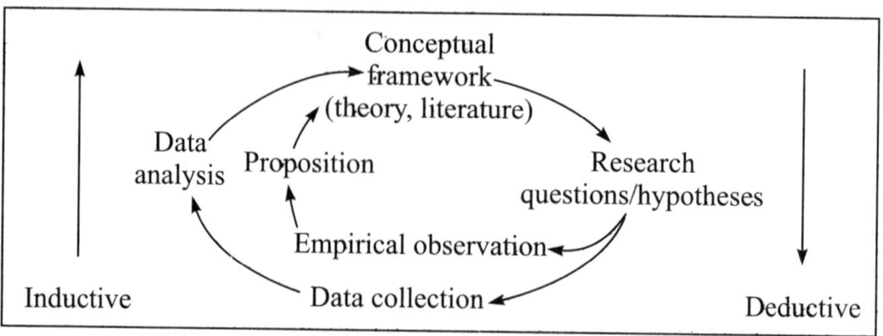

Exhibit 3.1: Theory building

A hypothesis is a proposition that is empirically testable. It is an empirical statement concerned with the relationship among variables. The abstract proposition "Reinforcements will increase the Academic Achievement" may be tested empirically with a hypothesis. Exhibit 3.2 shows that the hypothesis "Reinforcement of medals and awards will be associated with enhanced academic achievement in high school students" is an empirical counterpart of the proposition.

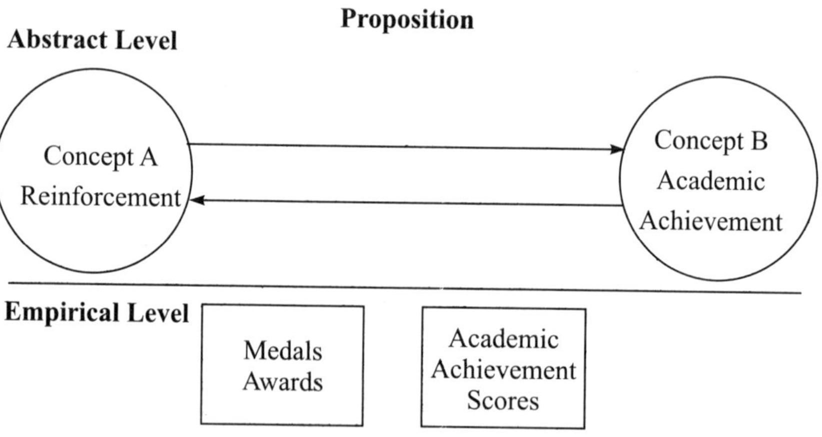

Exhibit 3.2: Hypotheses – The empirical counterparts of propositions

Reinforcements and academic achievement scores are variables, reflecting the concepts of reinforcement and academic achievement. As variables are at the empirical level, variables may be measured.

The Classical Approach to Hypothesis Construction

The classical approach consists of three stages.

Stage 1 takes place entirely on the conceptual level. Stage 2 bridges the gap between the conceptual and empirical levels. It consists of devising ways to measure the concepts empirically. This stage involves the writing of a testable hypothesis. The hypothesis in stage 2 is identical to the proposition in stage 1 except that stage 1 is at the conceptual level. The third stage consists of collecting data and analyzing it for verification of the hypothesis.

The relationships between the conceptual and empirical levels are shown in Exhibit 3.3. The empirical measures of the theoretical concepts X and Y are designated by the symbols X′ and Y′ respectively. Thus X′ is the measure of X and Y′ the measure of Y. In the Exhibit 3.3 X and Y are intelligence and happiness. X′ and Y′ are measures of X and Y respectively, that is, score on Intelligence test and score on Happiness Scale. The relationship between X and X′ and similarly Y and Y′ are signified by r_1 and r_2 respectively. These relationships between the conceptual and empirical levels are called epistemic relationships.

The possibility that the hypothesis will not be verified as first stated but must be either revised or abandoned leads many investigators to state the hypothesis initially in a tentative form. A hypothesis that is designed to be revised if necessary on the basis of findings is called a working hypothesis.

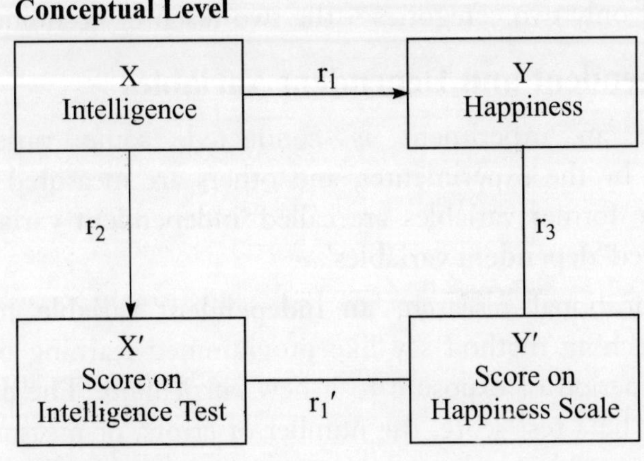

Exhibit 3.3: Classical approach to hypothesis construction

3.2 Constants, Variables and Operational Definitions

The effective conduct of research, as well as all communication, is complicated by the lack of agreement on concept meanings and the use of different abstraction levels. The problems of communication become even more difficult when a researcher decides to advance new concepts. For all these reasons, it is critical to the success of any research study that all persons involved have a common understanding of concept meanings. This is done by definitions.

A **constant** is a characteristic or condition that is the same for all individuals in a study.

A **variable** is a characteristic that takes on different values or conditions for different individuals.

Example: If a study is undertaken where the relative effectiveness of two new teaching techniques on the mathematics achievement of ninth standard students is undertaken, the standard level (***ninth***) is a ***constant***, as the sample comprises ninth standard students. However, each student would receive different scores on a test to measure the mathematics achievement. So, the mathematics achievement is a variable, because different students score differently on the same test. **Mathematics achievement in this case is a variable.**

There is another variable in the example above – the teaching technique. In this case, the teaching technique is a categorical variable consisting of only two categories – the two teaching techniques.

3.3 Independent and Dependent Variables

Where an experiment is conducted, some variables are manipulated by the experimenter, and others are measured from the subjects. The former variables are called '**independent variables**', the latter are called '**dependent variables**'.

In educational research, **an independent variable** may be a particular teaching method say like programmed learning or CAI, a reward or a period of exposure to a new curriculum. **The dependent variable** may be a test score, the number of errors, or measured speed in performing a task.

The dependent variables may mirror the measured changes on pupil performance attributable to the influence of the independent variable.

Examples

- A study of the effect of school location upon attitudes of sixth standard students toward school

  Independent variable: Location of school: urban, semi-urban and rural

  Dependent variable: Score on the investigator developed inventory to measure attitude
- A study of job stress of men and women teachers

  Independent variable: Gender of the teacher-male/female

  Dependent variable: Score on the tool to measure job stress

Different Types of Variables

- An ***organismic variable*** is a preexisting characteristic of the individuals under study. Gender and intelligence are examples
- An ***intervening variable*** is a hypothetical internal state that is used to explain relationships between observed variables, such as independent and dependent variables, in empirical research. An **intervening variable** facilitates in a better understanding of the relationship between the independent and dependent variables when the variables appear to not have a definite connection. They are studied by means of operational definitions and have no existence apart Examples of intervening variables include: motivation, intelligence, intention, and expectation.

  Example: An independent variable in a study on latent learning in rats is the number of practice trials received. Each rat receives an increasing number of trials, as one trial is given per day. The dependent variable is the number of wrong turns (errors) the rats make on a trial. As time, and number of practice trials, increases, the number of errors decreases. Theoretically, an internal state of "learning" intervened between the independent and dependent variables. It was this state that caused the errors to decrease, not the practice trials.
- A ***control variable*** is a variable other than the independent variable of primary interest whose effects are determined by the investigator. It is a variable held constant in order to assess or clarify the relationship between two other variables. Commonly used control variables for research on ***people*** include sex, age, caste,

education, and income. Commonly used control variables for research on ***organizations like schools*** include school size (number of students or teachers), mission, budget, and location of the school.

- A **moderator variable** is, in general terms, a qualitative (e.g., sex, class) or quantitative (e.g., level of reward) variable that affects the direction and/or strength of the relation between dependent and independent variables.

  Example: Considered is the case in which a variable **M** is presumed to change the X to Y causal relationship. So for instance, a certain form of psychotherapy may reduce depression more for men than for women, and so we would say that gender (M) moderates the causal effect of psychotherapy (X) on depression (Y).

Descriptions of variables are not mutually exclusive. For example, organismic variables may also be control variables.

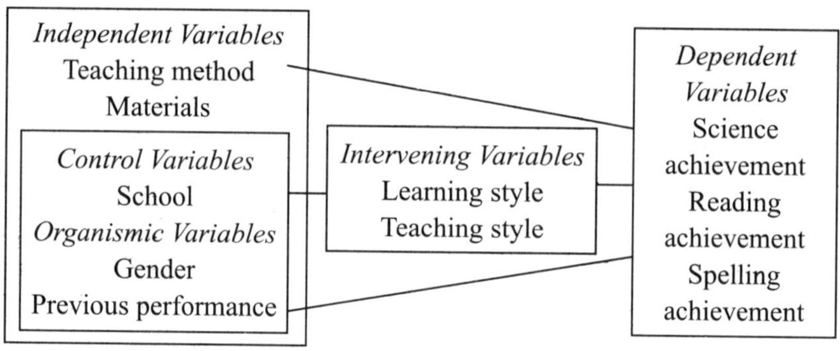

Exhibit 3.4: Different types of variables operating in a study

3.4 Operational Definitions

"An operational definition.... specifies the operation or characteristics necessary to identify the variable or condition being defined."

Wiersma and Jugs 2005

Intervening variables are studied by means of operational definitions, which are descriptions of procedures that are assumed to have some link to the internal state.

An Operational Definition

— Is stated in terms of specific testing criteria or operations.

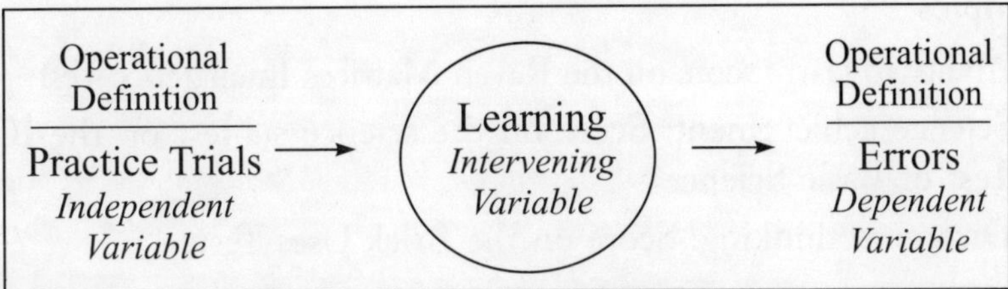

Exhibit 3.5: Operational definitions

— Must have empirical referents (that is, we must be able to count, measure or in some other way gather the information through our senses).

— Should specify the characteristics to be observed and how they are to be observed.

— The criteria or operations should be so objective that any competent observer should be able to define a person, action, condition or attitude in a specific situation and secure the same results.

While operational definitions are needed in the conduct of research, their use presents some problems. There is the ever-present danger of confusing the definition with the concept it represents. Definitions provide only limited insight into the meanings of the concepts and constructs they represent. In fact, operational definitions may be so narrow in meaning that more than one is required to express a concept fully. This narrowness is the price we pay for precision, and it complicates our measurement. By using several definitions we can tap more than one dimension of a concept, but how do we combine them? When, say, two definitions correlate well it supports the view that we are measuring the same concept. If there is little or no correlation it may mean we are tapping separate partial meanings of a construct, but it may also mean that one or both of the operational definitions are not measuring our concept. If the definitions correlate negatively, then we should reassess the nature of the concept and its proposed operational definitions.

Whatever the form of definition, its purpose in research is basically the same – to provide an understanding and measurement of concepts. We may need to provide operational definitions for only a few critical concepts, but these will almost always be the ones which we use to develop the concept relationship found in hypotheses and theories.

Examples

- Ability to learn: score on the Raven Matrices Intelligence Test
- Science achievement: Score on the science subtest on the IOWA Test of Basic Science
- Divergent thinking: Score on the Brick Uses Test
- Concept Attainment performance: time required to solve correctly five concept attainment problems

Conditions or characteristics of a research study may also require operational definition. For example, if high school students are to be surveyed, who is a high school student? An operational definition is this study may be a student who is enrolled in a Government aided high school and is currently in the Xth Standard of that school.

3.5 Hypothesis

In the literature of research and inference there are disagreements about the meanings of the terms "proposition" and "hypothesis." Here we define a proposition as a statement about concepts, which may be judged as true or false if it refers to observable phenomena. Linking the concepts of variables, constants, operational definitions as shown in Exhibit 3.6, we can now state our hypothesis so that it is more specific and gives direction to the research study.

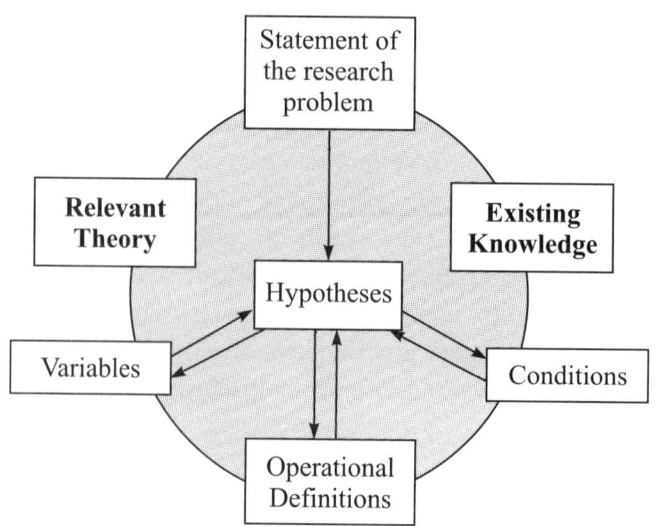

Exhibit 3.6: Linking hypotheses with what we know

- A hypothesis is a tentative prediction about the nature of the relationship between two or more variables.
- A hypothesis represents an educated guess about what will happen in an experiment.
- A research question is simply a hypothesis stated in a question form

3.5.1 Sources of Hypotheses

- Directly derived from the statement of the problem
- Based on research literature
- Ethnographic studies
- Data collection and analysis

3.5.2 Types of Hypotheses

Researchers use different kinds of hypotheses. A research hypothesis indicates what the investigator expects to find or substantiate with evidence.

- A **research hypothesis** is a tentative statement of expected outcomes.

  Example: Laboratory instruction enhances the student's understanding of scientific processes over the lecture method.
- A **statistical hypothesis** is given in statistical terms.

  Example: The mean reading achievement of the third standard students taught by Method A equals the mean reading achievement of the population taught by Method B.
- The **null hypothesis** is a hypothesis of no difference or no relationship. This is also called a nondirectional hypothesis because no direction is indicated for the results.
- The **alternative hypothesis**

  The means of the reading achievement of the population of third standard students taught by Method A and Method B are not equal.

Thus Null and Alternative cover all possibilities. Combining the two, we get the mean of the population of third standard students taught by Method A is less than or equal to the mean of the population taught by Method B.

Example of stating hypothesis in different ways

The achievement of ninth standard students taught chemistry through computer-aided instruction will equal or exceed that of ninth standard students taught by lecture method.

The hypothesis stated above is a research hypothesis. Researchers, however often use a second kind of hypothesis – the null hypothesis – for reasons of ease in statistical testing. *The null hypothesis states that no difference or relationship exists among the variables, regardless of whether or not the investigator believes that to be true.*

A null hypothesis for the same research would be:

There is no significant difference in achievement in chemistry between IXth standard students taught through computer aided instruction and through the lecture method.

If this null hypothesis is rejected, found to be untrue, the investigator concludes that differences do exist, and may then set out to identify those difference and their causes.

Experts in educational research have long believed that hypotheses are more useful than questions for problems statements, because of their testability and the direction and precision they give to the research. Today, however, questions are frequently used because they do not cause the investigator to concentrate on evidence for retaining or rejecting the hypothesis; rather, they leave the investigator open and receptive to a broad range of findings related to the topic. In general,

— Statistical hypotheses are used in analysis of data

— Research hypotheses indicate direction.

3.5.3 Questions and Sub-questions

Many researchers find it helpful to use questions rather than hypotheses for their problem statements. This is, because, the main question suggests a number of sub-questions, whose answers contribute toward answering the main question. These sub questions guide research efforts and suggest sources of data.

Take the research problem: Does it make any difference to hearing-impaired students later school success if they enter kindergarten at age four instead of six?

Sub-questions that could be posed from this are:

- Is there a relationship between age of entry into kindergarten and School Leaving Certificate scores for hearing-impaired students?
- Is there a relationship between School Leaving Certificate scores and later school success for hearing-impaired students?

In other words, problems stated as questions allow openness to a range of findings that might emerge from the research, while problems stated as hypotheses direct efforts towards testing the 'truth' of the relationships they describe. In historical and descriptive research, sub-questions are used to arrive at an answer to the main question.

You will not see sub-questions in reports of correlational research because the main question can be investigated directly.

3.5.4 Purposes that Hypotheses Serve

A hypothesis is a very powerful tool of educational inquiry. The purposes that hypotheses serve are:

- Hypotheses give statements of relationships that are empirically testable and can be found to be either probably true or probably false.
- Hypotheses give direction to the study and the experimenter.
- The hypotheses are evidence that the researcher has a sufficient background of knowledge to propose explanations to extend the body of educational knowledge.
- Hypotheses give continuity to the study by providing a basis for drawing conclusions for study.

A study may have more than one hypothesis. It might have a major hypothesis that is too broad to be tested in that form but other testable sub-hypotheses could be derived from it and tested separately. Thus the researcher will draw conclusions from them, and, in turn, conclusions about the major hypothesis.

3.6 The Role of the Hypothesis

In the research context, a hypothesis serves several important functions. Perhaps the most important is that it guides the direction of the study. A frequent problem in research is the proliferation of "interesting information." Unless the urge to include additional elements is curbed, a study can be diluted by a trivial concern, which does not answer the basic questions posed. The virtue of the hypothesis is that, if taken seriously, it defines what shall be studied and what shall not be. It defines which facts are relevant and which are not; in so doing, it suggests which form of research design is likely to be most appropriate. A final important role of the hypothesis is to provide a framework for organizing the conclusions that result from the study.

To consider specifically the role of the hypothesis in determining the direction of the research, consider the hypothesis **"Boys and girls agree in their perceptions of their respective roles in choice of school pupil leader."** The hypothesis specifies who shall be studied, in what context they shall be studied (their decision-making), and what shall be studied (their individual perceptions of their roles).

The nature of this hypothesis and the implications of the statement suggest that the best research design is probably a survey, as there are no other practical means to ascertain perceptions of people except to ask them in one way or another about their perception. In addition, only the roles that are assumed in the choice of school pupil leader is of interest in this study. The study should clearly, therefore, not involve itself in seeking information about other types of roles, which boys and girls might play. A third suggestion that might flow from a reflection on this hypothesis is that it might be found that boys and girls do disagree on their perceptions of roles but that these differences may be explained in terms of additional variables, such as age, social class, background, personality differences, and other factors not associated with their differences of sex.

3.6.1 What is Good Hypothesis?

A good hypothesis should fulfill three conditions. The most elementary requirement is that it be **adequate** for its purpose. For a descriptive hypothesis, this means that it clearly states the condition, size, or distribution of some variable in terms of values meaningful to the research task. If it is an explanatory hypothesis, it must explain the facts that gave rise to the need for explanation. Using the hypothesis, plus other known and accepted generalizations, one should be able to deduce the original problem condition.

A second major condition is that the hypothesis must be **testable**. A hypothesis is untestable if it calls for techniques, which are unavailable with the present state of the art. It is also untestable if it calls for an explanation, which defies known physical or psychological laws. Explanatory hypotheses are also untestable if there are no consequences or derivatives that can be deduced for testing purposes.

For explanatory hypotheses there is a third major condition. It must be better than its rivals. Generally speaking, the better hypothesis has a greater range; it explains more facts and a greater variety of facts than do its rivals. The better hypothesis is also the one, which informed judges accept as being the most likely. Their opinions can be highly subjective but depend chiefly on their judgment of which fits best with other information. Finally, the better hypothesis is the **simple** one requiring fewer conditions or assumption.

Hypotheses play an important role in the development of theory. While theory development has so far been an important aspect of educational research, it is likely to become more so in the future.

3.7 Classifications of Hypotheses

Hypotheses can be classified in several ways. We shall look into three ways of classifying them.

a) Simple versus Complex Hypothesis
   - Simple – states the relationship between two variables.
   - Complex – states the relationship between two or more independent variables and two or more dependent variables.

b) Directional versus Non-directional Hypothesis
   - Directional form – states the direction of the relationship between the variables.
   - Non-directional form – states a relationship, but not the direction.

c) On the Basis of Types: (Exhibit 3.7)

   Each of these types can be in simple or complex form.

- By its very nature, null hypothesis will be non-directional.
- Research hypothesis will be directional

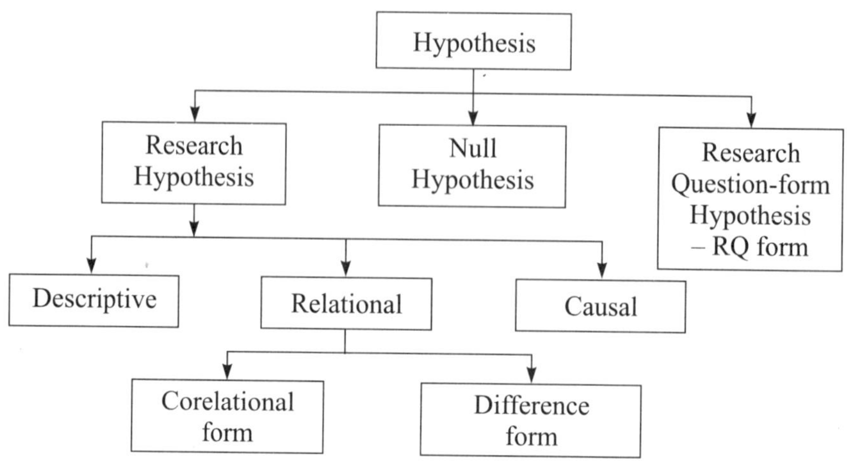

Exhibit 3.7: Types of Hypotheses

- Though research question form are usually non-directional, they can also be directional.

Hypotheses are of Three Types

— Research Hypothesis

— Null Hypothesis

— Question form Hypothesis. (Exhibit 3.7)

3.7.1 Research Hypothesis (Symbol H_1, H_a)

A research hypothesis is usually stated in a declarative form postulating the attributes of a phenomenon (***Descriptive Hypothesis***), the relationship between two variables (***Relational Hypothesis***) or explaining the cause and effect relationship among the variable (***Causal Hypothesis***). This can be used for:

- Prediction of statistically significant findings, like significant differences or correlations between groups or among variable.
- Significant difference in any direction
- Significant difference in the predicted direction.

Descriptive Hypothesis is stated when a study is designed primarily to describe what is going on or what exists. Public opinion polls that seek only to describe the proportion of people who hold various opinions are primarily descriptive in nature. For instance, if we want to know what per cent of the school student population would vote for a girl or a boy in the next School Public Leader election, we are simply interested in describing something.

Relational Hypothesis is used when a study is designed to look at the relationships between two or more variables. A school opinion poll that compares what proportion of girls and boys say they would vote for a girl or a boy candidate in the next School Public Leader election is essentially studying the relationship between gender and voting preference.

Causal Hypothesis is stated when a study is designed to determine whether one or more variables (e.g. a remedial programme or a new teaching technique) causes or affects one or more outcome variables. If we did an opinion poll among the teachers of the school to try to determine whether a recent student canvassing drive changed voting preferences, we would essentially be studying whether the canvassing drive (cause) changed the proportion of student voters who would vote a girl or a boy (effect).

These three types can be viewed as cumulative. That is, a relational study assumes that you can first describe (by measuring or observing) each of the variables you are trying to relate. A causal study assumes that you can describe both the cause and effect variables and that you can show that they are related to each other. Causal studies are invariably the most demanding of the three.

3.7.2 Null Hypothesis (Symbol H_0)

The hypotheses we have discussed thus far are called research or substantive hypotheses. Research hypotheses cannot be tested directly by available statistical procedures.

The null hypothesis is a statement about a status quo that asserts that any change from what has been thought to be true will be due entirely to random sampling error. The null hypothesis relates to a statistical method of interpreting conclusions about population characteristics inferred from the variable relationship observed in sample. The null form is a statement that asserts that observed differences or relationships merely result from chance errors inherent in the sampling process. It must be remembered that the null hypothesis is 'supported' if the results are not significant. The null hypothesis is never 'proven'.

Example of a null hypothesis

> There is no difference between the mean IQ's of athletes and non-athletes.

Here we are concerned only with establishing whether there is a difference or not, and not with the superiority or inferiority of either group. In empirical investigations where statistical tests are to be performed, the research hypothesis must be translated into another type of hypothesis known as a null hypothesis (symbolized as H_o). It is called null because it states that there is "no difference" or "no effect" or that there is "no relationship." A null hypothesis states a negation of what the experiment expects or predicts. A researcher may hope to show that, after an experimental treatment, two populations have different means, but the hypothesis would state that the populations' means are not different.

The null hypothesis is used because it enables researchers to compare their finding with chance expectations through statistical tests. The null hypothesis assumes that observed differences occurred because of chance alone and hence do not represent real differences at all. Statistical tests are used to determine the probability that the null hypothesis is true. If the tests indicate that observed differences had a very slight probability of occurring by chance, the null hypothesis becomes a very unlikely assumption. Therefore, it can be rejected in favor of an alternative hypothesis. The evidence is sufficient for tentatively concluding that the difference is real. If the observed differences could easily be a function of chance, the evidence is insufficient and the null hypothesis is retained. Testing a null hypothesis is analogous to the prosecutor's work in a criminal trial. In order to establish guilt, the prosecutor (in the legal system) must provide sufficient evidence to enable a jury to reject the presumption of innocence beyond reasonable doubt. It is not possible for a prosecutor to prove guilt conclusively, nor can a researcher obtain unequivocal support for a research hypothesis. The defendant is presumed to be innocent until there is sufficient evidence to indicate that he or she is not, and the null hypothesis is presumed to be true until there is sufficient evidence to indicate otherwise.

The null hypothesis always makes a statement about a characteristic of the population, not a sample. The Greek letter μ is used to represent the population mean.

Example

A researcher is interested in the difference between the anxiety levels of children of high and low IQ.

The research hypothesis might read:

Children with high IQs will exhibit more anxiety than children with low IQs.

The null hypothesis to be tested is:

The anxiety level of high-IQ children is not different from the anxiety level of low-IQ children.

In symbolic form, the null hypothesis is

$$H_o : \mu_A = \mu_B$$

where H_o is the null hypothesis

μ_A is the mean anxiety score of Population A (High-IQ children)

μ_B is the mean anxiety score of Population B (Low-IQ children)

The null hypothesis would be tested using one of the various statistical techniques to be discussed in a later chapter. If, when the study is completed, the empirical data indicate that the difference between the sample groups is large enough to be not due to chance, then the null hypothesis can be rejected. Rejection of the null hypothesis indicated that the anxiety level of the two groups of children is not likely to be equal. The researcher then adopts an alternative hypothesis (symbolized as H_1), which states: The mean anxiety scores of the two populations are not equal.

$$H_1 : : \mu_A \neq \mu_B$$

The alternative hypothesis (H_1) stated above is said to be non-directional because it does not state which group's average score will be larger. Although a non-directional hypothesis indicates that a difference is expected, it does not specify the direction of the difference. Probably most research in education begins with non-directional hypotheses. In some situations, however, the researcher may have a definite reason for stating a directional hypothesis, which, as the name implies, specifies the direction of the expected findings. An example of a directional hypothesis is $H_1 :: \mu_A > \mu_B$.

Testing the Null Hypothesis

A study begins with a research hypothesis, which should be a simple, clear statement of the expected relationship between the variables. We have explained earlier that hypotheses must be testable, which means that they are amenable to empirical verification. When researchers speak of testing a hypothesis, however, they are referring to the null hypothesis. Only the null hypothesis can be directly tested by statistical procedures. Testing a hypothesis involves the following steps:

Step 1 State, in operational terms, the relationships that should be observed if the research hypothesis is true.

Step 2 State the null hypothesis

Step 3 Select a research method that will permit the observation and/ or experimentation necessary to show whether or not these relationships do exist.

Step 4 Gather and analyze the empirical data.

Step 5 Determine whether the evidence is sufficient to reject the null hypothesis.

Example of Testing of Hypothesis

A teacher is interested in investigating the hypothesis that **praise or encouragement result in heightened motivation on the part of students.** If this hypothesis is correct, it should be logical to assume that teachers' encouraging comments on test papers (praise) would be followed by improvement in student performance, which implies the assumption that heightened motivation is indicated by improved test performance.

Step1

This deduced implication is stated as follows:

Teachers' comments on students' papers result in an improvement in pupils' performance on tests.

It is the relationship between the two variables—teachers' comments and pupil performance that will be investigated.

Step 2

For statistical testing, the above research hypothesis must be transformed into a null hypothesis. The null hypothesis is stated.

Teachers' comments on students' paper will not significantly improve pupils' performance on tests.

$$H_0 : : \mu_A = \mu_B$$

where

μ_A = the mean gain in performance for the population of students receiving teachers' comments on papers

μ_B = the mean gain in performance for the population of students not receiving teachers' comments on papers

Step 3

This type of hypothesis can be investigated by means of an experiment. The researcher could randomly select a number of classes to use in the study. Within each class, students would be randomly assigned to two groups: For those students assigned to Group A, their teachers would write encouraging comments concerning their test performance. (These comments would simply be words of encouragement to the student, such as "Excellent," "Keep up the good work." or "you're doing better." These comments should have nothing to do with content or the correction of particular student's errors: otherwise, the improvement could be attributed to the educational usefulness of such comments rather than to increased motivation.) The students assigned to Group B would receive no comments at all on their test papers.

Step 4

The teachers would administer an objective test covering a certain unit of content. The tests are scored and the experimental treatment introduced as described above. Then the teachers would administer a second test covering a unit comparable in difficulty to the previous unit and taught after the first test and the experimental treatment.

The change from the first test to second test would be ascertained for each students as well as the average gain for the group. It would then be possible through analysis of the data to determine whether average gains on the second test were related to the experimental treatment (teacher comments on paper).

Step 5

If it is found that, as a group, the students who had received comments, Group A, achieved statistically significantly higher gains than the group that did not receive comments, Group B, and then the null hypothesis can be rejected. Rejection of the null hypothesis would mean that the effects of the two methods are not equal. The researcher would tentatively conclude that teacher' comments on students' papers result in an improvement in students' performance in tests.

3.7.3 Research Question -Form Hypothesis (Symbol: RQ)

Formulating a research question allows a researcher to conduct more open-ended investigations. This form is useful if there is little previous research on the topic. It also allows a wider range of outcomes to be reported.

Example for a question form hypothesis:

Do athletes and non-athletes differ in their IQs?

3.8 Statement of Hypothesis

A hypothesis, in whichever form it is to be stated, should

- be in the form of an answer to the proposed question
- include an expressed relationship
- be testable through empirical investigation
- be stated clearly using the simplest terms to convey the thought
- be consistent with what is known
- if possible, be based on a common accepted theory.

If you find that it is difficult to write an acceptable hypothesis, check the problem question. A poorly presented question that does not meet the criteria may be difficult to answer with an acceptable hypothesis statement. Try rewriting the question, checking carefully against the criteria for problem questions. Avoid use of vague or nebulous wording. Always keep in mind that the hypothesis must be testable.

Exhibit 3.8 gives a few sample hypotheses.

Question Form Hypothesis

Will students who attended at least 2 years of Montessori preschool have better reading comprehension abilities at the end of first standard than those students who did not attend preschool at all?

Non-Directional Hypothesis

At the end of first standard there will be difference between the reading comprehension abilities of children who attended at least 2 years of Montessori preschool and children who did not attend preschool at all.

Null Hypothesis

At the end of first standard, there will be no difference between the reading comprehension abilities of children who attend at least two years of Montessori preschool and children who did not attend preschool at all.

Directional Hypothesis

At the end of first standard children who attended at least two years of Montessori preschool will have higher reading comprehension abilities compared to children who did not attend preschool at all.

Exhibit 3.8: Statement of hypothesis in different forms

Exhibit 3.9 gives a sample of how a problem question gives rise to research questions and research objectives.

Problem Question	Research Questions	Research Objectives
Should remedial programmes be offered to enhance science achievement in the primary sections of schools?	• Are teachers aware of Remedial Programmes? • How concerned are teachers about the need for enhance-ment of science in achievement primary schools?	• To determine teachers' awareness about the need for remedial programmes using questions. • To measure teachers' concern about the significance of such programmes. • To obtain ratings & rankings on different aspects of science concept mastery in primary schools.

Exhibit 3.9: Research problem translated into research objectives

SUGGESTED REFERENCES

- Best, John W. and Kahn, James V. Research in Education. 9th Ed. Prentice Hall of India Private Ltd., New Delhi. 2005
- Lomax, Richard G. An Introduction to Statistical Concepts for Education and Behavioural Science. Lawrence Erlbaum Associates. July 2000.
- Wiersma, William and Jurs, Stephen. Research Methods in Education. 8th Ed. Pearson Education. Boston. 2005.

USEFUL WEB SITES

- http://www.mnstate.edu/~wasson/ed603/ed6031esson6.htm
- http://www.hunter.cuny.edu/edu/apiccian/edstar02.htm1
- http://www2.n1.edu/proberts/Research questions hypothesse.pdf
- http://psych.fullerton.edu/navarick/

Sampling

4.0 The Nature of Sampling

An important research decision is the selection of subjects to study. We must determine how many people to interview, who they will be, what events to observe and how many there will be, or how many records to inspect and which ones. In research studies we often observe only a sample of the possible cases, but the selection of this sample is not a simple problem. Although sampling is commonplace in daily activities, most of these familiar samples are not of a scientific nature. The understanding of the concept of sampling may be intuitive, but the actual process of sampling can be quite complex. Because sampling is a central aspect of educational research, it requires careful study.

This chapter explains the nature of sampling and how to determine the appropriate design.

Most people intuitively understand the nature of sampling and use it on many occasions. One taste from a drink tells whether it is sweet or sour. If the people interviewed on a suburban street agree with a certain civic action we tend to think that most people will agree with that action. If some of our office staff favour a five-day week, we infer that others also would. Such examples may vary in their representativeness, but they are all samples.

The basic idea in sampling is that the analysis of some of the elements in a population provides useful information on the entire population. As used here, an element is the subject on which the measurement is being taken. It is the unit of study. For example, each office worker questioned about the five-day week is a population element, and each account analyzed is an element of an account population. Population is the total collection of elements about which we wish to make inferences. All staff members in the office might comprise the population of interest, or we might define the population in many other ways. The population takes whatever dimensions the researcher's objective dictates.

4.1 Sampling Terminology

The process of sampling involves any procedure using a small number of elements of the whole population to draw conclusions regarding the whole population.

A *sample* is a subset or some part of a larger population. The purpose of sampling is to enable researchers to estimate some unknown characteristic of the population based on a good representative sample.

A ***population*** or ***universe***, is any complete group of entities – people, schools, students, hospitals or the like – sharing some common set of characteristics. When a distinction is made between 'population' and 'universe', it is on the basis of whether the group is finite (population) or infinite (universe)

The term ***population element*** – refers to an individual member of the population.

A *census* is an investigation of all the individual elements that make up the population: a total count rather than a sample.

4.2 Why Sample?

Sampling is based on two premises. One is that there is enough similarity among the elements in a population that a few of these elements will adequately represent the characteristics of the total population. For example, we can estimate the attitudes in a large group by learning the attitudes of a few representative persons in that group. If this can be done there can obviously be a great saving in time and cost. However, improved economy alone is not the only value of sampling.

Deming argues that the quality of a study is often better with sampling than with a census. He suggests that "Sampling possesses the possibility of better interviewing (testing), more thorough investigation of missing, wrong, or suspicious information, better supervision, and better processing than is possible with complete coverage." The Bureau of the Census demonstrates its confidence in sampling by making sample surveys to check the accuracy of censuses.

Sampling also provides much quicker results than does a census. The speed of execution minimizes the time between the recognition of a need for information and the availability of that information. Then, too, some situations require sampling. For example, when we test the breaking strength of materials we must destroy them; a census would mean complete destruction of the materials. Sampling is also the only procedure possible if the population is infinite. We take a sample of throws of dice since the population of dice throws is infinite.

The members of a sample may not be fully representative of the population, and values calculated from sample data may vary from the population values. This problem of discrepancies between a population value (parameter) and its parallel sample value (statistic) calls up the second premise of sampling: while some sample items underestimate the parameter, others overestimate its value. When the sample is drawn properly, variations in item values tend to counteract each other; this counteraction tendency results in a statistic (sample value) that is generally close to the parameter (population value). For these offsetting efforts to take place, however, it is necessary (1) that there be enough members in the sample and (2) they must be drawn in a way to favour neither the overestimating nor the underestimating tendencies.

4.3 What is a Good Sample?

The ultimate test of a sample design is how well it represents the characteristics of the population it purports to represent. In measurement terms the sample must be valid. Validity of a sample depends upon two considerations.

Accuracy This is defined as the degree to which bias is absent from the sample. An accurate (unbiased) sample is one in which the underestimators and the overestimators are balanced among the members of the sample. There is no systematic variance with an accurate sample. Systematic variance has been defined as "the variation in measures due to some known or unknown influences that 'cause' the scores to lean in one direction more than another." For example, it has been said that homes on the corner of the block tend to be larger and more valuable than those within blocks. Thus, a sample in which we select corner homes only will cause us to overestimate home values in the area.

Precision The second criterion of good sample design is precision of estimate. No sample will fully represent its population in all respects. A sample statistic may be expected to differ from its parameter as a result of random fluctuations inherent in the sampling process. This is often referred to as error variance or sampling error and reflects the influences of chance in drawing the sample members. Error variance is that which is left over after all known sources of systematic variance have been accounted for. In theory, error variance consists of random fluctuation only although there may be some unknown systematic variance included.

Precision is measured by the standard error estimate, a type of standard deviation measurement. The relationship between the standard error of estimate and the precision of the sample is that the smaller the standard error of estimate, the higher is the precision of the sample. After giving due consideration to problem of overcoming bias, it is desirable that the sample design produce a minimum standard error of estimate. However, not all types of sample designs provide estimates of precision, and samples of the same size can produce different amounts of error variance.

Exhibit 4.1 demonstrates the concept of sampling size. Four photographs of Kavitalaya Krishnan are used to show how one can take different – size samples and produce a very generalisable conclusion. The first photograph is finely screened and is therefore printed with thousands of dots of ink. Because of the fineness of detail, one might say that this photograph contains nearly all of the detail, or information, that can be provided.

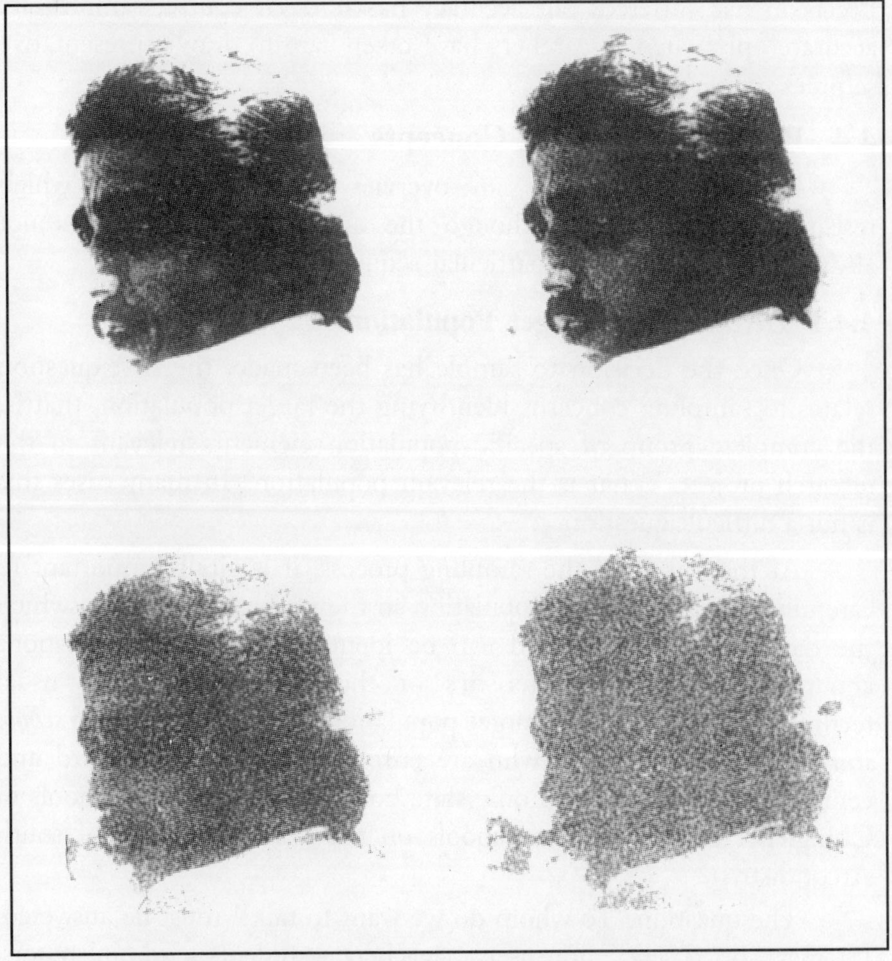

Exhibit 4.1: A photographic example of how sampling works

In other photographs, less detail is provided. Photograph 2 is made of approximately 2000 dots. The face is still very clear, but not as much so as in the first photograph; some detail is missing, but the face is still recognizable. Photograph 3 is made up of only 1000 dots, constituting a sample that is only half as large as that in Photograph 2; the face can still be recognized. In Photograph 4 the sample is down to 250 dots – yet if you look at the picture at a distance you can still make out a face and identify it as the one shown in Photograph 1. The 250 dot sample is still useful, despite the fact that is contains only a small fraction of the number of dots in the other photographs. Precision has suffered, but accuracy has not. Of course, samples are accurate only when researchers have taken care to draw representative samples properly.

4.4 Practical Sampling Concepts

Exhibit 4.2 presents an overview of the decisions which researchers must make, although the order of decisions does not always have to follow this particular sequence.

4.4.1 Defining the Target Population

Once the decision to sample has been made, the first question relates to sampling concerns identifying the target population, that is, the complete group of specific population elements relevant to the research project. What is the relevant population? In many cases this is not a difficult question.

At the outset of the sampling process, it is vitally important to carefully define the target population so the proper source from which the data are to be collected can be identified Answering questions about the critical characteristics of the population is the usual technique for defining the target population Does the term ***high school students*** include children who are enrolled in both state board and central board schools or in only state board schools? Do all schools in Chinglepet district include schools on the bordering areas of south Arcot district?

The question "To whom do we want to talk?" must be answered. It may be users, non-users, teachers, students, administrators, technicians and so on. To implement the sample in the field, tangible characteristics should be used to define the population.

4.4.2 The Sampling Frame

This is the list of elements from which a sample may be drawn. A sample example of a sampling frame might be the class attendance register. However, if the register is used as a sampling frame, it may exclude those students who registered late, students who have dropped out and the like. The sampling frame is also called the working population because it provides the list that can be worked with operationally.

The discrepancy between the definition of the population and a sampling frame is the first potential source of error associated with selection of a sample. A sampling frame error is associated with selection of a sample.

A sampling frame error occurs when certain sample elements are excluded or when the entire population is not accurately represented in the sample frame.

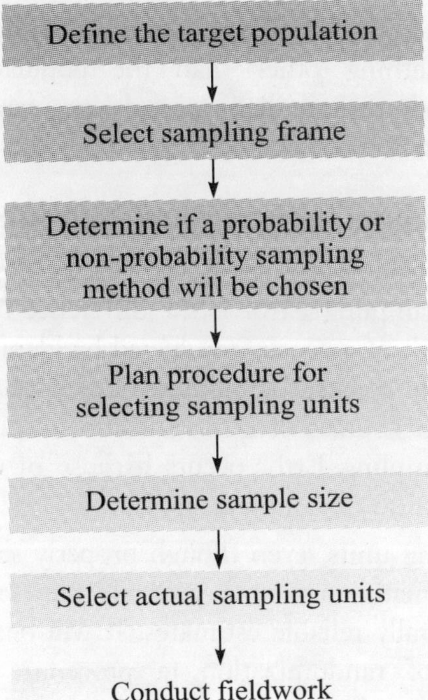

Exhibit 4.2: Stages in selection of a sample

4.4.3 Sampling Units

During the actual sampling process, the elements of the population must be selected according to a certain procedure. The sampling unit is a single element or group of elements subject to selection in the sample. For example, if a college wishes to sample science students, every 25th name on a complete list of students may be taken. In this case the sampling unit is the same as the element. Alternatively, the college could first select classes as the sampling unit, and then select certain students of the previously selected classes. In this case the sampling unit contains many elements.

If the target population has first been divided into units, such as science classes, additional terminology must be used. The term primary-sampling units (PSUs) designate units selected in the first stage of sampling. If successive stages of sampling are conducted, sampling units are called secondary sampling units or tertiary sampling units (if three stages are necessary).

When there is no list of population elements, the sampling unit is generally something other than the population element. For example, in a random-digit dialling study, the sampling unit will be telephone numbers.

4.5 Random Sampling Error and Non-sampling Error

Estimation from a sample is not exactly the same as a census count. Random Sampling Error is the difference between the sample result and the result of a census conducted by identical procedures. Of course, the result of a census is unknown unless one is taken, which is rarely done. Other sources of error can also be present (See Exhibit 4.3). Random Sampling Error occurs because of chance variation in the scientific selection of sampling units.

The sampling units, even though properly selected according to sampling theory, neither may nor perfectly represent the population, but they are generally reliable estimates. It will be seen, in discussion of the process of randomization (a procedure designed to give everyone in the population an equal chance of being selected as a sample member), that because random sampling errors follow chance variations, they tend to cancel each other out when averaged.

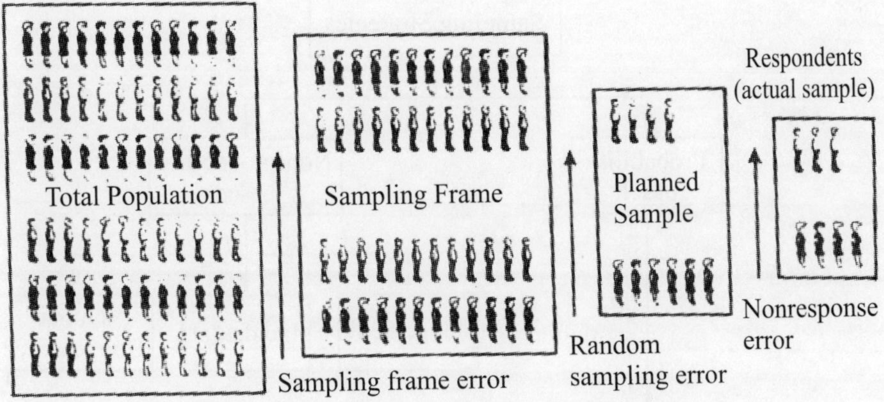

Exhibit 4.3: Errors associated with sampling

This means that samples, properly selected, are generally good approximations of the population.

There is almost always a slight difference between the true population value and the sample value, hence a small Random Sampling Error. Thus every once in a while a very unusual sample will be selected, because too many unusual people or companies were included in the sample, and this means there is a large Random Sampling Error.

The theory behind this concept of sample reliability and other basic statistical concepts is reviewed in detail in a later chapter. At this point, Random Sampling Error or sampling error is a technical term that refers only to statistical fluctuations that occur because of chance variations in the elements selected for the sample.

Random sampling error is a function of sample size. As sample size increases, sampling error decreases. The resources available, of course, will influence how large a sample may be.

Systematic (non-sampling) errors result from non-sampling factors, primarily the nature of a study's design and the correctness of execution. These errors are not due to chance fluctuations. For example, in mail surveys highly educated respondents are more likely to cooperate than poorly educated ones, for whom filling out forms is a more difficult task. Sample biases such as these account for a large portion of errors in educational research. The term sample bias is somewhat unfortunate, because many forms of bias are not related to the selection of the sample.

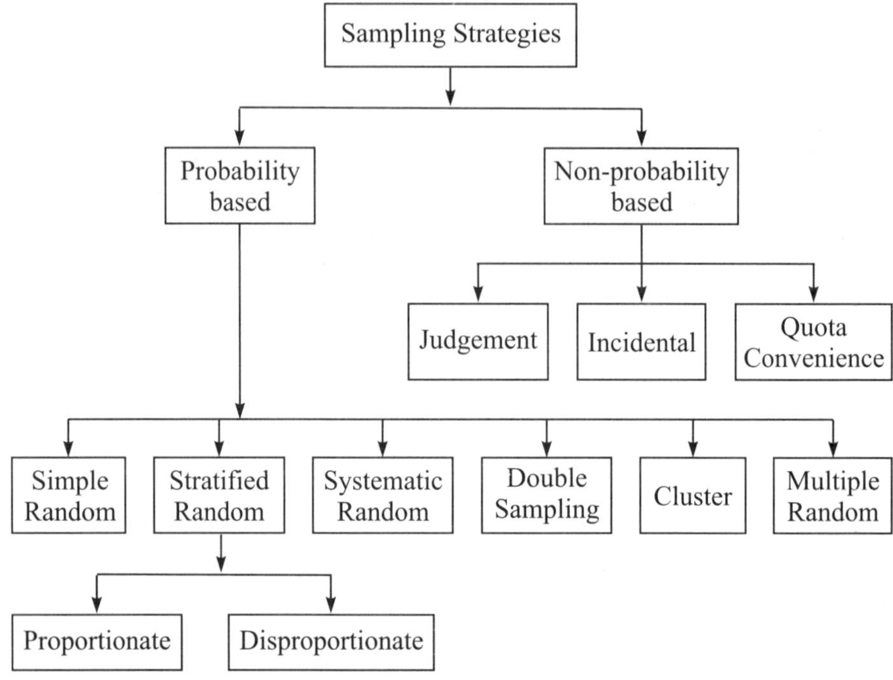

Exhibit 4.4: Types of sample design

It should be remembered that error due to sample selection problems, such as sampling frame error, are systematic (non-sampling) errors and should not be classified as Random Sampling Errors.

There are a variety of sampling techniques available. Which we select depends on the requirements of the projects, its objective, and funds available. The different approaches may be classified by their representation basis and the element selection techniques as in the accompanying table.

Representation Basis

Element Selection	*Probability*	*Nonprobability*
Unrestricted	Simple Random	Convenience
Restricted	Complex Random	Purposive
	Systematic	Expert choice
	Cluster	Quota
	Stratified	
	Double	

Representation. The members of a sample are selected either on a probability basis or by some other means. Probability sampling is based on the concept of random selection-a controlled procedure that assures that each population element is given a known non-zero chance of selection.

In contrast, non-probability selection is "non-random." That is, each member does not have a known non-zero chance of being included. Allowing interviewers to choose sample members "at random" (meaning as they wish or whether they find them) is not random sampling. Only probability samples provide estimates of precision.

Element Selection. Samples may also be classified by whether the elements are selected individually and directly from the population viewed as a single pool, or whether additional controls are placed on the process of element selection. When each sample element is drawn individually from the population at large, it is an unrestricted sample. Restricted sampling covers all other forms of sampling.

4.6 Probability versus Non-probability Sampling

There are several alternative ways of taking a sample. The major alternative sampling plans may be grouped into probability techniques and non-probability techniques. In probability sampling every element in the population has a known non-zero probability of selection. The simple random is the best known probability sample, in which each member of the population has an equal probability of being selected.

In non-probability sampling, the probability of any particular member of the population being chosen is unknown. The selection of sampling units in non-probability sampling is quite arbitrary, as researchers rely heavily on personal judgement. It should be noted that there are no appropriate statistical techniques for measuring Random Sampling Error from a non-probability sample. Thus projecting the data beyond the sample is statistically inappropriate. Nevertheless, there are occasions when non-probability samples are best suited for the researcher's purpose.

The various types of non-probability and probability samples will now be explored. Although probability sampling is preferred, non-probability sampling will be discussed first in order to illustrate some potential sources of error and other weaknesses in sampling.

4.6.1 Non-probability Sampling

4.6.1.1 Convenience Sampling

Convenience Sampling (also called incidental sampling) refers to the procedures of obtaining units or people who are most conveniently available. For example, the college professor who uses students has a captive sample-convenient but unrepresentative and perhaps unwilling.

Researchers generally use convenience samples to obtain a large number of completed questionnaires quickly and economically. Convenience samples are best utilized for exploratory research when additional research will subsequently be conducted with a probability sample.

Judgement or purposive sampling is a non-probability sampling technique in which an experienced individual selects the sample based upon his or her judgement about some appropriate characteristic required of the sample members. The researcher selects a sample to serve a specific purpose, even if this makes a sample less than fully representative.

Judgement samples are most useful in studying those cases, which we believe, are in the best position to provide us with information. For example, we may be interested only in those who hold extreme position, have had certain types of experiences within the last few years, and so forth. The subjects may be those, which are judged by some expert to be the best ones for study. In these cases we seek a particular type of subject and may not even be interested in securing a cross-section of a population.

4.6.1.2 Quota Sampling

The purpose of quota sampling is to ensure that the various subgroups in a population are represented on pertinent sample characteristics to the exact extent that the investigators desire.

In this type of sampling we are interested in selecting subjects to conform to certain predesignated control measures. For example, we may know that the student body at ABC University is 55 per cent male and 45 per cent female. We may require interviewees in this ratio.

In most quota samples we specify more than one control dimension, depending upon our opinions or evidence as to their importance. For example, we may believe that response to a question should vary, depending upon the sex of the respondent. If so, we seek proportional responses from both men and women. We may also feel that undergraduates differ from graduate students, so this would be a dimension. We may also choose dimensions such as the student's academic discipline, ethnic group, religious affiliation, and social group affiliation.

The logic behind quota sampling is that certain relevant characteristics describe the dimensions of the population. If the sample holds the same proportion of these dimensions as the population, then other information found from the sample members will also reflect the patterns in the population. This reasoning by analogy is obviously dangerous and gives no assurance that the sample is truly representative.

In spite of these weaknesses already mentioned, quota sampling is widely used by the opinion pollsters and researchers. Often it is viewed as the only practical method because of cost and time consideration. Its advocates feel that, while there is some danger of systematic bias, the risks are worth taking. They are interested in averages and these tend to be rather stable even if there is some bias involved.

4.6.1.3 Snowball Sampling

Snowball sampling refers to a variety of procedures in which initial respondents are selected by probability methods, but in which additional respondents are then obtained from information provided by initial respondents. This technique is used to locate members of rare populations by referrals.

Suppose a manufacturer of science equipment is considering the marketing of science teaching kits for B.Ed. Physical Science teacher trainees. An extremely large sample would be necessary to find 100 B.Ed. teacher trainees with Physical Science as optional. It would be much more economical to survey, say 300 teacher trainees, and find 15 with Physical Science as optional and ask them for the number who may require such kits.

Reduced sample sizes and costs are a clear advantage of snowball sampling. Bias is likely to enter into the study, however, because a person who is known to someone (also in the sample) has a higher probability of being similar to the first person. If there are major differences between those who are widely known by others and those who are not, there may be serious problems with snowball sampling.

4.6.2 Probability Sampling

All probability samples are based on chance selection procedures. This eliminates the bias inherent in the nonprobability sampling procedures because the probability sampling process is random. It is frequently forgotten that the term random refers to the procedure for selecting the sample; it does not describe the data in the sample. Randomness refers to a procedure the outcome of which cannot be predicted because it is dependent on chance.

The procedure of randomization should not be thought of as unplanned or unscientific. It is the basis of all probability-sampling techniques.

4.6.2.1 Simple Random Sampling

Simple random sampling assures that each element in the population has an equal chance of being included in the sample. Drawing names from a hat or selecting the winning raffle ticket from a large drum is typical of simple random sampling. If the names or raffle tickets are thoroughly stirred, each person (or ticket) should have an equal chance of being selected.

4.6.2.2 Systematic Sampling

To illustrate systematic sampling, suppose one wishes to take a sample of 1000 from a list consisting of 200,000 names of students. Using systematic sampling, every 200th name from the list would be drawn.

A random process selects an initial starting point, and then every nth number on the list is selected.

The sampling interval is the number of population elements between the units selected for the sample.

4.6.2.3 Stratified Random Sampling

According to Mendenhall, Ott, and Scheaffer (1971, p.53), ***a stratified sample is obtained by separating the population elements into***

non-overlapping groups, called strata, and then selecting a simple random sample from within each stratum.

Consider stratified sampling of groups that are rank-ordered, such as full professors, associate professors, and assistant professors. Stratified sampling consists of listing all full professors together in one homogeneous group, then all associate professors, and then all assistant professors. After that is done, random (or systematic) sample is drawn within each group. This procedure not only avoids the possible basis of taking a systematic sample from a non-stratified sampling frame (with periodic cycles of ranks) but can also save time and money. Although a random sample drawn from a non-stratified sampling frame should present all ranks adequately, it might require a much larger sample then would a stratified sample, which ensures that each rank is represented. The potential saving of time and money in interviewing is even greater if the variable that is stratified (e.g. military of professional rank) is correlated with other variables (age, sex, income). A stratified sample will thus assure representation not only of all ranks but simultaneously of all age and income ranks within the population being sampled.

Stratified sampling is not limited to stratification on only one variable. One can stratify on two or more variables simultaneously. For example, in addition to stratifying on professional rank, the investigator could simultaneously stratify on sex, providing six groups instead of three (female full professors; male full professors; female associate professors, male associate professors; female assistant professors; male assistant professors). After the six groups are formed, a simple random sample is taken within each group as before. Notice that correlation of sex with rank lessens the need for dual stratification and that the number of strata mushrooms rapidly with additional variables especially if these variables contain more than two categories.

4.6.2.4 Cluster Sampling

Mendenhall, Ott, and Scheaffer (1971, p.121) define a cluster sample as a random sample in which each sampling unit is a collection, or elements. For example, an investigator wishing to study students might first sample groups or clusters of students such as classes or dormitories, and then select the final sample of students from the clusters. Unlike stratified sampling, in which every stratum is sampled, cluster sampling samples among clusters. ***Cluster sampling, sometimes called area sampling, is generally used when it is impossible or impractical to construct a sampling frame in which the sampling units are the sampling elements themselves.***

For example, for a study of median educational levels of all adult females in Chennai, no adequate list of all females would be available, and direct field listing would be exorbitantly expensive and impractical. (By the time the list was completed half of the potential respondents could have moved out of town unless a tremendous number of listers were employed at great expense.) By multistage cluster sampling the investigator can first randomly sample census tracts from a sampling frame that lists all tracts in the city. Then in the second stage he or she can randomly sample city blocks from a sampling frame consisting of all city blocks within the census tracts drawn in the first stage of the sample. The third stage samples households from a sampling frame of all households contained in the blocks drawn in the second stage of the cluster sample. The fourth stage consists of choosing the adult females within each household drawn in the third stage (if two or more adult females reside in the same household, one of them is randomly selected).

The obvious advantage of cluster sampling is the great saving in time and money that it affords. The obvious disadvantage is that it is not a single sample but two or more, with a possibility for sampling error in each. For example, in simple random sampling there is always the possibility that the sample is not representative of the entire population. But in cluster sampling, if the first stage is representative, the second stage might not be. This means that the investigator must be concerned about sample size and sampling accuracy not once but in every stage of the cluster sample.

It should be clear that the sampling methods discussed here are not mutually exclusive, For example, clusters and then later elements can be drawn by either simple random or systematic procedures. In addition, stratified sampling and cluster sampling can be combined in a single procedure-stratified cluster sampling, in which one chooses the strata as before, then conducts cluster procedures within each stratum.

4.6.2.5 Multi-stage Area Sampling

Multi-stage area sampling involves two or more steps that combine some of the probability techniques already described. Typically, progressively smaller (lower-population) geographic areas will be randomly selected in a series of steps.

Exhibit 4.5 portrays a multistage area sampling process frequently used by a major academic research centre. Progressively smaller geographic areas are selected until a housing unit is selected for interviewing.

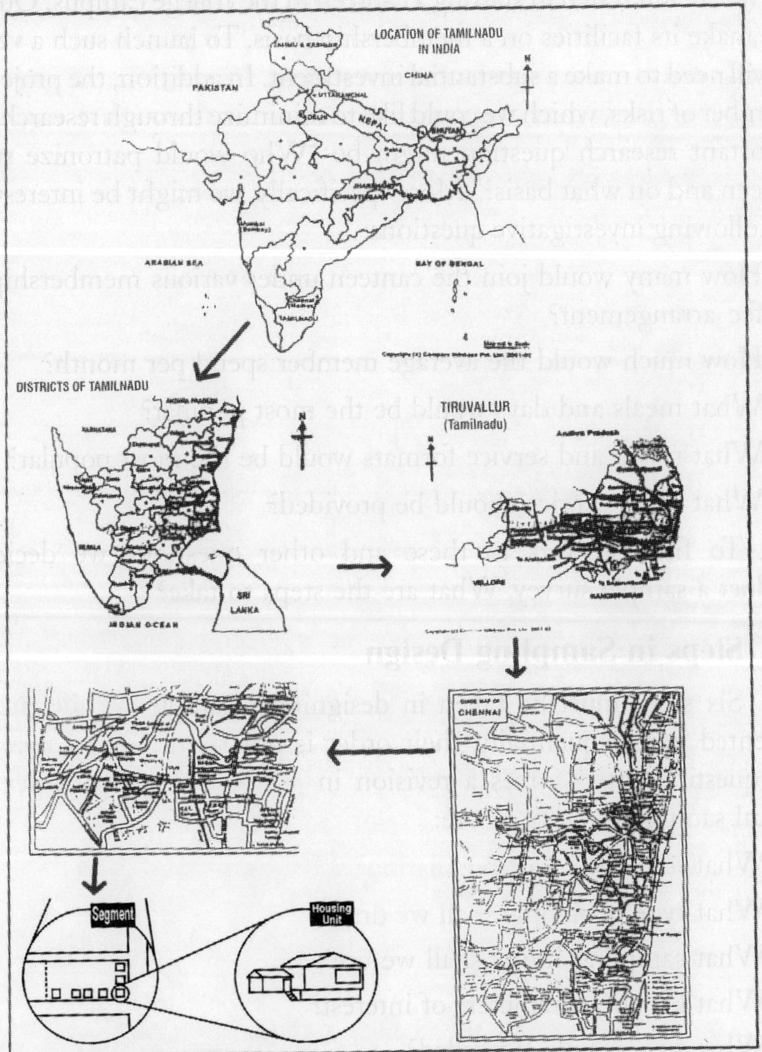

Exhibit 4.5: Multi-stage area sampling process

Exhibit 4.6 gives a summary comparing the sampling techniques. A researcher who must make a decision concerning the most appropriate sample design for a specific project will identify a number of sampling criteria and evaluate the relative importance of each criterion before homing in on a sample design.

4.6.2.6 Sampling Procedure

There are a number of design decisions that must be made. Assume that we are interested in starting a canteen in the college campus. Our idea is to make its facilities on a membership basis. To launch such a venture we will need to make a substantial investment. In addition, the project has a number of risks, which we could like to minimize through research. One important research question might be "Who would patronize such a canteen and on what basis?" More specifically, we might be interested in the following investigative questions:

— How many would join the canteen under various membership and fee arrangement?

— How much would the average member spend per month?

— What meals and days would be the most popular?

— What menu and service formats would be the most popular?

— What other service should be provided?

To find answers to these and other questions we decide to conduct a sample survey. What are the steps to take?

4.7 Steps in Sampling Design

Six steps must be taken in designing a sample. While they are presented here sequentially, their order is not fixed and an answer to one question often forces a revision in an answer given earlier. The critical sampling questions are:

- What is the relevant population?
- What type of sample shall we draw?
- What sampling frame shall we use?
- What are the parameters of interest?
- What size sample is needed?
- How much will the sample cost?

Exhibit 4.6: Comparison of sampling techniques

Non-probability Samples

Description	Cost and Degree of Use	Advantages	Disadvantages
1. Convenience: Researcher uses most convenient sample or most economical sample.	Very low cost, extensively used	No need for list of population	Variability and bias of estimates cannot be measured or controlled; projecting data beyond sample inappropriate
2. Judgement: An expert or experienced researcher selects the sample to fulfill a purpose; such as ensuring all members have a certain characteristic.	Moderate cost, average use	Useful for certain types of forecasting; sample guaranteed to meet a specific objective	Bias due to expert's beliefs may make sample unrepresentative; projecting data beyond sample inappropriate
3. Quota: Researcher classifies population by pertinent properties, determines desired proportion of sample from each class, and fixes quotas for each interviewer.	Moderate cost, very extensively used	Introduces some stratification of population; requires no list of population	Introduces bias in researcher's classification of subjects; non-random selection within classes means error from population cannot be estimated; projecting data beyond sample inappropriate

Description	Cost and Degree of Use	Advantages	Disadvantages
4. Snowball: Initial respondents are selected by probability samples; additional sample are obtained by referral from initial respondents.	Low cost, special situation	Useful in locating members of rare populations	High bias because sample units not independent; projecting data respondents beyond inappropriate

Probability Samples

Description	Cost and Degree of Use	Advantages	Disadvantages
1. Simple Random: Researcher assigns each member of the sampling frame a number, then selects sample units by a random digit method.	High cost, not frequently used in practice (expect random-dialling) sampling: respondents may be widely dispersed, hence higher cost	Only minimal advance knowledge of population needed; easy to analyze data and computer error	Requires sampling frame to work from; does not use knowledge of population that researcher may have; larger errors for same samples size than stratified
2. Systematic: Researcher uses natural ordering or order of sampling frame, selects an arbitrary starting point, then selects items at a preselected interval.	Moderate cost, moderately used	Simple to draw sample; easy to check	If sampling interval is related to a periodic ordering of the population, may introduce increased variability

Description	Cost and Degree of Use	Advantages	Disadvantages
3. Stratified: Researcher divides the population into groups and randomly selects sub-samples from each group. Variation includes proportional, disproportional, and optimal allocation of subsample sizes.	High cost, moderately used	Assures representation of all groups in sample; characteristics of each stratum can be estimated and comparisons made; reduces variability for same sample size	Requires accurate information on proportion in each stratum; if stratified lists are not already available, they can be costly to prepare
4. Cluster: Researcher selects sampling units at random, and then does complete observation of all units in the group.	Low cost, frequently used	If clusters geographically defined, yields lowest field cost; requires listing of all clusters but of individuals only within clusters; can estimate characteristics of clusters as well as of population	Larger error for comparable size than other probability samples; researcher must be able to assign population members to unique cluster, or duplication or omission of individual results
5. Multi-stage: Progressively smaller areas are selected in each stage. Researcher performs some combination of the first four techniques.	High cost, frequently used, especially in nation-wide surveys	Depends on techniques combined	Depends on techniques combined

What is the Relevant Population? The population of interest is normally apparent from the management problem and the research objectives. In the canteen example the population might be one or a combination of the following: students, faculty, non-academic personnel, area residents and/or workers, or the general public. Assume that the major need is for student facilities. Therefore, the relevant population might be "all currently enrolled students at XYZ College of Education."

What Type of Sample? What method should we use? Because the total student body is geographically concentrated, and there is a reasonably accurate list of this population, besides a major investment being planned, we conclude we would like to use a probability design of the simple random type. In a later section we will consider the application of other sampling techniques to this problem.

Choosing the simple random sampling technique has several consequences for us. With this sample design we can make probability-based confidence estimates of various parameters. In using this method we must also give careful attention to the execution of the sampling process. The selection must follow an appropriate procedure in which there is no chance for interviewers or others to modify the selections made. No one other than those selected can be included in the study; strong efforts must be made to include all of the elements in the original sampling frame. We must exclude substitutions except as clearly specified and controlled according to predetermined decision rules.

In spite of all of this care the actual sample achieved will not match perfectly the sample that is originally drawn. Some persons will refuse to participate and others will be difficult to find. The latter represent the well-known "not-at-home" problem and require that a number of callbacks be made to assure that they are adequately represented in the sample.

What Sampling Frame? The concept of sampling frame is closely related to the population. It is defined as the list of elements from which the sample is actually drawn. Ideally it is a complete and correct list of population members only. As a practical matter, however, the sampling frame often differs from the theoretical population.

Consider the canteen survey problem. The population is defined in terms of "currently enrolled students at XYZ College of Education." However, the college has two schools attached to it. Thus, we might redefine the population to be 'all students currently enrolled at the XYZ College campus."

The student directory would be a logical first choice as a list of population elements. This source may represent a sampling frame, which is too narrow.

We might redefine the population to include only those in the directory, but this would be a sampling frame that does not fully reflect our desired population. Therefore we would try other solutions first. These problems do not present great difficulties. Using the list of students in the college as well as the students on the roll in both the attached schools can retain the original population concept. One procedure in this case is to number consecutively all of the names on the college and school lists. Then use a table of random numbers to draw a sample of the desired size plus an additional list of replacement numbers, recorded in their order or selection. Names are selected for the sample from the list to correspond to the random numbers chosen. If a chosen student has left school or college that student is dropped from the study and replaced by the name chosen with the first unused number on the supplemental list. This process continues until the desired sample is secured. This procedure is often called sampling from a "too inclusive frame."

What Parameters to Estimate? In determining the nature of the sample design it is important that we determine what specific population parameters are of interest. Some of these will correspond to the investigative questions already asked. For example:

— The proportion of persons who express an interest in joining the canteen.
— The average expected expenditures per month per member.
— Average number of weekday lunches that will be demanded.

There may also be important subgroups in the population about whom we would like to make estimates. For example, we might want to draw conclusions about the extent of canteen use that could be expected from married students versus single students, residential students versus in-town students, and so forth. Such questions have a strong impact upon the nature of the sampling frame we accept, the design of the sample, and its size.

Parameters of interest may also be classified as variable or attributes data. Variables, as used in this special statistical sense, are normally computed from ratio or interval scale data such as, age, length, scores, and so on, and may be continuous or discrete. Continuous variables such as age and length, can take all possible values within the relevant ranges; discrete variables, such as family size and number of visits per month, can take only selected values. The most common measures of variables data are the arithmetic mean and the standard deviation.

Attribute measures are necessary for nominal data and are widely used for other measures as well. Examples of attribute measurement are the proportion of a sample that expresses an interest in joining the club, or the proportion of married students who report they now eat in restaurants five times a month or more. The most frequent concentration measure of attributes is the percentage; the variance measure is the pq ratio.

How Large a Sample? One false belief is that a sample must be large or it is not representative. This is much less true then most people believe. During prepoll survey or exit polls for elections, political partners question the sample size of 1000 or more of the electorate. Samples of 1,000 or more have been branded as totally inadequate by many critics but seldom if ever by a statistician. Sample size is only one aspect of representativeness. A sample of more than 1 million can be misleading while a sample of 1,000, drawn in the proper manner, can be more than adequate.

Casual observers generally feel that the size of sample must bear some proportional relationship to the size of the population from which it is drawn. One hears that a sample should represent 10 percent or more of the total population. This is a myth. The absolute number of people in a random sample is more significant than is the sample's size relative to the population size. A sample of 200 drawn from a population of 2,000 may be quite appropriate, but for many purposes the size of sample may need to be no more then, say 50 members. Again, a sample of 200 is, for most practical purposes, just as appropriate for a population of 100 millions as it is to a population of 2,000. If drawn correctly it will give almost the same precision in either case.

In simple random sampling there are a number of important factors, which affect the size of sample. Recall that a sample is only a partial reflection of the population from which it is drawn. It must be an acceptable representation of the population. But what is "acceptable? Ultimately this is determined by the researcher, who must determine (1) the desired size of the interval range around the estimated parameter and (2) an acceptable confidence level for the estimate.

Two other factors, which affect size of sample, concern the population. First is the size of the population variance. The greater this dispersion, the greater is the sample size needed to provide a given quality of representation. For example, if all members of a population hold the same view on a question then a sample of one will perfectly reflect the population on this question. On the other hand, if every member of the population were different on some characteristic, it would take a complete census to capture the full variety. A second population aspect, which can affect sample size, is the ***population*** size itself. Elementary sampling typically assumes an infinite population, but populations are often finite. Thus, a population of 50 obviously limits any sample size to no more than this amount.

Other considerations often weigh heavily upon the sample size decision. The conditions under which the sample is being conducted may indicate that only certain designs are feasible. For example, one type of sample may be the appropriate design because we have no list of population elements and must therefore sample geographic units. Since various designs have differing statistical and economic efficiencies, the choice of design coupled with the other requirements mentioned above will also affect the size of sample.

The researcher may also be interested in making estimates concerning various subgroups of the population; then the sample must be large enough for each of these subgroups to meet the desired quality level. We achieve this in simple random sampling by making the total sample large enough to assure that each critical subgroup meets the minimum size criterion. In more complex sampling procedures we sample the smaller subgroups more heavily and then weigh their effect on the total parameter estimates.

4.8 How Much Will it Cost?

Cost considerations have a major impact upon decisions about the size and type of samples as well as the data collection methods. Almost all studies have some budgetary constraint, and this can even dictate that a non-probability sample must be used. Probability sample surveys incur callback costs, listing costs, and a variety of other costs, which are not as important when more haphazard methods are used.

Costs also dictate the size of sample that we can draw. For example, if there is a Rs.2,000 budget for interviewing, and it costs an estimated Rs.10 to complete a personal interview using a simple random sample, it is obvious that the sample cannot exceed 200 respondents. By changing the design to a geographic cluster sample we might be able to reduce this to, say Rs.7.50 per interview, allowing a sample size of 300. A shift to a self-administered questionnaire might reduce costs to Rs.5 per interview, giving a sample of 400.

Cost factors may also dictate that we abandon personal interviewing in favour of either telephone or mail surveys. Thus, telephone interviews might cost Rs.2 each, allowing a sample of 1000. In changing the type of data collection method, of course, we must recognize that the amount and type of data, which can be secured, also changes.

4.9 What is the Appropriate Sample Design?

We have discussed the advantage and disadvantages of each of the various sampling techniques. A summary comparing the sampling techniques is given in Exhibit 4.6. A researcher who must make a decision concerning the most appropriate sample design for a specific project will identify a number of sampling criteria and evaluate the relative importance of each criterion before selecting a sample design. This section outlines and briefly discusses the most common criteria.

Degree of Accuracy

Selecting a representative sample is, of course, of importance to all researchers. However, the degree of accuracy required or the researcher's tolerance for sampling and non-sampling error may vary from project to project, especially when cost savings or another consideration may be a trade-off for a reduction in accuracy.

For example, when the sample is being selected for an exploratory research project, a high priority may not be placed on accuracy because a highly representative sample may not be necessary. For other, more conclusive projects, the sample result must be a precise representation of a population's characteristics, and the researcher must be willing to spend the time and money to achieve accuracy.

Resources

The costs associated with the different sampling techniques vary tremendously. If the researcher's financial and human resources are restricted, this limitation of resources will eliminate certain methods. For a postgraduate student working on a master's thesis, conducting a national survey is almost always out of the question because of limited resources. Educational administrators concerned with the cost of the research versus the value of the information often will opt for cost savings from a certain non-probability sample design rather than make the decision to conduct no research at all.

Time

Researchers who need to meet a deadline to complete a project quickly will be more likely to select simple, less time-consuming sample designs. A telephone survey utilizing a sample based on random-digit dialling takes considerably less time than a survey using an elaborate disproportionate stratified sample.

Advance Knowledge of the Population

Advance knowledge of population characteristics, such as the availability of lists of population members, is an important criterion. In many cases, a list of population elements will not be available to the researcher.

National versus Local Project

Geographic proximity of population elements will influence sample design. When population elements are unequally distributed geographically, a cluster sampling may become much more attractive.

Need for Statistical Analysis

The need for statistical projections based on the sample is often a criterion. Non-probability sampling techniques do not allow the researcher to utilize statistical analysis to project the data beyond the sample.

REFERENCES

- Best, John and Kahn, James. Research in Education. Prentice Hall of India. New Delhi. 2005.
- Cochran, W.G. Sampling Techniques. New York. John Wiley and Sons. 1963.
- Deming, W.E. Sample Design in Business Research. New York: John Wiley & Sons, 1960.
- Kerlinger, Fred. and Lee, Howard. N. Foundations of Behavioral Research. 4th Ed. Harcourt College Publishers. Toronto. 1999
- Kish, Leslie. "Selection of the Sample". Chapter 5 in Leon Festinger and Daniel Kart eds. Research Methods in the Behavioural Sciences. New York: Holt, Rinehart and Winston. 1953.
- Yamane, Taro. Elementary Sampling Theory. Englewood Cliffs, N.J. Prentice Hall, 1967.

Review of the Related Literature

5.0 Related Literature

Once a topic has been selected, the investigator is naturally eager for action. However, it is a mistake to rush headlong into planning and carrying out the study before making a thorough survey of what is already known in the area of interest. The topic must be related to relevant knowledge in the field. It is as important for educators, as it is for others engaged in research, to know how to locate, organize, and use the literature in their field. Basically, this chapter discusses.

- the role of related literature in a research project
- reference sources in education, and
- the task of organizing the related literature for presentation in the report.

5.1 Role of Related Literature in a Research Project

The review of related literature involves the systematic identification, location, and analysis of documents containing information relating to the research problem.

The search for related literature should be completed before the actual conduct of the study begins. This stage serves several important functions.

- *A knowledge of related research enables investigators to define the frontiers of their field.* To use an analogy, an explorer might say, "We know that beyond this river there are paddy fields for 2,000 kilometres west and beyond those fields a range of hills, but we do not know what lies beyond the hills. I propose to cross the fields, go over the hills, and proceed from there in a westerly direction." So the researcher in a sense says, "The work of X, Y, and Z has discovered this much about my question; the investigations of Z have added this much to our knowledge."
- *A thorough review of related theory and research enables researchers to place their questions in perspective.* One should determine whether one's endeavors would be likely to add to knowledge in a meaningful way. Knowledge in any given area consists of the accumulated outcomes of numerous studies conducted by generations of researchers and the theories designed to integrate this knowledge and to explain the observed phenomena. One should review the literature for the purpose of finding a link between one's study and the accumulated knowledge in one's field of interest. Studies with no link to the existing knowledge seldom make significant contributions to the field. Such studies tend to produce isolated bits of information that are of limited useful values.
- *Reviewing related literature helps researchers to limit their question and to clarify and define the concepts of the study.* A research question may be too broad to be carried out or too vague to be put into concrete operation. A careful review of the literature can help researchers to revise their initial question so that it can be investigated. It also helps in clarifying the concepts involved in the study and in translating these concepts into operational

definitions. Many educational and behavioural constructs as stress, creativity, frustration, aggression, achievement, motivation, and adjustment need to be clarified and operationally defined. These constructs, as well as many other educational and behavioural concepts, do not lend themselves to scientific research until they can be quantified. In reviewing literature one becomes familiar with previous efforts to clarify these concepts and to define them operationally. Successful reviews often result in the formation of hypotheses regarding the relationships between variables in one's study. Studies in which hypotheses are tested are usually more useful than those without hypotheses.

- *A critical review of related literature often leads to insight into the reasons for contradictory results in an area.* Contradictory results are not uncommon. The reasons for inconsistencies may be found in the kinds of approaches adopted for solving the problem, or the kinds of instruments employed, methodologies used, or analyses made. A comparison of the procedures of these studies may explain the inconsistent findings. To resolve such contradictions is not only a challenge, but it can also provide a significant contribution to one's knowledge.
- *Through studying related research, investigators learn which methodologies have proved useful and which seem less promising.* As one proceeds through the related literature and develops increasing sophistication, one may soon find oneself seeing better ways in which some of the studies could have been done. Of course, hindsight is always better than foresight, so perhaps it is inevitable that early studies in a field often seem crude and ineffective. Many research projects fail because of the use of inappropriate procedures, instruments, research designs, or statistical analysis. A thorough examination of the methodologies of previous studies often results in finding the reason for the failure of past studies as well as insight into the selection of an appropriate methodology for one's own research. Both the success and failures of past work provide insight for designing one's own study. By building on past investigations, we can develop increasing sophistication in our knowledge about educational research.

- *A thorough search through related research avoids unintentional replication of previous studies.* Frequently a researcher develops a worthwhile idea only to discover that very similar study has already been made. In such a case the researcher must decide whether deliberately to replicate the pervious work or to change the proposed plans and investigate a different aspect in the problem.
- *The study of related literature places researchers in a better position to interpret the significance of their own result.* Becoming familiar with theory in the field and with previous research prepares researchers for fitting the findings of their research into the body of knowledge in the field.

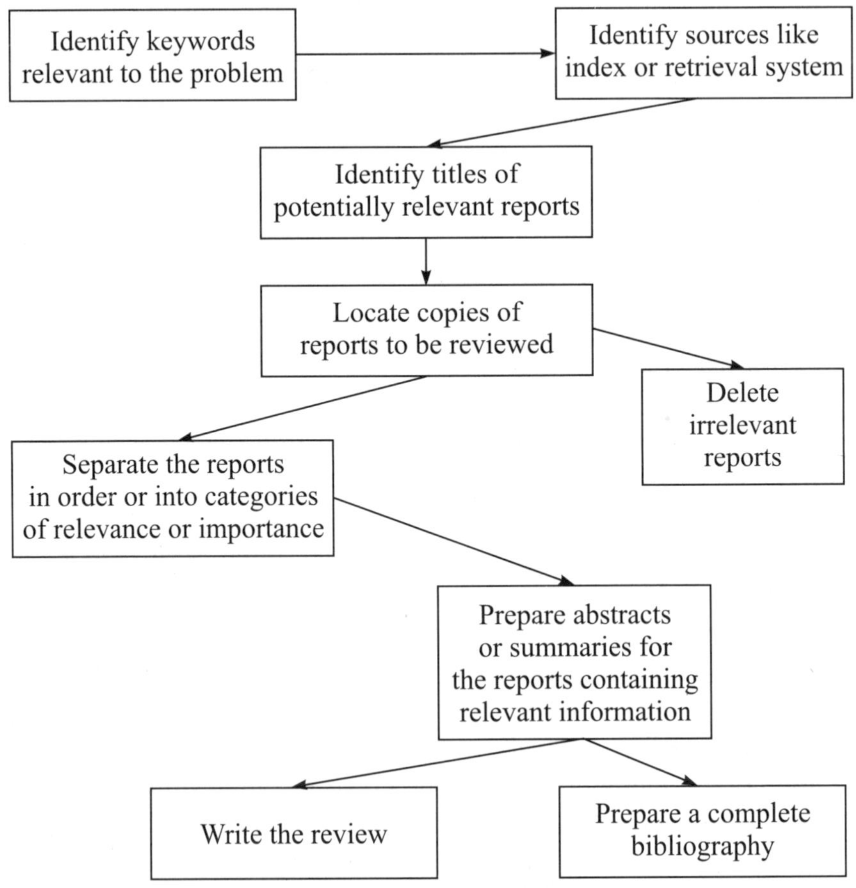

Exhibit 5.1: Activities of review process

Value of Research

- Limiting and identifying the research problem and hypotheses
- Informing the researcher of what has already been done
- Providing possible research design and methodology
- Identifying possible gaps in the research
- Providing a backdrop for interpreting the results

5.2 Sources of Information

The library is an invaluable source of information. Studies are published in books, journals, technical reports, working papers and theses. Many of these are accessible in electronic form.

5.2.1 Reference Sources in Education/Social Sciences

It is essential for scholars and researchers to know how to find previous work in their areas. To do this, one should know

— the sources of previous work
— what agencies collect such information and organize it into databases
— what form these databases
— what form these databases take, and
— efficient ways of finding the information one needs.

In order to use these sources, one must become familiar with available library facilities and services. Many libraries have printed guides describing their services and regulations or will schedule orientation tours. One should also find out whether the library can obtain books and other documents through inter-library loan. It is also necessary to know how to surf the Net and access relevant related literature, besides checking the authencity of the literature.

What do you look for in a library

- Periodical Literature
- Education Index
- Educational Resources Information Centre (ERIC)
- Other Indexes and Abstracts
- Review of Educational Research (RER)

- Reports of Meta Analysis
- Abstracts and Reports in Periodicals
- Theses and Dissertations
- Books

How do you use the library

Using the library effectively is a necessary skill for a researcher. A student should explore the following options before writing the review of the literature:

- Librarian – a fountain of information
- Catalogue – author/subject/title /keyword
- Browsing through computer databases
- On-line tutorials that many libraries provide

5.2.2 Basic Guides

To begin a search of research studies, it is useful to consult basic guide to the research literature. One of the most helpful of these guides is ***Berry's Bibliographic Guide to Educational Research.*** This guide lists major research sources and gives descriptive annotations for each, emphasizing recently published sources. It includes sections on different types of research materials such as books, periodicals, government publications, and tests. Other types of research reference sources described are encyclopedias, dictionaries, handbooks, statistical sources, yearbooks, directories, and biographical sources. A separate section on ERIC documents and computer searching of ERIC materials is included. Another section covers handbooks on the methodology of educational research and on form and style in writing research papers.

Woodbury's Guide to Sources of Educational Information is a comprehensive guide to locating information relating to education. It contains detailed descriptions of more than 700 published and institutional sources plus chapters on how to locate them and how and when to use them.

Hamilton's Directory of Educational Statistics lists 99 sources for educational statistics, both current and historical, on a wide range of topics. This guide describes publications by the United States Office of Education, U.S.Bureau of the Census, National Educational Association, UNESCO, and other governmental and nongovernmental organizations.

A comprehensive basic work is ***Sheehy's Guide to Reference Books*** which briefly describes and evaluates several thousand reference sources. This publication is kept up to date by means of biennial supplements.

5.2.3 Reviews of Education – Related Literature

Reviews that integrate and summarize research studies on specific topics can help to get one started on a literature search. There are several basic reviews that one can consult. **Mitzel's Encyclopedia of Educational Research** the fifth edition of an American Educational Research Association (AERA) project presents useful summaries and evaluation of research on a wide variety of topics. A new edition is published once every decade. **Review of Educational Research**, a quarterly published by AERA, summarizes research findings in education and related fields. From 1931 until 1970 the review concentrated in sequence on one of fifteen broad areas in education for each issue. In an attempt to provide summaries of research within broad subject areas in the profession, the editorial board of the American Educational Research Association launched publication of the series, **Review of Research in Education**, which has been published annually since 1972 (except 1973 and 1982). This series attempts to identify what research has been done, is being done, and needs to be done in the field. Emphasis is on current research.

Two other useful review sources are the **Handbook of Research on Teaching**, edited by Gage, and its second edition. Second Handbook of Research on Teaching edited by Travers. Both works list, summarize, and critically analyze research in the field of teaching. Written by over thirty specialists, each book contains lengthy articles on method variables, subject areas, and grade levels. Extensive bibliographies appear in each chapter.

For the field of special education, a basic review of research can be found in the First, Second, Third, and Fourth, **Review of Special Education,** edited by Lester Mann and David Sabatino. These books present comprehensive examinations of major fields and briefer, more restricted evaluations of special areas and concerns in special education.

Psychological studies that may also be of interest to educators are summarized.

5.2.4 Periodical Indexes, Abstract Journals and Citation

- **Indexes**

Having established a broad base of relevant research, theory, and opinion on a particular topic of interest, one can begin to locate additional material not cited in the basic review sources. Various periodical indexes, abstract journals, and citation indexes enable one to locate this information. These publications, which are issued in successive parts at regular intervals, serve as guides for finding information that is widely dispersed in journals and other sources. The publishers of these indexes employ professional readers who survey and classify papers into published and unpublished. These papers are then grouped by subject, sometimes with annotations, so that researchers are presented with a fairly comprehensive and reasonably up-to-date listing of work in their areas.

- **The ERIC Indexes**

Two of the most important indexes are produced by the Educational Resources Information Center (ERIC), which was established by the U.S.Office of Education (USOE) to collect, store, and disseminate information on education.

The ERIC System, now sponsored by the National Institute of Education (NIE), is a network of approximately sixteen clearinghouses, each devoted to collecting, evaluating, and abstracting resource material in its own area of specialization. Subject areas included are adult, career, and vocational education; counselling and personnel services; educational management; elementary and early childhood education; handicapped and gifted children, higher education, information resources; junior college; languages and linguistics; reading and communication skills; rural education and small schools; science, mathematics, environmental education, social studies and science education, teacher education, tests, measurement and evaluations; and urban education. In addition, there is a central processing facility that is in charge of storage and dissemination of materials. The results of this work are made available through two periodicals, **Current Index to Journals in Education** and **Resources in Education** plus other publications.

A carefully developed system of indexing is used for providing access to ERIC documents. This system is described in the Thesaurus of ERIC Descriptors (1980), which is available in most libraries or can be ordered from the publishers, the Onyx Press The ERIC thesaurus is a useful source for planning a comprehensive search for related studies in one's area.

Current Index to Journals in Education

The monthly journal Current Index to Journals in Education (CIJE) is compiled from the work of the specialists of the ERIC clearinghouses. Articles from over 700 journals are classified and indexed according to the system developed in the ERIC thesaurus.

CIJE is divided into four sections (1) subject index, (2) author index, (3) main entry section, and (4) journal contents index. One can find articles of interest by first looking in the subject index for the titles and numbers of relevant articles, then using these numbers to find the entries in the main entry section. If you cannot find your topic of interest in the subject index, look for synonyms for the topic. The vocabulary of the ERIC thesaurus is deliberately limited to provide a more systematic indexing system. The separate author index is useful to those wishing to find the work of a particular researcher. The journal contents index indicates the journals covered and the contents of each issue.

Exhibit 5.2 is a typical journal article citation taken from the main entry section, with explanation of its various parts, as provided by CIJE to illustrate the type of information in each entry. **Exhibit 5.3** is a typical document citation.

The annotation is particularly useful since it gives a brief description of the article. Note that in the example in Exhibit 5.3. the title alone gives only a partial idea of what the article is about. If the title for an article is considered sufficient to convey the main thrust of the article, the abstractors do not include an annotation. Publication of CIJE was begun in 1969. The journal is cumulated semi-annually and annually.

ERIC NO: EJ556860

TITLE: Small Schools: A Reform That Works.

AUTHOR: Raywid, Mary Anne

JOURNAL CITATION: Educational Leadership; v55 n4 p34-39 Dec-Jan 97-98

DESCRIPTORS: *Academic Achievement; *Change Strategies; *Educational Benefits; *Educational Improvement; Elementary Secondary Education; *High Risk Students; School Effectiveness; *Small Schools

IDENTIFIERS: Alaska; New Jersey; *Philadelphia School District PA

ABSTRACT: Recent research shows that students at all grade levels, **especially** at-risk youngsters, learn more in small schools; small schools are more violence-free; and bonds created in small schools are likely... (Note: This is a partial abstract.)

Exhibit 5.2: A sample journal article citation

ERIC NO: ED399990

TITLE: Opportunities and Challenges: Bridging the Two-Year Four-Year College Gap.

AUTHOR: Susskind, Tamar Y.

DESCRIPTORS: *Articulation (Education); *College Transfer Students; Community Colleges; *Educational Cooperation; *Transfer Policy; *Transfer Programs

ABSTRACT: Community colleges have been criticized with respect to both the low numbers of students who transfer to four-year institutions and the inadequate preparation of the students who do transfer...

PUBLICATION DATE: 1996

(Note: This is a partial abstract.)

Exhibit 5.3: A sample ERIC document citation

An efficient approach to the use of CIJE involves:

— Determine the ***keywords*** under which articles relevant to your study might be listed. These keywords will always include the ***population*** and the ***variables*** you have identified in your problem statement.

— Check the Thesaurus of ERIC Descriptors to find which of your key words are used as ***descriptors***. You may need to find synonyms for the key word you have listed.

— Begin your search with the most recent issue of CIJE and work back through earlier issues.
— Copy from CIJE the entire reference given for any title which may be useful. This procedure simplifies the task of finding the original articles.
— Search out the articles in their journals. If your library does not have the journal, the librarian may be able to obtain a xerographic copy of the article through inter-library loan.
— Read the abstract first – if one accompanies the journal article – to determine whether it will be useful to read the entire article. If there is no abstract, start with the summary and conclusion sections.

Exhibit 5.4 is an entry from the ERIC database, describing a **journal** article. This is typical of entries found in the printed version of Current Index to Journals in Education.

---

http://www.eric.ed.gov/ERICWebPortal/resources/html/publishers/bibliographic_record.pdf

ERIC Number: A unique accession number assigned to each record in the database. These are also known as the ERIC Document Number (ED Number) and ERIC Journal Number (EJ Number).

Full-Text Availability: Indicates document availability in electronic full-text (PDF image) from ERIC at no cost. Searchers may limit their search to retrieve only fulltext materials. A link to the publisher's Web site will appear here for materials indexed from 2004 forward, as well as a link to full text if available.

Descriptors: Terms from the Thesaurus of ERIC Descriptors, a controlled vocabulary used to describe the subject content of the document or article.

Note: Descriptors are not the same as keywords. Descriptors are Thesaurus terms used to describe the subject of a document or article.

Publisher: ERIC added this field in 2005 for materials published 2004 onward, and includes data provided by the publisher.

Abstract: A brief narrative description of the journal article, document, or resource.

The list of descriptors tells us terms that substantively describe the article and under which the article is listed in the subject index of CIJE. This information about descriptors, which at first might seem superfluous, is often helpful. By entering these terms we would have

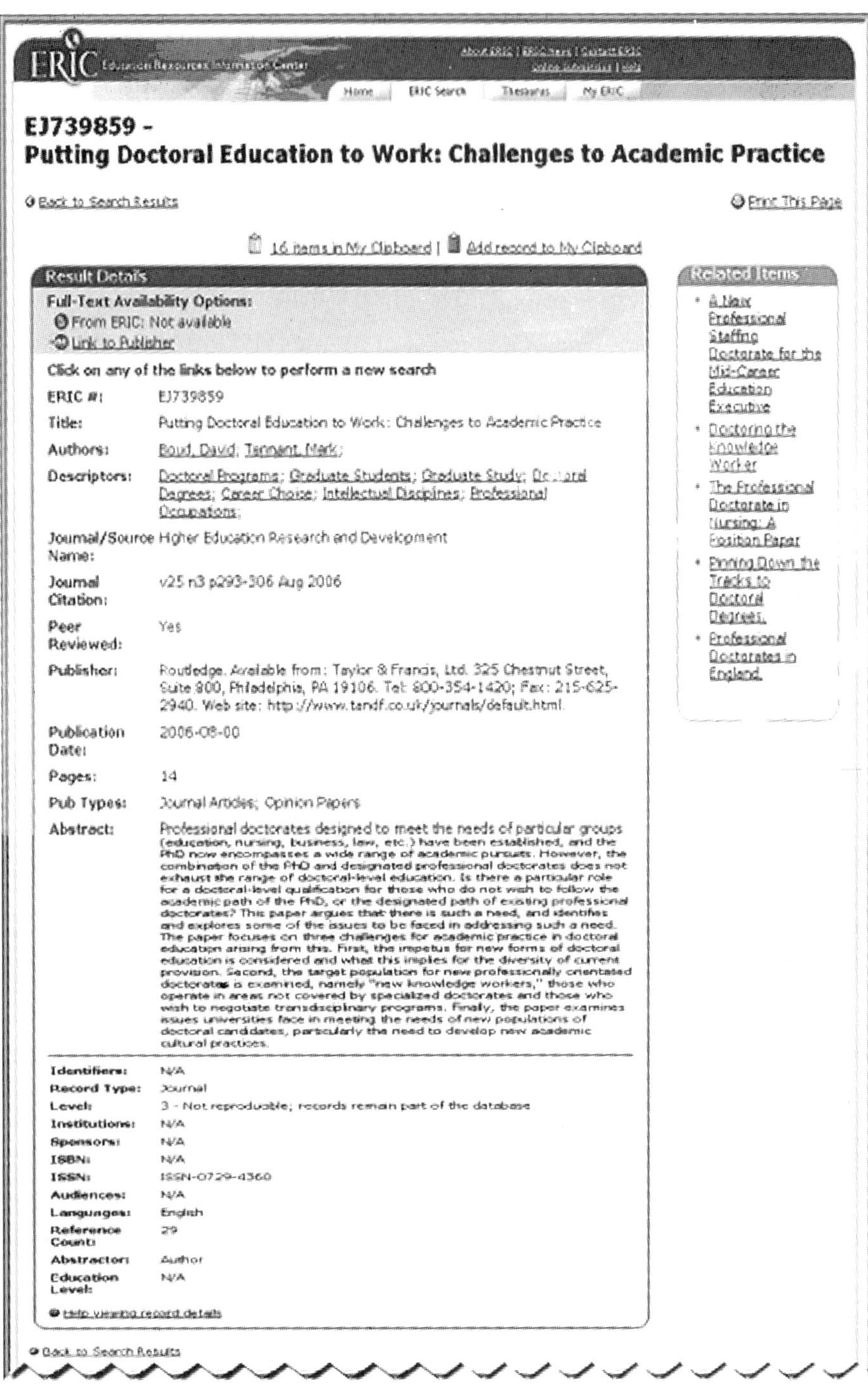

ERIC Education Resources Information Center

Home | ERIC Search | Thesaurus | My ERIC

EJ739859 -
Putting Doctoral Education to Work: Challenges to Academic Practice

Back to Search Results | Print This Page

16 items in My Clipboard | Add record to My Clipboard

Result Details

Full-Text Availability Options:
From ERIC: Not available
Link to Publisher

Click on any of the links below to perform a new search

ERIC #:	EJ739859
Title:	Putting Doctoral Education to Work: Challenges to Academic Practice
Authors:	Boud, David; Tennant, Mark;
Descriptors:	Doctoral Programs; Graduate Students; Graduate Study; Doctoral Degrees; Career Choice; Intellectual Disciplines; Professional Occupations;
Journal/Source Name:	Higher Education Research and Development
Journal Citation:	v25 n3 p293-306 Aug 2006
Peer Reviewed:	Yes
Publisher:	Routledge. Available from: Taylor & Francis, Ltd. 325 Chestnut Street, Suite 800, Philadelphia, PA 19106. Tel: 800-354-1420; Fax: 215-625-2940. Web site: http://www.tandf.co.uk/journals/default.html.
Publication Date:	2006-08-00
Pages:	14
Pub Types:	Journal Articles; Opinion Papers
Abstract:	Professional doctorates designed to meet the needs of particular groups (education, nursing, business, law, etc.) have been established, and the PhD now encompasses a wide range of academic pursuits. However, the combination of the PhD and designated professional doctorates does not exhaust the range of doctoral-level education. Is there a particular role for a doctoral-level qualification for those who do not wish to follow the academic path of the PhD, or the designated path of existing professional doctorates? This paper argues that there is such a need, and identifies and explores some of the issues to be faced in addressing such a need. The paper focuses on three challenges for academic practice in doctoral education arising from this. First, the impetus for new forms of doctoral education is considered and what this implies for the diversity of current provision. Second, the target population for new professionally orientated doctorates is examined, namely "new knowledge workers," those who operate in areas not covered by specialized doctorates and those who wish to negotiate transdisciplinary programs. Finally, the paper examines issues universities face in meeting the needs of new populations of doctoral candidates, particularly the need to develop new academic cultural practices.
Identifiers:	N/A
Record Type:	Journal
Level:	3 - Not reproducible; records remain part of the database
Institutions:	N/A
Sponsors:	N/A
ISBN:	N/A
ISSN:	ISSN-0729-4360
Audiences:	N/A
Languages:	English
Reference Count:	29
Abstractor:	Author
Education Level:	N/A

Help viewing record details

Related Items

- A New Professional Staffing Doctorate for the Mid-Career Education Executive
- Doctoring the Knowledge Worker
- The Professional Doctorate in Nursing: A Position Paper
- Pinning Down the Tracks to Doctoral Degrees.
- Professional Doctorates in England.

Back to Search Results

Exhibit 5.4: An entry from the ERIC database, describing a journal article

been able to find this article. In addition, by knowing what descriptors apply to the article we are currently examining, we can find out where similar articles are also likely to be found. All the descriptors listed after the citation is pertinent to the article in question, but the article was actually indexed in CIJE only under the descriptors marked by an asterisk.

Finally, the abstract describes the contents of the article. By reading this abstract we can decide whether we want to pursue the article any further. The initials in parentheses at the end of the abstract indicate who wrote the abstract. If the abstract had been written by the author, it would say so at this point.

Rather than merely plunging into CIJE to begin our search, we could be more systematic by referring first to the Thesaurus of ERIC Descriptors (Exhibit 5.3). By looking in this book we can find out what descriptors are actually used in CIJE. Moreover, we can find related terms, broader terms, and more specific terms, which would enable us to make our search more efficient and thorough. (In addition, the Thesaurus shows how many entries have been indexed under any descriptor in RIE and CIJE, and this information can be helpful in determining how many citations we would be likely to get by looking under that descriptor.)

A search of the ERIC system is an important step in the quest for related literature, but one cannot assure that when this step is finished the quest is completed. Material relevant to one's question may not have been entered

Useful websites

- Researching Topics in Education: A Tutorial http://www.lib.ncsu.edu/guides/education/ericintro.htm
- Using ERIC databases http://www.watsonlibrary.org/old/SubjectLinks/Education/ERIC.htm

5.2.5 Resources in Education

Abstracts of research reports from sources other than journals are indexed and published monthly by ERIC in Resources in Education (RIE). A semi-annual cumulative edition of the index sections is also published. Each clearinghouse collects materials related to its field of specialization, and then catalogs the documents and prepares indexes and abstracts. The original documents, together with the abstracts prepared by each clearinghouse, are sent on a regular basis to the Processing Facility, where they become part of the central data base on which users of the ERIC System can draw. The Processing Facility is responsible for collecting the input of all clearing-houses and publishing the combined abstracts monthly in RIE.

The sources covered include reports of all government funded educational research, abstracts, pamphlets, curriculum guides, significant papers from the proceedings of learned societies and institutes, bibliographies, exemplary course-related materials, teacher's guides and programme outlines, as well as various other research proposals and project reports. With such a far-ranging coverage it is clear that the documents in the ERIC collections are of vital interest to practitioners as well as researchers in education. Over 240,000 documents are now included, and the collection is growing at a rate of about 15,000 documents per year.

Each abstract is assigned its own accession number for the purpose of identification, and for ordering copies of the original documents. Three indexes are provided: author, institution, and subject. Using the appropriate index, one finds the titles of documents and their accession numbers, which one then uses to locate the individual abstracts.

The procedure for using RIE is similar to that used for CIJE. One typically begins with the most recent copy and works backward, looking under the subject or subjects of interest.

Exhibit 5.5 is an example of an entry in the main entry section of RIE.

Other Indexes

There are many other periodical indexes in the field of education that are useful for locating up-to-date information on research as well as contemporary opinion in education. One of the standard indexes for the field is the Education Index, which has been published regularly since 1929 by the H.W. Wilson Company. This index lists articles in more than 200 periodicals, year\books, bulletins, proceedings, and monographic series. Education Index is the best source for locating

Sample Resume Entry

ED 654 321
CE 123 456
Smith John
Johnson Jane
Career Education for Women
Central Unix - Chicago III
Spons Agency - National Inst of Education (DHEW) Washington D.C
Report No - CU2081.S
Pub date may 73
Contract- NIE -73-0001
Note -129p.
Presented National Conference on Career Education (3rd Chicago III. May 15/17/1973)
Available from - Campus bookstore 123 college Ave. Chicago -III 60690
EDRS: MF-50-83
HC 57-35
Description - Career Opportunity Career Planning, careers, Demand Occupations' Employment opportunities, females, labor force labor, market, manpower need, occupational aspiration occupational guidance, occupation, vocational counseling' working women

ERIC Accession Number- identification number sequentially assigned to documents as they are processed.

Clearinghouse accession number

Author(s)

Title

Organization where document Originated

Report Number- assigned by originator

Sponsoring Agency - Agency responsible for initiating, funding and managing the research project

Date published

Contract Grant Number

Descriptive Note (pagination first)

Alternate source for obtaining document

EDRS - availability through the ERIC document Reproduction Service MF means micratiche HC means hard copy reproduct paper copy when described as not Available From EDRS alternate sources are cited above prices are subject to change for latest price schedule see page on 'How to order ERIC Documents in the recent issue of RIE

Descriptions subject terms which characterize substantive content only the major terms. Printed in the subject index

Identifiers additional identifying terms not found in the Theasurus of ERIC descriptors only the major terms preceded by an asterisk are printed in the subject index.

Identifiers-consortium of states 'National Occupational Competence Testing institute III women's opportunity for employment will be directly related to the labor market demands through the remainder of the decade. The number of workers needed for all major occupational categories is expected to increase by about one-fifth between 1970 and 1980, but the growth rate will vary by occupational group professional and technical workers are expected to have the highest predicted rate (39 percent) followed by service workers (35 percent) clerical workers (26 percent, sales workers(24 percent) craftsmen and foremen (20 per cent, managers and administrators (15 percent) and operatives (11 percent) this publication contains a brief discussion and employment information concerning occupation for professional and technical worker managers and administrators skilled trades, sales workers clerical workers and service workers in order for women to take advantage of increased labor market demands, employer attitudes towards women need to change and women must (1) receive better career planning and counseling (2) change their career planning and fully utilize the sources of legal protection and assistance which are available to them. (SB)

Informative Abstract

Exhibit 5.5: Example of an RIE entry

journal articles prior to the establishment of Current Index to Journals in Education in 1969, as well as for very recent articles, as it typically lists articles about six months before CIJE does. A disadvantage of the Education Index is that it has no annotations.

In addition to these general indexes, a number of useful specialized indexes are available to the researcher. Exceptional Child Education Resources (formerly Exceptional Child Education Abstracts) published by the Council for Exceptional Children, lists journal articles from ERIC's CIJE and research materials from RIE concerning handicapped and gifted children. Psychological Abstracts lists the world's literature in psychology and related disciplines. This index includes books and doctoral dissertations as well as periodical articles. A summary of each article, book, dissertation listed is included, enabling the reader to determine the relevance of the material. Child Development Abstracts and Bibliography provides an author-and-subject approach to articles on the child covering the areas of infancy, clinical medicine and public health, developmental and comparative psychology, experimental psychology including learning phenomena, personality, and educational psychology and counseling. Sociology of Education Abstracts lists, by subject and author, periodical articles, books, and dissertations in its field, with a summary for each item. Educational Administration Abstracts provides an author-and-subject approach to specialized journals in the field of educational administration. Social Science Index lists, by author and subject, journal articles in the social sciences, covering education journals as well as journals from the field of psychology. sociology, political science, anthropology, law, and economics. Every discipline has its specialized indexes, such as business education, industrial arts, and medicine, to name only a few. Consulting the basic guides to the literature will give readers the names of the specialized indexes in other fields that they may need.

Indexes of Dissertations and Theses

Master's theses and doctoral dissertations are useful sources of information for researchers. In addition to the periodical indexes and abstract journals that list some dissertations and theses, such as ERIC's RIE and Psychological Abstracts, several specialized guides and indexes are very useful.

Dissertation Abstracts International published by University Microfilms in Ann Arbor, Michigan, contains the original author's abstracts of all doctoral dissertations accepted by over 150 universities across the United States and Canada Dissertation Abstracts International is published monthly, and indexes appear annually. Dissertations selected by University Microfilm from 1861 to 1972 are indexed but not abstracted in Comprehensive Dissertation Index 1861-1972. Many libraries that have online computer searching subscribe to DATRIX II and so have access to Dissertation Abstracts International's information.

American Doctoral Dissertations is a complete listing of all doctoral dissertations accepted by American Universities, compiled from commencement programs issued by universities and colleges. It includes a number of dissertations that are not included in Dissertation Abstracts International. It is published annually, is arranged by subject categories and institutions, and has an author index, but no abstracts of the dissertations are provided.

For master's theses, two useful indexes are Master's Abstracts: A Catalog of Selected Master Theses on Microfilm and Master's Theses in Education, edited by H.M. Silvey. Master's Abstracts, published by University Microfilms since 1962, provide abstracts for a selected list of master's theses submitted by various universities and colleges across the United States. Master's Theses in Education is an annual listing of theses from universities and colleges in the United States. For each thesis the author, title, and institution is given, but no abstracts are provided.

For studies done in Indian Universities, the reader is advised to refer Survey Of Educational Research brought out by the NCERT every five years. Besides this the Indian Council of Social Science Research brings out regular reviews.

Social Science Citation Index (SSCI)

A relevant article found by consulting one of these indexes will itself provide references to earlier work in the area. When one has found particularly relevant and important articles, a citation index can be used to move forward in time. For example, if you have read a particularly useful article published in 1976, through subsequent indexes you can identify articles that cite the article of interest in their bibliography. Many of these articles will describe continuations, expansions or modifications of the original work of interest.

Social Science Citation Index (SSCI), published in three volumes a year by the Institute for Scientific Information, can tell you which authors have been cited during the year in all areas of social science, including education, and what has been written in various areas, with the necessary bibliographic information for both citing and cited authors.

Many of the sources cited have been incorporated into computer data bases including ERIC, Exceptional Child Education Resources, Psychological Abstracts, Social Sciences Citation Index, and Dissertation Abstracts International. So have other data bases such as NIMIS (Instructional Materials for Education of the Handicapped), and Sociological Abstracts. Many institutions have librarians trained in the use of computer searching who can explain the services available and costs. Most researchers find computer searching well worth the price not only because of saving time and labour but because of the computer's capacity for doing highly complex searches combining many concepts and terms.

In a "manual" search through periodical indexes, for a particular topic, one can select a key term for the topic, follow it through the indexes, and find a few relevant subentries that combine that term with another. The computer, however, can search for any number of topics and any number of combinations of topics, and can do it thoroughly, quickly, and inexpensively. For example, the computer can quickly identify all articles and other materials that have the terms programmed instruction, mathematics, and secondary school among their descriptors.

Here are a few websites useful for education and the social sciences:

- http://gateway.library.uiuc.edu/
- http://www.icssr.org/
- http://ncert.nic.in/sites/publication/journals.htm
- http://padhaee.com/padhaee/htmlfiles/publication/indiancoucisocial.htm

5.3 Computer Searching

Many of the sources cited have been incorporated into computer databases including ERIC, Exceptional Child Education Resources, Psychological Abstracts, Social Sciences Citation Index, and Dissertation Abstracts International. Many institutions have librarians trained in the use of computer searching.

5.4 Inter-library Loan

Inter-library loan service can also be extremely helpful. If you find references to research studies in periodicals books or theses that are not available in the library you are using, it may be possible to borrow those materials from other libraries through interlibrary loan service.

INSDOC MALIBNET enables researchers in India to access literature from any part of the world. (http://www.angelfire.com/in/malibnet/services.html)

There are many other important sources of related literature:

Applied Social Sciences Index and Abstracts (ASSIA) is available online. It is an index of articles from over 600 international English language social science journals, from 1987 to the present. The database contains approximately 168,000 records and provides unique coverage of special educational and development aspects of children.

Australian Education Index (AEI) is produced by ACER and is an index to materials at all levels of education and related fields, dating from 1978 onwards. Source documents include journal articles, monographs, research reports, theses, conference papers, legislation, parliamentary debates and newspaper articles.

Book Bank OP is available on CD-ROM and contains details of UK and some American out of print books.

BOPCAS – British Official Publications Current Awareness Service is available on the internet via a password. It gives details of 9000 official government publication a year, with links to full text documents where available on the Internet.

British Education Index (BEI) is available on the Internet via an ATHENS account. It provides bibliographic reference to 350 British and selected European English – language journals in the field of education and training from 1986 onwards. Monographic, report and conference literature is limited, but increasing.

CBCA Full Text Education covers monographs and journal articles from over 200 Canadian education journals, many in full text from 1976 onwards. In addition, it includes Canadian federal and provincial government research reports, monographs from educational research communities across Canada, provisional curriculum guides, graduate dissertations and theses in education. It incorporates the ONTERIS database covering research reports and curriculum documents originating from sources in the province of Ontario. A comprehensive annual directory of education-related organizations, school and boards is also included.

Child Data Consists of four of the National Children's Bureau computerized information databases on CD-ROM. It provides information on the education, health and welfare of children and young people, including a comprehensive directory of organizations concerned with children, an index to all the key stories about children's issues that have appeared in the press since 1996, the holdings of the National Children's Bureau Library, and a conferences and events database.

The Cochrane Library is an electronic publication which includes 2 databases of systematic reviews and abstracts of systematic reviews, on the effects of health care, as well as a bibliography of controlled trials in the area and other sources of information on reviewing research and evidence – based health care.

ERIC is available on the Internet via an ATHENS account. It is the largest education database in the world, with files which extend back to 1966 and contain more than 700,000 records. ERIC indexes over 775 journals, mostly American, and provides good coverage of 'fugitive' literature, such as conference proceedings, speeches, theses and technical reports. Most records contain an abstract.

Global Books in Print is available on CD-ROM and consists of a listing of over 1.4 million English language book titles in print in the UK, Europe, USA, Australia, New Zealand and South Africa.

PsycINFO is available online. It contains references to the psychological literature from 1887 to the present, including articles selected from over 1,300 journals in psychology and related fields, as well as book chapters and books. This has now merged with the PsycLIT database, enhancing it with abstracts of dissertations and technical reports.

Social Research Methodology is available on CD-ROM. It contains approximately 39,000 references to literature on social and behavioural research methodology, statistical analysis and computer software. It dates from 1970 onwards and covers 100 international social science periodicals, books, monographs, research reports and Congress proceedings.

TES/THES is available on CD-ROM. It is a combination of the two Supplements containing the full text of the main editions from October 1994. Extracts are available on the TES and THES sites at http://www.tes.co.uk and http://www.thes.co.uk.

5.5 Government Publications

The Government of India, a major source of information, sponsors more research, conducts more surveys, and collects more statistics of all kinds than any other organization. This is true of Governments of most countries. The Department of Education, as well as the National Centre for Educational Statistics, disseminates a vast number of publications, including research reports, surveys, administrative actions and descriptive programmes.

For locating specific Indian government publications, the website of the NCERT ..... is a prime source to consult. Besides, State Governments have their own websites, which gives details of research projects and the like going on in the state.

A few of the publications are listed below:

Sixth Educational Survey. This survey is conducted once in 10 years. The Sixth Survey was conducted in 1990 and is being published by NCERT now. It contains statistical information on the status of education in India.

Indian Educational Abstracts: NCERT publishes twice a year (January and July) abstracts of published research in India in that period.

Primary Teacher: NCERT publishes a quarterly journal for primary teachers in English and Hindi .

School Science: NCERT publishes a quarterly journal for secondary teachers in English

DPEP Calling This is a DPEP monthly newsletter. It describes activities in the past months and plans for the future months.

Web sites giving details of Government of India's activities in education

- **http://www.education.nic.in/htmlweb/pub.htm**
- **http://www.education.nic.in/htmlweb/main.htm**
- **http://www.icssr.org/**
- **http://ncert.nic.in/sites/publication/journals.htm**

5.6 Test Sources

In conducting research, a test or measuring device is often required. This guide is a tool to help users identify and locate published and unpublished educational, psychological and vocational tests and measurements.

Steps in Finding a Test

1. Go to Mental Measurements Yearbook Database. **(http://library.bridgew.edu/mt/max/2008/02/database_trials_mental_measure_1.html)**
2. For a more comprehensive search, also go to the **ERIC /AE Test Locator** and to **Tests in Print.**
3. If you need to search further, check **Bibliographies** of Tests and Measurements.
   - **General Bibliographies**
   - **Subject-related Bibliographies**
4. If you are still unable to find a test that you want, there are several **Additional Options.**
   - Sources of Information on Testing / Source of Comprehensive Information about Specific Well-Known Tests

- Victor
- Indexes to Periodicals
- Reference Books
- Internet Resources
- Textbooks

ERIC / AE Test Locator [WWW. Site]

LOCATION: Access the following URL address: **http://ericae.net/testcol.htm**

This site actually comprises several usual tools, most notably the "The Educational Testing Service (ETS) Test Collection database. The ETS tool searches a database of more than 10,000 tests and research instruments, and provides descriptions and availability information for each.

- Murphy, Linda L., James C. Impara, and Barbara S. Plake, eds. Tests in Print V: An Index to Tests, Test Reviews, and the Literature on Specific Tests. Lincoln, NE: Buros Institute of Mental Measurements, 1999.

  This 2-volume set serves as a master index to all Buros publications. It attempts to provide a comprehensive listing of every test that is currently (i.e. at the time of compilation of the set) available for purchase, and of many out-of-print tests.

- Goldman, Bert Arthur, and John L. Saunders. Directory of Unpublished Experimental Mental Measures. New York, NY: Human Sciences Press, 1990 vol.

  This directory provides references to non standardized, experimental measures found in scholarly journals in the fields of education, psychology, and sociology.

- Hersen, Michel, and Alan S. Bellack, eds. Dictionary of Behavioral Assessment Techniques. Elmsford, NY: Pergamon Press, 1988.

  Not really a "dictionary," but rather an alphabetical list of individual essays of approximately 300 clinical measures.

- Keyser, Daniel J. and Sweetland, Richard C. eds. Test Critiques. Kansas city, MO: Test corp. of America, 1985.

Each volume of test critique contains approximately 100 critical reviews of commercially available tests – generally the most frequently used. Written for professionals and students alike.

- Maddox, Teddy, ed. Tests: A Comprehensive Reference for Assessments on Psychology, Education and Business. Austin, TX: Pro-ED. 1997.

  This is designed to provide 'quick reference' identification of a test to meet a specific need. More than 3000 psychology education and business tools are listed.

- Eliot, John and Ian Macfarlane Smith International Directory of Spatial Tests. Berkshire, UK: NFER-Nelson. 1983.

Attitudes

- Shaw, Marvin E. and Jack M. Wright Scales for the Measurements of Attitudes. New York, NY: McGraw-Hill 1967. This book actually reproduces 175 attitude measures that it discuses.
- Touliatos, John and Barry F. Pernutter and Murray A. Strauss. Handbook of Family Measurement Techniques. Newbury Park, CA: Sage Publishing 1990.

  This is the most extensive bibliography of tests that measure family functioning.

- Robinson,John P., Phillip R.Shaver and Lawrence S.Wrightsman. eds. Measures of Personality and Social Psychological Attitudes. Ann Arbor: MI: Survey Research Century 1968.

  These three works provide description of many cases including the entire measure or sample items of experimental attitude measures.

Reference Books

- Andrews, Frank M, et al. A. Guide for Selecting Statistical Techniques for Analyzing Social Science Data. Ann Arbor, MI: Institute for Social Research, University of Michigan, 1981.

  Provides a "decision tree" to help researchers and advanced students choose the appropriate statistical technique to meet their specific experimental needs.

- Goldstein, Gerald, and Michel Hersen, eds, Handbook of Psychological Assessment. New York, NY: Pergamon Press, 1990.

  This handbook attempts to provide an organized overview of the broad field of psychological assessment. Provides author and subject indexes.

- Kline, Paul. The Handbook of Psychological Testing. New York, NY: Routledge, 2000.

  Provides a comprehensive overview the whole field of psychometrics.

- Krug, Samuel E. Psychware Sourcebook. Kansas City, MO: Text Corporation of America, 1988.

  Describes the features of more than 450 software products designed for test interpretation, test administration, or clinical report generation.

- Miller, Delbert C. Handbook of Research Design and Social Measurement. Newbury Park. CA: Sage Publication, Inc, 2002.

  Comprehensive coverage of basic information about measurements for professions such as journalism, education, social work, business, and administration.

- O' Brien, Nancy Patricia,(compiler) Test Construction: A Bibliography of Selected Resources, Greenwood Publishing Group.1988.

  Comprehensive list of 2,759 times that deal with test design and construction.

- Reynolds, Cecil R., and Randy W. Kamphaus, eds. Handbook of Psychological and Educational Assessment of Children. New York. NY: Guildford Press, 1990

  This particular volume (of a two- volume handbook) focuses on all aspects of personality and behavior assessment of children.

- Rossi, Peter H., James D. Wright, and Andy B. Anderson, eds. Handbook of Survey Research. New York, NY: Academic Press, 1983.

Specialized guides to tests

- **Measures of Social Psychological Attitudes,**

  (A comprehensive guide to 65 Diagnostic Tests for Special Education along with assessment of selected Learning Disabled Instruments.)

Indian Psychological Tests

- Pestonjee,D.M. Second Handbook of Psychological and Social Instruments. South Asia Books. 1988.

5.7 Dictionaries

Good's Comprehensive Dictionary of Education gives concise definitions of terms in education and related disciplines. The **International Dictionary of Education** includes 10,000 educational terms from the preschool to the post-doctoral level. Famous educators and a wide range of international organizations and national institutions and associations are also included. There are many other specialized dictionaries for various subject areas, such a special education, reading, and educational technology.

5.8 Organizing the Related Literature

Once one is satisfied that a reasonably comprehensive study of the literature in the field has been carried out, one can proceed to the task of organizing it. A useful approach is to arrange the studies by topic and determine how each of these topics relates to one's own study.

The literature should be presented in such a way as to justify carrying out the study by showing what is known and what remains to be investigated in the topic of concern. The hypotheses provide a framework for such organization. Like an explorer proposing an expedition, the researcher maps out the known territory and points the way to the unknown territory to be explored. If the study includes several facets, or investigates more than a single hypothesis, the organization process is done separately for each one.

One should avoid the temptation to present the literature as a series of abstracts; rather, it should be presented in such a way as to lay a systematic foundation for the study.

It is almost inevitable that a number of the reports one has carefully studied and included in one's notes will, on reflection, prove to be only peripherally related to the topic. It is neither necessary nor desirable to include in a proposal every study encountered in a search through the literature. One's readers will not be impressed by mere quantity. Relevance and organization of the material are of prime importance.

The researcher who fails to approach the task of assembling the related literature in a systematic manner from the beginning can become much disorganized. The following suggestions may be of assistance.

- Begin with the most recent studies in your field and then work backward through earlier volumes. One obvious advantage of this approach is that you start with studies that have already incorporated the thoughts and findings of previous research. Earlier misunderstandings have been corrected and unprofitable approaches have been avoided. Another advantage is that these studies will include references to earlier works and, therefore, direct you to sources you might not otherwise encounter. Obviously, limits must be set to the process of gathering related research. On the one hand, laying meaningful groundwork for a study entails including all the important works in the field. On the other hand, devoting excessive time to this endeavor could result in boring the readers of your own report with superfluous details. Make sure that the related literature serves, but does not dominate, your own work.
- Read the abstract or summary sections of a report first to determine whether it is relevant top your question. Doing so can save much time that might be wasted reading unhelpful articles.
- Before taking notes, skim the report quickly to find those sections that are related to your question – another way to save reading time.
- Make notes directly on file cards as they are easier to sort and organize than sheets of paper, backs of envelopes, and so on. Many prefer 4-inch by 6-inch file cards, which provide a reasonable space for notes but are small enough to fit in a pocket or purse.

- Write out a complete bibliographic reference for each work. If you know which style manual will be used in the finished report, you can save time by using that reference from while note-taking. Add the library call number also to facilitate finding the work again, should it be necessary.
- To facilitate sorting and organizing, do not put more than one reference on each card. It is not possible to arrange your reference alphabetically or in any other way unless you record them singly.
- Be sure to indicate which parts of the notes are direct quotations from the author and which are your own paraphrases. Failure to make this distinction can lead to inadvertent plagiarism. It is also wise to clearly separate an author's evaluation of his research from your own.

Source	Content
Current Index to Journals in Education	Titles, authors and journal citations of journal articles related to education, with annotations where needed. Classification by subject by author, and by journal. No abstracts.
Resources in Education	Abstracts of research reports and other documents acquired by ERIC clearinghouses.
Thesaurus of ERIC Descriptors	System for classifying and indexing ERIC documents.
ERIC Microfiche Collection	Complete documents, the abstracts of which are in Resources in Education.
Education Index	Titles, authors and journal citations of journal articles related to education. Indexed by subject and title. No abstracts.
Readers Guide to Periodical	Title, author, and journal citations of articles in popular journals. Indexed by subject and title No abstracts.
Child Development Abstracts and Bibliography	Abstracts of journal articles in the field of child development.
Exceptional Child Education	Abstracts of journal articles in special education
Resources Psychological Abstracts	Abstracts of journal articles in psychology.

Source	Content
Review of Educational Research	Before June 1970: Review of research in selected topics in education in three – year cycle. Beginning June 1970: Unsolicited review on various topics in each issue.
Encyclopedia of Education Research	Summaries and evaluations of research of research in education, published at the end of each decade.
Dissertation Abstracts International	Abstracts of doctoral dissertations in the United States and Canada.
DATRIX II	Computerized sorting system for finding relevant dissertations listed in Dissertation Abstracts International.
Mental Measurements Yearbooks	Information and evaluation of commercially available tests.
Tests in Print III	Index and supplement to the first seven Mental Measurements Yearbooks.
Smithsonian Science Information Exchange	Information retrieval system for work currently in progress.
Social Science Citation Index	Bibliographic information for cited authors and topics.
Monthly Index to Government Publications	Subject listing of government publications.

Exhibit 5.6: Sources of related literature in education

5.9 Tips for Search Strategy on the Internet or Computer Database

There are two sets of factors which influences the way you search. They are which relates to

- you the researcher
- the resource you are about to use.

Before starting a search strategy you should be clear on time constraints, previous knowledge on the topic etc.

— You, your need, your topic, your prior knowledge, your time scale etc.

- Do you have time, or do you need to read widely?
- Do you already know the background? Or are investigating a new interest?
- How thorough do you need to be? Is it important that you are aware of "all" relevant work? Can you afford to miss some useful relevant research? Can you make do with just a few recent articles?
- Do you have an assignment to handle after the weekend, or Ph.D theses to complete in three years time?
- Are you looking for material specifically focussed on a precise question or do you need more general background material as well?
- Is your topic much researched/written about? Or is it a new developing field with very little published literature?

— The nature of the particular resource you are about to search

Your answers to the above questions will influence how thoroughly you need to search in any particular resource (and of course how wide a range of databases, search engines etc you need to search), but each one will need to be approached in a different way, on its own terms. You need to take into account the following:

- *What subject(s) does the resource/bibliography/database etc cover?*

  When using a well focused single subject database, like British Education index, your search strategy can often be less closely defined, simply because of the precise focus of the database. When using a multidisciplinary database, such as the International Bibliography of the Social Sciences, more care is needed to achieve the necessary focus in your search strategy itself.

- *What does it contain?*

  Does it consist of references to just whole books, or individual journal articles, or full text documents or website etc? When using a database of journal articles you will tend to find more items focused on relatively precise topics than overview of general themes – conversely a library catalogue will include books usually covering broader subjects. Your choice of search terms should take account of this.

- *What is searchable?*
  Just the titles of articles, books etc? Or are there Subject headings/ keywords that have been assigned to each item as well? The words and phrases used by authors in their titles are usually obvious indications of the major themes of the work. The subject heading or keywords used by the creators of the database will also be reliable indicators of the subject of each item (e.g. if the subject headings for an article are **"Parent Attitudes, National Curriculum, Primary Schools"** you can be pretty sure that the article is about parents' attitudes to the primary national curriculum.)

  If abstracts are searchable, you will need to be more careful and precise in your search-words or phrases that appear as part of a 500 word abstract, will not necessarily have the same weight or importance as those same words or phrases in titles or keywords. (e.g. "Since the introduction of the computer literacy in the school curriculum the attitudes of parents of primary school children towards secondary school selection procedures has changed...").

  This problem is magnified many times if full text is being searched – either full text documents, as in e.g. the full text of Agenda 21 of the UNESCO draft for wild life preservation or whole web pages, as indexed in some of the "Search engines".

- *How large is the resource?*
  How many items does it include? British Education Index contains less than 100,000 items, ERIC has almost 800,000. The smaller the database, the more generous or adventurous you can be in you are searching without fear of being overwhelmed.

- *How is the resource organized?*
  Does it use a consistent set of keywords or subject heading to describe the content of each item? Some databases and all search engines do not, but British Education Index, ERIC, Sociological abstracts and the International Bibliography of the Social Science all do.

- *What searching aids are available to you?*
  Are you able to search through the set of subject headings (often called the Thesaurus) before you start? Using British Education

Index through the BIDS service you cannot check the Thesaurus. Subject heading is automatically presented to you when you begin your search.

In general, the larger the database, the more abstracts there are, the more important it is to use the thesaurus or set of subject heading, if it is available to you.

Strategy Formulation

After you have considered the question relating to your need and to the resource you are about to search, you will have a clear idea of the probable complexity and scope of your search. You now need to prepare a structured strategy which aims to be as thorough and as focussed as you need it to be.

You can do this in three stages:

1. Analyze your question, being explicit about what you are trying to find, what it is you need, where your limits are etc. This is often more difficult than it sounds. It is always more difficult than with the artificial examples used here! You almost certainly will change your mind as you progress through the search and find things, but you do need to start with your ideas as clear as possible
2. Break down your question into its underlying, constituent concepts or ideas
3. Specify each of these concepts in turn as or as exhaustively as you need, using as many words, phrases, subject headings, thesaurus terms as you think you need to get the degree of coverage and relevance you want.

It often helps to imagine that you have already found your perfect set of references. Writing down a dozen "ideal" titles will help you clarify both the underlying concepts and get you started on thinking of alternative terminology which might be used to represent each of them. For example:

If you are interested in how parents might participate in their children's science learning or might influence the development of scientific attitude, you would be pleased to find titles such as:

- Parental involvement in science: an analysis of teacher's perceptions of parental involvement in science learning.

- Students' science development activities outside school.
- Playing games and learning science: the results of two intervention studies with parents.
- Does maternal scientific attitude affect students' scientific attitude on entry to school?
- Parent participation in science homework.

Having a list of "ideal titles" like this will make it easier:

- To see the underlying concepts. In this case one encompassing "parental involvement/participation/influence", another the idea of "science learning" and perhaps a third, "students"
- To give yourself a better idea of the range of alternative terms that you might have to use to retrieve the sorts of things you are looking for. For e.g.: you will need to find words or subject headings which specify not just "parental participation" but also "mothers' influence" or "fathers' involvement". Depending on how wide you want to stretch this concept, may be you need to include "grandparents" or of course "grandmothers", may be even "siblings...

The choice is yours – probably most of the literature will be dealing with parents rather than just mothers or fathers, and it is unlikely that there is much written about grandparental influence on mathematical learning, but if you do not explicitly ask for it, you will not retrieve it.

Similarly as well as specifying "science", a thorough search strategy would include "physics" "chemistry" the "high school", "primary school" "science concepts" and so on.

REFERENCES

- American Doctoral Dissertations. Ann Arbor, Mich.: Xerox University Microfilm 1961, 1963, 1964-1970.
- Annual Review of Psychology. Palo Alto, Calif.: Annual reviews, In., 1950.
- Guide to Reference Books. Robert Balay. Ed.: American Library Association. Z 1035. G85 1996 (11th ed.)
- Berry, Dorothea. A Bibliographic Guide to Educational Research. 3rd ed. Metuchen, N.J.: Scarecrow Press, Dec. 1990.

- Buch, M.B. (Ed.) Sixth Survey of Research in Education. NCERT. 1983-88.
- Child Development Abstracts and Bibliography (Washington, D.C. National Research Council, Committee on Child Development. 1927-1)
- Compton, C. A Guide to 65 Diagnostic Tests for Special Education Belmont, Calif.: Fearon-Pit-man Publishers, 1979
- Current Index to Journals in Education New York: Macmillan, 1969-1978; Phoenix, Ariz.: Onyx Press, 1979.
- Dissertation Abstracts International Ann Arbor, Mich.: Xerox University Microfilms, 1973
- Educational Administration Abstracts Columbus, Ohio: University Council for Educational Administration, 1966
- Education Index. New York: H. W. Wilson, 1929.
- Exceptional Child Education Resources. Reston, Va.: Council for Exceptional Children, 1969.
- Gage, N.L. ed., Handbook of Research on Teaching Chicago: Rand McNally, 1963
- Good, Carter V. Dictionary of Education. 3rd ed. New York: McGraw-Hill, 1973.
- Graham Page et al., International Dictionary of Education. London: Kogan Page/ New York: Nicholas Publishing, 1977.
- International Encyclopedia of Higher Education, Vol. 1. San Francisco, Jossey-Bass, 1977.
- Mann L. and D. Sabatino, Third Review of Special Education. Philadelphia, Pa.: JSE Press, 1976.
- Mann L. and D. Sabatino, Fourth Review of Special Education. New York: Grune.
- Mauser, A.J. Assessing the Learning Disabled: Selected Instruments San Rafael, Calif.: Academic Therapy Publications, 1977 & Stratton.
- Woodbury, Marda. A Guide to Sources of Educational Information. Washington, D.C.: Information Resources Press. Jan. 1982.
- Master's Abstracts: A catalog of Selected Master Theses on Microfilm Ann. Arbor, Mich.: Xerox University Microfilm, 1962.
- Master's Theses in Education Cedar Falls, lowa: Research Publications, 1952.

- Master's Theses in Education Cedar Falls, lowa: Research Publications, 1952.

- Mitchell, J.V. Tests in Print III: An Index to Tests, Test Reviews and the Literature on Specific Tests Lincoln, Ne: University of Nebraska Press, 1983
- Mitzel, H. ed., Encyclopedia of Educational Research, 5th ed. New York: Free Press, 1982.
- Psychological Abstracts Lancaster, Pa.: American Psychological Association, 1927.
- Resources in Education, Superintendent of Documents, U.S. Government Printing Office, Washington, D.C. 20402.
- Review of Educational Research. Washington, D.C. AERA, 1931.
- Review of Research in Education. Washington, D.C.: AERA, 1972.
- Robinson J.P. and P.R. Shaver, Measures of School Psychological Attitudes Ann Arbor, Mich.: Institute for Social Research, 1973.
- Sheehy, Eugene P. and Keckeissen Rita G., Mc Waine, Eileen and Winchell Constance M. ed. Guide to Reference Books. 9th edition. American Library Association, Chicago 1976.
- Sheehy, Eugene P. Guide to Reference Books. Chicago, American Library Association 1986.
- Social Sciences Citation Index Philadelphia, Pa.: Institute for Scientific Information, 1967.
- Social Science Index. New York: H.W. Wilson, 1974-1.
- Sociology of Education Abstracts Liverpool, 1965-1 Thesaurus of ERIC Descriptors Phoenix, Ariz: Onyx Press, 1980.
- Travers, Rober ed., Second Handbook of Research on Teaching. Chicago: Rand McNally, 1973.

CHAPTER 6

The Research Proposal

6.0 Introduction

A written proposal statement is often required when a study is undertaken. It assures that the investigator understands the study's purpose and proposed methods of investigation. Cost and time budgets are often spelled out. The length and complexity of research proposals ranges widely. A doctoral student may present a proposal that runs 20 pages or more. Applicants for UGC grants typically file a proposal request for a few pages, often in a standardized format specified by the granting agency.

Before the research proposal is prepared, it may be helpful to try out proposed procedures on a few subjects. This trial run or pilot study will, first of all, help the researcher to decide whether or not the study is feasible and whether or not it is worthwhile to continue. It provides an opportunity to assess the appropriateness and practicality of the data collection instruments. It permits a preliminary testing of the hypothesis, which may give some indication of its tenability and suggest whether or not further refinement is needed.

The pilot study will also demonstrate the adequacy of the research procedures and the measures that have been selected for the variables. Unanticipated problems that appear may be solved at this stage, thereby saving time and effort later. A pilot study is well worth the time required and is especially recommended for the beginning researcher.

6.1 The Research Proposal

After the question and the hypothesis have been formulated, one is ready to complete the tentative research plan. One needs to write out in detail what one proposes to do and just how one plans to do it.

Developing the research proposal is essential. It forces one to set down ideas in a concrete form. Many initial ideas seem promising until one has to spell them out in black and white; then the difficulties or the inadequacies become obvious.

The written form can also be given to others for their comments and criticism. It is much easier for another to detect flaws and errors in a proposal when it is written out than when it is communicated by word of mouth.

Typically the research at this stage is only a preliminary proposal and many changes will probably be needed before the final, formal proposal is written. However, it is helpful to keep in mind that the more complete and detailed this initial proposal is, the more useful it will be to the researcher and the more time will be saved later.

Exhibits 6.1 and **6.2** give the components of the proposal as well as the basic questions typically asked /checklist when planning a research study. A beginning researcher will be well advised to look through these exhibits so that s/he knows where s/he is heading.

- ***The rationale*** – why the research is needed and what is the general area of current concern.
- ***Existing research*** – what is already known about the general area of the proposed research.
- ***The research questions.***
- A discussion of information needed to answer the research questions.
- The methods appropriate to collect the required information.

- The sources of information (size and type of sample, etc)
- The *timescale* and sequence of various stages of the research.
- A statement of what you intend the outcomes to be (reports, discussion papers, contributions to theory, materials, etc)
- Description of who will do what and at what cost (if funding is being sought)
- References.

Exhibit 6.1: Components of the proposal

Decision to Make in the Research Process	Basic Questions
Problem definition	What is the purpose of the study? How much is already known? Is additional background information necessary? What is to be measured? How? Can the data be made available? Should research be conducted? Can a hypothesis be formulated?
Selection of basic research design	What types of questions need to be answered? Are descriptive or causal findings required? What is the source of the data? Can objective answers be obtained by asking people? How quickly is the information needed? How should survey questions be worded? How should experimental manipulations be made?
Selection of sample	Who or what is the source of the data? Can the target population be identified? Is a sample necessary? How accurate must the sample be? Is a probability sample necessary? Is a national sample necessary? How large a sample is necessary? How will the sample be selected?
Data gathering	Who will gather the data? How long will data gathering take? How much supervision is needed? What operational procedures need to be followed?

Decision to Make in the Research Process	Basic Questions
Data analysis and evaluation	Will standardized editing and coding procedures be utilized? How will the data be categorized? Will computer or hand tabulation be utilized? What questions need to be a answered? How many variables are to be investigated simultaneously? What are the criteria for evaluation of performance?
Type of report	Who will read the report? Are experts recommendations requested? How many presentations are required? What will be the format of the written report?
Overall evaluation	How much will the study cost? Is the timeframe acceptable? De we need outside help? Will this research design attain the stated research objectives? When should the research be scheduled to begin?

Exhibit 6.2: Basic questions typically asked when planning a research design

6.2 The Basic Framework of a Research Proposal

6.2.1 The Problem

The proposal begins with a clear statement of the question the research is supposed to answer. The problem gives the research its purpose.

The study rationale should answer the following questions:

- Has the study been done before?
- Will the study benefit researchers in better understanding the problem under investigation?

The criteria for a well selected problem are:

- Clear
- Logical
- Relevant
- Documented.

A brief description of the background of the problem should also be included. This discussion is typically presented in the review of the literature.

6.2.2 The Hypothesis

The question is followed by a concise statement of the hypothesis or hypotheses to be tested. The hypothesis gives the research its direction. All subsequent plans for the research project depend on the statement of the hypothesis. It is imperative that the researcher state the hypotheses and the supporting rationale with the greatest clarity. Identifying the research problem and developing a question to be answered are the fist steps in the research process. The research question will guide the remainder of the design process.

Research Objective is a clear statement of the specific purposes of the study, which identifies the key study variables and their possible interrelationships and the nature of the population of interest.

Research Question is the specific purpose stated in the form of a question.

Hypothesis is a tentative prediction or explanation of the relationship between two or more variables. It is a prediction of the answer to the research question

The functions of this section are to:

— Provide reviewers with a clear picture of what you plan to accomplish.
— Show the reviewers that you have a clear picture of what you want to accomplish.
— Form the foundation for the rest of the proposal
— Will be used to access the adequacy/appropriateness of the study's proposed methods.

The researcher should see that this section is clear and consistent, with key concepts / constructs identified including the independent and dependent variables (if applicable)

6.2.3 Operational Definitions

The variables chosen for the study should be defined in precise terms, so that the researcher's perception of the variables under study is clearly understood by the experts. Expressions such as academic achievement and science attitude scale are useful concepts, but they cannot be used as criteria unless they are described as observable sample of behaviour. Academic scores assigned by teachers on investigator devised achievement tests are operational definitions of achievement.

6.2.4 Assumptions and Limitations

Assumptions are statements of what the researcher believes to be facts, but cannot verify. A researcher must state his assumptions clearly.

Limitations are conditions beyond the control of the researcher that may place restrictions on the conclusions of the study and their applicability to other situations.

Delimitations are the boundaries beyond which the study is not concerned. A study of the attitudes towards Anglo-Indians may be concerned only with middle class, tenth standard students in Chennai city, and conclusions are not to be extended beyond this population sampled.

Literature Review

A critical summary of research on a topic of interest, generally prepared to put a research problem in context or to identify gaps and weaknesses in prior studies so as to justify a new investigation.

In searching related literature, the researcher should keep in mind the necessity of the following points:

- Thorough and complete review of closely related studies
- Logical analysis so that faults can be avoided
- Recent studies in the area of investigation have be reviewed
- Design of the study, including methods employed and tools used
- Variables that were defined
- Critical appraisal of extraneous variables that could have affected the findings
- Recommendations for further research, building case for new study.

6.2.5 The Research Design

The next section of the proposal presents a description of the research design – that is, a description of the procedures to be followed in testing the hypotheses. It is very important that an appropriate testing method be chosen. An experimental question cannot be answered by using descriptive methods and vice versa. This section should also include the measures or instruments to be used in gathering the data. Investigators must locate appropriate tests. scales, and other tools required to measure the variables and must assess the reliability and validity of these operations. The aim is to choose measures that are as objective and reliable as possible, without sacrificing the adequacy of their "fit" with the concepts they are supposed to represent.

6.2.6 The Sample

The proposal must include a description of the population of concern in the study – that is, the type of subjects to be included. The researcher must have given some attention to the availability of these subjects. It is also necessary to describe the sampling procedures to be followed. The universe to be sampled must be specified as well as the techniques to be followed in drawing the sample and the proposed sample size.

6.2.7 Statistical Analysis

This section will include the researcher's proposal for the statistical analysis of the data. Before one begins to collect data, one must identify the statistical procedure that will permit an answer to the research question or a test of the hypothesis. First, one will need to describe or summarize the data collected from the sample studied. Then one must be able to estimate the reliability or accuracy of the inferences and generalizations made from the sample findings to the total populations. Statistical methods serve both of these functions. The function of summarizing the obtained data is accomplished by descriptive statistics. Inferential statistics enables one to make inferences from sample data.

Many experienced researchers, as well as those who are just learning the process, find it necessary to consult with someone with expertise in statistics before completing their research plan. A brief discussion of the role statistical analysis plays in testing hypotheses is presented later in this book.

6.2.8 Time Schedule

The researcher should clearly state his work plan, giving details for each stage of the research.

Dividing the study into manageable parts and assigning time slots for their completion helps to streamline the study, ensuring completion on time.

6.2.9 Bibliography

References that the researcher used must be listed here, so that the experts can check out a few of the studies. Internet and web based resources should also be listed.

Many institutions suggest their own formats for the proposal. However, the key elements of a good research proposal are:

- Title
- Literature Review
- Study Problem
- Specific Study Objectives
- Relevance of the Project
- Research Methods

I. Study Design

II. Subjects
- Inclusion / Exclusion criteria
- Sampling
- Method of assignment to study groups

III. Data Collection
- Variables: independent and dependent
- Measures/instruments
- Procedures

IV. Intervention

V. Statistical Considerations
- Sample size
- Data analysis-descriptive and inferential
- Ethical Considerations
- Time Schedule
- Budget

Exhibit 6.3: Contents of a research proposal – elements

Overall Quality of the Study

- Good research question
- Appropriate research design
- Rigorous and feasible methods
- Qualified research team

Quality of the Proposal

- Informative title
- Self-sufficient and convincing abstract
- Clear research questions
- Scholarly and pertinent background and rationale
- Relevant previous work
- Appropriate measurement and intervention methods
- Quality control
- Adequate sample size
- Sound analysis plan
- Ethical issues well addressed
- Tight budget
- Realistic timetable

Quality of the Presentation

- Clear, concise, well-organized
- Helpful table of contents and subheadings
- Good schematic diagrams and tables
- Neat and free of errors

In general the following points must be kept in mind:

— Aim for clarity
— Establish the context
— Use a fresh approach
— Describe your methodology
— Specify your objectives
— Revise the text
— Go over the language, form and style

Exhibit 6.4: Criteria for a good research proposal (Adapted from Hulley & Cummings)

Rationale – WHY this research programme?

This section should contain a detailed account of the reasons(s) for undertaking this research.

- Why is this research important?
- What will be the benefits to the community or industry which are expected to result from the research?
- How will your research advance the understanding and perception of the issues involved?
- How will your research contribute to that body of knowledge that constitutes your field of study?

The benefits of the programme to your self-development are assumed and do constitute a sufficient rationale or reason for undertaking postgraduate research.

Academic research inevitably results in the production of original knowledge. Therefore it is important for the candidate to emphasize this aspect of their proposed research programme. This may pose more of a difficulty in certain disciplines than others, such as in the fine arts as compared with the science. It is therefore necessary for the candidate to clearly articulate the issues and debates within the realm that represents the focus of their work.

Methods – HOW will you undertake this research?

This section should clearly indicate the nature of the various stages of your programme. This is usually best achieved by creating a projected timeline to the duration of the programme (24 months maximum full – time or 48 months maximum part - time). Single line bullet points rather than lengthy description of each stage is best. List all the activities that will make up the programme, and divide them into appropriate stages or tasks. These steps should accord with what you have already detailed in your description.

- How long is each stage or task expected to take?
- Will some stages run concurrently?
- What information or data has to be gathered?
- Where will you gather this information from?
- How will you evaluate this information?

- How will this be implemented into your own work?
- What experimentation or testing has to be undertaken?
- Does your project rely on the cooperation of organisations other than the research institute?
- If so, what is the nature of the support?
- Are there any funding issues that need to be addressed?
- How will you determine when the aims of the programme have been achieved?

SUGGESTED REFERENCES

- Cohen, Louis, Lawrence Manion and Keith Morrison. Research Methods in Education. 5th Ed. Routledge Falmer. London. 2000.
- Guba, Egon "Guides for the Writing of Proposals". In Educational Research: New Perspectives, edited by J.A.Culbertson and S.P.Hencley. Darville,III: The Interstate. 1963.
- Madsen, David. Successful Dissertations and Theses – A Guide to Graduate-Student Research from Proposal to Completion. Jossey-Bass Higher and Adult Education Series. Nov. 1991.

WEB RESOURCES

- http://foundationcenter.org/getstarted/tutorials/shortcourse/index.html (This site is a primer on proposal writing.)
- http://www.research.umich.edu/proposals/pwg/pwgcontents.html (This Guide is intended for faculty and staff members with little or no experience in writing proposals for sponsored activities.)
- http://www.meaning.ca/archives/archive/art_how_to_write_P_Wong.htm (This paper focuses on proposal writing rather than on the development of research ideas.)
- http://globetrotter.berkeley.edu/DissPropWorkshop/ (This site comprises a collection of tips, samples, and links.)

Historical Research

7.1 What is Research?

Hamblin defines research as "... an unusually stubborn and persisting effort to think straight which involves the gathering and intelligent use of data". Educational research by its very nature is not easy to slot.

The categorization of educational research methods into logical and functional classes is a difficult proposition, as there is a lot of overlapping between the procedures.

Barr points out that "educational research methods can be categorized on the basis of end result (or goal), data-gathering technique, method of data-processing, degree of control and a number of other considerations.

Research can also be classified as

— Laboratory or field research

— Action or pure research

— Curriculum research, psychometric research or sociometric research (dimension wise)

However, in general, three basic categories can be considered:

- **Historical** describes what was. This is concerned with investigating, recording and interpreting the past events as a means of seeing the present in perspective.
- **Survey** describes what is. This is concerned with the present and attempts to determine the relationships between existing non-manipulated values.
- **Experimental** describes what will be. Here the focus is on discovering the basic relationships among phenomena as a means (Best) of producing and controlling their occurrence.

Looking at **Exhibit 7.1,** we have categorized the basic research methods into four-survey, experimental, observation and secondary data study.

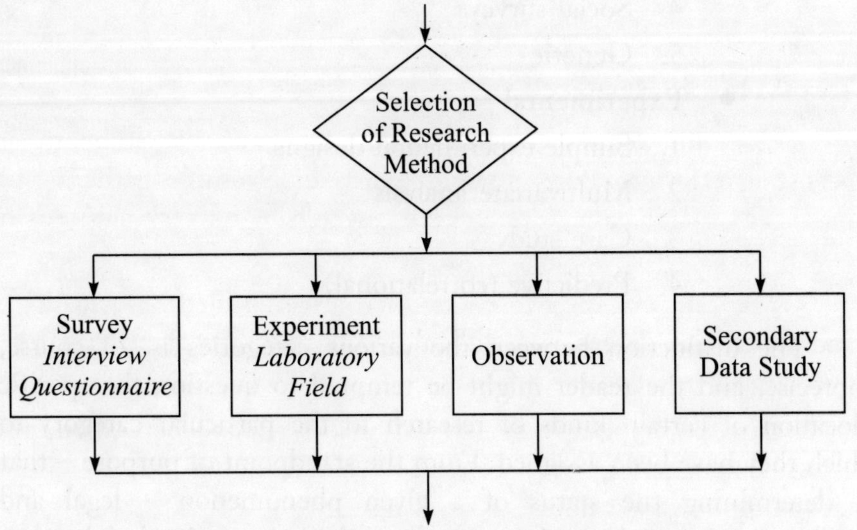

Exhibit 7.1: Categorization of research methods

Another categorization followed in some institutions is the following:

- **Historical**
  - Historical
  - Legal
  - Documentary
- **Survey**
  1. Descriptive
     - Survey testing
     - Questionnaire
     - Interview
  2. Analytical
     - Documentary-frequency
     - Observational
     - Rating
     - Critical incident
     - Factor analysis
  3. School surveys
  4. Social surveys
  5. Genetic
- **Experimental**
  1. Simple experimental designs
  2. Multivariate analysis
  3. Case study
  4. Predictive (correlational)

The distinction between the various categories is, of course, imprecise, and the reader might be tempted to question the specific allocation of certain kinds of research to the particular category to which they have been assigned. From the standpoint of purpose – that is, determining the status of a given phenomenon – legal and documentary research are, for example, perhaps more closely related to survey than to historical research. On the other hand, the particular problems encountered, and the specific techniques to be applied, in such research probably more closely resemble those of historical research, and, for the sake of organization, reader comprehension, and the avoidance of unnecessary repetition, they are discussed in that setting.

No one system of categorization can fit a field as complex as education. It appears quite futile to concentrate on the categorization of research methods. However, it is necessary to remember, that in all research methods, the basic steps remain the same:

- Problem definition
- Population definition
- Selection of sample
- Collection of data
- Validation
- Inferences drawn
- Report writing

Historical Research

Historical research is a procedure supplementary to observation in which the researcher seeks to test the authenticity of the reports or observation made by other. This is the systematic collection and objective evaluation of data related to past occurrences to determine causes, effects or trends of those events that may help explain present events and anticipates future events.

7.2 Purposes of Historical Research

Historical research can be undertaken for a variety of reasons. Despite some differences historical research is conducted in a logical and systematic manner.

Historians	Scientists
Study the past	Study the present
Lack of certainty in conclusions	Conclusions have higher degree of certainty
Writing often has storytelling format	Distinct format (purpose, methods, results, conclusions)
Often study social phenomena	Usually study natural phenomena

Exhibit 7.2: Historians and scientists

Despite some differences historians still try to have a "science like" approach and work to disprove findings. They approach their topics in a logical and systematic manner.

Historians have different views about social phenomena than scientists do about natural phenomena. Historians assume that humans make and give meaning to social phenomena. Historians are therefore less able to develop predictive theories than scientists who mostly deal with natural phenomena. Historians do however try to generalize (similar to scientists) based on their interpretations of the data they collect. These generalizations draw on social science theories and can be examined using data taken from other periods or places.

Historical research is done for the following reasons:

— Place events in logical sequence. Most events have a history, and it is generally profitable to acquaint ourselves with this history if we are really to appreciate their nature.

— Determine activities surrounding an event

— Preserve information that would otherwise be lost

— Answer why

— Make public information that has not been shared

— Have implications for the present and the future

An understanding of the historical background could save education from making the same mistakes.

7.3 Steps in Historical Research

Exhibit 7.3 gives a diagrammatic representation of the four steps involved in the methodology of historical research.

Historical Research must meet the same criteria and follow the same procedures as the other forms of research.

The steps are:

- Isolate the problem
- Collect source materials
    - Primary data
    - Secondary data

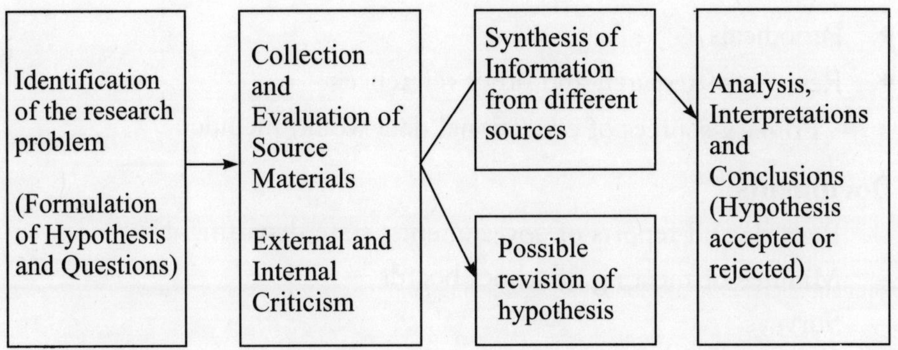

Exhibit 7.3: Steps involved in the methodology of historical research

- Evaluate source materials
- Formulate/Revise hypothesis
- Report and interpret findings

7.4 Sources of Historical Data

'Data' is defined as information organized for analysis or used as a basis for a decision. Historical data are usually classified as

- Primary sources, which are
  - Eye or ear witness accounts
  - Original objects
- Secondary Sources which are
  - Copies of objects
  - Second hand information

Thus first hand information such as the testimony of an eye witness, an original document, a relic, or a description of a study written by the person who conducted it, would be considered a primary source. On the other hand, second hand information, such as a description of historical events by someone not present, when the event occurred would be a secondary source.

Among secondary sources of historical data are

- Textbooks
- Encyclopedia
- Newspapers

- Periodicals
- Reviews of research and other references

Primary sources of educational data would include

Documents

— Records and reports of governments, state departments
— Minutes of meeting of school boards
— Surveys
— Charters, wills, deeds
— Bulletins
— Files, attendance roll, etc.
— Certificates
— Memo, diaries

Oral testimony like interviews, tapes, audio video presentations etc.

Relics include buildings, furniture, examination and the like.

Historical Criticism

Historical research requires a systematic data evaluation of the evidence. Generally, the data is subjected to careful analysis to sift the true from the false, irrelevant or misleading. Historical evidence derived from historical data by the process of criticism, which is of two types:

- External criticism
- Internal criticism

7.5 Primary Sources: Definitions

"By a 'source' the historian means material that is contemporary to the events being examined. Such sources include, among other things, diaries, letters, newspapers, magazine articles, tape recordings, pictures, and maps. Such material may have appeared in print before, edited or unedited, and still be a source. The term is meant to be restrictive rather than inclusive, in that it attempts to indicate that works of secondary scholarship, or synthesis, are not sources, since the data have been distilled by another person. One good way for the novice historian to lose credibility among his serious-minded fellows is to call a biography of Mahatma Gandhi or an analysis of the Magna Charta a 'source.'

"A primary source gives the words of the witnesses or the first recorders of an event. Primary sources include manuscripts, archives, letters, diaries, and speeches. Secondary sources are 'descriptions of the event derived from and based on primary sources'. The line between primary and secondary sources is often indistinct, for example, a single document may be a primary source on some matter and a secondary source on others." (Helen J. Poulton)

"A primary source is distinguished from a secondary by the fact that the former gives the words of the witnesses or first recorders of an event – for example, the diaries of Count Ciano written under Mussolini's regime. The researcher, using a number of such primary sources, produces a secondary source." (Jacques Barzun)

7.6 Writing the Historical Report

Having established the authority and accuracy of the facts, the researcher must address himself to the task of interpreting these facts in the light of the stated problem. Interpretation requires caution, a thorough review of the trends of the period under study, creative thinking and an understanding of the psychology of the human mind.

The writing of the historical report is a task involving the highest level of scholarship. Research reports should be written in a dignified and objective style.

In view of the difficulties inherent in historical research, the student must be particularly careful in selecting a topic.

7.7 Checklist of Evaluation for Historical Research

1. **Problem**
   - Has the problem been well defined?
   - Is it grounded in research and answerable?
   - Is it within the competence of the investigator?
2. **Data**
   - Are data of a primary nature available?
   - Is there over-dependence on secondary data?
   - *Analysis:* Historical researches tend to focus on description (what happened?) and analysis (why did it happen?)

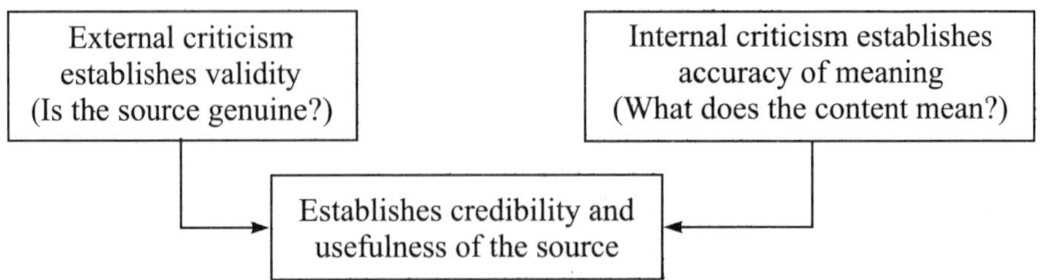

External Criticism establishes the genuinenessss and authority of data.

- Does the language and writing style conform to the period in question and is it typical of other work done by the author?
- Is there evidence that the author exhibits ignorance of things or events that she/he should have known?
- Did the author report things, event or places that could not have been known during that period?
- Has the original manuscript been altered either unintentionally or intentionally by copying?
- Is the document an original or draft copy? If it is a copy, was it reproduced in the exact words of the original?
- If the manuscript is undated or the author, unknown, is there any clues internally as to its origin?

Internal criticism determines if the contents of a document are accurate.

- What was meant by the author by each word and statement?
- How much credibility can the author be given?
- What was the author trying to say?
- How could the author's words be interpreted?

Exhibit 7.4: External and internal criticism in the evaluation of data

Historians follow three rules when applying the process of internal criticism.

Rule of context – does the information fit with what was said before and after?

Rule of perspective – did the source have a bias? Do the sources of information have an affiliation with a particular organization?

Rule of omission – was any information either intentionally or unintentionally omitted?

Exhibit 7.5: Rules to check for internal criticism

Description research: Constructs a map of the past and is often a first approach to a topic about which little is known.

— Has the investigator located events in time and place?

— Has a thorough review been done?

Analytic research

— Has the dependability of the data been adequately established?

— Has the relevance of the data been explored?

Interpretation

Historical evidence can be found in varying formats – literature, photos, relics etc

— Have all sources of data been evaluated for their validity?

— Has the external criticism been done? Is the document real or fake?

— Has the internal criticism been found?

— Is the information credible?

— Is it constant and accurate?

— Does the researcher display adequate historical perspective?

— Does s/he maintain objectivity?

— Are the stated hypotheses feasible?

— Has the researcher related the data with observed 'historical facts'?

Presentation

- Is the style of working lucid?
- Does the report make a contribution on the basis of newly discovered data?
- Does it reflect scholarliness?

7.8 Conclusion

> *"Whether historical research qualifies as a scientific endeavour depends on the criteria used. While historical research cannot meet some of the tests of the scientific method, interpreted in the narrow sense of its use in the physical sciences, it does qualify from the standpoint of its subscription to the same principles and the same general scholarship accuracy which characterizes all scientific research".*
>
> **Mouly (1976)**

SUGGESTED REFERENCES

- Barr, Arvil S. "Research Methods" in Chester W. Harris (ed.), Encyclopedia of Educational Research. New York: Macmillan, 1960.
- Barzun, Jacques. The Modern Researcher. Fifth edition. Boston: Houghton Mifflin, 1992.
- Green, Judith L. Gregory Camilli, Patricia B. Elmore and Audra Skukauskaite, Handbook of complementary methods in education research. Routledge. Taylor and Francis. 2006.
- McDowell, W. H. Historical Research. A Guide for Writers of Dissertations, Theses, Articles and Books Pearson Education Mar 2002.
- Mouly, George. Educational research: the Art and Science of Investigation. Boston. Allyn and Bacon. 1978.
- Poulton, Helen J. The Historian's Handbook Norman, OK: University of Oklahoma Press, 1972
- Prakash, Ravi. Historical Research in Education. New Delhi, Commonwealth, 2003, ISBN 81-7169-751-8.
- Winks, Robin. The Historian as Detective: Essays on Evidence. New York: Harper & Row, 1969.

WEB RESOURCES OF INTEREST

- http://www.dianahacker.com/resdoc/history.html

  A guide to historical research.

CHAPTER 8

The Experimental Method

8.1 The Experimental Method

It is now appropriate to focus on experiments, research studies designed for establishing causal relationships. This method begins with a question concerning the relationship between two or more variables. At the same time, the researcher advances one or more hypotheses stating the nature of the expected relationship. The experiment is the event planned and carried out by the researcher to gather evidence relevant to the hypotheses. The experimenter deliberately and systematically introduces changes into natural phenomena and then observes the consequences of those changes. The hypotheses express expectations as to the findings that will result from the changes that are introduced. In conducting an experiment, the researcher devotes great care to the manipulation and control of variables and to the observation and measurement of results. It is through such a research method that the researcher can obtain the most convincing evidence of the effect that one variable has on another.

In its simplest form an experiment has three characteristics:

1. an independent variable which is manipulated;
2. all other variables except the independent variable are held constant and
3. the effect of the manipulation of the independent variable on the dependent variable is observed.

Thus in an experiment the two variables of major interest are the independent variable and the dependent variable. The independent variable is manipulated or changed by the experimenter. The variable upon which the effects of the changes are observed is called the dependent variable, which is observed but not manipulated by the experimenter. The dependent variable is so named because its value is hypothesized to depend upon, and vary with the value of the independent variable. For example, to examine the effect of different teaching methods upon achievement in reading, an investigator would manipulate method – the independent variable – by using different teaching methods in order to ascertain their effect upon achievement, the dependent variable.

Illustration

Note carefully the italicized terms that appear in that outline since these terms will be used throughout our discussion of experimental research.

Ms XYZ reported a study that investigated the effect of the type of supplemental materials used in a school science class taught by traditional method. The experiment compared the use of a programmed booklet with two other techniques for presenting supplemental material in the class taught by traditional method.

Hypothesis The achievement of students who use programmed supplemental materials will be superior to the achievement of students who use non-programmed supplemental materials.

Or, stated in a null form: the achievement of students who use programmed supplemental materials will not differ significantly from the achievement of students using non-programmed supplemental materials.

Sample. All students enrolled in the school – Standard IX – were considered.

Independent variable. The independent variable was the type of supplemental material used in the science class-programmed instruction and puppetry.

Dependent variable. The dependent variable was the score on a science achievement test administered at the end of the study.

Controls. Subjects were randomly assigned to three groups, which differed only in the type of supplemental material used. To eliminate teacher differences, the experimenter was responsible for all three of the supplementary methods. To ensure a uniform presentation of material, the assigned homework problems were selected prior to the experiment and a complete set of solutions was prepared. These notes were used in the presentation to each of the three experimental groups.

The experiment used a simple randomized design with three treatment groups. Each group in a separate room was taught the same topic by the traditional method during the first half of each class period. This lecture was developmental in nature and based on a common reading assignment from the required textbook during the second half of the period, each group received instruction based on assigned homework problems.

Group I viewed a film of the solutions of the homework exercises. The students were instructed to compare their homework with the film explanation to verify their solutions or to obtain necessary assistance. Some review topics were discussed but no new developmental material was presented.

Group II participated in a classroom help session in which the experimenter answered questions pertaining to the assigned exercises. The students assisted the teacher in the solution of problems as he worked at the chalkboard. Other pertinent questions were answered, but there was no presentation of new material.

Group III studied a programmed booklet prepared by the experimenter and based on the assigned exercises. It was suggested that the students compare their solutions of the problems with those in the programmed materials. The last section of each lesson summarized concepts presented in the lecture, but included no new material.

After twelve class meetings of experimental instruction, the students were given an achievement test. The design of the study is summarized as follows (**R** indicates random assignment to groups).

	Group	Independent Variable	Dependent Variable
(R)	I	Film	Achievement test
(R)	II	Classroom discussion	Achievement test
(R)	III	Programmed booklet	Achievement test

Exhibit 8.1: Design of study with three groups – illustration

Results. The results indicated significant differences in the mean achievement of the three groups. In a comparison of Group III with Group I and with Group II, the mean achievement of Group III was significant at the .05 level in each case. The mean achievement of Group I and Group II did not differ significantly.

Conclusions. (1) The programmed material provided as supplement to traditional instruction was more effective than either of the other two supplementary methods. (2) The classroom discussion and the film problem session methods appeared to be equally effective.

From the description one can see the major aspects of an experiment:

a) A question for which the experimenter seeks an answer – a question concerned with the relationship between two variables;

b) Hypotheses as to the nature of the relationship between the two variables;
c) Introduction of the experimental conditions and measurement;
d) Analysis of data so that the researcher can decide whether or not there is a relationship between the variables

Experiments in education may be conducted in either a laboratory or in a field situation. The control of extraneous variables, which is so crucial to the experimental method, can usually be handled most adequately in the laboratory. In a laboratory, experimenters can control the environment in such a way that the independent variables of interest can be isolated. They can thus be very specific in the operational definition of variables. For these reasons laboratory experiments can be replicated with a high degree of precision.

Field experiments can be conducted in classrooms, playgrounds, interest club meetings, or other natural setting. The experimenter controls the extraneous variables as much as possible while manipulating the independent variable or variables, but in a field experiment control is inevitably less complete. However field experiments have certain advantages. First, experimental variables can be much stronger in field experiments than in laboratory over a short period of time, whereas a field experiment can encompass daily sessions for an entire school year. Second, because field experiments are conducted in a more realistic setting their results are more likely to provide solutions to the actual daily problems of educators.

> Experimental Method is an empirical research method used to examine a hypothesized causal relationship between independent and dependent variables.
>
> The antecedent event in a proposed causal sequence is called the independent variable.
>
> The measured effect in the causal sequence is called the dependent variable.

The main methodological rule of experimentation is that the experimenter must have precise control over the experimental situation.

Control involves the creation and variation (manipulation) of the independent variables. The values of the independent variable(s) define the experimental conditions or the design of the experiment. At a minimum, the design involves the application of a treatment to one group of participants and the withholding of the treatment from a comparison or control group. Aside from this manipulation, the situation in both groups must be identical. Accordingly, the dependent variable(s) has (have) to be assessed by consistent measures. In order to render the group samples comparable, participants must be randomly assigned to conditions. Differences that then occur on the measures of the dependent variable can be attributed to the factor which differentiates the groups systematically, the presence, absence or level of the independent variable. Without randomization the method is quasi-experimental (e.g. if gender is used as a factor in the design). Experiments can be conducted in the laboratory or in natural settings (field). Because it is easier to precisely control the experimental situation in the laboratory, this kind of experiment allows the experimenter to achieve a higher level of internal validity than in field experiment. However, if it is possible to sufficiently control the experimental situation in natural conditions, field experiments are more likely to be externally valid.

The purpose of experimentation is to derive verified functional relationship among phenomena under controlled conditions or, more simply, to identify the conditions underlying the occurrence of a given phenomena from an operational point. It is a matter of varying the independent variable in order to study the effect of such variation on the dependent variable.

Before you design an experiment or a survey, you must consider issues in hypotheses, whether your variables can approximate numbers or are clearly just categories, and whether your variables are independent or multidimensional.

In the hypotheses stage, we deal with conceptual variables: They are what you think the entity really is or what it means. Conceptual variables are about abstract constructs. Examples include "achievement motivation" or "endurance" or "group cohesion" You are describing a concept. On the other head, operational definitions of variable are how you actually measure this entity, or the concrete operations, measures or procedures that you use to measure the concept.

Example

Conceptual Variable	*Operational Variable*
Letter recognition	Scores on a particular test
Caste	According to Government categorization
Collective efficacy	Score on investigator constructed test
Attitude to science	SAS scores from Grewal standardized test
Leadership style	Score on an investigator devised test

A Confounded variable: is a multidimensional variable, a variable embedded. Care must be taken to see that each operational variable measures one and only one construct.

8.2 Nature of Variables Involved in Experiments

A variable is any measured characteristic or attribute that differs for different subjects. For example, if the weight of 30 subjects were measured, then weight would be a variable. Thus variables are the conditions or characteristics that the experimenter manipulates, controls or observes.

8.2.1 Quantitative and Qualitative Variables

Qualitative variables are sometimes called 'categorical variables'. Quantitative variables are measured on an ordinal, interval or ratio scale. Qualitative variables are measured on a nominal scale. If five year old kindergarten children were asked to name their favorite colour, then the variable would be qualitative. If the time it took them to respond were measured, then the variable would be quantitative.

8.2.2 Independent and Dependent Variables

Where an experiment is conducted, some variables are manipulated by the experimenter, and others are measured from the subjects. The former variables are called 'independent variables', the latter are called 'dependent variables'.

In educational research, an independent variable may be a particular teaching method say like programmed learning or CAI, a reward or a period of exposure to a new curriculum. The dependent variable may be a test score, the number of errors, or measured speed in performing a task. Thus the dependent variables are the measured changes on pupil performance attributable to the influence of the independent variable.

Experimental research design is where

- a researcher is able to manipulate exposure to the independent variable by the units of analysis and
- there is random assignment of units to groups exposed to different levels of the independent variable.

An independent variable is one whose values are chosen by the experimenter. In other words, the values of this variable are independent of the participant's behavior. For the independent variable to be manipulated, at least two levels must be present in an experiment. The most basic way to manipulate is by creating one experimental group (the group receiving the treatment) and a control group (exactly like the experimental group, except without the experimental treatment). The performances of the two groups in regard to the dependent measure are then compared to assess the effect of the independent variable.

8.2.3 Dependent vs. Independent Variables

Independent variables are those that are manipulated whereas dependent variables are only measured or registered. This distinction appears terminologically confusing to many because, as some students say, "all variables depend on something." However, once you get used to this distinction, it becomes indispensable. The terms dependent and independent variable apply mostly to experimental research where some variables are manipulated, and in this sense they are "independent" from the initial reaction patterns, features, intentions, etc. of the subjects. Some other variables are expected to be "dependent" on the manipulation or experimental conditions. That is to say, they depend on" what the subject will do" in response. Somewhat contrary to the nature of this distinction, these terms are also used in studies where we do not literally manipulate independent variables, but only assign subjects to "experimental groups" based on some pre-existing properties of the subjects. For example, if in an experiment, males are compared with females regarding their white cell count (WCC), Gender could be called the independent variable and WCC the dependent variable.

8.3 Measurement Scales

Variables differ in 'how well' they can be measured, i.e., in how much measurable information their measurement scale can provide. Variables are classified as (a) nominal (b) ordinal (c) interval (d) ratio.

a) **Nominal variables** allow for only qualitative classification. That is, they can be measured only in terms of whether the individual items belong to some distinctively different categories, but we cannot quantify or even rank order these categories.

   For example, all we can say is that 2 individuals are different in terms of variable A, (e.g.) they are of different castes, but we cannot say which one 'has more' of the quality represented by the variable. Typical examples of nominal variables are gender, race, color, city etc.

b) **Ordinal variables** allow us to rank order the terms we measure in terms of which has less and which has more of the quality represented by the variable, but still they do not allow us to say "how much more" a typical example of an ordinal variable is for socioeconomic status of families. For example, we know that upper middle is higher than middle but we cannot say that it is for example, 10% higher.

c) **Interval variables** allow us not only to rank order the terms that are measured, but also to quantify and compare the sizes of differences, between them. For example, IQ measured on the Stanford Binet scale constitutes an interval scale. We can say that a score of 100 is higher than a score 90, and that an increase from 80 to 90 is twice as much as an increase from 75 to 80 on the Stanford Binet is test.

d) **Ratio variables** are very similar to interval variables. In addition to all the properties of interval variables, they feature an identifiable absolute zero point. Typical example of ratio scales are measures of time and space. Interval scales do not have the ratio property.

8.4 Attribute Variable or Organismic Variable

Organismic variables are those variables that cannot be altered by the experimenter. Such independent variables as age, sex or caste have already been determined, but they can be introduced or removed as variables. The question of whether girls do better than boys in science in the NTSE examination provides an example of sex as an organismic variable. Criteria are the same for each group. Since sex is the variable it is not manipulated; it has already been determined.

8.5 Intervening Variables

An intervening variable is one that links the independent and the dependent variable. Thus an intervening variable is part of a causal chain.

Independent variable ⇨ Intervening variable ⇨ Dependent variable

Example

Educational level is a cause of science attitudes because educational level influences the type of occupation someone has (intervening variable), and it is the occupational type that affects income levels.

Intervening variables inform us about caused sequences or chains, thus explaining the causal process of a phenomenon.

Example

Educational level ⇨ Occupational type ⇨ Income level

Intervening variables certainly can be measured. They are critical to use in non-experimental research designs. Often they can specify what it is about the dependent variable that is important. Anxiety, fatigue, may be intervening variables and are difficult to define on operational terms.

8.6 Extraneous Variables

Extraneous variables are those uncontrolled variables (i.e. variables not manipulated by the experimenter) that may have a significant influence upon the dependent variable. If situational variables are not controlled on an experiment, one cannot be sure whether it is the independent variable or these incidental differences operating in the groups that are producing the difference in the dependent variable.

For instance, let us assume that an experimenter is interested in the effectiveness of a film in producing changes in attitude toward some issue. One group of children is selected at random from a classroom and sent off to see the film, leaving a comparable group in the classroom. Unknowingly, the experimenter may have set in motion a large number of forces. The children in the control group may be resentful, or feel rejected or inferior to the others. Such factors could have an effect on the outcome of the study. The difference that the experimenter wants to attribute to the use of the film could really be due to one of these incidental features. In this case steps must be taken to ensure that the control subjects also see a film of some sort and that both groups, and neither of the group, know that they are taking part in an experiment. This precaution is necessary in order to control what is known as the Hawthorne effect, which refers to the observation, first made at the Hawthorne plant of the Western Electric Company, that almost any changes, any extra attention, any experimental manipulation, or even the absence of manipulation but the knowledge that an experiment is being done, is enough to cause subjects to change. In short, any type of attention may lead subjects to respond.

8.7 Characteristics of Experimental Research

There are three essential ingredients with which the scientist is actively involved in the conduct of an experiment; ***control, manipulation,*** and ***observation.***

Control

Control is the essence of the experimental method. Without control it is impossible to evaluate unambiguously the effects of an independent variable. Let us examine briefly this concept of control in experimentation.

Basically the experimental method of science rests upon two assumptions regarding variables:

(1) If two situations are equal in every respect except for a variable that is added to or deleted from one of the situations, any difference appearing between the two situations can be attributed to that variable. This statement is called the ***law of the single variable.***

(2) If two situations are not equal, it can be demonstrated that none of the variables is significant in producing the phenomenon under investigation, or if significant variables are made equal, any difference occurring between the two situations after the introduction of a new variable to one of the systems can be attributed to the new variable. This statement is called the ***law of the only significant variable***. The purpose of control in an experiment is to arrange a situation in which the effect of variables can be investigated. The conditions underlying the law of the single variable are more likely to be fulfilled in the physical science than in education. Since educational research is concerned with human beings, there are always many variables present. To attempt to reduce educational problems to the operation of a single variable is not only unrealistic but perhaps even impossible. Fortunately such rigorous control is not absolutely essential since many aspects in which situations differ are irrelevant to the purpose of the study and thus can be ignored. It is sufficient to apply the law of the single significant independent variable. For example, in a study of the differential effects of two methods of teaching arithmetic, one would wish to have two groups of children who are identical in every respect except the way in which they are taught arithmetic. Since it is impossible to have two absolutely identical groups of children, the experimenter seeks to establish two groups that are as similar as possible in respect to those variables that are related to arithmetic achievement, such as reading ability, motivation, general intelligence, and the like. Other variables that are highly unlikely to be related to arithmetic, such as athletic ability, height, or color of hair, are ignored. Although the law of the single variable cannot be followed absolutely, the experimenter endeavours to approximate it as closely as possible in all relevant variables. Therefore in experimental studies in education we need procedures that permit us to compare groups on the basis of significant variables. A number of methods of control have been devised to make such comparisons possible.

Assume that we wish to test the hypothesis that children taught by the inductive method (Group/A) show greater gains in learning scientific concepts than children taught by the deductive method (Group B). In other words, we wish to study the relationship between teaching method (independent variable) and the learning of scientific concepts (dependent variable). In order for us to draw a conclusion concerning the relationship of the independent variable and the dependent variable, we must control the effects of any extraneous variables. An extraneous variable is a variable that is not related to the purpose of the study but may affect the dependent variable. Control is the term used to indicate an experimenter's procedure for eliminating the differential effects of all variables extraneous to the purpose of the study. The experimenter controls, for instance, when the groups are made comparable on extraneous variables that are related to the dependent variable. If a variable is known to be unrelated to the dependent variable, then it could not influence the dependent variable and we do not need to control for its effect.

In the experiment mentioned above, intelligence is a factor that certainly affects the learning of scientific concepts; therefore it would be considered an extraneous variable and must be controlled. Otherwise, if the children in Group A were more intelligent than those in Group B, the greater gains in learning by Group A could be attributed to intelligence and therefore we could not properly evaluate the effects of the teaching method on learning. In other words, intelligence has confounded the relationship between the variables in which we are interested. The term confounding refers to the "mixing" of the variables extraneous to the research problem with the independent variable(s) of the research study in such a way that their effects cannot be separated. It could not be clearly stated whether the relation found is (1) between the independent variable and the dependent variable of the study, or (2) between the extraneous variables and the dependent variable, or (3) a combination of (1) and (2). Confounding is eliminated by controlling for the effect of relevant extraneous variables.

Where there is no known relationship, as between the size of a student's shoes and his or her ability to learn science concepts, there would be no need for the experimenter to control for shoe size.

The first step must be directed towards controlling any relevant pre-existing differences between the subjects used in an experiment. Only in this way can the differences be attributed to the conditions of the experiment rather than to pre-existing subject differences. There are five basic procedures that are commonly used to increase equivalence among the groups that are to be exposed to the various experimental situations.

The five procedures for controlling inter subject differences are:

1. random assignment
2. randomized matching,
3. homogeneous selection
4. analysis of covariance,
5. use of subjects as their own controls.

Controlling Inter-Subject Differences

Random Assignment

Let us consider the experimenter's task. There is an available supply of subjects who for experimentation must be divided into two groups that will be treated differently and then compared. In assigning subjects to groups for the experiment, the experimenter needs a system that operates independently of personal judgment and of the characteristics of the subjects themselves. For example, the known high scores must not all be assigned to Group A and the low scorers, to Group B. A system that satisfies these requirements is random assignment. Random assignment is the assignment of subjects to groups in such a way that, for any given placement, every member of the population has an equal probability of being assigned to any of the groups. The randomization is often used as a synonym for random assignment.

Random assignment is not the same thing as random selection.

Random selection is the use of a chance procedure to select a sample from a population whereas random assignment is the use of a chance procedure to assign subjects to treatments.

For example, Ms XYZ has 2,000 subjects available for an experiment but only has sufficient facilities to include 100 in her experiment. By randomly selecting the 100 to include in the experiment, she avoids creating systematic differences between the subjects in the experiment and the population from which they were selected. By randomly assigning 50 of the 100 subjects to Treatment

A and 50 to Treatment B, she avoids systematic pre-treatment differences between the two groups.

To obtain randomized groups, the experimenter could number all the available subjects and then draw from a table of random numbers the number needed for the two groups. A coin flip could then determine which of the two groups is to get Treatment A and which is to get Treatment B.

When subjects have been randomly assigned to groups, the groups can be considered statistically equivalent. Statistically equivalent does not mean that the groups are absolutely equal, but it does mean that any difference between the groups is a function of chance alone and not a function of experimenter bias, subjects choices, or any other factor. A subject with high intelligence is as likely to be assigned to Treatment A as to Treatment B. The same is true for a subject with low intelligence. For the entire sample, the effects of intelligence on the dependent variable will tend to balance or randomize out. In the same manner subjects differences in political viewpoints, temperament, motivation, and other characteristics will tend to be approximately equally distributed between the two groups.

When random assignment has been employed, any pre-treatment differences between groups are a function of chance alone. When this is case, inferential statistics can be employed to determine how likely it is that post treatment differences are due to chance alone.

Note that not only known extraneous variables, but also other relevant extraneous variables unknown to or unimagined by the experimenter, can be expected to be randomized out.

Randomized Matching

An alternative procedure for assigning subjects to groups is to match individual subjects on as many extraneous variables as one thinks might affect the dependent variable and then to use some random procedure to assign one member of each matched pair to Treatment A and the other to Treatment B. If the groups are adequately matched on these variables, then there is reasonable assurance that any post-experimental differences can be attributed to the experimental treatment.

Although matching is a method for providing partial control of inter subject differences, there are several difficulties one may encounter. The first of these is to determine what variable or variables to use for matching. Variables such as IQ, socioeconomic status (SES), age, sex, reading score may be used. The variables on which subjects are matched must be substantially correlated to the dependent variable or else the matching is useless. As a general rule, we suggest that unless the variable correlates 50 or higher with the dependent variable, it should not be employed for the matching procedure since it would do little to increase the precision of the study. Ideally we would like to match on two or more variables that correlate well with the dependent variable and do not correlate significantly with each other. However, when we try to match on more than two variables, it becomes almost impossible to find subjects who are well matched on these several variables. Subjects are lost because no match can be found for them.

Another question that arises is how closely to match the subject on the variable(s). Matching closely increases the precision of the method but, at the same time, it also increases the number of subjects who cannot be matched. This, of course, also reduces the sample size and introduces sampling bias into the study.

8.8 Procedures for Matching

The researcher must decide what matching procedure is feasible in each particular situation. The usual method is to use a person-to-person procedure, in which an effort is made to locate two persons from the available subjects who score within the limits decided upon. For example, if the matching variable is IQ, then the researcher locates two subjects who are within, say, 5 points of each other on the IQ scale, and then randomly assigns one subject to Treatment A and the matching subject to Treatment B. It would not be too difficult to match subjects on just the IQ variable. But if sex and social class were also relevant variables, then it would become extremely difficult to find pairs who match on all three variables. Those subjects for whom no match can be found are lost to the experimenter.

Another method of matching is to place all subjects in rank order on the basis of their scores on the matching variable. The first two subjects are selected from the rank order list (regardless of the actual difference in their scores) to constitute the first pair. One subject of this pair is then randomly assigned to Treatment A and the other to Treatment B. The next two subjects on the list are selected, and again one is randomly assigned to A and the other to B. This process in continued until all subjects have been assigned. It is somewhat simple to match according to this procedure, but it is less precise than the person-to-person method. Note that randomized matching requires that the subjects be matched first and then randomly assigned to treatments. A study where subjects who are already experiencing one treatment are matched with subjects who are already experiencing another treatment cannot be classified as an experimental study. Such studies where matching is present, but random assignment to groups is not present, can lead researchers to erroneous conclusions.

Homogeneous Selection

Another method that can be used to make groups comparable on an extraneous variable involves selecting samples that are as homogeneous as possible on that variable. If the experimenter suspects that age is a variable that might affect the dependent variable, only children of a particular age would be selected. By selecting only six-year-old children, for instance, the experimenter would control the effects of age as an extraneous independent variable. Similarly if intelligence is likely to be a variable affecting the dependent variable of the study, then subjects would be selected from children within a restricted range of IQ, say 100-110. By this procedure the effects of IQ have been controlled. Then the experimenter randomly assigns individuals to groups from the resulting homogeneous population and can be confident that they were comparable on IQ. Beginning with a group that is homogeneous on the relevant variable eliminates the difficulty of trying to match subjects on that variable.

Although homogeneous selection is an effective way of controlling extraneous variables, it has the disadvantage of decreasing the extent to which the findings can be generalized to other situations. If a researcher investigates the effectiveness of a particular method with such a homogeneous sample, say, of children with average IQs, the results could not be generalized to children of other

IQ ranges. The effectiveness of the method with children of low intelligence or very high intelligence would not be known and the experiment would have to be repeated with subjects from different IQ strata.

As is the case with matching, a true experiment requires that the subjects be selected first and then assigned randomly to treatments.

Analysis of Covariance

Analysis of covariance (ANCOVA) is a statistical procedure that improves the precision of a research design by employing a pre-existing variable that is correlated with the dependent variable. For example, consider an experiment to study the effects of two methods of teaching reading. At the beginning of the term a pre-test is administered, and half of the subjects are randomly assigned to Method A and half to Method B. The **independent variable** is method of reading instruction and the **dependent variable** is the reading post-test. The reading pre-test is the covariate, the variable related to the dependent variable, which is used to add precision to the design.

Those subjects who are better readers will tend to score well on both pretest and the posttest, and those who are poorer readers will tend to score poorly on both tests; therefore, there will be a positive correlation between pretest and posttest scores. The ANCOVA technique removes the portion of each subject's posttest score that is in common with his or her pretest score.

Using this technique, we are not considering a subject's posttest score per se. We are able to analyze the difference between posttest scores and what we would expect the posttest score to be, given the score on the pretest and the correlation between pretest and posttest.

By removing that portion of the dependent variable score variance which is systematically associated with pretest variance, the precision of the experiment is improved. With part of the variance in the posttest scores that is not due to treatment removed, difference that is due to treatment stands out more clearly. The use of a covariate that is related to the dependent variable reduces the likelihood of **Type II error.**

Other measures besides pretest scores can be used as covariates. In our example, measures such as intelligence test scores or grade average could be used. To be useful, a covariate must be correlated with the dependent variable. In the example, basketball throw scores or shoe sizes would not be useful covariates, as they would be expected to have negligible correlation with the reading post-test.

Use of Subjects as their Own Controls

Still another procedure involves assigning the same subjects to all experimental conditions and then obtaining measurement of the subjects first under one experimental treatment and then under the other. The experimental treatment generally consists of selected values of an independent variable. For instance, the same subjects might be required to learn two different lists of nonsense syllables, one list with high association value and the other with low association value. The difference in learning time between the two lists is found for each subject, and the average difference in learning time for all subjects then can be tested for significance.

This is an efficient method of control when feasible, but there are circumstances in which it cannot be used. In some types of studies, exposure to one experimental condition would make it impossible to use the subject for the other experimental condition. We cannot teach children a spelling list one way and then erase their memory and teach it another way.

In the foregoing experiment, where one group of subjects was used to investigate the relative ease of learning high-association and low-association nonsense syllables, there could be a "learning to learn" effect, and thus whichever list appeared second would have an advantage over the first. Conversely, fatigue or interference effects might result in poorer performance on the second list. In this case, we would have a confounding-of-order effect and not reliable conclusions could be drawn. A more efficient procedure would involve a random division of the subjects into two groups; one group of the subjects would then be given one order and the second group, the other order.

Controlling Situational Differences

In addition to intersubject differences, it is also necessary to control any extraneous variables that might operate in the experimental situation itself. If situational variables are not controlled in an experiment, one cannot be sure whether it is the independent variable or these incidental differences operating in the groups that are producing the difference in the dependent variable.

In an experiment to study the effect of a drug on the performance of a manipulative skill, all groups must think that they are taking the drug. Therefore the experimenter must give every subject the same kind of substance as far as quantity, taste, and color are concerned. For some subjects this will be the drug under investigation and for the remainder, an inter chemical known as a placebo. Otherwise the experimenter would not know whether it was the effect of the drug or the subjects attitude or both which produced the result.

There are three methods commonly used to control potentially contaminating situational variables. One can (1) hold them constant, (2) randomize them, or (3) manipulate them systematically and separately from the main independent variable.

Holding extraneous variables constant means that all subjects in the various groups are treated exactly except for their exposure to the independent variable. For instance, in a reading experiment it would be necessary to control for the size of the groups since size of group is known to be a factor affecting reading achievement. One must see that the experimental and control groups have the same number of subjects. The teacher variable must be controlled since teacher efficiency and enthusiasm are factors that may affect the outcome of any learning experiment. Thus the same teacher should be used with two teaching methods that are to be compared.

In an experiment the various assistants must follow the same procedures; use the same instructions, apparatus, and tests and try to assume the same attitudes with all groups. All groups should meet at the same time of day and in the same room. One would not want the experimental group to meet during the first period in the morning of a school day and the control group during the last period of the day, Environmental conditions such as temperature, light intensity, humidity and furniture in the room, and the presence or absence of distracting noises, should be the same for all groups.

If conditions cannot be held constant, the experimenter must attempt to randomize or balance out certain situational variables. For instance, it if is not possible to have the same teacher for both treatments, an experimenter may divide the two major groups into two smaller groups and randomly assign half of the Method. A subjects and half of the Method B subjects to each teacher. The same could be done with other experimental conditions, such as apparatus. In this way situational variables are randomized; a variety of extraneous conditions is represented but is not allowed to affect the dependent variable systematically,

It is possible to control extraneous situational variables by manipulating them systematically. In many educational experiments it is necessary to use a sequence of experimental and control conditions in order to control progressive effects, like those of practice and fatigue. This is done by controlling the order in which experimental conditions are presented through a counterbalancing; half the subjects may receive an AB order and the other half a BA order. In this case an extraneous variable is being systematically manipulated. This procedure not only controls the potentially contaminating effect of order, but it can also provide an estimate to the size of the order effect by determining whether the average. A and B values obtained in the two sequences are different.

It should be mentioned here that other types of variables, such as those associated with the subjects themselves, can be built into an experimental design and thus controlled. For example, if sex is to be controlled in an experiment and it is not possible to use any of the methods for controlling intersubject differences, then one could add sex as another independent variable. This not only controls the extraneous variable, but also yields information about the effect of this variable on the dependent variable as well as its possible interaction with the other independent variables.

This method for controlling extraneous variable amounts to the same thing as adding more independent variables to the experiment. Although it increases the complexity of the study, it has the advantage of furnishing additional information about the effect of relevant variables on the dependent variable and their interaction with the main independent variable

The use of this method of control has been increasing since the introduction of electronic computer to handle the analysis of data in complex studies.

Manipulation

The manipulation of a variable refers to a deliberate operation performed by the experimenter. In educational research and other behavioral sciences, the manipulation of a variable takes a characteristic form in which the experimenter imposes a predetermined set of varied conditions on the subject. The set of varied conditions is referred to as the independent variable, the experimental variable or the treatment variable. The different conditions are designed to represent two or more values of the independent variable; these may be differences in degree or differences in kind. We may manipulate a single variable or a number of variables simultaneously. Multivariate analysis saves time and effort in that it permits the simultaneous investigation of a number of variables considered singly and in interaction – the latter often being the most significant aspect of the study.

Observation

In experimentation we are interested in the effect of the manipulation of the independent variable on a response variable. Observations are made with respect to some characteristic of the behavior of the subjects employed in the research. These observations, which are quantitative in nature if possible, are the dependent variable.

The dependent variable in educational research is often achievement of some type, such as learning. We are often interested in explaining or predicting achievement. Note that we cannot measure learning directly. We can only estimate learning through such measures as scores on a test. Therefore, strictly speaking, the dependent variable is scores or observations rather than achievement per se.

8.9 Experimental Comparison

For the simplest experiment, two groups of subject are required: the experimental group and the control group. The original definitions designated the experimental group as the one receiving a specific treatment, while the control group receives no treatment. In a pharmaceutical experiment, the experimental group receives the drug, while the control group receives no treatment or a placebo. The use of a control group enables the researcher to discount many alternate explanations for the effect of treatment. For example, a fertilizer might yield a bumper crop because of good weather conditions or rain. If an equivalent adjacent unfertilized field yields less, the effect of fertilizer on yield becomes credible.

It should be noted that the majority of educational experiments study the difference in the results of two or more treatments rather than the difference in the results of one particular treatment versus no treatment at all. For example, it would be pointless to compare the spelling achievement of an experimental group taught by Method A with a control group that had no spelling instruction at all. Instead, a comparison is made between groups receiving Method A and Method B. treatment. Comparison of groups receiving two treatments provides the same control over alternate explanations as do comparisons of treated and untreated groups. In order to simplify subsequent discussions, we will use the term control group to refer to either groups with no treatment or groups with alternate treatments. Comparison is essential in scientific investigation. Comparing a group receiving treatment with either an equivalent group receiving n treatment or an equivalent group or groups receiving alternate treatment makes it possible to draw well-founded conclusions from the results.

The experimental and control groups must be equivalent in all variables that may affect the dependent variable; they differ only in exposure to the independent variable. After the experimenter has imposed the different conditions on the subjects, each subject is measured on the dependent variable.

Measurement is followed by evaluation. Is there a difference between the two groups? Is the effect to Treatment. A different from that of Treatment B? This question implies and requires a comparison of the measures of the dependent variable in the one group with the measures of response in the other group. The comparison should tell the experimenter whether or not differences on the dependent variable are associated with differences on the independent variable as represented by the two conditions A and B.

8.10 Experimental Design

Experimental design refers to the conceptual framework within which the experiment is conducted. An Experimental design serves two functions: (1) it establishes the conditions for the comparison required by the hypotheses of the experiment and (2) it enables the experimenter through statistical analysis of the data to make a meaningful interpretation of the results of the study. If a design is to accomplish these functions, the experimenter, when selecting it, must keep in mind certain general criteria.

The most important criterion is that the design be appropriate for testing the particular hypotheses of the study. The mark of a sophisticated experiment is not complexity or simplicity but rather appropriateness. Will this design do the job it is supposed to do? Thus the first task for the experimenter is to select the design that best arranges the experimental conditions to meet the needs of the particular experimental problem.

If the research hypothesis is an interaction hypothesis, then it can be tested adequately only by means of a factorial type of design. Unfortunately, one often finds that educational researchers have tried to test an interaction hypothesis by performing two or more separate experiments. The latter type of design would be incapable of testing the hypothesis. Let us assume that a researcher is interested in the effects of programmed instruction on the learning of basic scientific concepts in elementary school science, believing that there may be differential effect of this method based on class size and the intelligence level of the students. This problem calls for a factorial type of design. The researcher could not answer the question by performing two or three separate experiments, each with a single independent variable.

Another example of an inadequate design is the attempt to use a matched-subjects design in cases when it is impossible for the experimenter to match the subjects on all the relevant extraneous variables. Even though matching may be successful on one or two variables, it cannot be assumed that the groups are equivalent on all relevant variables. A randomized subjects design would be superior in these circumstances.

A second criterion is that the design must provide adequate control so that the effects of the independent variable can be evaluated. Unless the design controls extraneous variables, one can never be confident of the relationship between the variables of the study. As mentioned earlier, randomization is the single best way achieve the necessary control. Therefore the best advice is to select a design that utilizes randomization in as many aspects as possible.

8.11 Validity of Research Designs

A very significant contribution to the evaluation of research designs has been made by Campbell and Stanley, who suggest that there are two general criteria of research design.

- **Internal validity and**
- **External validity**

8.11.1 Internal Validity

Internal validity is concerned with such questions as:

- Did the experimental treatment really bring about a change in the dependent variable?
- Did the independent variable really make a significant difference?

This question of internal validity cannot be answered positively by the experimenter unless the design provides adequate control of extraneous variable. That is, if the design provides control of variables, one is able to eliminate alternative explanations of the empirical outcome and interpret it as showing some kind of intrinsic relationship between variables. Internal validity is essentially a problem of control. The design of appropriate controls is a matter of finding ways to eliminate extraneous variables – that is, variables that could lead to alternative interpretations. Anything that contributes to the control of a design contributes to its internal validity.

Campbell and Stanley have identified eight extraneous variables that frequently represent threats to the internal validity of a research design. These variables must be controlled or else they might very well produce an effect that could be mistaken for the effect of the experimental treatment.

- **History**. Specific events, other than the experimental treatment, may occur between the first and second measurements of the subjects to produce changes in the dependent variable.
- **Maturation**. Processes that operate within the subject simply as a function of the passage of time may produce effects that could mistakenly be attributed to the experimental variable. Subjects may perform differently on the dependent variable measure simply because they are older, hungry, more fatigued, or less motivated than they were at the time of the first measurements.
- **Pretesting**. Exposure to the pretest may affect the subjects' performance on a second test, regardless of the experimental treatment.
- **Measuring instruments**. Changes in the measuring instruments, the scorers, or the observers used, may produce changes in the obtained measures. If the posttest is more difficult or if different observers are used for pre- and post- measures, these factors may account for observed differences in the two scores.
- **Statistical Regression**. If groups are selected on the basis of extreme scores, statistical regression may operate to produce an effect that could be mistakenly interpreted as an experimental effect. This regression effect refers to the tendency for extreme scores to regress or move toward the common mean on subsequent measures. For example, let us assume that the lowest fourth of the scores on an English proficiency test are selected for a special experimental program in English. The mean of this group will tend to move toward the mean of the population on a second test whether or not an experimental treatment is applied. Similarly high initial means would tend to go down toward the population mean on a second testing.
- **Differential selection of subject**. There may be important differences between the groups even before the application of the experimental treatment. For example, if the experimental group in a learning experiment is more intelligent than the control group, the former may perform better on the dependent-variable measure even if this group does not receive an experimental treatment.

— **Experimental mortality**. There may be differential loss of respondents from the comparison groups. If a particular type of subject drops out of one group during the course of the experiment, this differential loss may affect the outcome of the study. If, for example, several of the lowest scorers on a pretest gradually drop out of the experimental group, this group will have a higher mean performance on the final measure, not because of the experimental treatment but because the low-scoring subjects are absent.

— **Selection-maturation interaction**. This type of interaction may occur in a quasi-experimental design where the experimental and control groups are not randomly selected but instead are preexisting intact groups such as classrooms. Even though a pretest may show that the groups are equivalent, the experimental group may happen to have a higher rate of maturation than the control group and it is the increased rate of maturation that accounts for the observed effect. More rapidly maturing students are "selected" into the experimental group and it is the selection-maturation interaction that may be mistaken for the effect of the experimental variable.

For example, a group who elected to take an Advanced English class might show vocabulary growth than a group in a regular English class because their vocabulary growth was at a higher rate both before and during their freshman year. A comparison of pretest and post-test differences of the Advanced English and the regular English classes might lead one to conclude erroneously that the independent variable was responsible for a difference in gain which is due only to selection-maturation interaction. This problem also frequently arises when volunteers are compared with non-volunteers. The volunteers may be more motivated to make gains on the dependent variable than are the non-volunteers. And this difference in gains may be mistakenly attributed to the independent variables – as can happen even when the groups are equivalent on a pretest.

All the methods of control discussed earlier in this chapter are designed to control those extraneous variables that pose a threat to the internal validity of a design.

8.11.2 External Validity

External validity refers to the generalizability or representativeness of the findings. The experimenter asks the question: what population, settings experimental variables and measurement variables can these findings be generalized? Campbell and Stanley have identified four threats to external validity.

Any single study is necessarily performed on a particular group of subjects, with selected measuring instruments and under conditions that are, in some respects, unique. Yet the researcher wants the results of the study to furnish information about a larger realm of subjects, conditions, and operations than were actually investigated. In order to make generalizations from the observed to the unobserved, the researcher needs some kind of assurance that the sample of events actually studied represents the larger population to which results are to be generalized. To the extent that the results of an experiment can be generalized.to different subjects, setting, and measuring instruments, the experiment possesses external validity.

Web reference

Campbell and Stanley Research Design Summary
http://www.csupomona.edu/~tom/lib/senior_projects/research_design_summary.pdf

Bracht and Glass have identified two types of external validity: ***population validity*** and ***ecological validity.***

Population validity is concerned with the identification of the population to which the results of an experiment are generalizable. It asks the question: what population of subjects can behave in the same way as did the sample experimental subjects?

Ecological validity is concerned with generalizing experimental effects to other environmental conditions. It asks the question: under what conditions (that is, settings, treatments, experimenters, dependent variables, and so on) can the same results be expected?

1. Population Validity

A. Experimentally Accessible Population vs. Target Population: Generalizing from the population of subjects that is available to the experimenter (the accessible population) of the total population of subjects about whom s/he is interested (the target population) requires a thorough knowledge of the characteristics of both populations. The results of an experiment might apply only for those special sorts of persons from whom the experimental subjects were selected and not for some larger population of persons.

B. *Interaction of Personological Variables and Treatment Effects:* If the superiority of the experimental treatment over another would be reversed when subjects at a different level of some variable descriptive of persons are exposed to the treatments, there exists an interaction of treatment effects and personological variables.

2. Ecological Validity

A. *Describing the Independent Variable Explicitly:* Generalization and replication of the experimental results presuppose a complete knowledge of all aspects of the treatment and experimental setting.

B. *Multiple-Treatment Interference:* When two or more treatments are administered consecutively to the same persons within the same or different studies, it is difficult and sometimes impossible to ascertain the cause of the experimental results or to generalize the results to settings in which only one treatment is present.

C. *Hawthorne Effect:* A subject's behaviour may be influenced partly by his perception of the experiment and how he should respond to the experimental stimuli. His awareness of participating in an experiment may precipitate behaviour which would not occur in a setting which is not perceived as experimental.

D. *Novelty and Disruption Effects:* The experimental results may be due partly to the enthusiasm or disruption generated by the newness of the treatment.. The effect of some new programme in a setting where change is common may be quite different from the effect in a setting where very few changes have been experienced.

E. *Experimenter Effect*: The behaviour of the subjects may be unintentionally influenced by certain characteristics or behaviours of the experimenter. The expectations of the experimenter may also bias the administration of the treatment and the observation of the subjects' behaviour.

F. *Pre-test Sensitization*: When a pretest has been administered, the experimental results may partly be a result of the sensitization to the content of the treatment. The results of the experiment might not apply to a second group of persons who were not pretested.

G. *Post-test Sensitization*: Treatment effects may be latent or incomplete and appear only when a post experimental test is administered.

H. *Interaction of History and Treatment Effects*: The results may be unique because of "extraneous" events occurring at the time of the experiment.

I. *Measurement of the Dependent Variable:* Generalization of results depends on the identification of the dependent variables and the selection of instruments to measure these variables.

J. *Interaction of Time Measurement and Treatment Effects*: Measurement of the dependent variable at two different times may produce different results. A treatment effect, which is observed immediately after the administration of the treatment, may not be observed at some later time and vice versa.

Although internal validity is the sine qua non, the experimenter wants to select a design that is strong in both internal and external validity. However, in some cases, obtaining one type of validity tends to threaten the other types. For instance, as we arrange for more rigorous control in an educational experiment, we may increase its artificiality and cut down on the applicability of the findings to an actual classroom setting, In practice we try to reach a compromise between internal and external validity, which amounts to choosing a design that provides sufficient control to make the results interpretable, while preserving some realism, so that the findings will generalize to the intended settings.

8.12 Different Types of Experimental Design

Campbell and Stanley (1963) have discussed 16 designs ranging from the weakest to very strong ones which have proved very useful is psychological and educational researches. In discussing their 16 experimental designs, Campbell and Stanley have used some symbols with which a reader is expected to be acquainted.

R : Random selection of subjects or random assignment of treatment to Experimental Groups

X : Treatment or experimental variable which is manipulated. When treatments are compared, they are labelled as X_1, X_2, X_3.

O : Observation or measurement or test where there is more than one O, an arbitrary subscript O_1, O_2, O_3 and so on, is used.

When one or more X occurs in the same row, they indicate that these are being applied to the same persons. The left-to-right dimensions, in which X and O occur, indicate temporal order and when X and O occur in vertical order to each other, they indicate that these two are simultaneous. The parallel rows of symbols in separated by a dashed line indicate that groups have been equated by randomization and when separated by dashed lines, they indicate that groups have not been equated by randomization. There are three designs:

1. Pre-experimental,
2. True Experimental Designs
3. Quasi-Experimental Design

8.12.1 Pre-Experimental Design

The pre experimental design does not provide a control or the equivalent of a control group.

8.12.1.1 One Shot Case Study Design

Here a group is exposed to some form of intervention and then subsequently tested. This design might be illustrated as shown in Exhibit 8.2.

Experimental Group (X)	Process Observed or Measured (O)

Exhibit 8.2: One-off case study design

It has been described as lacking any form of control and therefore of being of no scientific value. The reason is that those factors which contribute to the internal invalidity of the findings are not controlled. Other experiences may have contributed to the scores subsequently obtained, whereas the impression is given that they were caused by the experimental intervention. In a similar way, the effects of maturation, test reliability and selection have not been ruled out and could account for the improvement. This design has weak external validity, and generalized conclusion from the setting cannot be safely made. However, though there is an absence of control factors, the process of observing experimental interventions is common practice in much educational research and evaluation, and is underpinned by a different set of assumptions about how we can research and understand social reality.

Example: Suppose the science teacher in a high school introduces the practice of giving a scholarship (X) to students of standard IX who regularly attend her classes. After this practice has been in operation for a year, the teacher observes that the students attend their classes regularly and science scores are improving (O). On this basis, the teacher concludes that with the practice of giving scholarships, the science scores are improving. However, this conclusion is dubious because the teacher does not know whether

i) there are other factors which may have contributed to the observed change and

ii) whether there was a real change in the observed score relative to their past score.

8.12.1.2 One Group Pre-test, Post-test Design

This design is an improvement over the above design because the effects of treatment (X) are judged by making a comparison between pre-test and post-test scores. However, no control group is used in this design.

The least complicated version of this type of research is the single-group pre-test and post-test design. An example might be the implementation of a curriculum programme which has been devised to improve AIDS awareness among Standard 8 pupils in a school. This consists of a week's intensive teaching, using interactive and didactic methods. Prior to its implementation, the pupils are tested about their knowledge of the effects of AIDS. After the intervention, the pupils are again tested. If a comparison between the scores on these two tests shows that these pupils now have knowledge of AIDS, it is possible to conclude that the teaching programme has been successful in its aims. Diagrammatically, single group experimental research can be shown as in **Exhibit 8.3.**

Experimental Group	Pre-test O_1	Special Treatment X	Post-test O_2

Exhibit 8.3: One group experimental design

There are several problems with this approach. Tests do not always measure what is intended. In the example above, the tests may not have measured the actual level of AIDS awareness amongst the pupils both before and after the intervention. Tests, in other words, can be invalid. They can also be unreliable. Since the pre-test and the post-test has to be either the same or at least similar because the researcher intends to make comparison between scores on the two tests, it is essential that pupils who take the first test do not discuss their answers with other pupils. If they do, it is difficult to determine whether learning has taken place as a result of the testing process or teaching programme.

Experimental subjects cannot be isolated during the experiment, but continue to lead normal lives and are subject to a variety of other influences. Learning opportunities, besides those provided in the teaching programme, occur naturally; pupils, for example, may watch a television programme on AIDS. These may act as more significant influences on learning than the teaching progrmmes. As a result, it is difficult for the researcher to be sure about the sources of any increase in AIDS awareness.

Furthermore, it is difficult to conceal from the pupils that they are taking part in a special teaching programme, and this may affect their behaviour. They may concentrate better than they normally would because they know that they are going to be tested at the end of the progrmme. This is known as pre-test sensitization.

Finally, if the findings from the experiment are to be applied to all eighth standard pupils in the country, then this creates problems. Are these pupils typical? Do they learn in similar ways to all other pupils of this age? Does the profile of this particular group of pupils fit the national profile? Is it legitimate to draw generalized conclusion from the sample? The answers to these questions determine the external validity of the findings.

8.12.1.3 The Static Group Comparison (intact group comparison)

The third pre-experimental design identified by Campbell and Stanley (1963) introduces the notion of a comparison group; this is an attempt to isolate the effects of the experimental intervention, and to clearly distinguish between them and those other factors which may contribute to the results. If the control group when it is tested shows different results from the experimental group, then it is possible to conclude that the intervention has had an effect. This design may be illustrated as shown in Exhibit 8.4.

Intervention with the experimental group	(X....O_1) Group tested (O_1)
No Intervention with the experimental group	Group tested (O_2)

Exhibit 8.4: Static group comparison design

Researchers are comparing here the experiences of the control group during the experiment with the experiences of the experimental group. They may conclude that, if they are measuring, for example, reading ages as a result of a programme designed specifically to accelerate reading skills, the experiences of the control group, though not directly related to the intervention, have contributed to gains recorded on standardized reading tests. One again with this design, because of the lack of controls, they may unjustifiably be attributing gains made on a reading test to the intervention when, for various reasons, those gains would have occurred anyway. They therefore cannot conclude that they have established a causal relationship between a programme and its effects in terms of increased skills amongst participants.

The dotted line indicates that the control group (O_1) has not been equated by randomization.

8.12.2 True Experimental Designs

There are three experimental designs, which are called true experimental designs. In these designs the control group and the experimental groups are formed, and their equivalence established through ***randomization***. As with the static group comparison design, it is important to be aware that the comparison which is made is not between a controlled intervention and nothing at all, but between two different types of experiences of two different groups, the one being planned and designed, and the other being what would have happened anyway.

8.12.2.1 Post-test Only Equivalent Group Design

This design is the most effective and useful true experimental design, which minimizes the threats to experimental validity

Randomly picked experimental (R)	Special Treatment (X)	Post-test (O_1)
Randomly picked control group (R)	No special treatment	Post-test (O_2)

Exhibit 8.5: Post-test only equivalent group design

In the above design there are two groups. One group is given treatment (X), usually called the experimental group, and the other group is not given any treatment called the control group. Both groups are formed on the basis of random assignment of the subjects, and hence they are equivalent.

Example

Suppose a researcher randomly selects 100 students out of a total of 1000 students, using a table of random numbers. These selected 100 students are then randomly assigned to two groups. The researcher is interested in evaluation of the effect of reward over retention of a verbal task. The hypothesis is that reward enhances the retention score. One group is given reward (X) while learning a task and another group receives no such reward while learning a task. Subsequently, both groups are given the test of retention. A simple test of ANOVA would help the researcher in making a decision on whether to accept or reject the hypotheses.

8.12.2.2 Pre-test, Post-test Control Group Design

These types of design have been described as true experimental designs because they always include the processes of randomization. As with the static group comparison design, it is important to be aware that the comparison which is made is not between a controlled intervention and nothing at all, but between two different types of experiences of two different groups, the one being planned and designed and the other being what would have happened anyway. The pre-test/post-test control group design is shown in Exhibit 8.6.

Randomly picked experimental group R	Pre-test O_1	Special treatment X	Post-test O_2
Randomly picked control group R	Pre-test O_3	No Special treatment	Post-test O_4

Exhibit 8.6: Pre-test, post-test control group-design

Exhibit 8.7 shows an experimental design to discover whether a new method of history teaching improves pupils' knowledge and understanding.

It is obvious from **Exhibit 8.6,** that the design has two groups' reviews. One group receives the treatment (X) and another group receives no such treatment. By use of the control group this design controls some sources of internal invalidity like history, maturation and statistical regression.

Group A	Tested for historical knowledge	Received-new method	Post-test
Group B	Tested for historical knowledge	Received-old method	Post-test

Exhibit 8.7: Pre-test, post-test control group design illustration

Having conducted the experiment, the researcher collected and tabulated the data as shown in Table 8.1

Table 8.1: Pre-test, post-test control group design illustration

	Pre-test (average group scores)	Post-test (average group scores)	Improvement
Group A	48%	68%	20
Group B	48%	53%	5

There are a number of problems, even if the conclusion was drawn that the new method seemed to have increased pupils knowledge and understanding. In order to be absolutely sure, it would be important to check that the two groups were similarly matched and that the conditions in which they were taught were the same.

A number of variables may have had an impact on how the old and new methods are received; for example, there may be a gender bias in one group compared with the order. If there is, is it a significant factor in the success or otherwise of the teaching programme? For the comparison between the scores obtained by the two groups to be valid, those other factors which may affect the amount and quality of learning have to be controlled . Only then can the researcher be certain that one method of history teaching (Method A) is a better method than the other (Method B). If less time is spent on Method B, or Method B is always taught in the last period in the afternoon when the children are less attentive, or in poorly ventilated and crowded conditions, then he or she cannot be certain that Group B has performed less well than Group A only because of the type of teaching method being employed. A partial solution to this problem is afforded by the process of random sampling. If two groups can be picked randomly (the one to act as the experimental group and the other to act as a control group), then it is possible to be fairly certain that internal characteristics of the two groups will be similar. The effect of randomly choosing experimental and control groups is that members of each group have an equal chance of being influenced by factors other than the intervention.

8.12.2.3 The Solomon Four-Group Design

The Solomon Four Group Design developed by Solomon (1949) is really a combination of the two equivalents – groups design, namely, the post-test only design and pre-test, post-test only design represents the first direct attempt to control the threats of the external validity. A two way analysis of variance is used to compare the four post-test scores; analysis of covariance to compare gains on O_2 and O_4 since this design provides for two simultaneous experiments, the advantages of replication being incorporated.

The effect of the intervention is replicated in four different ways. Experimentalists can compare pre-test and post-test scores with a single group (Group A) that has received the intervention. This will allow them to make a valid comparison but it may have weak internal and external validity. The second comparison they can make is between a group which has not been subject to the intervention

R Randomized group A	O_1 X Pre-test Receives intervention	O_2 Post-test
R Randomized group B	O_3 Pre-test No intervention	O_4 Post-test
R Randomized group C	Receives intervention	O_5 Post-test
R Randomized group D	No intervention	O_6 Post-test

Exhibit 8.8: Four-group design

(Group B) and one that has (Group A), though this does allow them to filter out the effects of testing – both its potential unreliability and its potential receptivity. They can therefore determine the differential between scores achieved by Group A and Group B, when one has been subjected to the experimental intervention and the other has not.

The third comparison they can make is between Group C and Group D, where the former has only been tested after the intervention, while the latter has received no intervention but has been post-tested. This allows them to make a judgement about the effects of the intervention when test-sensitizing effects have been eliminated. The children could not have behaved in unnatural ways because they were being tested, though there may still be a problem with the sensitizing effects of the intervention itself. This has the effect of increasing the ability of researchers to generalize to other settings. Finally, they can compare Group C and Group B, where the former has been but not pre-tested, while the latter has been pre-tested and post-tested even though it has been subject to any intervention Again, this allows them to be confident that the experimental mechanism which they have set in place is not responsible for the effects they observed and therefore allows them to be more confident about generalizing to other settings.

8.12.2 Quasi Experimental Design

Quasi experimental design is partly like true experimental designs. They control but not all extraneous variables, which give threat to the internal validity of the experiment. The quasi experimental designs provide control over when and to whom the measurement is applied but as subjects are not randomly assigned to the experimental and the control group, the equivalence of the groups is not maintained.

8.12.2.1 Time Series Design

The problem of time

One of the main problems with conducting experiments is that the effects of intervention may not show up, or the full implications of the intervention may be only partially revealed, at the moment of testing (post-testing). An example could be in the field of health education, where the experimenter is interested in testing for the effects of a smoking prevention programme, the intervention comprising a teaching programme with a group of 15-year-old school children. The intervention consists of lectures, seminars, workshops and written exercises. The aim is to reduce both the number of children who start smoking after age of 15 and the number who have already started. Because smoking take-up is heavily influenced by peer group pressure, the effectiveness of any health promotion intervention is likely to be compromised. However, in later life, when the influence of the peer group has considerably declined, learning which took place at an early age, but which had no immediate effect in terms of smoking cessation, influence later decision to stop smoking. In other words, the experimenter has to choose, in an arbitrary manner, the most likely moment to post-test the children, even though he or she is fully aware that the observed effects may be partial, incomplete and possibly misleading, Experimentalists have, therefore, devised a series of designs to compensate for this, though that compensation can be only partially effective. One such design is shown in Exhibit 8.9, and is known as the time-series experiment.

Test	Test	Test	Intervention	Test	Test	Test
O_1	O_2	O_3	X	O_4	O_5	O_6

Exhibit 8.9: Time-series experimental design

Sometimes it happens that a control group cannot be included in an experiment because of the situation in which the experiment is being conducted. Exhibit 8.9 shows one such design. A series of pretests are given to the group. Subsequently the treatment (X) is given and a series of post-tests are given to the same group. In analyzing the results of the time-series design, simple statistical comparisons between O_4 and O_5 are avoided. However, comparison among all other pairs of adjacent points is recommended.

8.12.2.2 Equivalent Time Samples Design

Another is the equivalent time-samples design, in which a series (random or regular alternation) of interventions are consecutively contrasted (over time) with a series of non-interventions. This is usually a single-group design (Exhibit 8.10).

$Time_1$	Intervention and post-test	X_1 O_1
$Time_2$	Non-intervention and post-test	X_0 O_2
$Time_3$	Intervention and post-test	X_1 O_3
$Time_4$	Non-intervention and post-test	X_0 O_4
$Time_5$	Intervention and post-test	X_1 O_5

Exhibit 8.10: Time-samples experimental design

The equivalent time – samples design is an extension of the time-series design with the repeated introduction of the treatment or the experimental variable. Like the time-series design, in equivalent time-samples design a single group is used and the group is exposed to repeated treatment in some systematic way. It is clear from Exhibit 8.9 that in the equivalent time-samples design the treatment (X_1), instead of being given for a single time, is introduced and reintroduced with some other experiments (X_0), which is available in the absence of the treatment. The variable history, which is the major limitation of the time-series design, is well controlled by presenting X on several separate occasions. Other extraneous variables (like maturation, testing, statistical regression,) are also well controlled.

Example: Suppose the experimenter wants to study the effect of showing a 20 minute Aids Awareness film on the attitude towards Aids for a group of grade IX students. The experimenter shows the film to a group of students (X_1). After a few days, the researcher briefly discusses the general usefulness of Aids awareness with them in their class (X_0). Again, the test of their attitude can be made (O_2). After a few days, the groups witness the same film (X_1) and the measure of attitude may be obtained (O_3). Following this, the researcher discusses in detail every aspect of AIDS awareness (X_0), Their attitude towards AIDS awareness is again measured (O_4). The statistical comparison of O_1 and O_3 with O_2 and O_4 helps the researcher to compare two experiences. The time effects are easily determined by comparing O_1 and O_2 to O_3 and O_4.

8.12.2.3 Counterbalanced Design

Finally, there is what is called counter-balanced designs, where four different experimental treatments are compared using four different groups over four different time periods. It can be displayed as shown in Exhibit 8.10

Such designs are also called cross-over designs (Cochran and Cox, 1957). The name "counter balanced designs" was given by Underwood (1949). For counter balancing the treatments, generally, the Latin square management wherein each treatment appears once and only once in each column and in each row, is made.

	Time$_1$	**Time$_2$**	**Time$_3$**	**Time$_4$**
Group A	Intervention$_1$ and post-test X_1O	Intervention$_2$ and post-test X_2O	Intervention$_3$ and post-test X_3O	Intervention$_4$ and post-test X_4O
Group B	Intervention$_2$ and post-test X_2O	Intervention$_4$ and post-test X_4O	Intervention$_1$ and post-test X_1O	Intervention$_3$ and post-test X_3O
Group C	Intervention$_3$ and post-test X_3O	Intervention$_1$ and post-test X_1O	Intervention$_4$ and post-test X_4O	Intervention$_2$ and post-test X_2O
Group D	Intervention$_4$ and post-test X_4O	Intervention$_3$ and post-test X_3O	Intervention$_2$ and post-test X_2O	Intervention$_1$ and post-test X_1O

Exhibit 8.11: Counterbalanced experimental design

A counterbalancing design in which four treatments have been randomly given to four groups at four different occasions is shown in Exhibit 8.11 Variables like history, maturation, testing, instrumental mortality posing threats to internal validity are well controlled by the counterbalanced designs.

Table 8.2: Factors jeopardizing the validity of experimental designs

Sources of Invalidity	**Pre-Experimental**			**True-Experimental**			**Quasi-Experimental**		
	1	**2**	**3**	**4**	**5**	**6**	**7**	**8**	**9**
Internal Validity									
Contemporary History		-	+	+	+	+	-	+	+
Maturation		-	?	+	+	+	+		+
Pretesting Procedure		-	+	+	+	+	+		+
Measuring Instrument		-	+	+	+	+	?		+
Statistical Regression		?	+	+	+	+	+		+
Differential Selection		+	-	+	+	+	+		+
Experimental Mortality		+	-	+	+	+	+		+
Interaction of Selection & Maturation		-	-	+	+	+	+		?
External Validity									
Interaction of Selection and Experimental Variable		-	-	?	?	?	?		?
Interaction of Pretesting and Experimental Variable	-		+	-	+	?		-	
Reactive Experimental Procedure		?		?	?	?	?		?
Multiple Treatment Interfering									

Designs are as follows:

Pre-experimental Design

1. One Shot Case Study
2. One Static Group Comparison
3. The Static Group Comparison

True Experimental Design

4. Post-test only, Equivalent Group Design
5. Pre-test, Post-test Control Group Design
6. Solomon Four Group Design

Quasi Experimental Design

7. Time Series Design
8. Equivalent Time Samples Design
9. Counterbalanced Design

A plus sign indicates that the factor is controlled; a minus sign indicates lack of control, a question mark indicates a possible source of concern, and a blank indicates that the factor is not relevant.

8.13 Validity Problems with Experimental Designs

Some of the sources of invalidity in experimental designs are summarized in Table 8.2. This brief summary must not be depended upon as the sole guide in selecting a design. It must be accompanied by a thorough consideration of the qualified presentation appearing in the text so that the reader understands the particular strengths and weaknesses that characterize each design.

SUGGESTED REFERENCES

- Bracht, Glenn H. and Gene V. Glass. External Validity of Experiments, p. 438. Copyright by American Educational Research Association, Washington D.C. The reader is referred to this source for a more extended discussion of the treats to externals validity.
- Campbell Donald T. and Julian C. Stanley. "Experimental and quasi-Experimental Designs for Research on Teaching," in N.I. Gage, ed., Handbook of Research on Teaching (Washington, D.C..: American, Washington, D.C. This material also appears in Campbell and Stanley, Experimental and quasi Experimental Designs for Research (Skokie, III.: Rand McNally, 1996) The author is indebted to the work of Campbell and Stanley for the terminology and designs used in this section of the chapter.
- Cochran, W.G. and C.M. Cox. Experimental Design. New York. John. Wiley. 1957.
- Edwards, Allen L. Experimental Designs in Psychological Research. 3rd ed. (New York: Holt Rinehart and Winston, 1968, ch. 16).
- Fisher, R.A. The Design of Experiments. 7th ed. New York. Hafner Publishing Co. 1960.
- Kelly, Anthony (Editor) and Richard A. Lesh (ed.) Handbook of Research Design in Mathematics and Science Education. Lawrence Erlbaum Associates. Aug. 2000.
- Mill. John Stuart. A System of Logic (New York); Harper & Brothers, 1846), P. 224.
- Thorndike, Edward L. "Mental Discipline in High School Subjects", Journal of Educational Psychology. 15 (1924): 1-22, 83-98.

❖ ❖ ❖

Descriptive Research

Descriptive Research "describes and interprets what is. It is concerned with conditions or relationships that exist, opinions that are held, processes that are going on, effects that are evident, or trends that are developing. It is primarily concerned with the present, although it often considers past events and influences as they relate to current conditions.". – Best and Kahn (2005).

9.1 Introduction

The major purpose of ***descriptive research*** is to tell **what is.** There are several subcategories of Descriptive Research:

— Case Studies

— Surveys

— Developmental Studies

— Follow up Studies

— Content / Document Analysis

— Secondary Analysis
— Trend Analysis
— Correlational Studies
— Qualitative Observational Research
— Ex Post Facto Studies

Descriptive Research asks questions about the nature, incidence, or distribution of educational variables.

Examples

- What do high school students know about the process through which political parties select candidates for president?
- What is the best way to provide access to computer equipment in schools?
- Do teachers hold favourable attitudes toward using computers in schools?
- What have been the reactions of school administrators to technological innovations in teaching?

9.2 Conducting a Descriptive Research Study

The process of conducting a descriptive research study would include the following:

1. State the hypotheses or questions you hope to answer with your descriptive study.
2. Define subjects.
3. Develop the instrumentation for your study. Usually this involves selecting or more often developing a questionnaire.
4. Validate the questionnaire.
5. Prepare a cover letter
6. Pretest the questionnaire
7. Plan how you will deal with non-respondents and with items not completed.
8. Description and analysis of results.

9.3 Advantages of Descriptive Research Studies

- Educational research often contains many variables that cannot be realistically controlled.
- Educational research may require observations of life experiences.
- Data collection may be spread over a large number of people over a large geographic area.

9.4 Steps involved in Descriptive Research

The process of descriptive research may be summarized in the following steps:

1. **Statement of the problem**

   As in the case of experimental research, the researcher must start with a clear statement of the problem. This statement identifies the variable to be involved in the study and specifies whether the study is merely seeking to determine the status of these variables or whether it will also investigate relationships between the variable.

2. **Identification of information needed to solve the problem**

   The researcher lists the information to be collected, states whether this information is of a qualitative or a quantitative nature, and identifies the form the information will take (interviews, questionnaires, personal data sheets, tests)

3. **Selection or development of instruments for gathering data**

   Questionnaires, interviews, tests and scales of various types are the most frequently used instruments for descriptive research. If the researcher plans to use existing tests, the reliability, validity meaning the variable under study and the suitability for population of interest must be investigated. If a tool is to be devised, a pilot study should be conducted and the reliability and validity, for measuring of the variables of concern should be evaluated.

4. **Identification of the target population and determination of any necessary sampling procedure**

   The researcher determines the group about which information is being sought. In a census this is typically a well-defined local group such as the students in a particular school. Sample surveys usually deal with groups identified by specific characteristics, such as hearing-impaired students, headmasters of higher secondary schools and so forth. In a sample survey the researcher attempts to select a sample that will adequately represent the population.

5. **Design of the procedure for data collection**
   The researcher lays out the practical schedule for obtaining the sample and using the instruments.
6. **Collection of data**
   This involves detailed planning, including getting permission from the schools or persons concerned, timetabling, getting photostat copies of questionnaires and the like. The revised questionnaires (after the pilot study) are readied for administration. The timetable helps the researcher to collect data in an organized manner.
7. **Analysis of data**
   The statistical techniques to be used will have to be planned. A little foresight is necessary so that the data coding can be done properly. The researcher should be familiar with the different categories of measurement scales and use the most suitable, so that appropriate tests can be carried out.
8. **Preparation of the report**

Exhibit 9.1 is an example of a descriptive study . The researcher decides the final format of the descriptive study.

9.5 Sub-categories of Descriptive Research

9.5.1 Case Studies

Case studies and single-subject experiments—both study a single individual or single, discrete social unit such as a family, club, or gang. However, single-subject experiments focus on a single behaviour or a very limited number of behaviours, where as case studies attempt to describe the subject's entire range of behaviours and the relationship of these behaviours to the subject's history and environment. In a single-subject experiment the investigator introduces a specific treatment for the purpose of studying the effect of this treatment on the subject, whereas in case study the investigator observes the subject's reaction to naturally occurring events.

ED059980

A Descriptive Research Study of Cooperating Teachers and Student Teachers in Biracial Situations. Final Report.

Shoudel, Pearl W.

Attitude Change; Black Teachers; Cooperating Teachers; Racial Attitudes; Teacher Attitudes; Whites

This study was designed to determine if the attitudes of cooperating teachers toward another race are changed by their experiences with student teachers of the opposite race. Two rating scales were devised to measure the attitudinal responses of cooperating teachers to items of bias. A control group of 33 black teachers and 32 white teachers who had not worked in biracial situations were tested. The experimental group of 42 white teachers and 41 black teachers, who had been assigned student teachers of the other race, were tested before and after the student teaching program. The most dramatic differences occurred between the control and experimental groups rather than among the experimental groups. Accounting for the lack of change among the latter are the previous experiences of experimental group teachers with students of the opposite race and their voluntary acceptance of the student teacher. However, Caucasian and Negro teachers in the experimental group changed their attitudes about the characteristics of children of the other race in a number of areas. In addition, differences in attitudes between Negro and Caucasian teachers were noteworthy in the following areas: acceptance of the minority teacher by the faculty, ease of communication with the other race, professionalism in relationship to all faculty members and administrators regardless of race, and equality between the races in inherent intelligence and children's behavior patterns. (Author/LP)

Philander Smith Coll., Little Rock, AR.

Office of Education (DHEW), Washington, DC. Bureau of Research.

Exhibit 9.1: ED059980 – A descriptive research study of cooperating teachers and student teachers in biracial situations: final report

In a case study the investigator attempts to examine an individual or unit in depth. The investigator tries to discover all the variables that are important in the history or development of the subject. The emphasis is on understanding why the individual does what he or she does and studying behaviour changes as the individual responds to the environment. This requires detailed study for a considerable period of time. The investigator gathers data about the subject's present state, past experiences, environment, and how these factors relate to one another.

Many case studies arise from endeavours to solve problems. The well-known case studies of Freud began with his attempt to assist his subjects in solving their personality problems. As he attempted to probe deeply into the dynamics of his patients' personalities, he reasoned that the relationships that he observed between them and their environments might also be characteristic of other individual with similar problems. He published detailed accounts of his interviews with patients and his interpretations of their thoughts, dreams, and actions, on the assumption that far-reaching generalizations could be made from the studies

The greatest advantage of case study is the possibility of depth; it attempts to understand the whole child or the whole adult in the totality of that individual's environment. Not only can the present actions of an individual but his or her past, environment, emotions, and thoughts be probed. The researcher attempts to determine why an individual behaves as he or she does and not merely to record behaviour.

Case studies often provide an opportunity for an investigator to develop insight into basic aspects of human behavior. The intensive probing characteristic of this technique may lead to the discovery of previously unsuspected relationships.

On the other hand, the advantages of the case study are also its weaknesses. Although it can have depth, it will inevitably lack breadth. The dynamics of one individual or social unit may bear little relationship to the dynamics of others. In practice most case studies arise out of counselling or remedial efforts and therefore will provide information on exceptional rather than representative individuals.

The opportunities for insight in case study are also opportunities for subjectivity or even prejudice. The pre-conceptions of an investigator can determine which behaviours are observed and which are ignored as well as the way in which the observations are interpreted.

The reputation of the case study approach has suffered because some investigators in the past have explained their observations in constructs that are impossible either to confirm or refute through empirical study.

Since the extent to which case studies can produce valid generalizations is extremely limited, their major usefulness is not as tools for testing hypotheses but rather in the production of hypotheses, which can then be tested through more rigorous investigation. For example, the insights Jean Piaget gained in his famous case studies have been investigated through other methods.

Title: Word Processing in Elementary Schools: Seven Case Studies. Education and Technology Series

Author: Jack Murray and others.

Abstract: As a result of preliminary observations of word processing in elementary level language the seven case studies presented in this report reveal the effectiveness of current word processing (WP) activities within their respective instructional contexts. Each study is presented separately, detailing the classroom context, tasks and outcomes, program effectiveness and results. Generally, the studies indicated that the type and / or degree of success students attain using contextual variables identified in the studies were age, equipment availability, and location.

Source: This information can be found in ERIC Document (ED297317)

Exhibit 9.2: Sample of case studies

9.5.2 The Survey Technique

9.5.2.1 Characteristics of a Good Survey

- Good questioning techniques
- Use of complete sentences
- A limited set of options in the questioning
- Interesting
- Worded without ambiguity
- The option “I do not know” used carefully

9.5.2.2 Steps in Survey Research

Survey research involves a number of steps:

1. *Planning* involves the determination of what population is to be studied and what topic is to be investigated. In this stage, one also decides on the methods and procedures that will be used to gather the data.
2. *Sampling* involves decision-making about which people from the population of interest are to be included in the survey. If one is to generalize from the sample to the population, it is essential the sample selected be representative. The sampling procedure that is most likely to yield a representative sample is some form of random sample (see Chapter 6.)
3. *Construction of the data-gathering instrument* involves writing the questions and planning the format of the instrument to be used. Among the data-gathering techniques used in surveys are personal interviews, questionnaires, and telephone interviews.
4. *Executing* the survey includes pre-testing the instrument to determine whether it will obtain the desired data, training the users of the instrument (for example, interviewers,) interviewing subjects or distributing questionnaires to them, and verifying the accuracy of the data gathered.
5. *Processing* the data includes the coding of the data, computer processing of the data, interpreting the results and reporting the findings.

9.5.2.3 Data-gathering Instruments used in the Survey Technique

The interview and the questionnaire, both utilize the question-asking approach. These instruments can be used to obtain information concerning facts, beliefs, feelings, intentions, and so on. Although both the interview and the questionnaire make use of the question approach, there are important differences between the two methods.

In an interview, data are collected through face-to-face or telephone interaction between the interviewer and the respondent. The questionnaire obtains information through the respondent's written responses to a list of questions. Each method has advantages as well as the disadvantages. The researcher must decide which of the two methods is more appropriate for the needs and characteristics of a particular study.

Useful websites for Survey

Survey Research http://www.socialresearchmethods.net/kb/survey.htm This is part of the Trochim site that discusses survey research. Information on the most current version of this web site or a printed copy of the text can be found at http://www.atomicdog.com/trochim. Information is also available on the use of this version of the site at http://www.socialresearchmethods.net/kb/.

What Is a Survey? http://www.whatisasurvey.info/ This site was developed by the American Statistical Association to provide a brief introduction to many aspects of survey research. The topics of ten short papers include defining a survey, planning survey research, data collection, mail surveys, focus groups, designing questionnaires, and telephone surveys.

9.5.2.4 Interviews

One of the important aspects of the interview is its flexibility. The interviewer has opportunity to observe the subject and the total situation in which he or she is responding. Questions can be repeated or their meanings explained in case they are not understood by the respondents. The interviewer can also press for additional information when a response seems incomplete or not entirely relevant.

A greater completion rate is another obvious advantage of interview. Personal contact increases the likelihood that the individual will participate and will provide the desired information. The low return rate typical for mailed questionnaires (35% per cent is common) not only reduce the sample size but also may bias the results. Missing data represent a serious problem for the mailed questionnaire.

Another advantage is the control that interviewee has over the order with which questions are considered. In some cases it is very important that respondents not know the nature of later questions since their responses to these questions might influence earlier responses. This problem is eliminated in an interview, where the subject does not know what questions are coming up and cannot go back and change answers previously given. For individuals who cannot read and understand a written questionnaire, interviews provide the only possible information-gathering technique.

The main disadvantage of interviews is that they are more expensive and time-consuming than questionnaires.

Two basic types of questions, open-ended or closed are used in an interview, according to the nature of the response desired from the respondent. The open-ended question permits a free response from the subject rather than restricting the response to a choice from among stated alternatives. The individual is free to respond according to his or own frame of reference. The interviewer simply reads the question and records the respondent's answer verbatim. An example of an ***open-ended question*** is:

> What are the most prominent computational problems that you have observed among your Standard IX students?

With the ***closed-question format***, the interviewer reads the question and presents the respondent with the various alternative response options. From the list of stated options, the individual picks the response that best represents his or her own belief or opinion. An example of a closed question is:

> What type of laboratory work is typically required in your science class?
>
> 1) hands on 2) model making 3) seminars
> 4) others (please specify)

The open-ended response format permits greater freedom of expression for the respondent and provides a wider range of responses. However, open-ended questions require time for both interviewer and respondent. It is difficult for the interviewer to record the responses verbatim and later classify and code the data for analysis. The closed question is easier and quicker for the subject to respond to and easier for the interviewer to code and analyze. A closed format also ensures that all subjects will have the same frame of reference in responding and may also make it easier for subjects to answer questions dealing with topics of a sensitive or private nature.

A limitation of the closed question is that it does not provide much insight into whether respondents really have any information or any clearly formulated opinions about an issue. It is easier for the uninformed respondent to choose some of the suggested answers than to admit to lack of knowledge on an issue. For example, in response to the question. What aspects of the Finance Minister's new economic package do you think will be most helpful?, The respondent without any knowledge of the Finance Minister's programme could easily select a reasonable answer from among those provided. On the other hand, respondents who have the information or who have well-informed opinions on the issue may dislike being restricted to simple response categories that do not permit them to qualify their answers.

Of course, a combination of open-ended and closed questions may be used in a single interview. Closed questions are recommended for securing factual information or opinions on issues where it is possible to identify a limited number of alternative responses. The open-ended question is preferred for more complex questions where the researcher is interested in identifying the subject's understanding of an issue, the frame of reference used in responding, or the motivations underlying the response.

In practice, a researcher in the process of constructing an interview schedule often begins with an interview made up of open-ended questions administered to a few subjects strictly for the purpose of identifying the possible alternative responses to the questions. Then on the basis of the results from this small sample, an interview schedule made up mainly of closed questions can be prepared.

Conducting the Interview

The interviewer's main job is to ask the questions in such a way as to obtain valid responses and to record the responses accurately and completely. The initial task for the interviewer is to create an atmosphere that will put the respondent at ease. After introducing himself or herself in a friendly way, the interviewer should state briefly the purpose of the interview but should avoid giving too much information about the study, which could bias the respondent.

The interviewer also has the responsibility of keeping the respondent's attention focussed on the task and for keeping the interview moving along smoothly. This can best be done if the interviewer is thoroughly familiar with the questions and their sequence so that he or she can ask the questions in a conversational tone and without constantly pausing to find what question is coming next. Of course the interviewer must refrain from expressing approval, surprise, or shock at any of the respondent's answers.

If comparable data are to be obtained, it is important that the same questions be asked in the same order and with the same wording for all respondents. If the respondent starts to hem and haw, moves away from the topic, or gives an irrelevant response, or if he or she has obviously misinterpreted the question, then the interviewer may probe by saying, "explain your answer a little further' or "can you tell me a little more then that?" Of course, the interviewer must be careful not to suggest or give hints about possible responses.

A complete and accurate recording of the respondent's answers must be made. On the open-ended questions the respondent's exact words must be recorded verbatim while he or she is responding. This recording can be facilitated by abbreviating words and sentences or by using a tape recorder. Taping has the obvious advantage of recording the subjects' responses verbatim along with the added advantage of freeing the interviewer to participate in the dialogue rather than having to concentrate on note taking. However, many people feel uncomfortable about their answers being taped and may become inhibited and excessively cautious about what they say. Of course, ethics demands that the subject's permission be obtained before a tape recorder is used.

Training the Interviewer

It is essential that potential interviewers receive training before being sent out to use this technique. They should first spend time observing sample interviews being conducted by trained individuals and then should be required to conduct interviews under the direct supervision of instructor. In the practice interviews, the interviewees should be individuals drawn from the same population that will be used in the research study.

9.5.2.5 Questionnaires

Web reference

- Questionnaires in Usability Engineering
  http://www.ucc.ie/hfrg/resources/qfaq1.html

The direct one-on-one contact with subject involved in the interview process is time-consuming and expensive. Often, much of the same information can be obtained by means of a questionnaire. Because a questionnaire is designed for self-administration and is often mailed, it is possible to include a larger number of subjects as well as subjects in more diverse locations than is practical with the interview.

Another advantage is that a questionnaire that can guarantee confidentiality may elicit more truthful responses than would be obtained with a personal interview. In the interview, subjects may be reluctant to express unpopular points of view or to give information that they think might be used against them later. Furthermore, the interviewer, whose personal appearance, mood, or conduct may influence the results of an interview, is not present when the questionnaire is completed.

A disadvantage of the questionnaire is the possibility of misinterpretation of the questions by the respondents. It is extremely difficult to formulate a series of questions whose meanings are crystal-clear to every reader. The investigator may know exactly what is meant by a question, but because of poor wording or differential meaning of terms, a significantly different interpretation is made by the respondent. Furthermore, large segments of the population may not be able to read and respond to a mailed questionnaire. Only people with considerable education may be able to complete a very complex questionnaire.

However, questionnaires do not elicit as high a completion rate as the interview. It is easy for the individual who receives a questionnaire to lay it aside and simply forget to complete and return it. A low response rate limits the generalizability of the results of questionnaire study. It cannot be assumed that non-response is randomly distributed throughout a group. Studies have shown that there are usually systematic differences in the characteristics of respondents and non-respondents to questionnaire studies. Response rate is often higher among the more intelligent, better educated, more conscientious, and more interested or generally more favourable to the issue involved in the questionnaires.

A number of factors have been found to influence the rate of returns for ***a mailed questionnaire.***

Some of these are:

- ✓ the length of the questionnaire,
- ✓ the cover letter,
- ✓ the sponsorship of the questionnaire,
- ✓ the attractiveness of the questionnaire,
- ✓ the ease of completing it and mailing it back,
- ✓ the interest aroused by the content, and
- ✓ the follow-up procedure used.

Constructing the Questionnaire

Constructing a good questionnaire is a difficult and time-consuming task. But we know that a well-constructed questionnaire is more likely to elicit a good response than a poorly constructed one. The following are a few guidelines for constructing a mailed questionnaire.

1. *Construct the instrument in such a way that it reflects quality.* A questionnaire that appears to have been thrown together quickly will not elicit high returns. During the process of constructing the questionnaire, numerous revisions may be necessary in order to eliminate ambiguous or unnecessary items.
2. *Keep the questionnaire as brief as possible so that it requires a minimum of the respondents' time.* Respondents are much more likely to complete and return a short questionnaire. The researcher must make an effort to eliminate all unnecessary items, especially those whose answers are available from other sources. All the items of a questionnaire should serve a specific research problem function. For example, a question that asks the respondent's age in a study where this information is not needed in the data analysis can be eliminated.

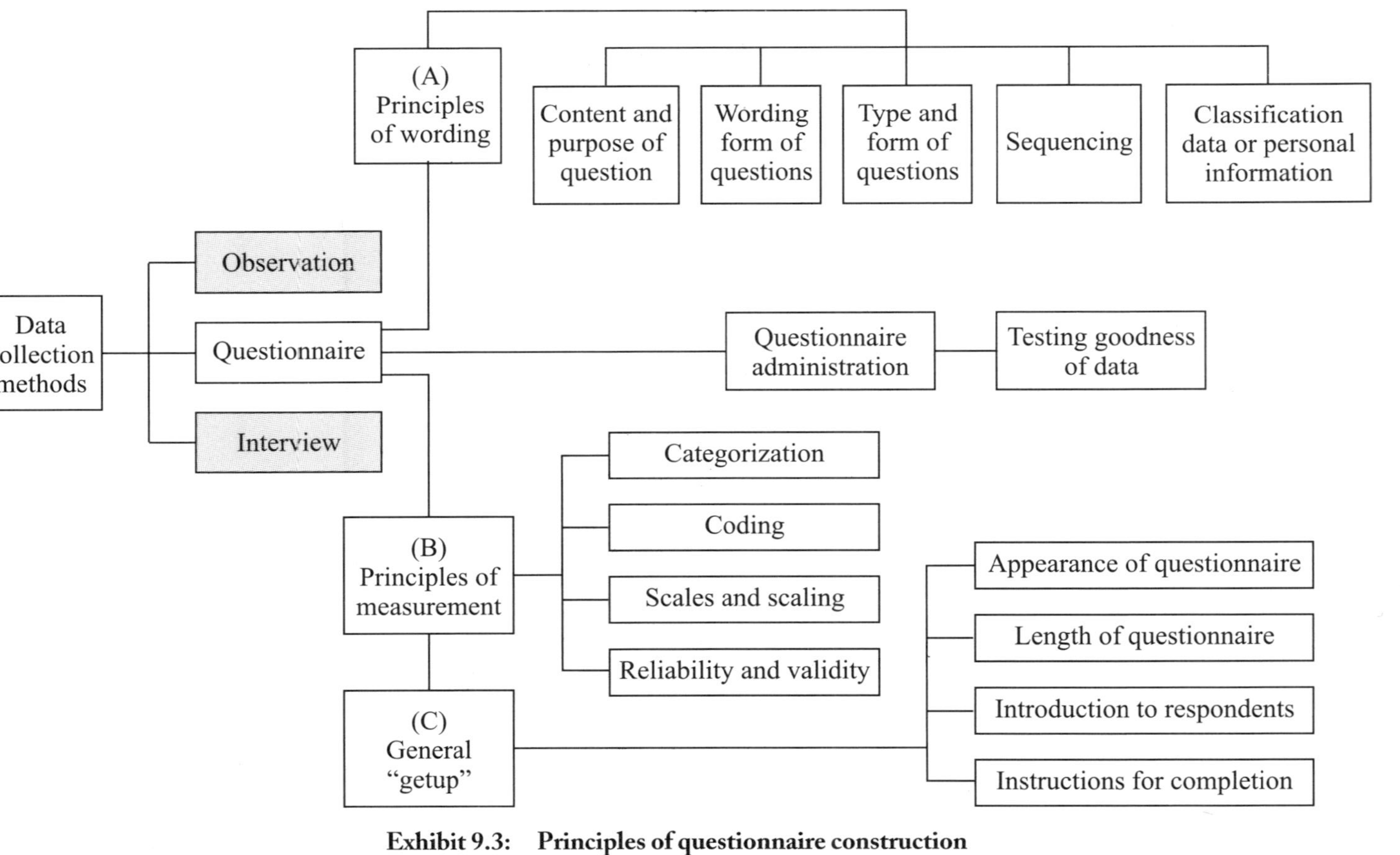

Exhibit 9.3: Principles of questionnaire construction

3. ***Make sure that the respondents have the information necessary to answer the questions.*** Avoid questions dealing with experiences or topics known to be unfamiliar to your sample.
4. ***Phrase questionnaire items so that they can be understood by every respondent.*** The vocabulary used should be non-technical and should be geared to the least-educated respondent. At the same time, the researcher should avoid talking down to respondents or choosing words that sound patronizing. It is a good idea to have some other people, preferably ones whose background is similar to those who will be included in study, read and give their interpretation of the content of each question. The researcher should also be careful not to use abbreviations or acronyms that might not be familiar to all.
5. ***Keep individual questionnaire items as short and simple as possible.*** Eliminate any words and phrases not essential to the clear meaning of the question. Carefully choosing the words to be used is very important if the questionnaire is to be used with a cultural or socioeconomic group other than that of the researcher.
6. ***Phrase questionnaire items so as to elicit unambiguous answers.*** Whenever possible, responses should be quantified. For example, instead of having respondents check sometimes, often, or always, state the alternative number of times per week. Words like often and sometimes have different meaning for different people.
7. ***Phrase questionnaire items so as to avoid bias that might predetermine a respondent's answer.*** That is, the wording of a question should not influence the respondent in certain direction. For this reason, stereotyped, prestige-carrying, emotionally loaded or superlative word should be avoided. Some words have such an emotional appeal in our culture that tend to bias questions regardless of how they are used. Dillman says that words such as freedom, equality, private enterprise, justice, and honesty have a strong positive appeal in our culture. Words such as bureaucrat, socialist, boss, and government planning have a strong negative appeal. Such words should be avoided if at all possible.
8. ***Avoid questionnaire items that might mislead because of unstated assumptions.*** The frame of reference for answering the question

should be clear and consistent for all respondents. If any assumptions have to be made before respondents give an answer, then questions designed to inquire into these assumptions should also be included.

For example, in a survey designed for teacher trainees the question: Do you think your training college has adequately prepared you for teaching? assumes that teacher trainee is going to training college and that he knows what is required in way of preparation.

9. ***Make sure that the alternatives to each questionnaire item are exhaustive; that is express all the possible alternatives on the issue.*** For example, what is your marital status? should include not only the alternatives married or single, but also widowed, divorced separated.

   In developing the alternatives for questionnaire items designed to identify attitudes or opinions on issues, it is good idea first to present the question in an open-ended form to small sample of respondents. Their answers can then be used as alternatives in the final product. On questions for which there is wide variety of possible responses, one should always include the alternative other along with a request that the respondent explain that choice. For example, the question 'what is your position in the school system?' might be followed by the alternatives: administrator, teacher, librarian, non-teaching staff (please specify).

10. ***Avoid questions that might elicit reactions of embarrassment, suspicion, or hostility in the respondent.*** Questions should not put the respondent on the defensive. For example, people often resent question about their age, income, religion, or education status. Instead of asking a subject's age the researcher can ask for his or her year of birth. People seem less concerned about giving their year of birth than about giving their age

11. ***Avoid "double-barreled" questions that attempt to ask two questions in one.*** For example, the question: do you feel that the university should provide vocational-skills courses for students and give credit for these courses? is a double-barreled question. When a respondent answers a double-barreled question, the researcher does not know whether the answer applies to both parts of the question or to just one. A yes answer to the above question may

mean that the respondent believes either that university should offer vocational-skill courses and should give credit for them or that it should offer the courses but not give credit for them.

Types of Questions

Both open-ended and closed questions are used in questionnaires. We have already discussed in connection with interviews the advantages and disadvantages of these question formats. Questions can be structured in several ways.

1. *Completion or fill-in items* are open-ended questions to which respondents must supply their own answers stated in their own words.
2. *Checklists* are questions that present a number of possible answers and the respondents are asked to check those that apply. For example

> What type of audiovisual aids do you use in your classes? (Check as many as apply)
>
> ☐ blackboard ☐ video tapes ☐ speakers
>
> ☐ films ☐ audio tapes ☐ books
>
> ☐ other (please specify)
>
> Responses to these items are also classified into nominal categories.

3. *Scaled items* ask respondents to rate a concept, event or situation on such dimensions as (a) quantity or intensity, indicating "how much" or (b) frequency, indicating "how often." For example:

> How would you rate the students you are teaching on science model making skills? (Circle number)
>
> 1. very poor
> 2. less than adequate
> 3. adequate
> 4. more than adequate
> 5. excellent
> 6. insufficient information

> How frequently have you observed lack of psychomotor coordination while performing titration among Standard XII Chemistry students? (Circle number)
>
> 1. very infrequently
> 2. infrequently
> 3. sometimes
> 4. frequently
> 5. very frequently
> 6. insufficient information

4. ***Ranking*** questions ask respondents to indicate the order of their preference among a number of opinions. Rankings should not involve more than five or six options because it becomes too difficult for respondents to make the comparisons. An example of a ranking item follows.

> Do your M.Ed. students have differential difficulty level while reviewing literature for selection of problem for their dissertation? Please rank the order of difficulty of the following materials, with 1 being the most difficult and 4 the least difficult.
>
> ____ textbooks
>
> ____ other reference books
>
> ____ journal articles
>
> ____ other (please specify)

Arrangement of Questions

It is recommended that special attention be given to the very first question because it may determine whether the respondents continue with the questionnaire or toss it aside. The first question needs to be interesting and easy enough for all respondents to interpret and answer. Being able to answer the first question increases the subjects' motivation and their confidence about the ability to complete the questionnaire. However, being easy does not mean that the question is trivial or insignificant. It is essential that the first question seeks worthwhile information on the topic under consideration. For this reason, one should avoid beginning with questions relating to age, sex, education, occupation, ethnic origin, marital status, and the like. The respondents may regard these questions as irrelevant or as an invasion of privacy and may therefore not continue with the questionnaire. It is also recommended that the first few questions be of the closed type, which the respondents can complete quickly, rather than open-ended ones, which may require a long written response.

Questions that are similar in content should be grouped together. For example, in a questionnaire asking university faculty about the basic academic skills of their students, all the questions on reading comprehension would be placed together. Then questions on spatial ability would appear together, followed later by questions related to mathematics skills. Within the content areas, the items should be grouped according to the type of question. For example, the questions requiring a simple yes or no answer would be placed together, as would items requiring subjects to rank or to indicate the extent of the agreement or disagreement.

Within each of the topic areas, the questions should be arranged in good psychological order. A logical or psychological arrangement contributes to better-thought-out answers on the part of the respondents. For example, one would first ascertain whether or not respondents were satisfied with the training provided before asking for changes that they would recommend. If both general and specific questions are asked on a topic, place the general questions first. Objective items on an issue or situation should precede the more subjective questions. Questions that are less likely to be objectionable should precede items that are more objectionable. People are sometimes reluctant to answer questions about attitudes, preferences, motives, behaviour, personal feelings, etc., but if objective questions can be used first to clarify and specify the situation, it may be easier for individuals to respond. For example, a researcher who wanted to survey students on the extent of cigarette smoking might begin by asking more objective question questions first, such as

- Do you consider smoking a serious, moderate, slight, or no problem at all in our university?
- Do you think the frequency of smoking has increased, stayed about the same, or decreased this year?
- Do you know students who smoke?
- Do you ever smoke cigarettes?....

An implication of the above principle of placing less objectionable questions before more objectionable ones is that the items dealing with biographical data such as age, sex, and occupation should be placed at the end of the questionnaire rather than at the beginning. There will be fewer objections of giving this personal information after the individual has completed the rest of the questionnaire and can see why these kinds of data would be relevant.

Layout of the Questionnaire

The questionnaire should be laid out so that it is attractive, easy for the respondent to read and answer, and convenient for the researcher to code and score.

1. ***Number questions consecutively throughout the questionnaire without any repetitions or omissions.*** Having a unique number for each question avoids confusion in coding responses.
2. ***Questions can be differentiated from answer categories by using lowercase letters for the questions, uppercase letters for the answers.*** Any specific directions for responding are put inside parentheses and are in lower case.

> Example:
>
> a. Do you favour setting standards by having a cut-off point for entry into teacher training colleges?
>
> A. No B. Yes

3. ***Use numbers to identify the various answer categories.*** Numbers are preferable to letters, blanks, or boxes because the numbers assigned to the options represent a form of pre coding that will facilitate processing of the data.

> What is the highest level of education that you have completed?
>
> 1. Primary
> 2. Eighth Standard
> 3. High School
> 4. Higher Secondary
> 5. Degree/Technical Education
> 6. Postgraduation/Technical Education
> 7. Doctoral/Other

The 5 indicates that the individual has completed college, and a count can easily be made for that category. Because of the varying lengths of the options, it is recommended that number for the options be placed to the left of the response categories rather than at the right.

4. ***Be consistent in assigning numbers to the various answer categories.*** That is, always use the same number for the same answer throughout the questionnaire. It is conventional to assign lower numbers to negative responses and higher numbers to the positive responses. For example, **1** is assigned to **No** and **2** is assigned to **Yes; 1** is assigned to **unfavourable** and **2** to **favourable.** Whatever number scheme is chosen, it must be used throughout since it is confusing for a respondent to associate 1 with no in the first part of the questionnaire and then find 1 associated with yes in another part.
5. ***Responses categories must be arranged in a vertical rather than horizontal format.*** The vertical arrangement makes the questionnaire appear less crowded and eliminates the common error of checking the space on the wrong side of the answer.

What is your present marital status?		
1. Never married	2. Married	3. Divorced
4. Śeparated	5. Widowed	

The above confusing arrangement could be improved in the following way:

What is your present marital status? (Circle number)

a. never married
b. married
c. divorced
d. separated
e. widowed

6. ***Have the questionnaire reproduced by high-quality method such as electronic typing or computer word processing.*** Quality printing gives the questionnaire a more professional appearance and will make a more favourable impression on respondents.

Pre-testing

Before the final printing, it is essential that the questionnaire be pre-tested in order to identify ambiguities, misunderstandings, or other inadequacies. First, it is a good idea to ask colleagues who are familiar with the study to examine a draft of the questionnaire and give their opinions on whether the instrument will obtain the desired data and whether there are any problems that may have been overlooked.

Next, the questionnaire should be administered personally and individually to a small group of persons drawn from the population to be considered in the study. Respondents answer the questions one at a time and provide feedback to the researcher on any difficulties they have with the items. Attention would be paid to comments like "I don't know what you mean here" and "More than one of these answers apply to me." The researcher should try to ascertain whether questions are interpreted in the same way by all respondents. The questionnaire can be given to 10 judges who can be requested to categorize all the questions as ***most appropriate/appropriate/not appropriate***. Whenever the judges disagree on an item, that item can be rejected. Most appropriate questions can be retained. Appropriate questions can be grouped under different components and a few questions slightly modified to suit the objectives of the study, then included in the questionnaire.

Observations made of the respondents as they fill out questionnaire can also be enlightening. Spending an undue amount of time on a question or leaving a question blank and returning to it later shows that there are problems with some of the items.

The results of pre-testing can be used to clarify the items or perhaps to eliminate some. It is especially important to determine whether the questions will operate equally well in the different social classes and culture groups of the population to be studied.

Some specific questions that should be answered as a result of pre-testing are:

— Do the respondents appear to be comfortable with questionnaire and motivated to complete it?
— Are certain items confusing?
— Could some items result in hostility or embarrassment on the part of respondents?
— Are the instructions clear?
— How long will it take a respondent to complete the questionnaire?
— Do all respondents interpret the items in the same way?

Distributing the Questionnaire

Researchers may find it useful to mail an introductory letter to potential respondents in advance of the questionnaire itself. This procedure alerts the subject to the study so that he or she is not overwhelmed by the questionnaire package. In any case, a cover letter addressed to the respondent by name and title must accompany the questionnaire. The cover letter serves to introduce the potential respondents to the questionnaire and "prepares" them on responding. The cover letter should include the following elements:

1. *The purpose of the study*. The first paragraph of the letter should explain the purpose of the study and its potential usefulness. It will be helpful to relate the importance of the study to the reference group with which the individuals may identify.
2. *A request for cooperation*. The letter should explain why the potential respondent was included in the sample and should make an appeal for the respondent's cooperation. Respondents should be made to feel that they can make an important contribution to the study.
3. *The protection provided to the respondent*. The letter must not only assure the respondents that their responses will be confidential but must also explain how that confidentiality will be maintained. In order to facilitate the follow-up procedure necessary for a high return rate, it is recommended that identification numbers be used on the questionnaires. If identification numbers are used, it is essential that the respondents are told that the numbers are there simply to enable the researcher to check the respondents' names off the mailing list when the questionnaires are returned. The respondents must be assured that their names will never be placed on the questionnaires themselves; thus there will be no reason to associate particular responses with any individual. If the researcher intends to destroy the questionnaire immediately after the responses have been coded, this information should be conveyed in the letter in order to reassure the respondents of their anonymity.
4. *Sponsorship of the study*. The signature on the letter is important in influencing the return of the questionnaire. If the study is part

of a doctoral dissertation, it would be helpful if a person is well known to the respondents, such as the head of a university department or the principal of the school/college, signs or countersigns the letter. If there is a sponsor (say the UGC or some NGO) for the study, this should be mentioned. A university or agency letterhead should be used.

5. *Promise of results.* An offer may be made to share the findings of the study with the respondents if they are interested. They should be told how to make their request for the results known to the researcher. One method is to provide place for checking on the back of the return envelope as a place for the respondent's name and address.
6. *Appreciation.* An expression of appreciation for their assistance and cooperation with the study should be included.
7. *Recent date on the letter.* The cover letter should be dated near the day of mailing. A potential respondent will not be impressed by a letter dated several weeks before receipt.
8. *Request for immediate return.* It is also important to urge immediate return of the questionnaire. If a time period such as two weeks or month is suggested, the respondent may lay the questionnaire aside and.inspite of good intentions, forget about it. A questionnaire that fails to receive attention within a week is not likely ever to be returned.

Follow-ups

In order to reach the maximum percentage return, follow-up mailings are essential. Several steps are typically taken in the follow-up:

✓ **First reminder.** If the questionnaire has not been returned in a week or ten days after the initial mailing. a postcard should be sent to the respondent. This card serves as a polite reminder that a questionnaire was sent earlier and that the response is very important for the study. Urge respondents to complete and return the questionnaire immediately ('today'). Of course a word of thanks should be expressed to those who may have already mailed the questionnaire.

✓ **Second follow-up.** This follow-up, which should be sent about three weeks after the original mailing, involves a letter, another copy of the questionnaire, and addressed return envelope. The letter should first tell the non-respondents that their questionnaires have not been received and should reiterate the usefulness of the study. The enclosure of a replacement questionnaire should be emphasized, along with a strong appeal to complete and return it. The respondents should be told not to respond a second time if they have already mailed the questionnaire.

✓ **Third follow-up.** The third and final follow-up is sent out six to seven weeks after the initial mailing. It is similar to the second, having both a letter and a replacement questionnaire. Many researchers send this follow-up by under certificate of posting mail. If a researcher has 75 to 90 per cent returns after three follow-ups he or she may be ready to terminate the survey and to declare the remaining subjects non-respondents. The researcher must decide whether the responses obtained through additional follow-up effort would be worth the cost and the time involved.

Dealing with Non response

The usual approach is to try to interview either personally or by telephone a small random sample (perhaps 10 percent) of the non-respondents for the purpose of learning something of their characteristics as well as obtaining their responses. The mean responses or proportion of responses of the respondents and non-respondents to the items may be compared to see whether the two groups differ significantly. If no significant difference is found when the responses of the initial respondents are compared with those of the interview sample, then one could reasonably assume that the respondents represent an unbiased sample of all who received the questionnaires. If there are meaningful differences, some type of weightage procedure can be applied to the non-returns in the final analysis of data, ***Aiken shows that the extent to which the responses of the respondents to survey items are representative of the responses of the total sample is a function of the sample size, proportion of returns and proportion of respondents responding to items in a specified direction.*** He provides a formula for determining the minimum proportion of people who must return a survey in order for the researcher to feel confident that the responses of the respondents are representative of the total sample

If one finds that certain clearly identifiable subgroups did not return the questionnaire, it may be necessary to change the original research question to exclude these subgroups. For example, if secondary teachers showed much lower rate of return than did primary school teachers in a survey, the researcher might conclude that the questionnaire had little relevance or interest for secondary teachers and decide to restrict the study to primary school teachers. The research question would be tested to indicate the change.

Group-Administered Questionnaires

The self-administered questionnaire is usually used in groups assembled for a specific purpose (e.g., the parents of entrants to training college attending pre registration day on campus) or to gather information in a specific situation (e.g., in a hostel). The administrator of the survey is present and can provide assistance, if necessary. The sample is usually quite specific (e.g., parents of teacher trainees) and generalizable only to that population.

9.5.2.6 The Telephone Interview

The telephone interview has become popular as a source of data. Its major advantages are lower cost and faster completion with relatively high response rates. Telephone interviews can be conducted with persons scattered over a large geographic area in a short period of time. National polling organizations often use the telephone to obtain national opinions among voters near election time. Other large-scale surveys in major cities use the telephone instead of sending interviewers into areas where they could be exposed to dangers. Another advantage of the telephone interview in a large city is that one is able to reach people who might not open their doors to an interviewer, but who would be willing to talk on the telephone.

Its main disadvantage is the lack of opportunity for establishing the rapport with the respondent that is possible in a face-to-face situation. A great deal of skill is required to construct a telephone questionnaire and carry out the interview so that good results are obtained. Another disadvantage is that households without telephones are automatically excluded from the survey which may bias results.

Validity

Some attention must be given to the validity question – that is, whether the interview or questionnaire is really measuring what it is supposed to measure. The most obvious type of validity is content validity, which may be assessed by having some competent colleagues who are familiar with the purpose of the survey, examine the items to judge whether they are adequate for measuring what they are supposed to measure and whether they are a representative sample of the behaviour domain under investigation.

Some studies have used observation of behaviour to assess criterion-related validity of responses. After responses were obtained, observations were made to see whether the actual behaviour of the subjects agreed with their expressed attitudes, opinions or other answers. Other data sources, such as third parties, may also be used as criteria.

Some factors that influence the validity of questionnaire are:

- ***How important is the topic to the respondent*?** We can assume more valid responses from individuals who are interested in the topic and/or are informed about it.
- ***Does the questionnaire protect the respondents' anonymity?*** It is reasonable to assume that greater truth-fulness will be obtained if the respondents could remain anonymous, especially when sensitive questions are asked.

Reliability

Having two different interviewers interview the same individual to check on the consistency of the results is one procedure for assessing reliability of questionnaires or interviews.

Internal consistency may be checked by building some redundancy into the instrument. That is, items on the same topic may be rephrased and repeated in the questionnaire or interview.

It is also possible to repeat a questionnaire or interview with the same individual after a period of time or to administer two different forms of the questionnaire to the same individuals. Such procedures are often expensive and time-consuming and somewhat impractical because it is not easy to find subjects willing to repeat the questionnaire or interview a second time.

Its main disadvantage is the lack of opportunity for establishing the rapport with the respondent that is possible in face-to-face situation. It may be difficult to overcome the suspicions of the surprised respondents, especially when personal or sensitive questions are asked. An advance letter which informs the potential respondents of the approaching call is a good way to deal with this problem. A great deal of skill is required to construct a telephone questionnaire and carry out the interview so that good results are obtained. Another disadvantage is that households without telephones are automatically excluded from the survey, which may bias results.

9.5.2.7 Statistical Analysis in Surveys

Data analysis in a descriptive survey may simply consist of determining the frequencies for the major variable involved in the study. For example, a survey of laboratory resources may report the number of consumable items, amount of non-consummable items, chemicals, cupboards, furniture, ventilation and the like. A survey of people's attitudes on an issue may report the number of people falling in different response categories. Data analysis in a descriptive survey may simply consist of determining the frequencies for the major variable involved in the study. For example, a survey of laboratory resources may report the number of consumable items, amount of non-consummable items, chemicals, cupboards, furniture, ventilation and the like. A survey of people's attitudes on an issue may report the number of people falling in different response categories.

In an explanatory survey, however, there is interest in exploring the relationship between the variables of the study. The relationship is generally explored by setting up frequency distributions of one variable against another variable by means of cross-tabulations. The simplest cross-tabulation contains two variables with two categories for each variable. More complex forms are possible, such as 2 × 3, 2 × 4, 3 × 4, and so on. But frequency analysis and interpretation become more difficult as the number of variables increases. A cross tabulation shows how frequently various combinations of the variables occur, from which one can "see" the relationship between the variables. In order to better show the strength of the relationship, the frequencies are usually converted to percentages. Cross-tabulations can be used with almost any kind of data, but are usually with categorical or nominal data.

Consider the hypothetical results on a survey in a college of attitudes toward a new library fee for improving and expanding the library. A cross-tabulation of frequency data on two variables is shown in Table 9.1.

Table 9.1 shows that 66.6 per cent (160/240) of hostel residents favour the library fee, compared with 33 per cent (86/260) of the day students. One must conclude from the data in the table that there is direct relationship between place of residence and attitude towards the library fee. A majority of hostel students favour the library fee, while the majority of day students are against it. A more cautious observer, however, might point out that the hostel students will have ready access to the library even after college hours, whereas for the day students it may not make much of a difference. There may be a third variable, educational level, since the more highly educated (postgraduate) are more likely to live in the hostel and are more likely support the library fee.

In order to explore this alternative explanation, we would need to "control" this third variable. In order to control the third variable that is related to the two major variables in survey, it is necessary to hold that variable constant and then see whether the relationship between the first variable is not free to vary.

The simplest way to hold a variable constant is to divide the subject into separate groups, each having a different value on that variable, and to do the same analysis with each of these groups. That is, one observes whether within each of these groups a relationship exists between the first two variables. If there is still a relationship between the variables, that cannot be due to variation in the third variable, because within each of the group the third variable has been held constant. To control the third variable (educational level) in the above example, we would categorize the respondents into postgraduates and graduates (assuming this information was available) and look at the relationship for these separate groups. Table 9.2 shows the data.

The data in Table 9.2 shows that the alternative explanation is correct. That is, if holding it constant controls college education, there is no relationship between the variables place of residence and attitude toward the library fee. Among the postgraduates, 85.7 per cent (120/140) of the hostel residents favors the fee, and so do 79.1 per cent (76/96)

Table-9.1: Attitudes toward library fees

	Hostel students	*Day*	*Total*
Favour	160	86	246
Against	80	174	254
Total	240	260	500

Table 9.2: Attitudes toward library fees by education

	Post graduates		
	Hostel	*Day*	*Total*
Favour	120	76	196
Against	20	20	40
Total	140	96	236
	Graduates		
	Hostel	*Day*	*Total*
Favour	40	10	50
Against	60	154	214
Total	100	164	264

Table 9.3: Attitudes toward library fees by level of education

	Postgraduates				
	Hostel		*Day*		
	Boy	*Girl*	*Boy*	*Girl*	*Total*
Favour	60	20	15	5	100
Against	10	30	10	30	80
Total	120		60		180
	Graduates				
	Hostel		*Day*		
	Boy	*Girl*	*Boy*	*Girl*	*Total*
Favour	50	20	54	22	146
Against	24	26	24	100	174
Total	120		200		320

of the day students favour the fee. As for the graduates, 40 per cent of the hostel students favor the new library fee.

Suppose the data had been as shown in Table 9.3. Even though educational level has been held constant within each table, the relationship between the variables residence and attitude is evident. Among the post graduate, 66.7 per cent (80/120) of the hostel residents favour the fee, compared with 33.3 per cent (20/60) of the day students. Among the graduates, 58.3 per cent of the hostel students favor the fee, compared with 38 per cent of the day residents. In this case there is something about the hostel and day respondents, other than their education, that leads them to feel differently about the library fee.

Social class can be controlled by categorizing subjects into separate groups on the basis of appropriate criteria and analyzing the data within each of the groups. In planning and survey, the need to control variables should be anticipated as far as possible and questions needed for such analysis should be included.

We may need to control many variables in a survey study. For example, sex may need to be controlled before a relationship could be explained. In this case, one would separate the subjects into two groups, male and female, and look at the data for each of the groups separately.

The survey is a widely used research method for gathering data ranging from physical counts and frequencies to attitudes and opinions. Surveys should involve careful planning, unbiased sampling of a population, development of data-gathering instruments, and careful analysis of the results. Surveys are classified according to their ***purpose, focus,*** and ***scope.*** Interviews and questionnaires are the major means of data collection for a survey. Both procedures involve asking questions of selected subjects, but each has unique advantages and disadvantages. It is important that the instruments used be reliable. Various follow up procedures have proved effective in increasing returns from mailed questionnaires.

9.5.3 Developmental Studies

It is important to have reliable information about what children are like at various ages, how they vary from one another within age levels, and how they grow and develop. Knowledge of physiological, intellectual, and emotional growth is important for numerous practical as well as theoretical questions. The physical facilities, curriculum, and teaching methods must take into consideration the relevant characteristics of learner, as must any comprehensive theory of learning or instruction. Two complementary techniques have emerged for investigating the characteristics of children and the ways in which these characteristics change with growth. These are generally referred to as the longitudinal method and the cross-sectional method.

The Longitudinal Method

In the longitudinal method the same sample of subjects is studied over an extended period of time. Researchers studying the development of quantitative concepts of elementary school pupils, for example, would start by measuring the quantitative skills of a group of first-graders and would continue by making annual measurements of their skills at each successive grade level. Thus the researchers could assess how these skills develop over a period of time for this group. Since they are dealing with same individuals, such factors as initial ability will remain constant and the difference observed between two grade levels can be interpreted as changes in quantitative skills related to the growth of the subjects.

Using the longitudinal method, Honzik, Macfarlane, and Allen studied the fluctuations of IQ scores of children from age 2 to 18. They found that the IQ scores of over half the group changed 15 or more points, the scores of 9 per cent of the group changed 30 or more points, and scores separated by a short period correlated more highly than scores separated by long period. When they studied individuals who showed consistent upward or downward trends, it was found that such changes tended to be in the direction of the family's socioeconomic status; that is, those children whose IQ scores showed consistent downward trends came predominantly from lower socioeconomic groups and those whose scores exhibited consistent upward trends were large from higher socioeconomic groups.

The longitudinal method allows for intensive studies of individuals because the investigator accumulates data for the same subjects at various levels. However, longitudinal studies have inherent practical difficulties. To begin with they demand an extended commitment from an individual or institution willing to spend time, money, and other resources for several years before completing the project. If the sample selected should prove to be a poor one, there is nothing that can be done to remedy it, nor can new longitudinal variables for investigation be introduced after the study has matured. Keeping up with subjects who move, may become extremely difficult. In some cases, also, it proves difficult to maintain the cooperation of subjects for an extended period.

Web references

The Seattle Longitudinal Study

http://geron.psu.edu/sls/researchers/index.htm

The Cross-Sectional Method

Many of the practical difficulties of the longitudinal method are not characteristic of the cross-sectional method. This approach studies subjects of various age levels at the same point in time. For example, a cross-sectional study of the development of quantitative skills would employ a different sample and of the standard levels. It would compare the statistics derived from the samples and draw conclusions about the growth of children with these skills.

A major disadvantage of the cross-sectional method is that chance differences between samples may seriously bias the results. One may by chance draw a sample of first-standard students who are more mature than average and sample of second-standard students who are less mature than average, with the result that the difference between the groups appears to be much smaller than it really is. However, it is usually possible to obtain large samples for cross-sectional studies than can be obtained for longitudinal studies, and the advantages of these large samples may in many cases outweigh the disadvantages of the cross-sectional approach.

A further disadvantage of the cross-sectional approach lies in the possibility of extraneous variables creating difference between the populations sampled. For example, suppose investigators are studying the vocabulary development of high school students. The Standard X students will probably be a less diverse group than the Standard VIII students, as the less capable students tend to drop out in greater proportion than the more capable students. Consequently, comparisons of vocabulary will tend to reflect this selection factor as well. However, the investigator with longitudinal data will know which subjects have been lost and how they differ from the remaining sample and can then take these differences into account in interpreting the results.

When we want to learn the characteristics of typical children at various stages, the cross-sectional method is preferred because of the greater possibility of obtaining large samples with this technique. It would also be preferred if we want to know how contemporary first standard students differ from contemporary high school students since a longitudinal study would be comparing first-graders of eight years ago to eighth-standard students of today.

If we want to study change per se, the longitudinal method is preferred since it follows the same subjects through their development. Spurts and plateaus of growth cannot be observed in a cross-sectional study.

Web references

- Prevalence and patterns of smoking in Delhi: cross sectional study

K M Venkat Narayan et al.

http://www.bmj.com/cgi/content/abstract/312/7046/1576

9.5.4 Follow-up Studies

The follow-up study somewhat resembles the longitudinal method. Studies of this type are concerned with investigating the subsequent development of subjects after a specified treatment or condition. Among the best known are the studies by Terman and his associates of subjects who had been part of an original sample of gifted children in 1921-22. The subjects were studied six years later and again in 1936, 1940, and 1945. Among other things it was found that as adults these subjects had better physical and mental health than the general population. Only four of the 1,467 subjects served terms in penal institutions. Approximately 90 per cent of the males entered college and 70 per cent of these graduated, 40 per cent with honours. About 80 per cent of the woman entered college and 67 per cent of these graduated, 32 per cent with honors. In general, the gifted children matured into gifted and successful adults. Follow-up studies are frequently conducted to evaluate the success of particular programmes.

9.5.5 Content / Document Analysis

Although the discipline of education is primarily concerned with people, many interesting and useful research projects in the field have been concerned with information obtained by examining records and documents.

Researchers interested in the more traditionally scientific or quantitative sort of hypothesis testing will find the highly structured technique of content analysis used by Kimberly A. Neuendorf (2001) to their liking. ***The basic goal of content analysis is to take a verbal, non-quantitative document and transform into quantitative data.*** The results of content analysis can generally be presented in tables containing frequencies or percentages, in the same manner as survey data. How does one perform this analyses that can turn words into numbers? The answer is often as simple as mere word counting.

Content analysis is a research technique for the objective, systematic and quantitative descriptions of the manifest content of communication (Berelson 1954,p.489).

Purpose of Content Analysis

Content analysis is the equivalent of document study to survey research. It is conducive to the use of formal hypothesis, large scientifically drawn samples, and the quantitative data that can be analyzed with computers and modern statistical techniques. Thus the purposes of content analysis cover virtually all areas of specialization encompassed by survey techniques. In addition, content analysis has some special purposes, such as the determination of authorship for documents whose authority is questionable.

Holsti (1969, p.43) lists seven purposes for content analysis in addition to scientific hypothesis testing:

— To describe trends in communication content

— To relate known characteristics of sources to messages they produce

— To audit communication content against standards
— To analyze techniques of persuasion
— To analyze style
— To relate known attributes of the audience to messages produced for them
— To describe patterns of communication

Documentary analysis, often referred to as content analysis, is not confined to simple counts but can also be used to study sociological and psychological variables. In comparing McGuffey readers of the 1870s with elementary reading texts of the 1930s, Estensen found many interesting differences in cultural and ethical values. A thorough treatment of the conduct of documentary analysis and its uses will be found in a book by Berelson.

The five chief tasks facing a content analyst are:

a) Draw the sample of documents.
b) Define the content of categories. The actual content depends upon the purpose of the study.
c) Define the recording unit.
d) Define the context unit.
e) Define the system of enumeration.

Advantages of Document Study

- *Inaccessible subjects.* One of the advantages of document studies is that they allow research on which the researcher does not have physical access, and cannot study by any other method. The most obvious group of people who are completely inaccessible can be read only after their death, than in an interview or mailed questionnaire study. Thus a study of documents such as diaries, posthumously published autobiographies, and suicide notes may be the only way to obtain such information.
- *Relatively low cost.* Although the cost of documentary analysis can vary widely depending on the type of document analyzed, how widely documents are dispersed, and how far one must travel to gain access to them, documentary analysis can be inexpensive compared to large-scale surveys. Many times documents are

gathered together in centralized location such as a library or newspaper morgue where the analyst can study them for only the cost of travel to the repository.

- *High quality*: Although documents vary tremendously in quality, many documents, such as newspaper columns, are written by skilled social commentators and may be much more valuable than, for example, poorly written responses to mailed questionnaires.

Web references

Content Analysis Resources

http://academic.csuohio.edu/kneuendorf/content/

Disadvantages of Document Study

- **Bias:** Many documents used in social research were not originally intended for research purposes. The various goals and purposes for which documents are written can bias them in various ways. For example, personal documents such as confessional articles or autobiographies are often written by famous people or people who have had some unusual experience, such as having been a witness to the Indira Gandhi assassination or claiming to have been taken for a ride in a spaceship to Mars. While often providing unique and valuable research data, these documents usually are written for the purpose of making money. Thus they tend to exaggerate and even fabricate to make a good story. They also tend to include those events that make the author look good and exclude those that cast him or her in a negative light.
- *Selective Survival* Since documents are generally written on paper, they do not withstand the elements well unless care is taken to preserve them. Thus while documents written by famous people are likely to be preserved, day-to-day documents such as letters and diaries written by common people tend either to be destroyed or to be placed in storage and thus become inaccessible. It is relatively rare for common documents that are not about some event of immediate interest to researchers (e.g., suicide) and not about some famous occurrence or by some famous person to be gathered together in a public history repository that is accessible to social researchers.

- *Incompleteness*: Many documents provide an incomplete account to the researcher who has had no prior experience with or knowledge of the events or behaviour discussed. A problem with many personal documents such as letters and diaries is that they were not written for research purposes but were designed to be private or even secret. Both of these kinds of documents often assume specific knowledge that researchers unfamiliar with certain events will not possess. Diaries are probably the worst in this respect, since they are usually written to be read only by the author and can consist more of "soul searching" and confession than of description. Letters tend to be a little more complete, since they are addressed to a second person. Still, many letters assume a great amount of prior information on the part of the reader.
- *Lack of availability*: In addition to bias, incompleteness, and selective survival of documents, there are many areas of study for which no documents are available. In many cases the information simply was never recorded. In other cases it was recorded, but the documents remain secret or classified, or have been destroyed.
- *Sampling bias*: The first task is to construct a sampling frame or complete list of all potential respondents from which the sample could be drawn. One of the problems of bias occurred because persons of lower educational or income levels were less likely to be on available lists (e.g. voter-registration lists) from which sampling frames could be compiled. After the sample was drawn, surveys, particularly mailed surveys, encountered problems posed by the limited ability of poorly educated persons to read the questionnaire and to express themselves in writing. The problem of sampling bias by educational level is even more acute for document study than for survey research. It is a safe generalization that poorly educated people are much less likely than well-educated people to write documents. In addition, poorly educated people read much less frequently than well-educated people. Thus the mass media are not aimed at them, and it is likely that their viewpoints are not well represented in such publications.
- *Limited to verbal behaviour*. By definition, documents provide information only on a respondent's verbal behaviour, and provide

no direct information on the respondent's non-verbal behaviour. The document being analyzed may contain a description of non-verbal behaviour, either that of the document's author or of another person. However, in direct contrast to the observational method, the experiment, and even the survey where direct observation by the researcher is common, the document analyst cannot possibly observe the non-verbal behaviour of his or her respondents, as they typically are not personally present with only their written accounts to work with.

- *Lack of a standard format*. Documents differ widely in regard to their standardization of format. Some documents, such as newspapers, appear frequently in a standard format. Large dailies always contain such standard components as the opinion-editorial page, obituaries, comics, sports, and whether report. Such standardization facilitates comparison across time for the same newspaper, and comparison across different newspapers at one point in time. However, many other documents, particularly personal documents, have no standard format. Comparison is difficult or impossible, since valuable information contained in a document at one point in time may be entirely lacking in an earlier or later document.
- *Coding difficulties*: For a number of reasons, including differences in purpose for which the documents were written, differences in content or subject matter, lack of standardization, and differences in length and format, coding is one of the most difficult tasks facing the document analyst.

9.5.6 Secondary Analysis

Many researchers use data from the available data archives (either in the form of documents or survey results and codebooks) for secondary analysis. Secondary analysis is the analysis of a document or data gathered or authored by another person. The secondary analyst generally has a research goal different from that of the first researcher. For example as a sociologist interested in studying stratification, you might find in a data archive a codebook from a study of voting behaviour conducted by a political scientist, and discover upon examination that the study gathered sufficient (as yet unanalyzed) data on social class to enable you to conduct a perfectly adequate stratification study.

Hyman (1972) presents a comprehensive treatment of secondary analysis. Among the benefits of secondary analysis listed by Hyman are:

- A saving of time and money by use of available data rather than collection of original new data;
- Less invasion of privacy by using existing data rather than collecting new data;
- Ease in making comparative analyses (for example, comparing different countries through the secondary analysis of data collected in the respective countries).

These are also obvious disadvantages to secondary analysis. The major disadvantages are:

- Some of the data that the researcher needs may simply not be available.
- The original data may contain errors that the secondary researcher is not able to detect.

Example

Consider the secondary analysis conducted by Hunt and Hunt (1977). They were interested in the effect that the absence of a father in the household has on the development of children. More specifically, they were interested in the effect that the father's absence has. They were also interested in the effect of race.

Collection of data for this study obviously would have taken a long time and would have been very expensive. Fortunately, the Hunts were able to use data that had previously been collected for a study of racial esteem by Rosenberg and Simmons (1972). Those data comprised interviews from 1,917 Baltimore public school students in grades 3 through 12 in 1968. They included interviews from both blacks and whites and males and females. There was information on father absence, social class, personal esteem, academic activities, dating, and future orientation.

Hunt and Hunt (1977) concluded that father absence does have an effect on a daughter's development and that there are some racial differences. For white daughters, for example, sex role identification and dating are slightly lower when the father is absent, and marriage plans are reduced significantly. The effects of father's absence are not as pronounced for black daughters but are present. A black father's absence leads not only to diminished marriage plans, but also to lower self-esteem.

Another factor to consider in secondary analysis is that even though the original data may be excellent and may contain all the information the researcher needs, the task of working with masses of data may still be considerable. Some researchers think that because the data are already collected and stored, for example on computer cards or a computer tape, they can begin analysis immediately. This is not always the case by any means. Hunt and Hunt (1981, p.318) reported difficulty in "achieving focus" or moving from the mass of available data to a set of specific questions and their operationalization.

9.5.7 Trend Studies

In order to plan as effectively as possible, schools (as well as governmental agencies and other institutions) need to project the demands that will be made on their services in the future. Through documentary analysis or surveys repeated at intervals they are able to study the rate and direction of changes and use these trends to predict future status. For example, a large school district will attempt to locate new schools in the areas where the home building rates and population growth indicate there will be the greatest need. Projections made from the findings of studies made in the 1950s warned colleges and universities to expect an extremely increased demand for their services during the 1960s. This prediction was based on such factors as the increasing birthrate, the increasing proportion of students completing high school, and the increasing need for a college-trained labour force.

Short-term predictions are often very reliable. For example, to predict first standard enrollment ten years from now, one must first predict birthrate five years hence. Birthrate is difficult to predict since it is subject to many economic, technological, and social changes. Hence long term prediction is in practice a matter of estimating as well as possible.

9.5.8 Correlational Studies

Correlational studies are concerned with determining the extent of relationship existing between variables. They enable one to measure the extent to which variation in one variable is associated with another. The magnitude of the relationship is determined through the use of the coefficient of correlation. They may be classified as descriptive studies if the intent is to describe relationships or to generate a study. An investigator takes measure on a number of variables and computes coefficients between them in order to see which variables appear to be related. **The purpose of such studies is exploration rather than theory testing.**

Example

Revathi conducted an exploratory study to investigate variables that might be related to the degree of performance improvement in science manifested in a remedial programme. She hoped to identify the variables that would have predictive value in the selection and grouping of poor performers for remedial programmes. Revathi correlated each student's degree of improvement (the difference between pre and post-test scores on the Investigator Constructed Test): with several other variables: chronological age, degree of performance retardation, father's occupational level, socio-economic status, vocabulary, IQ, kind of school the student was enrolled in, medium of instruction, and the like. Statistically, significant correlation coefficient were found between performance improvement in science and the four variables of IQ, kind of school, medium of instruction and socio-economic status. It was concluded that these four variables would have the highest efficiency for predictive purposes.

In a hypotheses-testing study investigators have a priori basis for expecting to observe a correlation between variables. They base their selection of variables for investigation on previously developed theory and can hypothesize the direction of the expected relationship.

Typically, correlation studies do not require large samples. It can be assumed that if a relationship exists, it will be evident in a sample of moderate size, for instance 50 to 100. If one is interested in making an inference about the relationship in a population, then the sample selected should be representative sample of that population. ***It is well to recall, at this point, that the variability in the sources that are being correlated affects the size of the coefficient of correlation.*** A restricted range of the sources on one or both variables will result in a smaller coefficient that would be obtained with a wide range of sources on the variables.

It is important to select or develop measures that are an appropriate indicator of the variables to be correlated. It is especially important that these instruments have reliability and are valid for measuring the variables under consideration. The size of a coefficient of correlation is influenced by the adequacy of measuring instrument for its intended purpose. An instrument, for instance, that is too easy or too difficult for the subject of study would not discriminate among them and would result in a small correlation coefficient. Studies using instruments with low reliability and questionable validity are unlikely to produce evidence of any significant relationship.

It must be borne in mind that a correlation does not necessarily indicate a cause-and-effect relationship between the two variables. Correlation must not be interpreted to mean that one variable is causing the scores in the other variable to be what they are. Frequently there are other factors that influence both of the variables under consideration. For example, it may be that there is a negative correlation between measures of anxiety and measures of intelligence. It should not be interpreted that there is a causative relationship between anxiety and intelligence; that is, that pupils are anxious because they are unintelligent or that pupils appear unintelligent because they are anxious. It might be that there are other underlying characteristics of individuals that tend to make some appear unintelligent and anxious and others, intelligent and not anxious. Interpretation of such a correlation is difficult without experimental confirmation. It is recommended in many instances that a relationship study be supplemented by an experimental study in which the alternative interpretation can become hypothesis for experimentation. For example, the relationship between anxiety and intelligence measures could be investigated experimentally by deliberately inducting anxiety situation and determining the effect on intelligence test sources.

The Value of Correlational Studies

Fox writes:

> *What we need is a massive series of studies whose primary function is to learn the nature and extent of the relationship between matrices of educational characteristics on the one hand and psychosocial characteristics on the other. If such studies were conducted, the researcher on any particular educational problem would then be able to know what characteristics were critical for him as he prepared to establish a sampling plan.*

- In planning the control in experimental and ex-post-facto studies, the researcher must be able to identify the critical variables, that is, those variables that have a substantial correlation with the dependent variable of the study. For example, if one were investigating the effect of certain experience on creativity sources then it would be necessary to know what other variables are substantially correlated with the dependent variable of creativity in order that these variables might be controlled. Information such as correlation can be obtained through exploratory relationship studies.
- A related use of the coefficient of correlation is in deter-mining the validity and reliability of measuring instruments.
- Computation of the correlation coefficient gives a more useful tool for describing the strength of the relationship between two variables. However, care must be exercised in conducting and interpreting this type of research if any meaningful conclusions are to be reached.
- The possibility of the existence of relationships between variables is a reasonable question to investigate in educational research since there are numerous situations where such information is valuable in decision-making. This is especially true in exploratory studies in an area. In the sampling aspect of a study one of the problems is securing representative ness in terms of the variables that are known to be related to the phenomena under investigation. But what are the factors "known to be related"? Unfortunately one does not always know the characteristics that are related to the phenomena that one wishes to study.

- Correlation techniques are particularly useful in making predictions. If we know that there is a correlation between two variables, then we can predict from one variable to the other. For example, since we know that IQ and SSLC scores are positively correlated, we can predict with some degree of accuracy that an individual with a high IQ will probably have a high SSLC scores. To be valuable for prediction the extent of correlation between two variables must be substantial, and of course the higher the correlation, the more accurate the prediction.
- When we try to introduce a new technology to any environment, it is likely that we will confront uncertainty in adaptation not knowing what effects it may cause. When the situations are educational sites, the reluctance to introduce technology can be more complicated.
- To know what is going on in the classroom before bringing in new technology and to know what has changed after adapting technology, the ethnography, qualitative method, is a well-suited one to use.

9.5.9 Qualitative Observational Research

Qualitative Research study lends itself to thick narrative description, and it may be intensive given the complexity of group interactions. It takes place on site, in the group's natural environment, and ***attempts to be non-manipulative of group behaviours***. The purpose is to aim for objectivity, while it must take into account the view of the participants.

Qualitative observational research describes and classifies various cultural, racial and/or sociological groups by employing interpretive and naturalistic approaches. It is both observational and narrative in nature and relies less on the experimental elements normally associated with scientific research (***reliability***, ***validity*** and ***generalizability***). Connelly and Clandinin (1990) suggest that qualitative inquiry relies more on ***apparency***, ***verisimilitude*** and ***transferability***. On the other hand, Lincoln and Guba (1985) emphasize the importance of ***credibility***, ***transferability***, ***dependability*** and ***conformability*** in qualitative studies. ***Because the field of qualitative research is still evolving, the criteria and terminology for its evaluation are not yet agreed upon.***

What is agreed upon is that qualitative observational research is ***systematic inquiry*** into the nature or qualities of observable group behaviours in order to learn what it means to be a member of that group. The researcher's job, rather than to describe a stable entity, is to give continually updated accounts of observations on multiple level of group interactions that occur on both a temporal and continuous basis simultaneously.

This type of research attempts to identify and explain complex social structures within the study group. Typically, qualitative research methodologies are combined with each other in order to provide comparative results. A triangulation of methods (also called multiple methods), where three or more methodologies are used and the results compared against each other, is common and can provide a more complete understanding of the behavior of the study group.

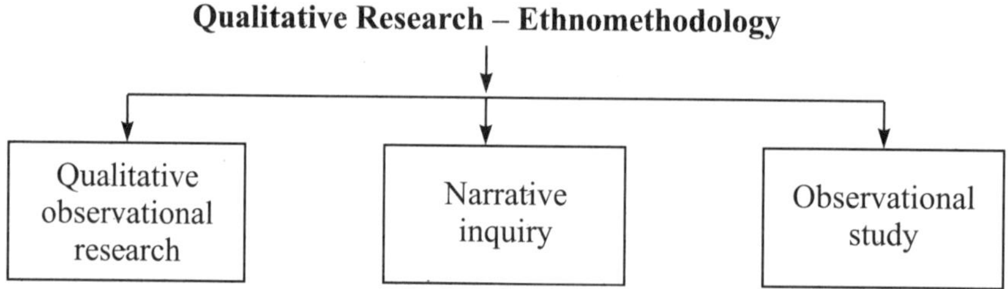

According to Coulon (1995), "ethno methodology is the empirical study of methods that individuals use to give sense to and.... to accomplish their daily actions: communing, making decisions, and reasoning" This approach is actually a form of ethnography, which specifically studies activities of group members to see how they make sense of their surroundings. Usually an ethnomethodologist will see or hear things in a group that participants are not consciously aware of.

In sum, the qualitative observational researcher must attempt to maintain a non-judgemental bias throughout the study. The researcher's goal is to observe and describe group patterns, similarities and differences as they occur. Preconceptions or expectations of an individual or group's behavior interfere with researcher's ability to tell the group or culture's story in a fair and accurate manner. In addition, preconceived expectations preclude the researcher from observing subtle nuances of character and speech that may be important to understand group behaviours or interactions. While absolute objectivity is impossible, it is paramount that researchers enter the field or study group with an open mind, an awareness of their own biases, and a commitment to detach from those biases as much as possible while observing and representing the group.

Qualitative research expands the range of knowledge and understanding of the world beyond the researchers themselves. It often helps us to see why something is the way it is, rather than just presenting a phenomenon. For instance, a quantitative study may find that students who are taught composition using a process method receive higher grades on papers than students taught using a product method. However, a qualitative study of composition instructors could reveal why many of them still use the product method even though they are aware of the benefits of the process method.

Any group that is studied is altered to some degree by the very presence of the researcher. Therefore, any data collected is somewhat skewed. (Heisenberg Uncertainty Principle)

Ethical issues should always be considered when undertaking data analysis. Because of the nature of qualitative observational research that requires observation and interaction with groups, it is understandable why certain ethical issues may arise. Miles and Huberman (1994) list several issues that researchers should consider when analyzing data. They caution researchers to be aware of these and other issues before, during and after the research had been conducted. Some of the issues involve the following:

Ethnography

Ethnography is a part of anthropological approach seeking to understand and describe the points of view of the members of a particular culture by conducting intensive field works such as careful observations and in-depth interviews to describe in detail in the points of view of the informants.

Ethnography has been frequently used to examine educational settings and the cultural transmission processes to make of familiar strange (Spinder)

When we try to introduce a new technology to any environment, it is likely that we will confront uncertainty in adaptation not knowing what effects it may cause. When the situations are educational sites, the reluctance to introduce technology can be even more complicated. To know what is going on in the classroom before bringing in new technology and to know what has changed after adapting technology, one could use the ethnography, qualitative method. Thus, for the introduction of e-learning into the classroom, a science teacher would do well to study her class using ethnomethodology before bringing in the new technology.

Ethnography research offers an orientation to under-standing the process and the structure of a social setting and employs research techniques consistent with this orientation. Spradley (1980) describes ethnography as "the study of both explicit and tacit cultural knowledge " Culture is defined as the acquired knowledge people use to interpret experience and generate behavior"; whereas explicit cultural knowledge can be communicated at a conscious level and with relative ease, tacit cultural knowledge remains largely outside of people's awareness. An example of tacit cultural knowledge would be the way in which individual of a given culture defines space.

Spradley (1980) further infers that the role of an ethnographer is to make inference about what people know by listening carefully to what they say [and] by observing their behavior: This is why ethnographers must participate as well as observe. As Spardley maintains "participation allows you to experience activities directly, to get the feel of what events are like, and to record your own perceptions".

According to Taft (1988), Ethnography is "***naturalistic enquiry***". In fact, the emphasis on subjective realities as the focus of the investigator's attention has much in common with the philosophy of naturalism which purports that "there exist multiple realities which are, in the main, constructions existing in the minds of people" (Guba & Lincoln 1988,p.81). Since these constructions are intangible, they can best be studied in "holistic and idiosyncratic fashion"

The assumptions underlying much of naturalistic, ethnographic research, emphasize the subjective reality of individuals and stresses the relativistic nature of the social world which can be understood by adopting the point of view of the individuals who are directly involved in the activities which are to be studied. Thus the stress on understanding human activities lies in the frame of reference of the participant in action (Burrel & Morgan, 1979). This approach highlights the importance of knowledge as something which is personally experienced and which can thus be best understood from the inside i.e. from the subjective experience of individuals.

Ethnography can be understood by examining the theoretical assumptions which underly it. Blumer (1969) posits that "the concept of culture as acquired knowledge has much in common with symbolic interactionism, a theory that seeks to explain human behavior in terms of meanings"

These meanings are derived from the social interaction between individuals and groups and are "modified through an interpretive process used by the person dealing with the things he encounters" This process can be seen in terms of the interpretive paradigm which attempts "to understand and explain the social world primarily from the point of view of the actors directly involved in the social process" (Burrell & Morgan, 1979). The methods of investigation based on the interpretive paradigm "seek to understand human beings, their inner minds and their feelings, and the way these are expressed in their outward actions and achievements". The subjective realities of individuals thus become the focus of the investigator's attention.

Goetz and LeCompte (1984) describe ***the high degree of internal validity inherent in ethnographic research.*** They note that participant observation provides the opportunity for continual data analysis and comparison to refine constructs and to ensure the match between scientific categories and participant reality It is also "conducted in natural settings that reflect the reality of the life experiences of participants more accurately than do more contrived or laboratory settings" They argue as well that informant interviews are "less abstract than many instruments used in other research designs"

Taft (1988) describes validity as being a "***quality of the conclusions and the processes through which these were reached***". However, he argues that the exact meaning of validity depends on "the particular criterion of truth that is adopted" and that "***in ethnographic research, the most appropriate criterion is credibility***" He further indicates that credibility can be enhanced by and is dependent on the apparent accuracy of the data and the way the study is communicated to the audience.

In reference to ***external validity***, the aim of many Ethnographic studies is not to make generalizations on the basis of the data gathered. The aim is to uncover idiographic knowledge of the world. Guba and Lincoln (1988) posit that this type of "knowledge is best encapsulated in a series of 'working hypotheses' that describe the individual case". Kennedy (1979) argues that, in Ethnographic research, ***the onus of generalization lies not with the researcher but with the reader of the research report.***

Clearly the study of a single case with no replications limits the strength and the range of generalization arguments considerably. But, in fact, the range of generalization simply cannot be known to the evaluator. That the range cannot be known, however, does not mean that a range does not exist. The range of evaluation is a matter of judgement. For studies of single cases, however, that judgement should not be made by the evaluator. Instead, it should be made by those individuals who wish to apply the evaluation findings to their own situations. That is, the evaluator should produce and share the information, but the receivers of the information must determine whether or not it applies to their own situation.

Ethical considerations in Ethnography, Observational Research and Narrative Inquiry

Ethical issues should always be considered when undertaking data analysis. Because the nature of qualitative observational research requires observation and interaction with groups, researchers have to exercise caution regarding the following issues:

— Informed consent (Do participants have full knowledge of what is involved?)

— Harm and risk (Can the study hurt the participants?)

— Honesty and trust (Is the researcher being truthful in presenting data?)

— Privacy and confidentiality and anonymity (Will the study intrude on the privacy of the group?)

— Intervention and advocacy (What happens if the participants indulge in illegal behaviour?)

Advantages of Qualitative Observational Research

Qualitative observational research, especially ethnographies, can:

- Account for the complexity of group behaviours
- Reveal inter-relationships among multifaceted dimensions of group interactions
- Provide context for behaviours

Narrative inquiry, especially ethnographic, can:

- Reveal qualities of group experience in a way that other forms of research cannot
- Help determine questions and types of follow-up research

Observational study can:

— Reveal descriptions of behaviour in context by stepping outside the group

— Allow qualitative researchers to identify recurring patterns of behaviour that participants may be unable to recognize.

Qualitative research expands the range of knowledge and understanding of the world beyond the researchers themselves. It often helps us see why something is the way it is, rather than just presenting a phenomenon. For instance, a quantitative study may find that students who are taught problem-solving using inductive reasoning score higher on tests than students taught using deductive reasoning. However, a qualitative study of the teachers teaching mathematics may reveal why many of them still use a particular method even though they are aware of the benefits of the other method.

Disadvantages of Qualitative Observational Research

- Researcher bias can bias the design of a study.
- Researcher bias can enter data collection.
- Sources or subjects may not all be equally credible.
- Some subjects may be previously influenced and affect the outcome of the study.
- Background information may be lacking.
- Study group may not be representative of the larger population.
- Analysis of observation can be biased.

- Any group that is studied is altered by the very presence of the researcher.
- It takes time to build trust with participants that facilitates full and honest self-representation.

Disadvantages of Ethnographic studies

- The quality of the data alone is problematic
- Ethnographic research is time-consuming, potentially expensive and requires a well trained researcher.
- Too little data can lead to false assumptions about behaviour patterns.
- Data collector's first impressions can bias collection.

Disadvantages of Narrative Inquiries

- Narrative inquiries do not lend themselves well to replicability and are not generalisable.
- Narrative inquiries are considered unreliable by experimentalists. However, ethnographies can be assessed and compared for certain variables to yield testable explanations; this is as close as ethnographic research gets to being empirical.
- Qualitative research is neither prescriptive nor definite. While it provides significant data about trends and groups, it does not answer any question.

Title: Societal Issues and School Practices: An Ethnographic Investigation of the Social Context of School Computer Use

Author: Batya Friedman

Abstract: This study examines the relationship between social forces and school computer use in the context of two issues surrounding computer technology: computer property and computer privacy. Methods employed were naturalistic observation, informal interviews, historical document analysis and structured interviews. Finding two issues surrounding computer technology helps explain why students neither asserted nor protected the privacy of their files and why the classroom projects a nonchalant attitude toward accessing electronic information despite the societal climate. Source: This information can be found in ERIC Document (ED321740)

Exhibit 9.4: Sample 1 – An ethnographic study

Title: Mixed Methods in a Study of Implementation of Technology-Based Materials in the Elementary Classroom.

Author: Bernadette Russek

Abstract: Barriers to the implementation of technology-based materials in elementary school mathematics classrooms were studied using naturalistic inquiry and multiple methods of data collection in keeping with ethnographic principles. Implementation of the elementary school mathematics curriculum materials that incorporate technology and studies the effects of these curricula was studied in 16 teachers' classrooms in one school district. The ethnographic techniques offered a valuable perspective on barriers in implementation.

Source: This information can be found in ERIC Document (ED327230)

Exhibit 9.5: Sample 2 of qualitative observational technique

Title: Implementation of an Interactive Videodisc Program: An Ethnographic Study

Author: Hsun-Fung Kao

Abstract: This ethnographic study examines the process of implementing an interactive videodisc program in a senior high school. The research questions were: What happened during the implementation process and what factors facilitated or hindered the implementation of the innovation? Descriptive data were collected through participant observation, interviews and artifact collections. Study results revealed that implementing an educational innovation is a complex, multidimensional process involving the organization, the people and the innovation. Effective implementation depends on the combination of all the factors described in the study, including initiation, planning and support; communication and collaboration; planning policies; teacher's realities; students' characteristics; change strategies; and characteristics of the innovation.

Source: This information can be found in ERIC Document (ED373769)

Exhibit 9.6: Sample 3 – An ethnographic study

9.5.10 Ex-post Facto Research

The designation ex-post facto, Latin for "from after the fact" serves to indicate that the research in question is conducted after variations in the independent variable have already been determined in the natural course of events. Kerlinger has defined ex post facto research as:

> *systematic empirical inquiry in which the scientist does not have direct control of independent variables because their manifestations have already occurred or because they are inherently not manipulable. Inferences about relations among variables are made, without direct intervention, from concomitant variation of independent and dependent variables.*

If we wish to investigate the influence of such variables as home environment, intelligence, parental T.V. watching habits and the like, we cannot randomly assign students to different categories of these variables. Independent variables such as these are called attribute variables. ***An attribute variable is a characteristic that a subject possesses before the study begins.***

In contrast, an independent variable that an investigator can directly manipulate is an ***active variable.*** An investigator can determine which students will have access to a hands on laboratory class and which will use Program A to study a unit in physics and which will use Program B. When active independent variables are involved, we can employ experimental or quasi-experimental research. When we have attribute independent variables, we must turn to ex post facto research (sometimes called causal-comparative research).

Researchers achieve the variation they want, not by direct manipulation of the variable itself but by selection of individuals in whom the variable is present or absent, strong or weak, and so on. They present hearing impaired and non-hearing impaired (normal) children with the same perceptual task; or they compare the performance of high-IQ and low IQ children on the same measure of anxiety.

Ex-post Facto and Experimental Approaches Compared

In both types of research, interest is focused upon discovery or establishment of relationships among the variables in one's data. Ex-post facto research, as well as experimental research, can test hypotheses concerning the relationship between an independent variable, X and a dependent variable Y. The aim of both is to compare two groups, similar on all relevant characteristics but one, in order to measure the effects of those characteristics. However, with an experiment it is possible to obtain much more convincing evidence for causal or functional relationships among variables than can be obtained with ex-post facto studies. The effects of extraneous variables in an experiment are controlled by the experimental conditions, and the presumably antecedent dependent variable. If Y is observed to vary concomitantly with the variation in X in this controlled situation, then one has obtained evidence for the validity of the hypothesized antecedent consequence relationship between X and Y.

In ***an ex-post facto situation***, on the other hand, the researcher cannot control the independent variables by manipulation or by randomization. The term ex post facto indicates that changes in the independent variable have already taken place; the researcher is faced with the problem of trying to determine the antecedents of the observed consequence. Because of the lack of control, it is more hazardous to infer that there is a genuine relationship between X and Y in an ex-post facto study.

Let us illustrate the difference between an ex post facto an experimental approach by examining these two approaches to the same research question. Consider the question of the effect that student' anxiety in an achievement-testing situation has on their examination performance. The ex-post fact approach to this problem would involve measuring the already existing anxiety level at the time of the examination, then comparing the performance of "high anxious' and 'low anxious' students. The weakness of such an approach is that one could not necessarily conclude that it was the student' anxiety that produced the observed difference in achievement examination performance. Both sets of scores may have been influenced by a third factor, such as general intelligence or achievement motivation. General intelligence may be the major cause of both the level of anxiety and the achievement test results.

An experimental approach to the same problem would involve the administration of the examination under two conditions that are identical in every respect except that one is anxiety-arousing and the other, natural. The experimenter can induce anxiety by telling the subjects that their final grade is dependent upon their performance, that the test is extremely difficult, or that the test will be used to identify the incompetent. The neutral group would merely be told that their cooperation is needed for the experiment. The investigator could randomly assign subjects to the two conditions. Then if the anxious group performed better than the neutral, it could be concluded that the anxiety had a facilitating effect on test performance. Such a conclusion could be legitimately drawn because of control provided by the random assignment of group to treatments and the direct manipulation of the independent variable by experimenter. Anxiety is one of the few variables that can be either be an active or an attribute independent variable. That is, one can manipulate it actively, as described (experimental approach), or one can take subjects and classify them on the basis of their scores on an anxiety measure (ex-post facto approach).

In a sense the ex-post facto study can be viewed as a reverse approach to experimentation. Instead of taking groups that are equivalent and exposing them to different treatments, the ex post facto study starts with groups that are different and tries to determine the antecedents of these differences. An ex-post facto study begins with a description of present situation, which is assumed to be an effect of some previously acting factors, and attempts a retrospective search to determine the assumed accident factors, which began operating at an earlier time. Such a procedure does not provide the safeguards, typical in experimentation, that are necessary for making inference about causal relationships. An investigator, who finds a relationship between the variables in an ex-post facto study, has secured evidence only of some concomitant variation. Because the investigator has not controlled X or other possible variables that may determine Y, there is no basis for inferring a causal relationship between X and Y. In order to be able to make a type of antecedent-consequent relationship between the variables, one must gather evidence to show that it has not controlled X or other possible variables that may determine Y, there is no basis for inferring a causal relationship between X and Y. In order to be able to make a type of antecedent-consequent relationship between the variables, one must gather evidence to show that Y did not precede X or that the Y effect has not been produced by some other factor that is related to the presumed antecedent factor. For example, if we give children with brain damage and children without damage a perceptual test, the differences in their performance might reflect the effects of brain damage or they might reflect such other factors as differences in anxiety associated with certain types of illness.

Ex-post facto research, though not a satisfactory substitute for experimentation, does provide a method that can use the circumstances under which much of educational research must be conducted. It remains a useful method that can supply much information of value in educational decision-making.

Conditions necessary for inferring Causal Relationship

If one wishes to reach a conclusion that one variable (X) is the cause of another variable (Y), three kinds of evidence are necessary:

1. A statistical relationship between X and Y has been established
2. X preceded Y in time
3. The other factor did not determine Y

Because of the safeguard built into an experimental design, experimental studies provide evidence on all of these, so that causal inference can be made. In ex-post facto studies, however, the safeguards of the experimental situation are lacking and interpretation of causal relationship is much more nebulous.

The investigator must establish the time sequence; that is, one must consider whether Y might have occurred before X and hence could not be an effect of X. Decisions about the time relationship between X and Y can be made either on a logical basis or as a result of measurements that show the groups did not differ on Y before exposure to X.

It is also extremely important that the investigator consider whether or not factors other than X might have determined Y. One proceeds to check this possibility by introducing other relevant variable into the analysis and observing how the relationship between X and Y is affected by these additional variables.

Possibilities for Spurious Result in Ex-post Facto Research

The difference between an active independent variable and an attribute independent variable is exceedingly important. When investigators can control the treatment (X) and then observe the dependent variable (Y), they have reasonable evidence that X influences Y. If they cannot control. X, they may have a spurious relationship that is due to other causes, not because of X influencing Y. Among the possible origins of spurious relationships are common cause, reverse causality, and the presence of other independent variables.

Common Cause

In an ex-post facto investigation, one must consider the possibility that both the independent and dependent variables of the the study are merely two separate results of the third variable.

It is well established that the average income of management graduates from premier institutions is much higher than the average income of other management institutes. Does this mean that premier institutions better prepare students for financial success? Or is the difference due to the fact that those families with enough money to send their children to these premier institutions are also able to finance their children's career interest subsequently?

Investigations on the effects of child- rearing practices have revealed that there is more aggressive behavior on the part of children who are frequently punished. Does this mean that one can conclude that parental punishment leads to aggressive children, or is it that aggressive children are more likely to be punished?

The hypothesis of reverse causality is easier to deal with than the hypothesis of common cause. With the latter there may be numerous common causes in each case that could produce a spurious relationship. With reverse causality there is only one possibility in each case; Y caused X instead of X caused Y.

In any situation when X always precedes Y in time, the very nature of our data rules out the possibility of reverse causality. For example, numerous studies have shown that the average annual income of college graduates is not any higher than the average annual income of post-graduates. We can rule out hypothesis of reverse causality since graduation or postgraduation precedes the subsequent annual income. We cannot rule out a variety of possible common causes.

Other Possible Independent Variables

There may be independent variables other than the one under consideration in the ex-post facto study that could bring about the observed effect on the Y variable. That is, in addition to X_1, other variables, X_2 and X_3, might also be antecedent factors for the variation in the dependent variable.

Partial Control in Ex-post facto Research

There are strategies for improving the credibility of ex-post facto research although none of them can adequately compensate for the inherent weakness of such research, namely, lack of control of the independent variable. They are

- change scores
- matching
- analysis of covariance
- partial correlation
- homogeneous groups
- building extraneous variables into the design.

Change Scores

With change scores one takes into account previous scores on the Y variable rather than just present scores on Y. When one compares how much a treatment group changes in comparison with a control group, one may be somewhat less likely to be misled than when only present scores are used. However, the use of change scores is a partial solution and the results of such studies must be treated with caution. For example, principal A has introduced a new remedial programme in eighth standard and after it has been in use for a year she wants to compare its effectiveness with the effectiveness of the traditional supervised study programme it replaced. In the same district Principal B's school is still using the traditional supervised study programme. Both schools give the same standardized science test at the end of each school year. Principal A compares the mean science scores for eighth standard with the mean for principal B's eighth standard students. Is this evidence of the effectiveness of the new method? Principal A realizes that the difference between means could be due to difference between the pupils when they began the eighth standard in the two schools. She obtains scores for the science test administered when the pupils were finishing fourth standard. Can Principal A now conclude that the new method is more effective than the old one? Given the nature of change scores, she cannot. Differences in change scores may be due to the continuation of previous patterns. An inherent weakness in change scores is that an apparent greater gain in one group compared with another group may well be a continuation of a previous and not due to the treatment at all.

Consider another example. It hypothesizes that the study of Sanskrit improves high school students' English vocabulary. The investigator has eighth standard and ninth standard vocabulary scores for both those who took and those who did not take Sanskrit. The gain in the vocabulary scores from eighth standard to ninth standard for the Sanskrit group (from 80 to 95 points) is greater than the eighth standard to ninth standard for the non Sanskrit group (from 54 to 63 points).

Change scores adjust for groups beginning at different points but not for pre-existing differences in growth rates.

Matching

A common method of providing partial control in ex-post facto investigation has been to match the subjects in the experimental and control groups on as many extraneous variables as possible. The matching is usually done on a subject –to- subject basis to form matched pairs. For example, if one is interested in the relationship between camping experiences and delinquency, one could locate two groups of boys classified as delinquent and non-delinquent according to specified criteria. It would be wise in such a study to select pairs from these groups matched on the basis of socioeconomic status, family structure, and other variables to determine whether or not scouting characterizes the non-delinquent and is absent in the background of the delinquent. The matching in an ex-post facto study assumes that one knows what the relevant factors-that is, the factors that may have some correlation with the dependent variable. Furthermore, matching is likely to reduce greatly the number of subjects that can actually be used in final analysis. The loss of case inherent in the matching process is an even more serious problem in ex post facto research than in experimentation, where matching precedes the introduction of the independent variable. At least in the experimental approach there may be a possibility (although it is not recommended) of adding new case to replace the ones that do not match. This cannot be done in ex-post facto research.

This all sound very good. Can we now attribute difference in eighth standard science to difference in the effectiveness of the old and new method?

Matching looks good since it provides experimental and control groups that are equal on a pretreatment variables. However, when two matched groups are drawn from different populations, regression toward the original population means will be expected to create spurious result whenever the two populations are not equal. Matching pairs from within a single population is often a useful strategy. Matching subject from one population is a bad strategy. As is the case with change scores, matching only partly adjusts for pre-existing differences between groups. This underadjustment can mislead us in the same manner that the under adjustment in change score can mislead us.

Analysis of Covariance

Analysis of covariance, like matching, can be used to partially adjust for pre-existing differences between groups. An advantage of ANCOVA is that data from all subjects can be used rather only data from matched pairs. ANCOVA is an excellent procedure for improving the precision in a randomized experiment. ANCOVA is also sometimes used to partially adjust for initial difference in an ex post facto design. However, as the adjustment in ex-post facto research is only partial, ANCOVA does not 'solve" the problem of initial difference between groups; it only lessens it. When interpreting ex-post facto research, it is inappropriate to assume ANCOVA has satisfactorily adjusted for initial difference.

Homogeneous Groups

You may recall from the discussion of control in experimentation that it is possible to control the effects of a variable by selecting samples that are as homogeneous as possible on that variable. A similar procedure can be followed in ex post facto research. Instead of taking a heterogeneous sample and comparing matched subgroups within it, an investigator may control a variable by including in the sample only subjects who are homogeneous on that variable. If intelligence is a relevant extraneous variable, the investigator could control its effect by using subjects from only one intelligence level. This procedure serves the purpose of disentangling the independent variable in which in the investigator may be interested from other variables with which it is commonly associated so that any effects that are found can more justifiably be associated with the independent variable.

Suppose one wishes to investigate whether having a quiet room at home, with desk, books, and so on, in which to study affects the grades of high school students. If one simply selects a cross section of high school students, ask them whether or not they have a quiet room in which to study, and then compare the grades of those who have a room and those who do not, one may erroneously conclude that having a quiet room in which to study leads to good grades. An alternative explanation is that there are other factors associated with social class that may influence both one's study arrangements and grades received in school. Low-income families, for instance, are more likely to be over crowed and are less likely to put emphasis on scholastic achievement than are middle-and upper-class families. If one wants to control the effects of social class, one can limit the study to subjects of one socioeconomic level. If one finds a relationship between study arrangements and grades within the one social class, one would have somewhat more confidence in the conclusion that the difference in grades is due to study arrangements and not to socioeconomic differences. Of course, this procedure limits the generalizability of the findings to the one social class used in the study; one would not know whether the relationship exist in other social classes.

The use of homogeneous samples is only a partial solution to the problems inherent in ex-post facto research. We can control some common cause variables by selecting samples who are alike on a suspected common cause variable. We cannot be sure we have subjects who are homogenous on all suspected or unsuspected common cause variables. In our example it is quite possible that within middle-class families both having or not having a quiet room and academic achievement are a function of family size or other variables. Regression can also be a problem with homogenous sample. For example, if Principal A in our earlier example had used only children in the two schools who scored exactly 4.0 on the fourth-grade reading test, regression would cause the A group to regress up and the B group to regress down, as they did when subjects were matched.

Building Extraneous Variables into the Design

It may be possible to build relevant extraneous independent variables into the ex-post facto design and use a factorial analysis-of-variable and it is not feasible to control it through any other means. In such a case intelligence could be added to the design as another independent variable and the subjects of the study classified in terms of intelligence levels. The dependent variable measures would then be analyzed through the analysis of variance, and the main and interaction effects of intelligence might be determined. Such a procedure would reveal any significant difference among the groups on the dependent variable, but no causal relationship between intelligence and the dependent variable could be assumed. Other extraneous variables could be operating to produce both the main effect and any interaction effect.

For example, many studies have reported a relationship between birth order and intellectual attainment and occupational achievement: first born doing better than second born, second born doing better than third born, and so forth. After a thorough review of the literature, Schooler concluded: "The most frequently reported differences of between birth ranks – the greater occurrence of first born among group marked by unusual intellectual attainment or occupational; achievement – seems to be most parsimoniously explained in terms of difference among social class trends in family size. "Since there is an inverse relationship between social class and family size, the average social-class standing of fifth children would be lower than the average social-class of fourth children, and so forth. As social class is related to achievement, the apparent relationship between birth order and achievement might be due solely to differences in average social-class standing and not to birth order per se.

Later Belmont and Marolla studied birth order and scores on the Raven Progressive Matrices test (a non-verbal intelligence test) for nearly 400,000 young men in the Netherlands. They found that within each family size intelligence declined with birth order. Since they were comparing scores only within five-child families, within four-child families, and so forth, difference in social class could not account for their results.

Do the Belmont and Marolla result now enable us to say that birth order per se is related to intelligence? We would be wise to treat this as only a tentative conclusion. Certainly the average age of the parents of fourth children is older than the average age of parents of third children and this may have something to do with the phenomenon. Perhaps it is accounted for by something we cannot even imagine.

Building other variables into an ex-post facto design is a partial solution, but we can never be sure that we have selected the right variables or that we have employed all the variables that should have been considered.

As a result of the inadequate control in an ex-post facto study, interpretation of the findings may be particularly hazardous. The risk of incorrect interpretation is great. when a relationship between two variables has established in the course of an ex-post facto study, the analysis has, in a sense, taken only its first step. The investigator must consider and test any plausible alternative hypotheses, and even after doing so, must realize that an apparent relationship may be due to some other unfathomable cause. Procedures such as the use of change scores, matching, analysis of covariance, partial correlation, homogeneous groups, and building extraneous variables into a study, can help avoid gross errors in ex post facto studies, but they all underadjust for pre-treatment differences among groups. Listing alternative hypotheses (common cause, reverse causality, and alternate independent variables) can help one asses more realistically ex-post facto results.

Designing the Ex-post Facto Investigation

The two basic modes of ex-post facto research are

— Begin with subjects who differ on an independent variable and test hypotheses concerning how they will differ on dependent variable and

— Begin with subjects who differ on a dependent variable and test hypotheses concerning possible independent variables.

Example

Consider a study to compare the problem-solving performance of creative and non-creative college of education students. The hypothesis would read: Creative college students will exhibit greater speed and accuracy on a problem-solving task than will non-creative college students. This hypothesis clearly indicates the need for an ex-post facto design since the investigators can neither manipulate creativity nor assign students randomly to groups. They must start with two groups who already differ on the independent variable, creativity, and compare them on the dependent variable, problem-solving performance.

The investigators must define a creative college student and a non-creative college student in precise operational terms. The creative college student might be defined as those undergraduates in the school of education scoring above the upper quartile on both the Guilford Test of Alternate Uses and Consequences and an anagram test. Those students scoring below the first quartile on the tests would be defined as non-creative.

The investigators should try to identify variables other than creativity that could affect the dependent variable of problem-solving performance and take steps to equate the experimental and control groups on these variables by matching or by statistical means. For example, in this study other independent variables that should be controlled are intelligence, sex, and perhaps college subject main or college year. A bright male student in the creative group might be matched with his counterpart in the non-creative group.

After the formation of the matched groups, both groups would be given a measure of the dependent variable, a problem-solving task. Further analysis of the data by means of a t-test would reveal any significant differences in the problem-solving performance of the two groups and perhaps show a relationship between creativity and problem-solving performance. Although one may conclude from such a study that there is a relationship, one cannot assume a causal connection between creativity and problem-solving performance. There may be other uncontrolled variables that singly or in combination could influence problem-solving. The alert investigator is aware of the need to examine other plausible alternative explanations of an ex-post facto finding.

The Role of Ex-post Facto Research

Despite its weaknesses much ex post facto research must be done in psychology, sociology, and education simply because many research problems in the social sciences and education do not lend themselves to experimental inquiry.

– Kerlinger

It can even be said that ex post facto research is more important than experimental research. This is, of course, not a methodological observation. It means, rather, that the most important social, scientific and education research problems do not lend themselves to experimentation, although many of them do lend themselves to controlled inquiry of the ex-post facto kind. Consider Piaget's studies of children's thinking. The ex-post facto design is used when investigators are not in a position to test a hypothesis by assigning subjects to different conditions in which they directly manipulate the independent variable. In ex-post facto studies the changes in the independent variable have already taken place and the researchers must study them in retrospect for their possible effects on an observed dependent variable.

Although there are many disadvantages of the ex-post facto approach, it nevertheless is frequently the only method by which educational researchers can obtain necessary information about characteristics of defined groups of students or information needed for the intelligent formulation of programmes in the school. It permits researchers to investigate situations in which it is impossible to introduce controlled variation. Attributes such as intelligence, creativity, socioeconomic status, and teacher personality cannot be manipulated and hence must be investigated through ex-post facto research rather than through the more rigorous experimental approach.

Many ex-post facto investigations have been notable in their influence on education. Variables such as home background, genetic endowment, brain damage, and early experiences are very important educational variables even though they are beyond the control of educators.

The possibility of spurious relationships is always present in ex-post facto research. Considering the possibilities of common cause, reversed causality, and possible alternate independent variables can help us evaluate such research more realistically. Several partial control strategies can help us avoid gross errors in ex-post facto designs, but none can entirely solve the problems inherent in those designs. We must always exercise caution in interpreting ex post facto results.

SUGGESTED REFERENCES

- Aiken, Lewis R. Rating Scales and Checklists. Wiley. ISBN 0-471-12787-6. Good general introduction including discussions of personality and achievement questionnaires. 1996,
- Best, John and James Kahn. Research in Education. Prentice Hall of India, New Delhi. 2005.
- Blumer, H. Symbolic Interactionism. New Jersey: Prentice Hall. 1969.
- Burrel G. & Morgan. Sociological Paradigms and Organizational Analysis. London: Heinemann Educational Books Ltd. 1979.
- Campbell Donald T. and Albert Erlebacher. "How Regression Artifacts in Quasi-Experimental Evaluation Can Mistakenly Make Compensatory Education Look Harmful", in Compensatory Education: A National Debate, vol. 3. Disadvantaged Child, ed., J. Hellmuth (New York: Brunner / Mazel). 1970.
- Dillman, Don A. Mail and Telephone Surveys: The Total Design Method. New York: Wiley, 1978.
- Glock, Charles Y. Survey Research in the Social Science. New York: Russell Sage Foundation. 1967.
- Goetz, J.P. & LeCompte, M.D. Ethnography and Qualitative Design in Educational Research. Orlando Academic Press Inc. 1984.

- Guba, E.G. & Lincoln, Y.S. Naturalistic and Rationalistic Enquiry, pp.81-84. In J.Keeves (Ed.) (1988). Educational Research, Methodology, and Measurement: An international handbook. Oxford: Pergamon Press. 1988.
- Holsti, Ole R *Content Analysis for the Social Sciences and Humanities.* Reading, Mass. 1969
- Hyman, Herbert H. et al. Interviewing in Social Research. Chicago. University of Chicago Press. 1975.
- Hymes, D. What is Ethnography? Sociolinguistics Working Paper #45, Texas: Southwest Educational Development Laboratory 1978.
- Kennedy, M.M. Generalizing from Single Case Studies. Evaluation Quarterly. 3(4), 661-66. 1979.
- Kerlinger, Fred N. Foundation of Behavioral Research, 2nd ed. (New York: Holt, Rinehart and Winston, 1973.
- Spardley, J. Participant Observation, New York: Holt, Rinehart and Winston. 1980.
- Taft, R. Ethnographic Research Methods. Pp.59-63. In J.Keeves (Ed.) Educational Research, Methodology, and Measurement: An International Handbook. Oxford: Pergamon Press. 1988.
- Warwick Donald P. and Charles Lininger, The Sample Story: Theory and Practice chs. 6 and 7. New York: McGraw-Hill, 1975.

Data Collection in Educational Research

This chapter describes the different methods of gathering data for educational research.

10.1 Observation Method

When is Observation Scientific?

Observation becomes a tool for scientific inquiry when it

- serves a formulated research purpose
- is planned systematically
- is recorded systematically and related to more general propositions rather than being presented as reflecting a set of interesting curiosities.
- is subjected to checks or control on validity and reliability

Scientific Observation is the systematic process of recording the behavioural patterns of people, objects, and occurrences without questioning or communicating with them.

What can be Observed?

Exhibit 10.1 indicates seven kinds of content that can be observed.

Phenomenon	Example
Human behaviour or action	Students' movement patterns in a class or in a field trip
Verbal behaviour	Statements made by parents waiting in the parlour for their ward
Spatial relations	Proximity of teachers staff room to the principal's office
Temporal patterns	How long students take to perform a task
Physical objects	How much paper office staff recycle
Verbal and pictorial records	How many illustrations appear in a unit being taught
Expressive behaviour	Facial expressions, tone of voice, and other forms of body language

Exhibit 10.1: Content that can be observed

Although the observation method may be used to describe a wide variety of behaviours, cognitive phenomena, such as attitudes, motivations, expectations, intentions, and preferences, cannot be observed. Another limitation is that observed behaviour is generally of short duration. Observing behaviour patterns over a period of several days or several weeks generally is either too costly or too difficult.

The Nature of Observation Studies

As a data gathering device, observation studies score over descriptive studies, which contain self-reported data from respondents. The data are recorded when the actual behaviour takes place.

Human or mechanical observation may be unobtrusive in that communication with the respondent may not be necessary. For example, one may study the characteristics of a school laboratory by observing and recording the plinth area, water, gas and other service facilities, ventilation, storage of chemicals, furniture, presence and absence of fume cupboards, antidotes, first aid box, and other such relevant aspects. Adequacy could then be determined by comparing these facilities with reasonable standards, determined by experts.

Similarly, during a practical class, a chemistry teacher can record the performance of the students, by splitting the tasks to sub-tasks and observing the presence or absence of certain psychomotor skills.

The unobtrusive or non-reactive nature of the observation method often generates data without the knowledge of the subjects. Situations where the observer's presence is known to the subject are ***visible observation***. Situations where the observer is unaware that observation is taking place are ***hidden observation***. With hidden, unobtrusive observation, respondent error is minimized. Asking subjects to participate in the research is not required when those subjects are unaware that they are being observed. However, hidden observation raises an ethical issue concerning respondents' privacy.

Behavioural scientists have recognized that non-verbal behaviour can be a communication process by which meanings are exchanged between individuals. Head nods, smiles, raised eyebrows, and other facial expressions or body movements have been recognized as communication symbols. Observation of non-verbal communication has considerable promise for the researcher. For example, in a classroom situation, the non-verbal communication between peers, between teacher and taught, can give vital clues on the classroom climate. Exhibit 10.2 could help in observation of the classroom situation.

10.1.1 Direct Observation

Direct observation can produce a detailed record of an event or what people actually do. The observer plays a passive role; that is, there is no attempt to control or manipulate a situation. The observer merely records what occurs.

Direct observation is a straightforward attempt to observe and record what naturally occurs; the investigator does not create an artificial situation.

Researchers using the direct observation method compile data by recording events as they occur. An observation form is often used to help keep the observations consistent and to ensure that all relevant information is recorded. A respondent is not required to recall (perhaps inaccurately) an event after it has occurred. The observation is instantaneous.

	Between Status Equals (Peers)		Between Status Non equals (Teacher and student)		Between Men and Women (classmates, staff etc)	
Behaviour	**Intimate**	**Non intimate**	**Used by Superior**	**Used by Subordinate**	**Used by Men (boys)**	**Used by Women (girls)**
Posture	Relaxed	Tense	Relaxed (less relaxed)	Tense	Relaxed	Tense
Personal space	Closeness	Distance	Closeness (optional)	Distance (optional)	Closeness	Distance
Touching	Touch	Don't	Touch (optional)	Don't touch	Touch	Don't touch
Eye gaze	Establish	Avoid	Stare, ignore	Watch	Stare, ignore	Avert eyes
Demeanor	Informal	Circumspect	Informal	Circumspect	Informal	Circumspect
Emotional expression	Show	Hide	Hide	Show	Hide	Show
Facial expression	Smile*	Don't smile*	Don't smile	Smile	Don't smile	Smile

* Behaviour not known

Exhibit 10.2: Non-verbal communication: Status and power gestures

Certain data may be more quickly or easily obtained by direct observation. For example, in a quality-of-job survey, respondents were asked a series of questions that were compiled into an index of job satisfaction. Direct observation was also used by the interviewers because the researchers wanted to investigate whether environmental conditions influenced people's answers. The researchers quickly and easily observed and recorded environmental conditions, including outside weather conditions on the day of the interview, as well as the temperature and humidity in the building where the interviews were taken.

Errors Associated with Direct Observation

Although there is no interaction with the respondent, direct observation is not error-free; the observer may add subjectivity to the recording. The same visual cues that may influence the interplay between an interviewer and respondent (e.g., the subject's age or sex) may also come into play in some types of direct observation settings. For example, the observer may subjectively attribute a particular economic status or educational background to the subject. A distortion of measurement resulting form the cognitive behaviour or actions of the witnessing observer is called ***observer bias***. In Exhibit 10.3 an excerpt from the observation section of a survey shows how fieldworkers may be required to rely on their own interpretations of people or situations during the observation process.

If the observer does not record every detail that describes the persons, objects, and events in a given situation, accuracy may suffer. As a general guideline, the observer should record as much detail as possible. However, the pace of events, the observer's memory, and the observer's writing speed, and other factors will limit the amount of detail that can be recorded.

Interpretation of observation data is another major limitation. Facial expression and other non-verbal communication may have several meanings. Does a smile always mean happiness? Because someone is standing or seated in close proximity to the principal, is it necessarily a direct indication of status?

Response Latency

The decision time necessary to make a choice between two alternatives is a relatively simple, unobtrusive measure. The term

	(R=Respondent)
Q3 Rate R's Physical appearance:	
	1. Strikingly handsome or beautiful 2. Good looking (above average for age and sex) 3. Average looks for age and sex 4. Quite plain (below average for age and sex) 5. Homely
Q4 How tall would you say R was? _..... _Feet__ inches	
Q5 Rate R's apparent intelligence?	
	1. Very High 2. Above Average 3. Average 4. Below Average 5. Very Low

Exhibit 10.3: Part of an observation form

response latency refers to the recording of choice time as a measure of the strength of the preference between alternatives. It is hypothesized that the longer a decision maker takes to make a choice between two alternatives, the closer the two alternatives are in terms of preference. However, if a quick decision is made, it is assumed that the "psychological distance" between alternatives is considerable. The response latency measure is growing more popular now that computer – assisted data collection methods are becoming more common (i.e., the computer records the decision time).

Response Latency is the amount of time necessary to make a choice between two alternatives; used as a measure of the strength of preference.

10.1.2 Scientifically Contrived Observation

Most observations take place in natural setting. Intervention by the investigator to create an artificial environment to test a hypothesis is called contrived observation. This increases the frequency of certain behaviour patterns. For example, a parent, complaining about poor teaching in physics to the teacher may actually be a researcher recording the teacher's reactions. If the situation wasn't contrived, the research time spent waiting and observing situations would expand considerably. The term mystery shopper is used by a number of retailers to describe this type of research, where an unknown shopper comes into a store and pretends to be interested in a particular product or service. After leaving the store, the shopper (observer) evaluates the performance of the salesperson.

Contrived observation is observation in which the investigator creates an artificial environment in order to test a hypothesis.

10.1.3 Participant Observation

This refers to situations in which observer gains firsthand knowledge by being in or around the social setting that is being investigated. The individual who joins a group, for example, may be a known or unknown observer. In either case the observer generally uses a combination of direct observation and interviewing.

Interview questions may be asked during the course of a conversation or discussion, rather than in any structured format. Long and involved personal interaction with the subjects of the research is the prime advantage of participant observation. Increased contact with the subjects allows the subjects to feel comfortable in the participant observer's presence.

The participant observer must develop a system for recording his or her observations. Generally, the observer takes mental notes and jots down field notes where possible. At the end of the day more detailed field notes are recorded to summarize and synthesize the events and activities of the day.

10.2 Attitude Measurement

There are many definitions for the term *attitude*. An *attitude* is usually viewed as an enduring disposition to respond consistently in a given manner to various aspects of the world, including persons, events, and objects. One conception of attitude is reflected in this brief statement: "Gopal loves working at XYZ College of Education.

He believes it is conveniently located, and has the best wages in town. He intends to work there until he retires." In this short description three components of attitude have been disclosed: ***affective***, ***cognitive*** and ***behavioural***.

The ***affective component*** reflects an individual's general feelings or emotions toward an object. Statements such as "I love my job;" "I liked that book – The Fifth Discipline." Or "I hate apple juice" reflect the emotional character of attitudes.

The way one feels about a product, person, or object is usually tied to one's beliefs or cognitions. The *cognitive component* represents one's awareness of and knowledge about an object. A woman might feel happy about her job because she "believes that the pay is great" or because she knows "that my job is the biggest challenge in Chennai".

The third component of an attitude is the ***behavioural component***. Intentions and behavioural expectations are reflected in this component, which therefore reflects a predisposition to action.

To measure an attitude, we must infer from the way an individual responds (verbal expression or overt behaviour) to some stimulus. The term ***hypothetical construct*** describes a variable that is not directly observable but is measured by an indirect means, such as verbal expression or overt behaviour.

A ***ranking*** task requires that the respondents rank order a small number of items in overall preference or on the basis of some characteristic of the stimulus. ***Rating*** asks the respondents to estimate the magnitude of a characteristic or quality than an object possesses. Quantitative scores, along a continuum that has been supplied to the respondents are used to estimate the strength of the attitude or belief. In other words, the respondents indicate the position, on a scale, where they would rate the object.

A ***sorting technique*** might present respondent with several product concepts, printed on cards, and require that the respondents arrange the cards into a number of piles or otherwise classify the product concepts. The ***choice technique***, choosing one of two or more alternatives, is another type attitude measurement. If a respondent chooses one object over another, it is assumed the chosen object is preferred over the other.

The most popular for measuring attitudes are presented in this section.

10.2.1 Attitude Rating Scales

Using rating scales to measure attitudes is perhaps the most common practice in educational research. This section discusses many rating scales designed to enable respondent to report the intensity of their attitudes.

Simple Attitude Scaling

In its most basic form, attitude scaling requires that an individual agree or disagree with a statement or respond to a single question.

The Job Descriptive Index (JDI) is a modified checklist with a large number of items. The Job Descriptive Index measures several dimensions of satisfaction: pay, promotion co-workers, supervision, and quality of work. Some sample items appear below.

Directions

Think of your present work. What is it like most of the time?

Circle YES if it describes your work.

Circles NO if it does NOT describe it.

Circle ? If you cannot decide.

Fascinating	YES	NO ?
Routine	YES	NO ?
Satisfying	YES	NO ?

> ***Category scale*** is an attitude scale consisting of several response categories to provide the respondent with alternative ratings.

Category Scales

Some rating scales have only two response categories: agree and disagree. Expanding the response categories provides the respondent more flexibility in the rating task. Even more information is provided if the categories are ordered according to a descriptive or evaluative dimension. Consider the question below asked by a researcher to a teacher.

How often is your principal courteous and friendly to you?

❑ Never ❑ Rarely ❑ Sometimes ❑ Often ❑ Very often

If you could choose, how much longer would you stay at your present job?

- ❑ Less than six months
- ❑ Six moths to one year
- ❑ Longer than one year

Each of these category scales is a more sensitive measure than a scale with only two response categories. It provides more information.

Wording is an extremely important factor in the usefulness of these scales. Exhibit 10.4 shows some common wordings for category scales.

Quality				
Excellent	Good	Fair	Poor	
Very good	Fairly good	Neither good nor bad	Not very good	Not good at all
Importance				
Very important	Fairly important	Neutral	Not so important	Not at all important
Interest				
Very Interested		Somewhat Interested		Not very Interested
Satisfaction				
Very Satisfied	Somewhat Satisfied	Neither Satisfied nor dissatisfied	Somewhat dissatisfied	Very dissatisfied
Very Satisfied	Quite Satisfied		Somewhat satisfied	Not at all satisfied
Frequency				
All of the time	Very often	Often	Sometimes	Hardly ever
Very often	Often	Sometimes	Rarely	Never
All of the time	Most of the time		Some of the time	Just now and then
Truth				
Very true	Somewhat true	Not very true	Not at all true	
Definitely true	More true than false	More false than true	Definitely not true	

Exhibit 10.4: Common wordings for category scales

10.2.2 Summated Ratings Method: The Likert Scale

Educational researchers' adaptation of the summated ratings method, developed by Rensis Likert, is extremely popular for measuring attitudes because the method is simple to administer . With the Likert scale, respondents indicate their attitudes by checking how strongly they agree or disagree with carefully constructed statements that range from very positive to very negative toward the attitudinal object. Individuals generally choose from five alternatives; strongly agree, agree, uncertain, disagree, and strongly disagree; but the alternatives may number from 3 to 9.

> *Likert scale* is a measure of attitudes ranging from very positive to very negative designed to allow respondents to indicate how strongly they agree or disagree with carefully constructed statements relating to an attitudinal object.

A Likert scale may include several scale items to form an index. Each statement is assumed to represent an aspect of a common attitudinal domain. The total score is the summation of the weights assigned to an individual's total response.

In Likert's original procedure a large number of statements are generated and then an item analysis is performed. The purpose of the item analysis is to ensure that final items evoke a wide response and discriminate among those with positive and negative attitudes. Items that are poor because they lack clarity or elicit mixed response patterns are eliminated from the final statement list.

10.2.3 Semantic Differential

The semantic differential is a series of attitude scales. This popular attitude-measurement technique consists of identification of a company, product, brand, job or other concept followed by a series of seven-point bipolar rating scales. Bipolar adjectives, such as "good and bad," "modern and old-fashioned," or "clean and dirty," indicate the beginning and end (or poles) of the scale.

Modern |___|___|___|___|___|___|___|___| Old Fashioned

The subject makes repeated judgments of the concept under investigation on each of the scales. For example, Exhibit 10.5 shows a

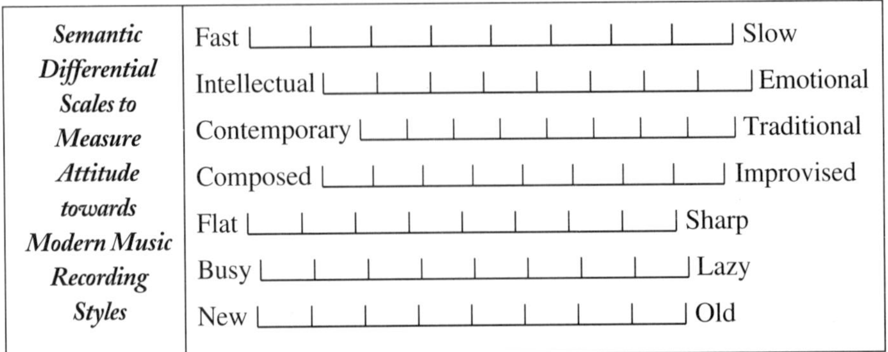

Semantic Differential Scales to Measure Attitude towards Modern Music Recording Styles	
	Fast ⎿⎯⎯⎯⎯⎯⎯⎯⎯⏌ Slow
	Intellectual ⎿⎯⎯⎯⎯⎯⎯⎯⎯⏌ Emotional
	Contemporary ⎿⎯⎯⎯⎯⎯⎯⎯⎯⏌ Traditional
	Composed ⎿⎯⎯⎯⎯⎯⎯⎯⎯⏌ Improvised
	Flat ⎿⎯⎯⎯⎯⎯⎯⎯⎯⏌ Sharp
	Busy ⎿⎯⎯⎯⎯⎯⎯⎯⎯⏌ Lazy
	New ⎿⎯⎯⎯⎯⎯⎯⎯⎯⏌ Old

Exhibit 10.5: Measuring attitudes

series of scales related to measuring attitudes toward jazz saxophonists' recording styles.

10.2.4 Numerical Scales

Numerical Scales (Exhibit 10.6) have numbers as response options, rather than "semantic space" or verbal descriptions, to identify categories (response positions). If the scale items have five response positions, the scale is called a 5-point numerical scale; when seven response positions, it is called a 7-point numerical scale; and so on.

10.2.5 Graphic Rating Scales

A graphic rating scale presents respondents with a graphic continuum. The respondents are allowed to choose any point on the continuum to indicate their attitudes. The scale illustrated in Exhibit 10.7. shows a traditional graphic scale, ranging from one extreme position to the opposite position. Typically, a respondent's score is determined by measuring the length (millimeters) from one end of the graphic continuum to the point marked by the respondent. Many researchers believe scoring in this manner strengthens the assumption that graphic rating scales of this type are interval scales. Alternatively, the researcher may divide the line into predetermined scoring categories (lengths) and record respondents' marks accordingly. In other words, the graphic rating scale has the advantage of allowing the researchers to choose any interval they wish for purpose of scoring. The disadvantage of the graphic rating scales is that there are no standard answers.

I. P. C. Least Preferred Co-Worker Scale of Leadership Effectiveness	Think of the person with whom you can work least well. The person may be someone you work with now or may be someone you knew in the past. The individual does not have to be the person you like least well, but should be the person with whom you had the most difficulty in getting a job done.

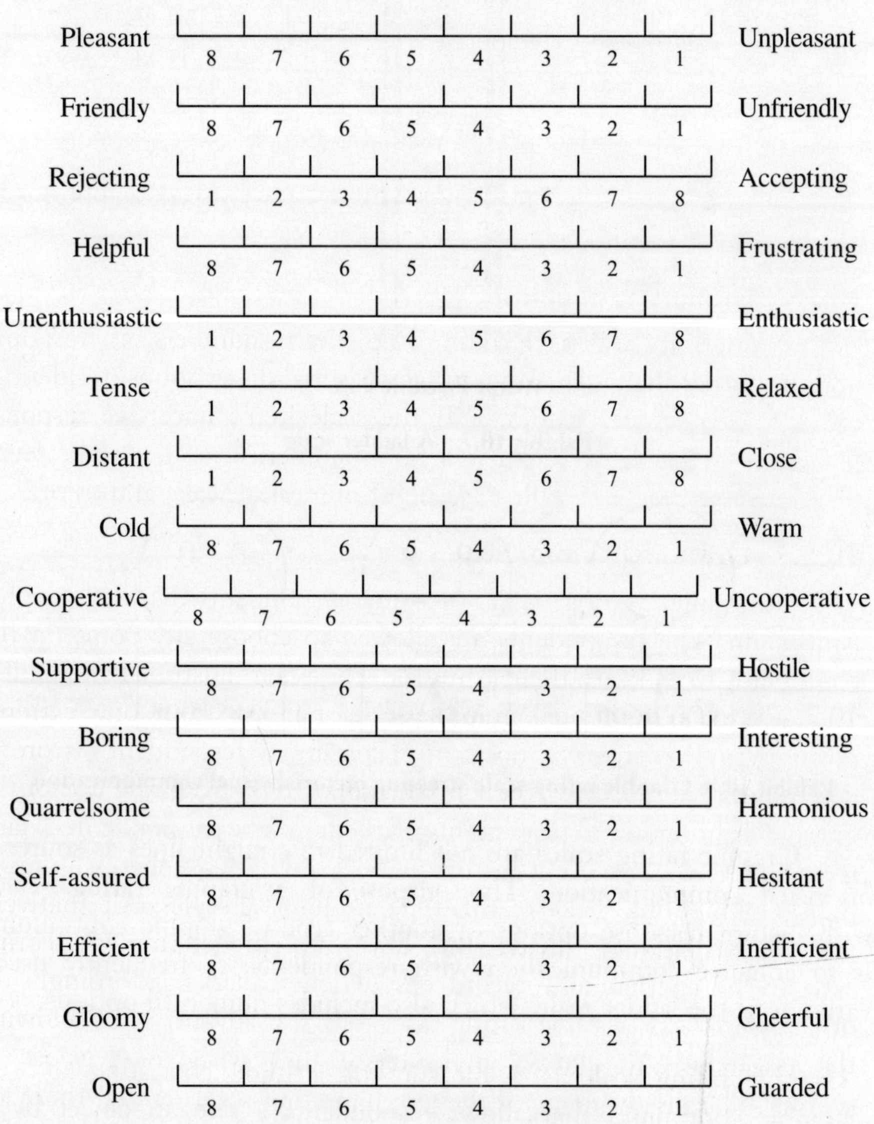

Pleasant	8	7	6	5	4	3	2	1	Unpleasant
Friendly	8	7	6	5	4	3	2	1	Unfriendly
Rejecting	1	2	3	4	5	6	7	8	Accepting
Helpful	8	7	6	5	4	3	2	1	Frustrating
Unenthusiastic	1	2	3	4	5	6	7	8	Enthusiastic
Tense	1	2	3	4	5	6	7	8	Relaxed
Distant	1	2	3	4	5	6	7	8	Close
Cold	8	7	6	5	4	3	2	1	Warm
Cooperative	8	7	6	5	4	3	2	1	Uncooperative
Supportive	8	7	6	5	4	3	2	1	Hostile
Boring	8	7	6	5	4	3	2	1	Interesting
Quarrelsome	8	7	6	5	4	3	2	1	Harmonious
Self-assured	8	7	6	5	4	3	2	1	Hesitant
Efficient	8	7	6	5	4	3	2	1	Inefficient
Gloomy	8	7	6	5	4	3	2	1	Cheerful
Open	8	7	6	5	4	3	2	1	Guarded

Exhibit 10.6: Numerical scales

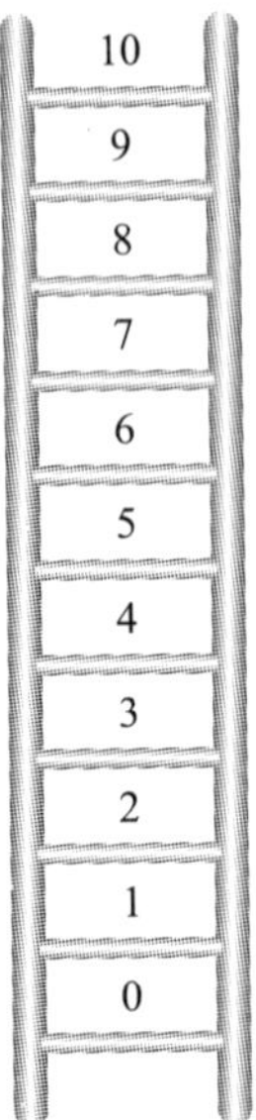

Exhibit 10.7 A ladder scale

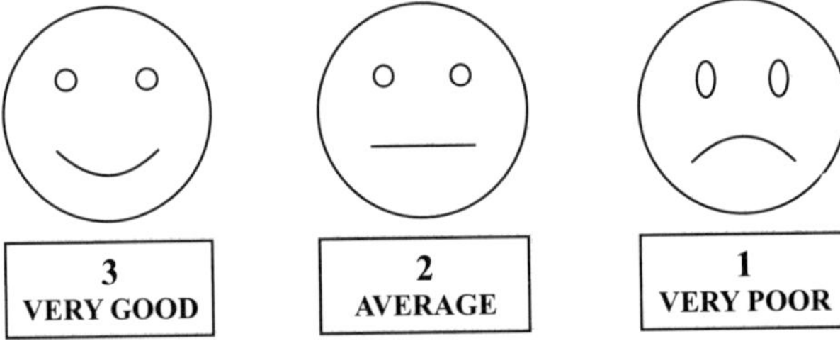

Exhibit 10.8: Graphic rating scale stressing pictorial visual communication

Graphic rating scales are not limited to straight lines as sources of visual communication. The purpose of a graphic rating scale with picture response options or another type of graphic continuum is to enhance communication with respondents. A frequently used variation is the ladder scale, which also includes numerical options.

Graphic rating scale is a measure of attitude consisting of a graphic continuum that allows respondents a rate an object by choosing any point on the continuum.

Rating Measure	Subject Must	Advantages	Disadvantages
Category scale	Indicate response category	Flexible, easy to respond	Items may be ambiguous, with few categories, only gross distinctions can be made
Likert scale	Evaluate statements on 5-point scale	Easiest scale to construct	Hard to judge what a single score means
Semantic differential and Numerical scales	Choose points between bipolar adjectives on relevant dimensions	Easy to construct; norms exist for comparison	Bipolar adjectives must be found; data may be ordinal, not interval
Constant sum scale	Divide a constant sum among response alternative	Scale approximates interval measure	Difficult for respondents with low education levels
Stapel scale	Choose points on a scale with a single adjective in center	Easier to construct than semantic differential, easy to administer	End points, not verbal, labels
Graphic scale	Choose a point a continuum	Visual impact, unlimited scale points	No standard answers
Graphic scale (Pictorial)	Choose a visual picture response	Visual impact	Verbal explanation to picture response

Exhibit 10. 9: Summary of the advantages and disadvantages of rating scales

10.2.6 Questions to be Asked Before Selecting a Measurement Scale

1. Is a ranking, sorting, rating, or choice technique best?
2. Should a monadic or comparative scale be used?
3. What type of category labels, if any, should be used?
4. How many scale positions are needed?
5. Should a balanced or unbalanced scale be chosen?
6. Should respondents be given a forced-choice or a no forced-choice scale?
7. Should a single measure or an index measure be used?

10.3 Three Criteria for Good Measurement

There are three major criteria for evaluating measurements: reliability, validity, and sensitivity.

Reliability

A tailor measuring fabric with a tape measure obtains a "true" value of the fabric's length. If the tailor takes repeated measures of the fabric and each time estimates the same length it is assumed that the tape measure is reliable. When the outcome of the measuring process is reproducible, the measuring instrument is reliable.

> Reliability is the degree to which measures are free from error and therefore yield consistent results.

Reliability applies to a measure when similar results are obtained over time and across situations. Broadly defined, reliability is the degree to which measures are free from error and therefore yield consistent results. For example, ordinal-level measures are reliable if they consistently rank order subjects in the same manner; reliable interval-level measures consistently rank order and maintain the distance between subjects.

Imperfections in the measuring process that affect the assignment of scores or numbers in different ways each time a measure is taken, such as a respondent who misunderstands a question, are the cause of low reliability. Suppose a respondent understands a question but does not know the real reason for his or her behaviour and so cannot give any of several responses with truthfulness. The actual choice between plausible responses may be governed by such transitory factors as mood, whim, or the context set by surrounding questions. Measures of this type will not be error-free and stable over time.

Two dimensions underlie the concept of reliability: repeatability and internal consistency. Assessing the repeatability of a measure is the first aspect of reliability.

The test-retest method involves administering the same scale or measure to the same respondents at two separate times to test for stability. If the measure is stable over time, the reported test, administered under conditions similar to the first test, should obtain similar results. For example, suppose a researcher measures job satisfaction and finds that 64 per cent of the population is satisfied with their jobs. If the study is repeated a few weeks later under similar conditions, and the researcher again finds that 64 per cent of the population is satisfied with their jobs, it appears that the measure is reliable. The high stability correlation or consistency between the two measures at Time 1 and Time 2 indicates a high degree of reliability.

At the individual (rather than aggregate) level, assume that a person does not change his or her attitude about the job. If repeated measurement of that individual's attitude toward the job is taken with the same attitude, a reliable instrument will produce the same results each time the attitude is measured. When a measuring instrument produces unpredictable results from one testing to the next, the results are said to be unreliable because of error in measurement.

There are two problems with measures of test-retests reliability that are common to all longitudinal studies. First, the premature (or first measure) may sensitize the respondents to their participation in a research project and subsequently influence the results of the second measure. Further if the time between measures is long, there may be attitude change or other maturation of the subject. Thus it is possible for reliable measure to indicate a low or moderate correlation between the first and the second administration, if this low correlation is due to an attitude change over time rather than to a lack of reliability.

The second dimension of reliability concerns the homogeneity of the measure. An attempt to measure an attitude may require asking several similar (but not identical) questions or presenting a battery of scale items. To measure the internal consistency of a multiple-item measure, scores on subsets of the items within the scale are correlated.

The technique of splitting halves is the most basic method for checking internal consistency when a measure contains a large number of items. In the split-half method the researcher may take the result obtained from one-half of the scale items (e.g., odd-numbered items) and check them against the results from the other half of the items (e.g., even numbered items).

Split-half method is the method that measures the degree of internal consistency by checking one half of the results of a set of scaled items against the other half.

In the equivalent-form method two alternative instruments are designed to be as equivalent as possible. Each of the two measurement scales is administered to the same group of subjects. If there is high correlation between the two forms, the researcher concludes that the scale is reliable. However, there is a problem if there is low correspondence The researcher will be uncertain whether the measure has intrinsically low reliability or whether a single equivalent form has failed to be similar to the other form.

Equivalent-form method is a method that measures the correlation between alternative instruments, designed to be as equivalent as possible, administered to the same group of subjects between the two instruments.

Both the equivalent-form and the split-half approaches to measuring reliability assume that the concept being measured is uni-dimensional. They measure homogeneity, or inter-item consistency, rather than stability over time.

It should be noted that reliability is a necessary condition for validity, but a reliable instrument may not be valid. A reliable but invalid instrument will yield consistently inaccurate results.

Validity

The purpose of measurement is to measure what we intend to measure – but this obvious goal is not as simple as it sounds at first. Consider the student who takes a test (measurement) in a statistics class. After receiving a poor grade, the student may say: "I really understood that material because I studied hard. The test measured my ability to do arithmetic and to memorize formulas rather than my understandings of statistics." The student's complaint is that the test did not measure her understanding of statistics-what the professor had intended to measure; the test may have measured something else.

> Validity is the ability of a scale or measuring instrument to measure what is intended to be measured.

A researcher who wonders if rate of staff absenteeism might be utilized to measure morale illustrates another validity issue. It is possible that this is not a valid measure of morale because absenteeism might reflect either a wave of illness in the community or dissatisfied teachers not coming to work.

Researchers want to know if their measure is valid, and the question of validity expresses their concern with accurate measurement. Validity addresses the problem of whether a measure (for example, an attitude measure) measures what it is supposed to measure. If it does not measure what we designate it to measure, there will be problems.

Researchers have attempted to assess validity in a variety of ways; including asking questions such as "Is there a consensus among my colleagues that my attitude scale measures what it is supposed to measure?" "Does my measure correlate with other's measures of the 'same' concept?" or "Does the behaviour expected from my measure predict the actual observed behaviour?" Researchers expect the answers to provide some evidence of a measure's validity. This section discusses the three basic approaches to dealing with the issue of validity.

Face validity or content validity refers to the subjective agreement among professionals that a scale logically appears to reflect accurately what it purports to measure. The content of the scale appears to be adequate. When it appears evident to experts that the measure provides adequate coverage of the concept, a measure has face validity. Clear understandable questions such as "How many children do you have?" are generally agreed to have face validity. However, in scientific studies researchers generally prefer strong evidence because of the elusive nature of measuring attitudes and other cognitive phenomena.

Criterion validity is an attempt by researchers to answer the question "Does my measure correlate with other measures of the 'same' construct? Consider the physical concept of Length. It is possible to measure length utilizing a tape measure, calipers and variations of the ruler. If a new measure of length were developed (for example, through laser technology), finding that the new measure correlated with the other measures of length could provide some assurance that the new measure was valid. A researcher wishing to establish criterion validity for a new measure of absenteeism, such as a measure utilizing co-worker's ratings of employee absenteeism, should correlate it with other traditional measures of absenteeism, such as total days absent.

Criterion validity may be classified as either concurrent validity or predictive validity, depending on the time sequence of associating the "new" measurement scale and the criterion measure. If the new measure is taken at the same time as the criterion measure, the method is called concurrent validity. Predictive validity is established when an attitude measure predicts a future event. The two measures differ only on the basis of a time dimension, that is, only if the criterion is separated in time from the predictor measure.

Concurrent validity is a classification of criterion validity whereby a new measure correlates with criterion measure taken at the same time.
Predictive validity is a classification of criterion validity whereby a new measure predicts a future event or correlates with a criterion measure administered at a later time.
Construct validity is established by the degree to which the measure confirms a network or related hypotheses generated from a theory based on the concepts.

Establishing constructs validity occurs during the statistical analysis of the data. In construct validity the empirical evidence is consistent with the theoretical logic about the concepts. In its simplest from, if the measure behaves the way it is supposed to, in pattern of inter correlation with a variety of other variables; there is evidence for construct validity.

For example, a researcher developed a personality scale to measure several interpersonal response traits that education theorists had previously related to occupational preference. Testing the new scale against occupation preference would be evidence for construct validity.

To achieve construct validity, the researcher must have already determined the meaning of the measure by establishing what basic researchers call convergent validity and discriminate validity. Convergent validity is synonymous with criterion validity. The criterion may be a construct that one would logically expect to be associated with the new measure. Thus, to establish validity, the new measure should "converge" with other similar measures; a measure of a theoretical concept has convergent validity when it is highly correlated with different measures of similar constructs. A measure has discriminant validity when it has a low correlation with measures of dissimilar concepts. This is a complex method of establishing validity and of less concern to the applied researcher than to the basic researcher.

Reliability and Validity

The concepts of reliability and validity should be compared. Although a tailor, using a ruler, may obtain the same measurements over time, it is possible that he is using a bent ruler. A ruler, one that does not provide perfect accuracy, is not a valid measure. Thus reliability, although necessary for validity, is not in itself sufficient. A measure of a subject's physiological reaction to a reward (for example, pupil dilation on receiving a chocolate) may be highly reliable, but it does not necessarily constitute a valid measure of motivation.

The differences between reliability and validity can be illustrated by the rifle targets in Exhibit 10.10 An expert marksman fires an equal number of rounds with a century-old rifle and with a modern rifle. The shots from the century-old gun are considerably scattered, but the shots from the new gun are closely clustered. The variability of the old rifle, compared to the new weapon, indicates it is less reliable. Target C illustrates the concept of a systematic bias influencing validity, The new rifle is reliable (Little variance), but the sharpshooter's vision is hampered by glare from the sun. Although consistent, the marksman is unable to hit the bull's eye.

Validity	Description
Content validity	Does the measure adequately measure the concept?
Face validity	Do "experts" validate that the instrument measures what its name suggests it measures?
Criterion-related validity	Does the measure differentiate in a manner that helps to predict a criterion variable?
Predictive validity	Does the measure differentiate individuals in a manner as to help predict a future criterion?
Constructive validity	Does the instrument tap the concept as theorized?
Convergent validity	Do two instruments measuring the concept correlate highly?
Discriminant validity	Does the measure have a low correlation with a variable that is supposed to be unrelated to this variable?

Exhibit 10.10: Reliability and validity on target

Many quality checks on measurement involve examining two or more scoring or categorizations of the same cases, using similar statistical procedures. Exhibit 10.11 attempts to summarise the main situations in simple terms.

Exhibit 10.12 summarizes the kinds of formal check on quantification that can be done, as a function of what you have to have available, to perform them.

Sensitivity

The sensitivity of a scale is an important measurement concept, particularly when changes in attitudes or other hypothetical constructs are under investigation. Sensitivity refers to an instrument's ability to accurately measure variability in stimuli or responses. A dichotomous response category, such as "agree or disagree", does not reflect subtle

Substance	Facts	Quality control
The sets of scores are assumed to reflect:	**The means of quantification of each is meant to be:**	**As a check you aim to quantify:**
The same variable repeated in some way	Identical but for random variation within choices on facets (e.g. parallel items, different market of same sort, same setting on a different day)	How great an effect on measurement does this sort of intra-facet choice variation have? **Random measurement error**
The same variable or slightly different but heavily overlapping in substance school setting)	Identical but for a few facet choices altered (e.g. different kind of marker, open choice instead of m/c items, home versus	Do different choices like these alter the measurements obtained? **Systematic measurement error**
One variable and another overlapping in substance (dedicatory)	Quite different (e.g. native speaker rating instead of m/c test). Usually one is quicker and easier to do than the other or precedes and predicts it	Does the quick measure produce similar measurement to the other one? **Criterion validity**
One variable and others which together are components of complex invariable (complementary)	Could be similar means but different substance (e.g. counts of grammar errors, spelling errors and vocabulary errors	Do the components disagree with each other but agree with the whole as expected? **Construct validity - internal**
One variable and a different but related one (e.g. oral communicative competence and written communicative competence)	Could be similar or different facet choices, as well as different substance	Do the measures agree as expected? **Construct validity - convergent**

Exhibit 10.11: Checklist for use of correct measurements

Substance	Facts	Quality control
The sets of scores are assumed to reflect:	**The means of quantification of each is meant to be:**	**As a check you aim to quantify:**
One variable and a different and unrelated one (e.g. communicative competence and spelling)	Could be similar or different facet choices, as well, as different substance	Do the measures show no relationship, as expected **Construct validity - divergent**

Testing Goodness of Measures: Forms of Reliability and Validity

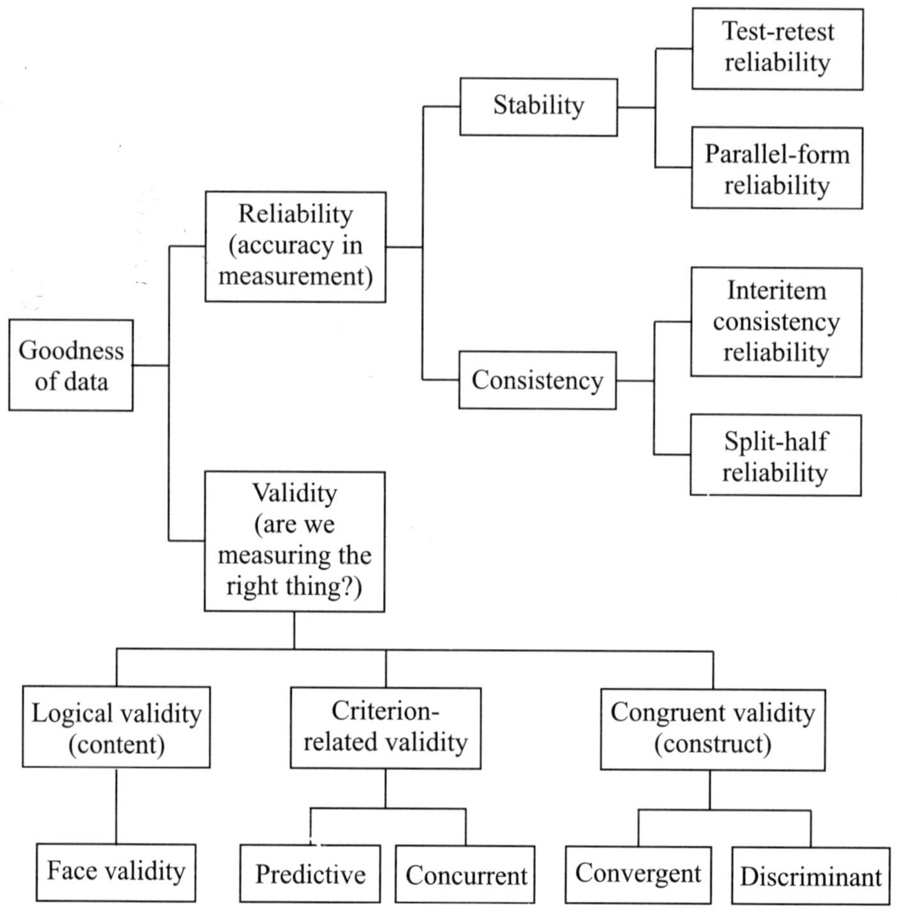

Exhibit 10.12: Formal check to be done by researcher

attitude changes. A more sensitive measure, with numerous items on the scale, may be needed. For example, adding "strongly agree", "mildly agree", "neither agree nor disagree," "mildly disagree" and strongly disagree" as categories increases a scale's sensitivity.

The sensitivity of a scale based on a single question or single item can also be increased by adding additional questions or times. In other words, because index measures allow for a greater range of possible scores, they are more sensitive than single-item scale

10.4 An Overview of the Stages of Data Analysis

The process of analysis begins after the data have been collected. During the analysis stage several interrelated procedure are performed to summarize and rearrange the data. The research steps related to processing and analysis are presented in Exhibit 10.3 We now turn our attention to this process of data reduction and analysis.

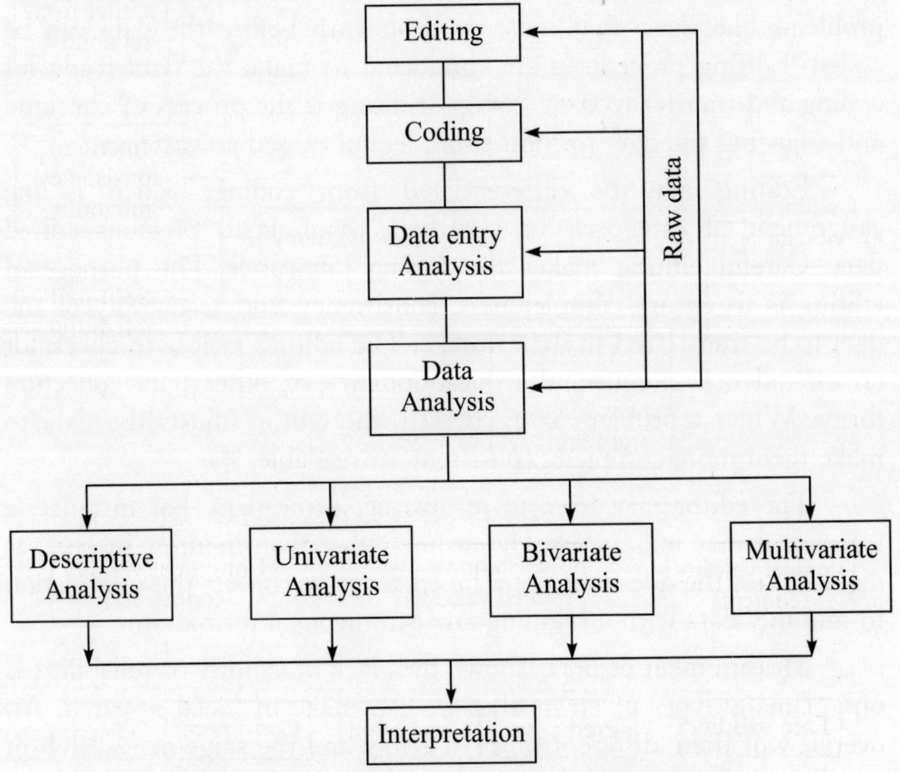

Exhibit 10.13: Overview of the stages in data analysis

The goal of most research is to provide information. Information refers to a body of facts that are in a format suitable for decision making, whereas data are simply recorded measures of certain phenomena. The raw data collected in the field must be transformed into information that will answer the researcher's question. The conversion of raw data into information requires that the data be edited and coded so the data may be transferred to a computer or other data storage medium.

If the database is large, there are many advantages to utilizing a computer. Assuming a large database, entering the data into the computer follows the coding procedure.

Occasionally, a fieldworker makes a mistake and records an impossible answer (e.g., birth year. 1843) or interviews an intelligible respondent (e.g., too young to qualify). Seemingly contradictory answers, such as "no automobile ownership" but an expenditure on automobile insurance, may appear on a questionnaire. There are many problems like these that must de dealt with before the data can be coded. Editing procedures are conducted to make the data ready for coding and transfer to data storage. Editing is the process of checking and adjusting the data for omissions, legibility, and consistency.

Editing may be differentiated from coding, which is the assignment of categories or classifying symbols to previous edited data. Careful editing makes the coding job easier. The purpose of editing is to ensure completeness, consistency, and readability of the data to be transferred to data storage. The editor's task is to check for errors and omissions on the questionnaires or other data collection forms. When a problem is discovered, the editor adjusts the data to make them more complete, consistent, or readable.

The editor may have to reconstruct some data. For instance, a respondent may indicate weekly income rather than monthly income, as requested on the questionnaire. The editor must convert the information to monthly data without adding any extraneous information.

Measurement error, as shown by a lack of validity or reliability, is one of many types of errors that we can make in social research. An overview of these different types of errors and the stage or research in which each is most likely to be made is provided in Exhibit 10.14.

Stage of Research	Type of Error
1. Concept and hypothesis construction (including choice of operational definitions)	Lack of face validity
2. Construction of research instrument (questionnaire)	Lack of reliability (faulty or ambiguous wording on question)
3. Sampling	Lack of external validity (sampling error)
4. Data gathering	Error due to failure to control a) Environment b) Personal characteristics of respondent (fatigue etc) c) Relationship between respondent and researcher d) Defect of research instrument (fautly sound recording, equipment failure, etc) e) Interviewer misunderstood answer
5. Coding	Incorrect information recorded due to missing data, illegible data, or simple coding error
6. Data analysis	Misuse of statistics or faulty interpretation of data

Exhibit 10.14: Types of errors

Even before research begins, the researcher can in a sense make an error by choosing an irrelevant or unimportant research topic. But by error we mean here the failure to collect the data accurately. In stage 1 of Exhibit 10.14 the construction of ambiguous and a poor operational definition of the concept can cause lack of face validity. In addition, ambiguous or poorly worded hypotheses may never be properly tested, ensuring total error and a worthless study, since the latter is dependent upon the former. But even it the concept is clear and well defined and the hypothesis is well written, poorly worded items in the measuring instrument (stage 2) can ensure lack of reliability if the respondent cannot understand them. Further, different respondents may understand the same question to mean different

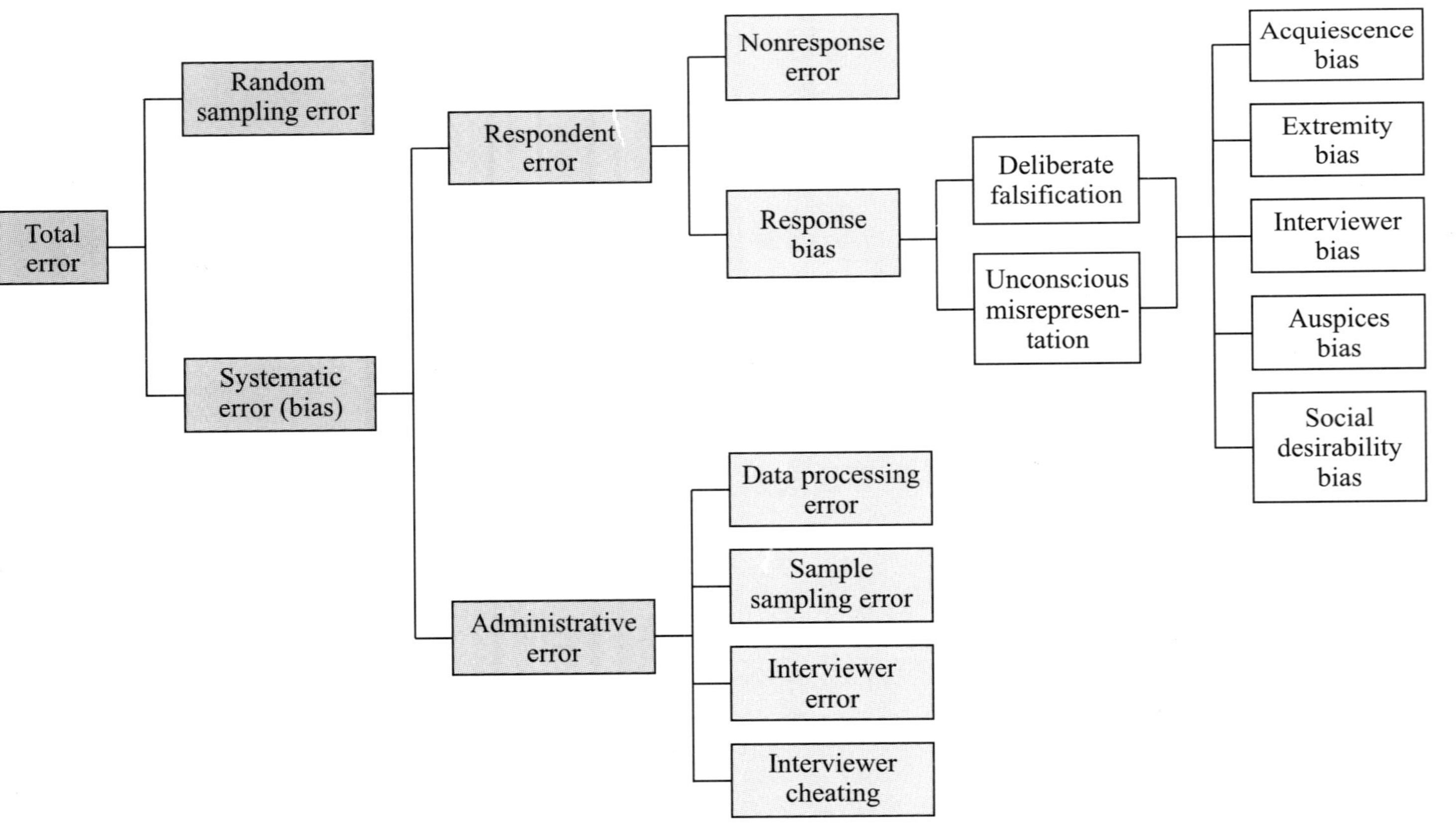

Exhibit 10.15: Tree diagram of total survey error

things, thus leading to invalid and unreliable data. In the third stage poor sampling procedures can lead to unrepresentative data, comes from such sources as samples bias, mistake in recording response, and non-responses from person not contacted or refusing to participate.

Sample bias is a persistent tendency for the results of a sample to deviate in one direction from the true value of the population parameter.

Most surveys try to portray a representative cross section of a particular target population. Even with technically proper random probability samples, statistical errors will occur because of chance variation. Unless sample size is increased, these statistical problems are unavoidable. However, **random sampling errors** can be estimated.

Systematic error results from some imperfect aspect of the research design or from a mistake in the execution of the research. Because all sources of error or biases are also called nonsampling errors. A sample bias exists when the results of a sample show a persistent tendency to deviate in one direction from the true value of the population parameter.

SUGGESTED REFERENCES

- Guildford, J.P. (1975). *Psychometric Methods*. Tata McGraw-Hill. 2nd edition.
- Kerlinger, F.N. 1986. Foundations of Behavioural Research. 3rd ed. New York. Rinehart and Winston.
- Plake, B.S. and Impara, J.C. (Eds.) 2003. Fifteenth mental measurement yearbook. Lincoln University of Nebraska Press: Buros Institute for Mental Measurements.
- Summers, Gene F. (Ed.) Attitude Measurement. Chicago: Rand McNally and Co. 1970.
- Thorndike, Robert L. and Hagen, Elizabeth P. Measurement and Evaluation in Psychology and Education. 4th ed. New York: John Wiley and Sons. 1977.

❖ ❖ ❖

Data Analysis

11.1 Introduction

Best and Kahn define statistics as "a body of mathematical techniques or processes for gathering, organizing, analyzing, and interpreting numerical data". Thus statistics are a set of mathematical techniques used to organize and manipulate data to answer questions and testing theories. If one does not understand the basics of a language, you will have problems conversing in it. Statistics is the language of the researcher. Educational researchers use statistics as a means of communication.

11.2 Reviewing Some Basic Terminology

The first portion of this chapter summarizes several key statistical concepts necessary for helping students selecting appropriate statistics. After selecting and computing a statistic, students need to develop the ability to interpret statistics. Many students, even those who received distinction in their statistics classes, will benefit from a quick review of the basic statistical concepts.

11.2.1 Descriptive and Inferential Statistics

The Statistical Abstract of India presents table after table of figures associated with the number of births, number of employees of each state and other data that the average person calls statistics. These are descriptive statistics. Another type of statistics, inferential statistics, is used to make an inference about a population from a sample.

There are two applications of statistics:

- *to describe characteristics of the population or sample, and*
- *to generalize from the sample to the population.*

Starting with a set of data, two main types of analysis emerge:

- Descriptive analysis
- Inferential analysis

Descriptive analysis refers to the transformation of the raw data into a form that will make them easy to understand and interpret. Describing responses or observations is typically the first form of analysis. The calculation of averages, frequency distributions, and percentage distribution is the most common form of summarizing data. As the analysis progresses beyond the descriptive stage, researchers generally apply the tools of inferential statistics.

Exhibit 11. 1 outlines the most common descriptive statistics associated with each type of scale. ***It is important to remember that all descriptive statistics appropriate for a lower order scale are also appropriate for higher order scales.***

Tabulation refers to the orderly arrangement of data in a table or other summary format. Counting the number of responses to a

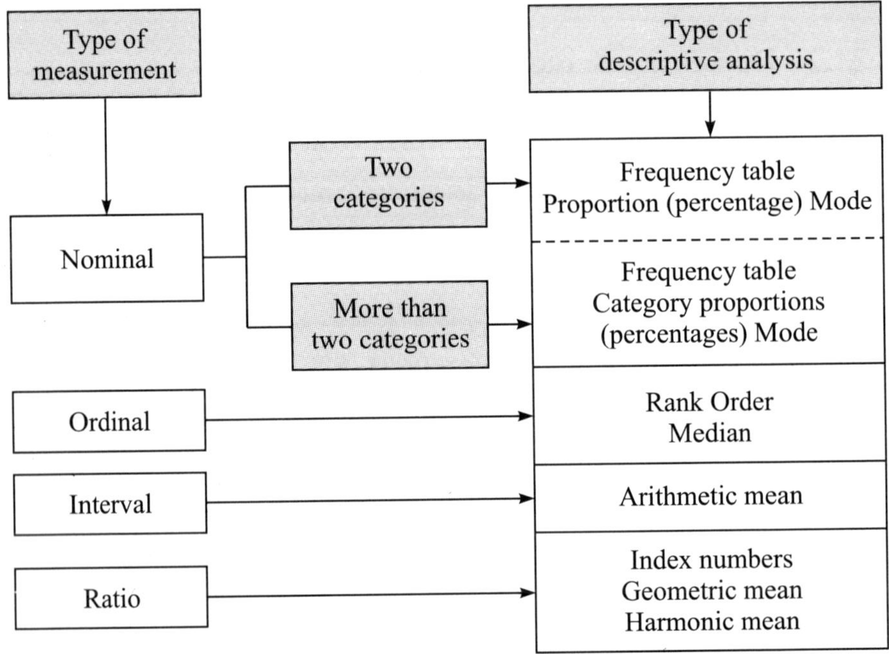

Exhibit 11.1: Descriptive statistics permissible with different types of measurements

question and putting them in a frequency distribution is ***a simple***, or ***marginal tabulation***. Simple tabulation of the responses or observations on a question-by-question or item-by-item basis provides the most basic form of information for the researcher and in many cases the most useful information. It tells the researcher how frequently each response occurs. This starting point for analysis requires the counting of responses or observations for each of the categories or codes assigned to a variable. Table 11.1 illustrates a frequency table. When this tabulation process is done by hand, it is called tallying. Large samples sizes generally require computer tabulation of the data.

Percentage

Whether the data is tabulated by computer or by hand, it is useful to have percentage and cumulative percentages as well as frequently distributions.

Table-11.1: Frequency table

Do you shop at Nilgiris?

Response	Frequency
Yes	330
No	120
Total	450

Tables11.2 and **11.3** shows how the variable (Psychology scores) has been grouped in order to reduce it to a manageable form.

Table-11.2: Scores obtained by 60 B.Ed. students in a psychology test in January 2000

48	71	52	53	36	41	69	58	47	60
53	29	41	72	81	37	43	58	68	42
73	62	59	44	51	53	47	66	59	52
34	49	73	29	47	16	39	58	43	29
46	52	38	46	80	58	51	67	54	57
58	63	49	40	54	61	58	66	47	50

Table-11.3: Frequency distribution of test scores

Scores in the Psychology Test (a)	No. of students (Frequency) (b)	Relative frequency (%) (c)
10 - 19	1	1.7
20 - 29	3	5.0
30 - 39	5	8.3
40 - 49	16	26.7
50 - 59	20	33.3
60 - 69	9	15.0
70 - 79	4	6.7
80 - 89	2	3.3
	60	100

Note that the table consists of the following:

- A number of groups (*Classes*), each of which covers a range of the psychology scores obtained in each *class interval* shown in (a)
- *Class frequencies* (the number of B.Ed students with psychology scores falling within each class interval) – shown in (b)
- *Relative frequencies*, in which each absolute frequency is shown as a proportion of the total frequency – shown in column (c)

11.2.2 Mathematical and Statistical Analysis of Scales

The type of scale that is utilized in research will determine the form of the statistical analysis. For example, a number of operations, such as calculation of the mean (mathematical average), can be conducted only if the scale is of an interval or ratio nature; they are not permissible with nominal or ordinal scales.

Exhibit 11.2 shows the appropriate descriptive statistics for each type of scale. The most sophisticated form of statistical analysis for nominal scale data is counting. Because numbers are merely labels for classification purpose, they have no quantitative meaning. The researcher tallies the frequency in each category containing the highest number of observations (individuals, objects, etc.). An ordinal

Type of Scale	Numerical Operation	Descriptive Statistics
Nominal	Counting	Frequency in each category/Percentage in each category/Mode
Ordinal	Rank ordering	Median Range Percentile ranking
Interval	Arithmetic operations on intervals between numbers	Mean Standard deviation Variance
Ratio	Arithmetic operations on actual quantities	Geometric mean Coefficient of variation

Note: All statistics that are appropriate for lower-order scales (nominal is the lowest) are appropriate for higher-order scales (ratio is the highest).

Exhibit 11.2: Descriptive statistics for types of scales

scale provides data that may be rank ordered from lowest to highest. Thus observations may be associated with a percentile rank such as the median. Because all statistical analysis appropriate for lower-order scales is appropriate for higher-order scales, an interval scale may be used as a nominal scale to uniquely classify or as an ordinal scale to preserve order. In addition, an interval scale's property of equal intervals allows researcher to compare differences between scale values and to perform arithmetic operations such as addition and subtraction. Numbers may be changed, but the numerical operations must preserve order and relative magnitudes of differences. The mean and standard deviation may be calculated when true interval-scale data are obtained. Ratio scales have all the properties of nominal, ordinal, and interval scales. In addition, researchers may make comparisons of absolute magnitude because the scale has an absolute zero point. Arithmetic operations on actual quantities are permissible. The ratio of scale values is meaningful.

Population Parameters and Sample Statistics

The primary purpose of inferential statistics is to make a judgment about the populations or the collection of all elements about which one seeks information. The sample is a subset or relatively small fraction of the total number of elements in the population. It is useful to distinguish between the data computed in the sample and the data or variable in the population. We use the term sample statistics to designate variable in the sample or measures computed from the sample data. The term population parameter is used to designate the variable or measured characteristics of the population. Sample statistics are used to make inferences about population parameters. In our notation, we will generally use Greek lower-case letters (m or s for example) to denote population parameters and we will use English letters to denote sample statistics (X or S, for example).

- Sample statistics refers to variables in a sample or measures computed from sample data.
- Population parameter refers to the variables in a population or measured characteristics of the population.

Making Data Usable

Frequency Distributions

Suppose a survey has been conducted for categorizing students in a district according to socioeconomic status. The data have been recorded on large number of questionnaires. To make the data usable this information must be organized and summarized. Constructing a frequency distribution, or frequency table, is one of the most common means of summarizing a set of data. The process begins by recording the number of times a particular value of a variable occurs. This is the frequency of that value. In our survey example, **Table 11.4** represents a frequency distribution of respondents' answers to the question asking what parents income is.

It is also quite simple to construct a distinction of relative frequency, or a percentage distribution. In **Table 11.5** the frequency of each value in **Table 11.4** has been divided by the total number of observations. Multiplying each of the relative class frequencies by 100 we convert them to percentages and obtain a frequency distribution of percentages.

Probability is the long-run relative frequency with which an event will occur. In inferential statistics, we use the concept of a probability distribution, which is conceptually the same as a percentage distribution except that the data have been converted into probabilities (see Table 11.6).

Table-11.4: Frequency distribution of income

Amount	Frequency (Number of people with income in Each Range)
Less than Rs.5,000	811
Rs.5,000 - Rs.9,999	530
Rs.10,000 - Rs.14,999	562
Rs.15,000 - Rs.19,999	718
Rs.20,000 or more	499
	3120

Table-11.5: Percentage distribution of income

Amount	Percent of People Making Deposits in Each Range
Less than 5,000	26%
5,000 - 9,999	17
10,000 - 14,999	18
15,000 - 19,999	23
20,000 or more	16
	100%

Table-11.6: Probability distribution of amount of income

Amount	Probability
Less than 5,000	.26
5,000 - 9,999	.17
10,000 - 14,999	.18
15,000 - 19,999	.23
20,000	.16
	1.00

Frequency distribution (table) is organizing a set of data by summarizing the number of times a particular value of a variable occurs.

Percentage distribution is the organization of a frequency distribution into a table (or graph) that summarizes percentage values associated with particular values of a variable.

Probability distribution is the organization of probability values associated with particular values of a variable into a table (or graph).

Proportions

When frequency distribution portrays only a single characteristic as a percentage of the total, the proportion of occurrence is defined. A proportion, perhaps the proportion of doctors in the workforce, may be expressed as a percentage, fraction, or decimal value. A proportion, such as the proportion to management faculty at a university, indicates the percentage of population elements that successfully meet some standard on the particular characteristic.

Proportion is the percentage of population elements that successfully meet some criterion.

11.2.3 Central Tendency

On a typical test, a certain teacher counts the scores of his students. He wishes to inspect the data to see the "centre" or "middle area" of the frequency distribution. There are three ways to measure this central tendency, and each of these "averages" has a different meaning.

11.2.3.1 Mean

The mean is an average that all of us have been exposed to. The mean is simply the arithmetic average, and it is a very common measure of central tendency. At this point it is appropriate to introduce the summation symbol, the Greek capital letter sigma (Σ).

Mean is a measure of central tendency: the arithmetic average.

A typical use is the following $\sum_{i=1}^{n} = X_i$

This is a shorthand way to write the sum:

$$X_1 + X_2 + X_3 + X_4 + X_5 + \dots + X_n$$

Researchers generally wish to know the population mean, m (lowercase Greek letter mu), which is calculated as follows:

$$\mu = \sum_{i=1}^{n} X_i / N$$

where N = number of observations in the population.

Often we will not have enough data to calculate the population mean μ, so we will calculate a sample mean, $\overline{X}$ (read as "X bar"), with the following formula:

$$\overline{X} = \sum_{i=1}^{n} X_i / N$$

n = number of observation in the sample.

Distinguishing between the symbols Σμ and X is necessary for an understanding of statistics. In our introductory discussion of the summation sign (Σ) we have used very detailed notation that included the subscript for the initial value (i) and final index value (n). However, from this point on, references to Σ will not use the subscript for the initial index value (i) and final index value (n) unless there is unique reason to highlight these index values.

11.2.3.2 Median

The next measure of central tendency, the median, is the midpoint of the distribution, or the 50th percentile. In other words, the median is the value below which half the values in the sample fall.

Median is a measure of central tendency that is the midpoint, the value below which half the values in a sample fall.

11.2.3.3 Mode

In statistics, the mode is the measure of central tendency that merely identifies the value that occurs most often.

Mode is a measure of central tendency, that is, the value that occurs most often.

11.2.4 Measures of Dispersion

The mean, median, and mode summarize the central tendency of frequency distributions. Calculating the dispersion of the data, or how the observations vary from the mean, is another way of summarizing the data. Consider, for instance, the 12-month inventory-level of two textbooks shown in Table 11.7. Both have a mean inventory level of 200 units, but the dispersion of observations for Textbook B is much greater than for Textbook A. There are several measures of dispersion.

11.2.4.1 The Range

The range is the simplest measure of dispersion. It is the distance between the smallest and the largest values of a frequency distribution. Thus for Textbook A the range is between 196 units and 202 units (6 units), whereas for Text book B the range is between 150 units and 261

Table 11.7: Inventory levels for textbook A and B (both average 200 units)

	Units of Text book A	Units of Text book B
January	196	150
February	198	160
March	199	176
April	200	181
May	200	192
June	200	200
July	200	201
August	201	202
September	201	213
October	201	224
November	202	240
December	202	261

units (111 units). The range does not take into account all the observations. It merely tells us about the extreme values of the distribution.

Range is the distance between the smallest and largest values of a frequency distribution.

It can be observed that for Textbook A the observations are close together and reasonably close to the mean.

The interquartile range encompasses the middlemost 50 percent of the observation, that is, the range between the bottom quartile (lowest 25 percent) and the top quartile (highest 25 percent).

11.2.4.2 Deviation Scores

A method of calculating how far away any observation is from the mean is to calculate individual deviation scores. To calculate a deviation from the mean, the following formula is used:

$$d_i = (X_i - \bar{X})$$

where

d_i = a deviation score.

If the value of 150 units for Textbook B represents the month of January, we calculate its deviation score to be –50. If the deviation scores are large, we will find that the distribution exhibits a broad spread.

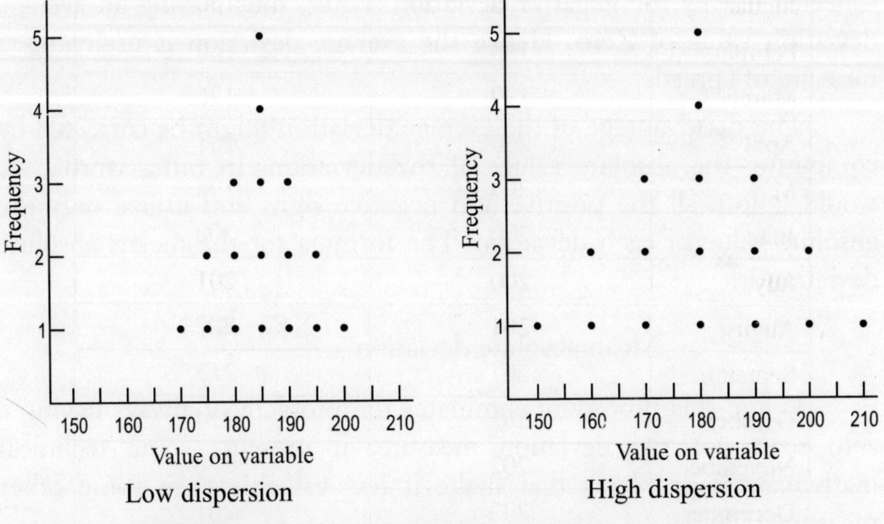

Exhibit 11.3: Low dispersion versus high dispersion

Why Use the Standard Deviation?

Statisticians have devised several quantitative indexes to reflect a distribution's spread or variability. ***The standard deviation is perhaps the most valuable index of spread or dispersion.*** Students often have difficulty understanding this concept. Learning about the standard deviation will be easier if we present several other measures of dispersion that may be used. Each of these has certain limitations that the standard deviation does not.

Standard deviation is a quantitative index of a distribution's spread or variability. It is the square root of the variance.

The average deviation is computed by calculating the deviation score of each observation value, that is, its difference from the mean, and summing up each deviation score, then dividing by the samples size (n):

$$\text{Average deviation} = \Sigma(X_i - \overline{X}) / n$$

Average deviation is a measure of dispersion that is computed by calculating the deviation score of each observation value, summing up each deviation score, and dividing by the sample size.

While this method of calculating a measure of spread seems of interest, it is never used. The positive deviation scores are always canceled out by the negative deviation scores, thus leaving an average deviation value of Zero. Hence the average deviation is useless as a measure of spread.

The disadvantage of the average deviation might be corrected by computing the absolute values of the deviation. In other words, we would ignore all the positive and negative signs and utilize only the absolute value of each deviation. The formula for the means absolute deviation is:

$$\text{Mean absolute deviation} = \frac{\Sigma X_i - \overline{X}}{n}$$

While this procedure eliminates the problem of always having a zero score for the deviation measure, it presents some technical mathematical problems that make it less valuable than some other measures.

Variance: There is another means of eliminating the sign problem caused by the negative deviations cancelling out the positive deviation. The procedure is to square the deviation scores. In the formula below, the mean squared deviation is given:

$$\textbf{Mean squared deviation} = \frac{\Sigma(X_i - \overline{X})^2}{n}$$

This measure is useful to describe the sample variability. However, we typically wish to make an inference about a population from the sample. The divisor n – 1 is used (rather than n) in most pragmatic research problems. This new measure of spread is called the sample variance, and the formula is given below:

$$\textbf{Variance, } S^2 = \frac{\Sigma(X_i - \overline{X})^2}{n-1}$$

The variance is a very good index of the degree of dispersion. The variance, S^2, will be equal to zero if and only if each and every observation in the distribution is the same as the mean. The variance will grow larger as the observations tend to differ increasingly from each other and from the mean.

Variance is a measure of variability or dispersion, the square root of which is the standard deviation.

Standard Deviation

While the variance is frequently used in statistics, it does have one major drawback. The variance reflects a unit of measurement that has been squared. For instance, in measures of sales (say,of the textbooks in Table 11.7) in a territory in rupees, then the mean number is reflected in rupees but the variance will be squared rupees. The square root of the variance for distribution is called the standard deviation. This eliminates the drawback of having the measures of dispersion in squared units rather than in the original measurement units.

The formula for the standard deviation is:

$$S = \sqrt{S^2} = \sqrt{\frac{\Sigma(X_i - \overline{X})^2}{n-1}}$$

Indexes of central tendencies, such as the mean, help us interpret the data. In addition, we wish to calculate a measure of variability that will give us a quantitative index of the dispersion of the distribution. We have looked at several measures of dispersion and have arrived at two adequate means of measuring dispersion: ***the variance and the standard deviation.***

At this point we should note that the formula is for the sample standard deviation, S. The formula for the population standard deviations, which is conceptually very similar, has not been given. Nevertheless, the reader should understand that s measures the dispersion in the population while S measures the dispersion in the sample.

11.3 The Normal Distribution

One of the most useful probability distributions in statistics is ***the normal distribution***, which is also called the normal curve. This mathematical and theoretical distribution describes the expected distribution of sample means and many other chance occurrences. The normal curve is bell-shaped and almost all (99 per cent) of its values are within +3 standard deviations from its mean. An example of a normal curve, the distribution of IQ scores, appears in Exhibit 11.4. In our examples a standard deviation for IQ equals 15. Notice that we can identify the proportion of the curve by measuring a score's (in this case standard deviation) distance from the means (100).

Normal distribution is a symmetrical, bell-shaped distribution that describes the expected probability distribution of many chance occurrences.

The Standardized normal distribution is a specific normal curve that has several characteristics:

1. It is symmetrical about its mean;
2. The means of the normal distribution identifies its highest point (the mode) and vertical line about which this normal curve is symmetrical;
3. The normal distribution has an infinite number of cases (it is a continuous distribution), and the area under the curve has a probability density equal to 1.0; and (4) the standardized normal distribution has a mean of zero and a standard deviation of 1. Exhibit11.5 illustrates these properties. Table 11.7 is a summary version of the typical standardized normal table found at the end of most statistics textbooks.

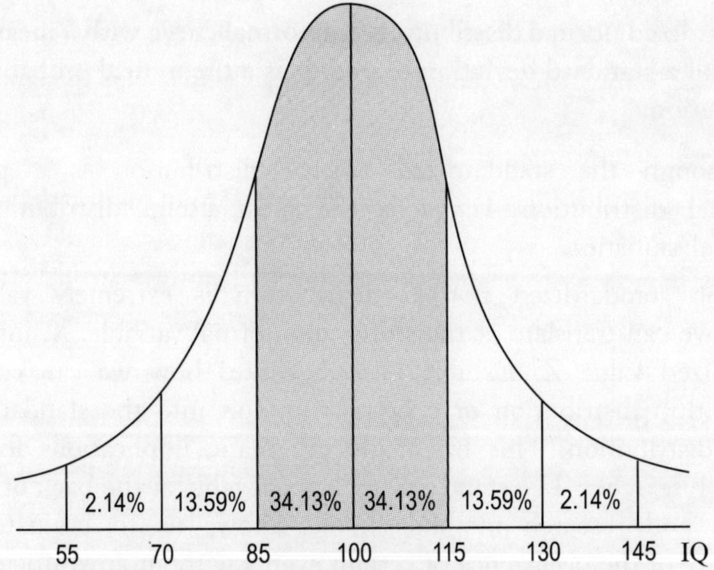

Exhibit 11.4: The normal distribution: An example of the distribution of Intelligence Quotient (IQ) scores

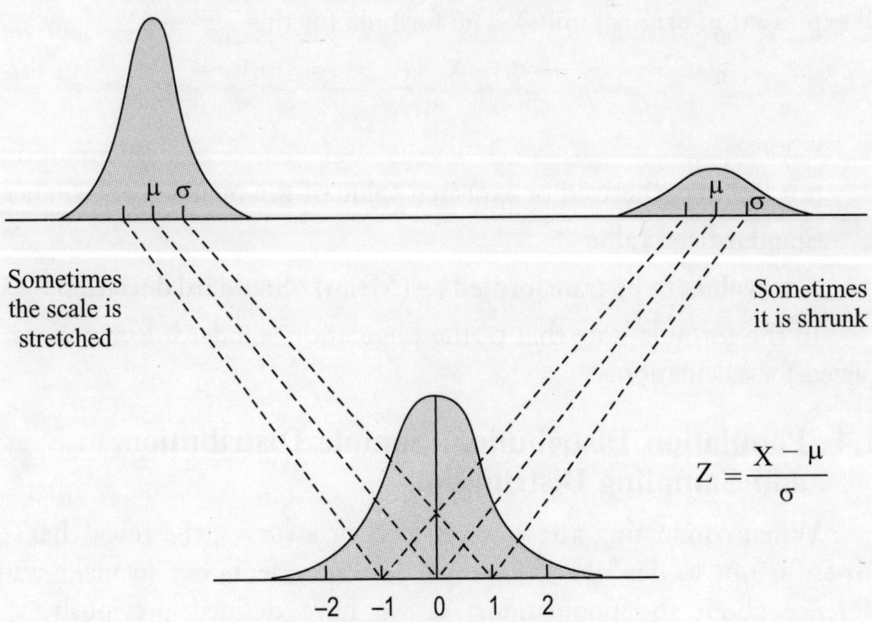

Exhibit 11.5: Linear Transformation of any Normal Variable into the Standardized Normal Variable

Standardized normal distribution is a normal curve with a mean of zero and a standard deviation of one. It is a theoretical probability distribution.

Though the standardized normal distribution is a purely theoretical distribution, yet it is the most useful distribution in inferential statistics.

The standardized normal distribution is extremely valuable because we can translate or transform any normal variable. X, into the standardized value Z. Exhibit 11.5 illustrates how we can convert either a thin distribution or a fat distribution into the standardized normal distribution. This has many pragmatic implications for the business researcher. The standardized normal table at the back of most statistics and research methods books allows us to evaluate the probability of the occurrence of certain events without any difficulty.

The computation of the standardized value, Z, of any measurement expressed in original units is simple. Subtract the mean from the value to be transformed and divide by the standard deviation (all expressed in original units). The formula for this

$$Z = \frac{X - \mu}{\sigma}$$

where

μ = the hypothesized or expected value of the mean.

Standardized value

= (values to be transformed) – (Mean) / Standard deviation.

In the formula note that σ, the population standard deviation, is utilized for calculation.

11.4 Population Distribution, Sample Distribution, and Sampling Distribution

When conducting a research project or a survey, the researcher's purpose is not to describe the sample of respondents but to make an inference about the population. As we have defined previously, a population or universe is the total set or collection of potential units for observation. The sample is a smaller subset of this population.

A frequency distribution of the population elements is called ***a population distribution.*** The population distribution has its mean and standard represented by the Greek letters μ and σ. A frequency distribution of a sample is called a *sample distribution*. The sample mean is designated X and the sample standard deviation is designated S. The concept of the population distribution and the sample distribution are relatively simple. However, we must now introduce another distribution, the sampling distributing of the sample mean.

Understanding the sampling distribution is the basis for understanding statistics. ***The sampling distribution is a theoretical probability distribution that in actual practice would be calculated.*** Assuming that the large number of samples were randomly selected, the sample means, Xs, could be arranged in a frequency distribution. Because different people or sample units will be selected in the different samples, the sample means will not be exactly equal. The shape of the sampling distribution is of considerable importance to statisticians. If the sample size is sufficiently large and if the samples were randomly drawn, the distribution of the mean will be approximately normally distributed.

A sampling distribution is a theoretical probability distribution that shows the functional relationship between the possible values of some summary characteristic of n cases drawn at random and the probability (density) associated with each value over all possible samples of size n from a particular population.

Sampling distribution is a theoretical probability distribution of all possible samples of a certain size drawn from a particular population. The sampling distribution's mean is called the ***expected values of the statistic.*** The expected values of the mean of the sampling distribution are equal to μ. The standard deviation of the sampling distribution of X is called the standard error of the mean (SX) and is approximately equal to

$$S_{\overline{X}} = \frac{\sigma}{\sqrt{n}}$$

Exhibit 11.7 shows the relationship among a population distribution, the sample distribution, and three sampling distribution of varying sample size.

Distribution	Mean	Standard Deviation
Population	μ	σ
Sample	$\overline{X}$	S
Sampling	$\mu_{\overline{X}} = \mu$	$S_{\overline{X}}$

Exhibit 11.6: Characteristics of three important distributions

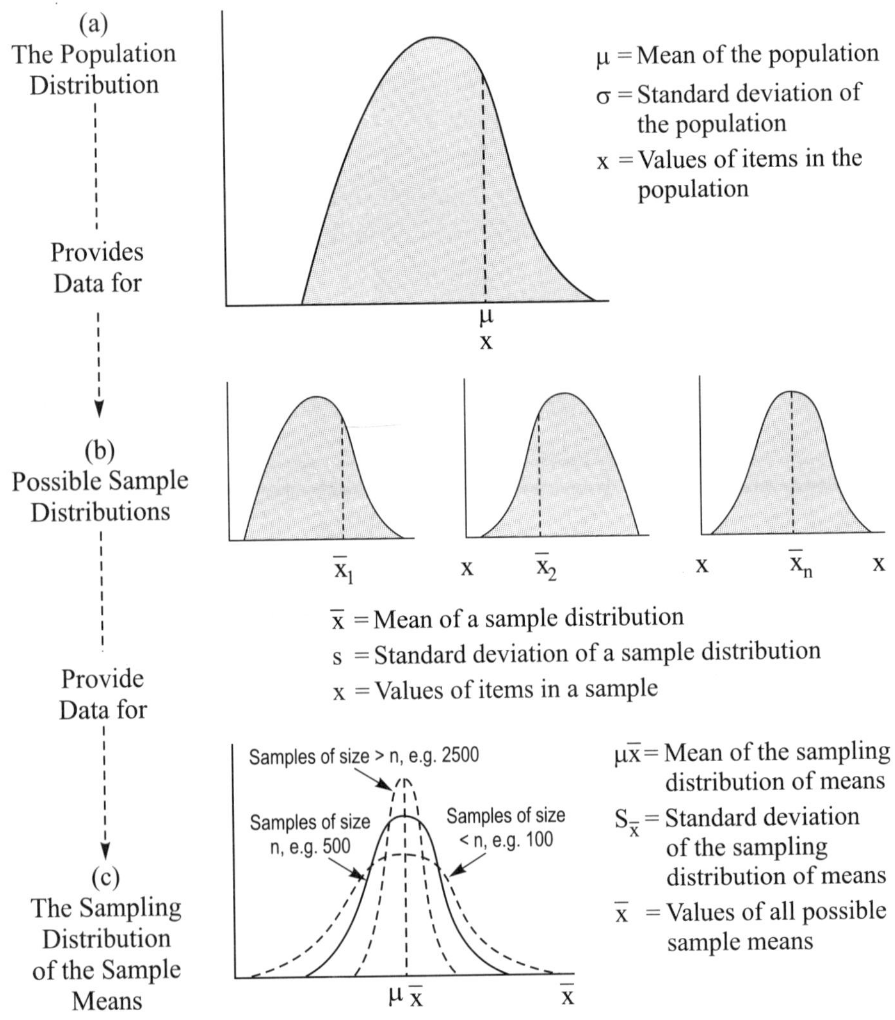

Exhibit 11.7: Schematic representation of the three fundamental types of distribution

In Part (a) of this exhibit we note that the population distribution is not a normal distribution.

In Part (b) we note that the sample distribution resembles the distribution of the population; however, there may be some differences.

In Part (c) we note that each of the sampling distributions is normally distributed and that the means of each of these sampling distributions are the same. It can be seen that as samples increase, the spread of these sample means around μ decreases. Thus with a larger samples size we will have a thinner sampling distribution.

Point estimate is an estimate of the population mean using a single value, usually the sample mean.

Confidence Interval

Confidence interval estimates is a specified range of numbers within which a population mean should lie. It is the set of acceptable hypotheses or the level of probability associated with an interval estimate.

If we specify a range of numbers or an interval within which the population mean should lie, we may be more confident that our inference is correct. Making a Confidence interval estimate is based on the knowledge that the confidence interval for $\mu = \overline{X} \pm$ a small sampling error. After calculating an interval estimate, we will be able to determine how probable it is that the population mean will fall within a range of statistical values.

The crux of the problem for the researcher is to determine how much random sampling error will be tolerated. In other words, what should the confidence interval be? How much of a gamble should be taken that m will be included in the range: 80 per cent, 90 percent, 99 per cent? The Confidence level is a percentage indicating the long-run probability that the results will be correct. Traditionally, researchers have utilized the 95 per cent confidence level. While there is nothing magical about the 95 per cent confidence level, it is useful to select 95 percent confidence level in our examples.

Confidence level is a percentage or decimal value that tells how confident a researcher can be about being correct. It states the long-run percentage of the time that a confidence interval will include the true population mean.

Calculating a Confidence Interval

The point estimate does not give us any information about the possible magnitude of random sampling error. The confidence interval gives an estimate plus or minus the estimated value of the population parameter. We may express the ideas of the confidence interval as:

$$\mu = \overline{X} \pm \text{a small sampling error}$$

More formally, assuming the researchers select a large sample (more than 30 observations), the small sampling error is equal to:

Small Sampling error = $Zc.\ell.S_{\overline{X}}$

where

$\overline{X}$ = sample mean

$Zc.\ell$ = value of Z, our standardized normal variable, at a specified confidence level (c.ℓ.)

$S_{\overline{X}}$ = standard error of the mean

The population of our estimate is indicated by the value of $Zc.\ell S_{\overline{X}}$. It is useful to define the range of possible random error, E, as follows:

Range of possible random error is the potential difference between a population mean and an observed value.

$E = Z_{c.\ell}S_{\overline{X}}$

Thus $\mu = \overline{X} \pm E$ or $\mu = \overline{X} \pm Z_{c.\ell}S_{\overline{X}}$

It should be noted that the confidence interval (+E) is always stated as half of the total interval.

The following is a step-by-step procedure for calculating confidence intervals:

1. Calculate X from the sample.
2. Assuming σ is unknown, we must estimate the population standard deviation by finding S, the sample standard deviation.

3. Estimate the standard error of the mean, utilizing the following formula:

$$S_X = \frac{S}{\sqrt{n}}$$

4. Determine the Z - values associated with the confidence level desired. The confidence level should be divided by 2 to determine what percentage of the area under the curve must be included on each side of the mean.
5. Calculate the confidence interval.

11.5 Sample Size

Random Sampling Error and Sample Size

When asked to evaluate a research project, most people, even those with little research training, will begin by asking. "How big was the sample?" Intuitively, we know that the larger the sample the more accurate the research. This is in fact a statistical truth; that is, *random sampling error varies with sample of different sizes. In statistical terms, increasing the samples size decreases the width of the confidence interval at a given confidence level.* When the standard deviation of the population is known, a confidence interval is calculated by using the following formula:

$$\overline{X} \pm Z\frac{S}{\sqrt{n}}$$

Observe that the equation for the plus or minus error factors in the confidence interval includes n, the sample size:

$$E = Z\frac{S}{\sqrt{n}}$$

If n increases, E is reduced. **Exhibit 11.8** illustrates that the confidence interval (or magnitude of error) decreases as the sample size, n, increases It is not necessary to take a census of all elements of the population to conduct an accurate study. The laws of probability provide investigators with sufficient confidence regarding the accuracy of collecting data from a sample. Knowledge of the theory concerning the sampling distribution helps researchers make reasonably precise estimates.

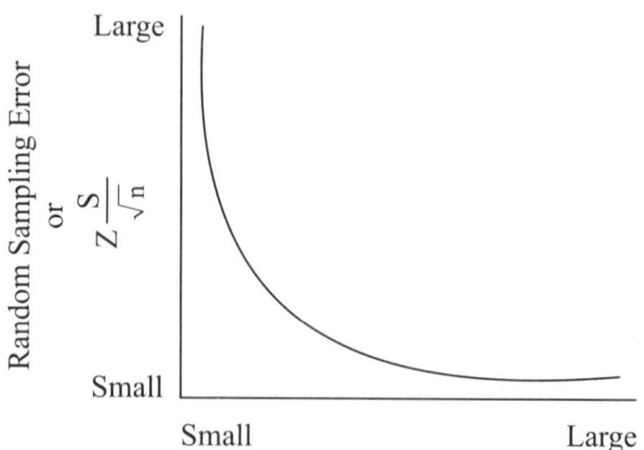

Exhibit 11.8: Relationship between sample size and error

Students familiar with the "law of diminishing returns" in economics will easily grasp the concept that increase in sample size reduces sampling error at a decreasing rate. For example, doubling the sampling from 1000 to 2,000 will reduce sampling error by only another ½ percentage point. More technically, ***random sampling error is inversely proportional to the square root of n.*** **Exhibit 11.8** gives an approximation of the relationship between sample size and error. Thus the main issue becomes one of determining the optimal sample size.

Determining Sample Size

Three factors are required to specify sample size:

a) Variance or heterogeneity of the population
b) Magnitude of acceptable error
c) Confidence level

Suppose a researcher wishes to find out whether nine-year-old girls are taller than four-year-old girls. Even with a very small sample size, the correct information will probably be obtained. Intuitively, we know this is logical. The logic is based on the fact that the determination of sample size depends on the research question and the variability within the sample.

The *variance* or *heterogeneity* of the population is the first necessary bit of information. In statistical terms, this refers to the standard deviation of the population parameter. Only a small sample is required if the population is homogeneous. For example, predicting the average age of the college students requires a smaller sample size than predicting the average age of people visiting the temple on a given Sunday afternoon.

The *magnitude of error*, or the confidence interval, is the second necessary bit of information. Defined in statistical terms as E, the magnitude of error (range of possible random error) indicates how precise the estimate must be. It indicates a certain precision level.

The third factor of concern is the confidence level. In educational research. we use the 95 per cent confidence level. This, however, is an arbitrary decision, based on convention. There is nothing sacred about the 0.5 chance level (i.e., the probability of the true population parameter being incorrectly estimated). Exhibit 11.9 summarizes the information required about these factors to determine sample size.

Variable	Symbol	Typical Source of Information
Standard deviation	S	Pilot study or rule of thumb
Magnitude of error	E	Judgement of experts or calculation (ZSx)
Confidence level	Zc.i.	Judgement of researcher

Exhibit 11.9: Statistical information needed to determine sample size

Estimating the Sample size

Once the above concepts are understood, determining the actual size for a simple random sample is quite easy. To estimate Sample Size, the researcher does the following:

1. Estimates the standard deviation of the population
2. Makes a judgement about the desired magnitude of error
3. Determines a confidence level.

Sample size is the size of a sample; the number of observations or cases specified by

1. the estimated variance of the population
2. the magnitude of acceptable error and
3. the confidence level.

The only problem is that of estimating the standard deviation of the population. Ideally, similar studies conducted in the past will be used as a basis for judging the standard deviation. In practice, a researcher without prior information conducts a pilot study for the purpose of estimating the population parameter so that another larger sample, with the appropriate sample size, may be drawn. This procedure is called ***sequential sampling*** because the researcher takes an initial look at the pilot study results before deciding on a larger sample that provides more precise information.

A rule of thumb for estimation of the value of the standard deviation is to expect it to be one-sixth of the range.

Analysis begins for most projects with some form of descriptive analysis to reduce the raw data into a summary format. Often researchers wish to go beyond the simple tabulation of frequency distributions and the calculation of averages: They frequently conduct univariate tests of statistical significance. The foundations of univariate statistical estimation of parameters involve hypothesis testing when the research focuses on one variable at a time.

11.6 Stating a Hypothesis

Let us recapitulate a few key definitions.

- **A hypothesis is an unproven proposition or supposition that tentatively explains certain facts or phenomena. It is a proposition that is testable.**
- **A null hypothesis is a statement about a status quo that asserts that any change from what has been thought to be true will be due entirely to random error.**
- **An alternative hypothesis is a statement indicating the opposite of the null hypotheses.**

Hypothesis Testing

We generally assign the symbol H_0 to the null hypothesis and the symbol H_1 to the alternative hypothesis. The purpose of hypothesis testing is to determine which of the two hypotheses is correct. The procedure of hypothesis testing is slightly more complicated than estimating parameters because the decision maker must make a choice between the two hypotheses.

Hypothesis – Testing Procedure

The process of hypothesis testing goes as follows.

- A statistical hypothesis is determined. Then we imagine what the sampling distribution of the mean would be if this hypothesis were a true statement of the nature of the population.
- An actual sample is taken and the sample mean (or appropriate statistic, if we are not concerned about the mean) is calculated. The difference between the sample mean and the population mean is examined to determine if the deviation between the obtained value of the sample mean and its expected value (based on the statistical hypothesis) would have occurred by chance alone, say 5 times out of 100, if the statistical hypothesis were true.
- Ask the question: "Has the sample mean deviated substantially from the mean of the hypothesized sampling distribution by a large enough value to conclude that this large a deviation would be somewhat rare if the statistical hypothesis were true. Before we can conclude that these results are improbable (or possibly probable), we must have some standard or decision rule to determine if, in fact, we should reject the null hypothesis and accept the alternative hypothesis. Statisticians have defined the decision criterion as the significance level.
- Set the decision criteria and significance level. The significance level is a critical probability in choosing between the hypothesis and the alternative hypothesis. The level of significance determines the probability level, say .05 or .01, which is to be considered too low to warrant support of the null hypothesis. On the assumption that the hypothesis being tested is true, if the probability of occurrence of the observed data is smaller than the level of significance, then the data suggest the null hypothesis should be rejected. In other words, there is evidence to support contradiction of the null hypothesis, which is equivalent to supporting the alternative hypothesis.

The terminology utilized in discussing confidence intervals identifies what is the confidence level or a confidence coefficient. The confidence interval may be regarded as the set of acceptable hypotheses or the level of probability associated with an interval estimate. However, when discussing hypothesis testing, statisticians change their terminology and call this the level of significance α (Greek letter alpha).

- Accept or reject the null hypothesis based on the decision criteria.

Example of Hypothesis Testing

Suppose that the ABC School is concerned about its image. One aspect of its image deals with the amount of co-operation within the school. In a personal interview, customers of the school parents, teachers, general public including Senior Citizens – were asked to indicate their perception of co-operation on a five point scale, where 1 indicates very unco-operative and 5 indicates very co-operative. The scale was assumed to be an interval scale, and experience has shown that previous distribution of this attitudinal measurement for assessing image of a school (co-operation) was approximately normal. Suppose the researcher entertains the hypothesis that the perception of co-operation of the school is neither very co-operative nor very unco-operative. The researcher formulates the null hypothesis that the mean is equal to 3.0:

$$\boxed{H_0 : \mu = 3.0}$$

The alternative hypothesis is that the mean does not equal 3.0.

$$\boxed{H_1 : \mu \neq 3.0}$$

Next, the researcher must decide upon a region of rejection. Exhibit 11.10 shows a sampling distribution of the mean assuming the null hypothesis, that is, assuming μ = 3.0. The shaded area shows the region of rejection when α = .025 in each tail of the curve. In other words, the region of rejection shows those values that are very unlikely to occur if the null hypothesis is true, but relatively probable if the alternative hypothesis is true. The values within the unshaded areas are called acceptable at the .95 percent confidence level (or 5 percent significant level, .05 alpha level), and if we find that our sample mean lies within this region of acceptance, we would conclude that the null hypothesis is true. More precisely, we fail to disprove the null hypothesis.

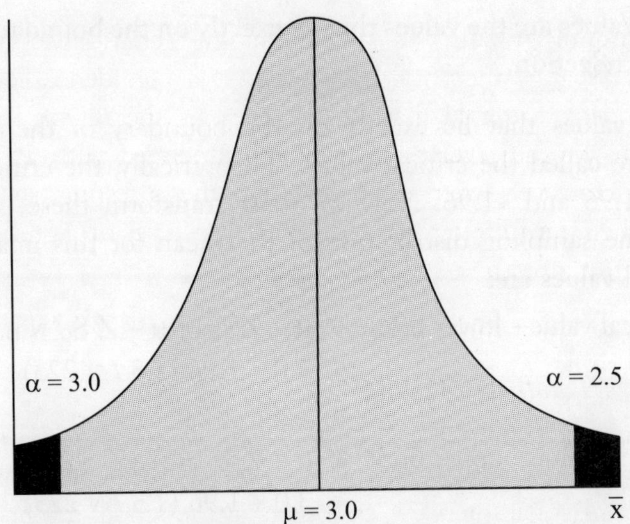

Exhibit 11.10: A sampling distribution of the mean assuming μ = 3.0

The range of acceptance

- *Identifies those acceptable values with a difference between the hypothesized mean in the null hypothesis and*
- *Shows a difference in this range to be so small that we would conclude that this difference was due to random sampling error rather than a false null hypothesis.*

In our example the ABC School hired research consultants who collected a sample of 225 interviews. The mean score on the five-point scale, X, equated 3.78. If a is known, then this is utilized in the analysis; however, this is rarely true, and was not true in this case. The sample standard deviation was S = 1.5. Now we have enough information to test the hypothesis.

The researchers decided that the decision rule would be to set the significance level at the .05 level. This means that in the long run the probability of making an erroneous decision when H_0 is true will be fewer than 5 times in 100(.05). From the standardized normal distribution table, the researchers find that the Z-score of 1.96 represented a probability of .025 that a sample mean will lie above 1.96 standard errors from μ. Likewise, the table shows that about .025 of all sample means will fall below −1.96 standard errors from μ.

Critical Values are the values that lie exactly on the boundary of the region of rejection.

The values that lie exactly on the boundary of the region of rejection are called the critical values. Theoretically, the critical values are Z = −1.96 and +1.96. Now we must transform these critical Z-values to the sampling distribution of the mean for this image study. The critical values are:

$$\text{Critical value - lower limit} = \mu - ZSx \text{ or } \mu - Z\, S / \sqrt{n}$$
$$= 3.0 - 1.96\,(1.5 / \sqrt{225})$$
$$= 2.804$$

$$\text{Critical value - upper limit} = \mu + ZSx \text{ or } \mu + Z\, S / \sqrt{n}$$
$$= 3.0 + 1.96\,(1.5 / \sqrt{225})$$
$$= 3.196$$

Based on the survey, $\overline{X}$ = 3.78. In this case the sample mean is contained in the region of rejection (Exhibit 11.11). Thus, since the sample mean is greater than the critical value, 3.196, the researchers

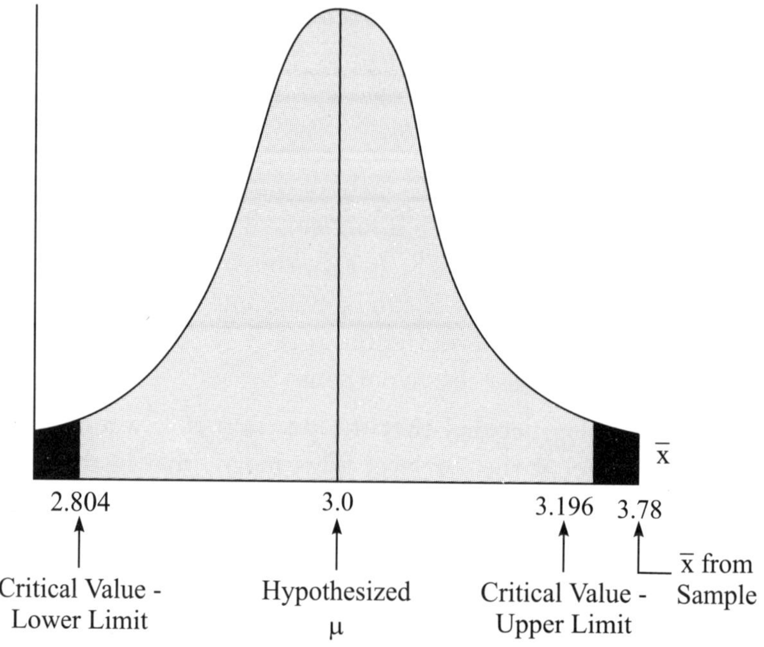

Exhibit 11.11: The sampling distribution of X under the hypothesis of μ = 3.0

say that the sample result is statistically significant beyond the .05 level. In other words, fewer than 5 of each 100 samples would show results that deviate this much from the null hypothesis, when in fact the H_0 is actually true.

What does this mean to the management of the ABC School? The results indicate that customers – parents, community, students and the public – believe the image is friendly. It is unlikely (less than 5 times in 100) that this result would occur because of random sampling error. It means that the school should worry about factors other than the friendliness of the service personnel.

An alternative way of testing the hypothesis is to formulate the decision rule in terms of the Z-statistic. Using the formula below, we can calculate the observed value of the Z-statistic, given a certain sample mean, X:

$$Z_{obs} = \overline{X} - \mu \sqrt{S\overline{x}}$$

$$Z_{obs} = 3.78 - \mu \sqrt{S\overline{x}}$$

$$Z_{obs} = 3.78 - 3.0 / .1 = .78 / .1 = 7.8$$

In this case the Z-value is 7.8, and we find that we have met the criterion of statistical significance at the .05 level. As a matter of fact, this is statistically significant at the .000001 level.

11.7 Type I and Type II Errors

Hypothesis testing, as we have previously stated, is based on probability theory. Because we cannot make any statement about a sample with complete certainty, there is always the chance that an error can be made. In fact, the researcher runs the risk of committing two types or errors. **Exhibit 11.12** summarizes the state of affairs in the population and the nature of Type I and Type II errors. The four possible situations in the table result because the null hypothesis can be either true or false, and the statistical decision will be either to accept or to reject the null hypothesis.

If the decision has been made to reject the null hypothesis and, in fact, the null hypothesis is true, we have made what is called a Type I error. A Type I error has the probability of alpha (a), the level of

State of Null hypothesis	Decision	
In the population	**Accept Ho**	**Reject Ho**
Ho is true	Correct–no error	Type 1 error
Ho is false	Type II error	Correct–no error

Exhibit 11.12: Type I and Type II errors in hypothesis testing

Type I and Type II Errors in the Legal Profession

Although most attorneys and judges do not concern themselves with the statistical terminology of Type I and Type II errors, they do follow this logic. For example, our legal system is based on the concept that a person is innocent until proven guilty. Assume that the null hypothesis is that the person in innocent. If we make a Type I error, we send an innocent person to prison. Our legal system takes many cautions to avoid Type I errors. A person is innocent until proven guilty. A Type II error would occur when a guilty party is set free (the null hypothesis is accepted). Our society places such a high value on avoiding Type I errors that Type II errors are more likely to occur.

statistical significance that the decision maker has set up. Simply put, Type I error occurs when the researcher concludes that there is a statistically significant difference when, in reality, one does not exist.

Type I error is an error caused by rejecting the null hypothesis when it is true.

Type II error is an error caused by failing to reject the null hypothesis when the alternative hypothesis is true.

If the alternative hypothesis is, in fact, true and the null hypothesis is actually false but the decision maker concludes that we should not reject the null hypothesis, then we have made what is called a Type II error. The probability of making this incorrect decision is called beta (β). No error is made if the null hypothesis is true and the decision is made to accept it. A correct decision is also made if the null hypothesis is false and the decision is made to reject the null hypothesis.

Unfortunately, without increasing sample size, the researcher cannot simultaneously reduce Type I and Type II errors because there is an inverse relationship between these two types of errors. Thus reducing the probability of a Type II error increases the probability of a Type I error.

Choosing the Appropriate Statistical Technique

Now that one statistical technique for hypothesis testing has been illustrated, it should be noted that there are a number of appropriate statistical techniques to assist the researcher in interpreting data.

The choice of the method of statistical analysis depends on

- the type of question to be answered,
- the number of variables, and
- the scale of measurement.

Type of Question to Be Answered

The type of question the researcher is attempting to answer is a consideration in the choice of statistical techniques. For example, a researcher may be concerned about the central tendency of a variable or the distribution of that variable. Comparison of two divisions' average sales will require a t-test of two means, whereas a comparison of the quarterly sales distributions over a year's period will require a chi-square test.

The choice of research design and the type of data to collect should anticipate the method of statistical analysis. Once the data are collected, the initial orientation toward analysis of the problem is reflected in the research design.

Number of Variables

The number of variables that will be simultaneously investigated is a primary consideration in the choice of statistical techniques.

Univariate data analysis is conducted when the researcher assesses the statistical significance of a hypothesis about a single variable.

Bivariate data analysis refers to data analysis and hypothesis testing when the investigation concerns simultaneous investigation of two variables using tests of differences or measures of association between two variables at a time.

Multivariate data analysis is the statistical methods that allow the simultaneous investigation of more than two variables.

11.8 Scale of Measurement

The scale of measurement on which the data are based or the type of measurement reflected in the data determines the permissible statistical technique and the appropriate empirical operation that may be performed (see **Exhibit 11.13**). Testing a hypothesis about a mean, as we have just discussed, requires interval – or ratio – scaled data. Suppose a researcher is concerned with a nominal scale that identifies members versus non-members of the Science club. The researcher must use the modes as the measure of central tendency, because of the type of scale.

In other situations the median may be used as the average, or percentiles may be used as measures of dispersion because the data are measured on an ordinal scale.

Type of Scale	Measure of Central Tendency	Measure of Dispersion
Nominal	Mode	None
Ordinal	Median	Percentile
Interval or ratio	Mean	Standard deviation

Exhibit 11.13: Measures of central tendency and dispersion permissible with each type of measurement scale

11.9 Parametric versus Non-parametric Hypothesis Tests

The terms parametric statistics and non-parametric statistics refers to the two major groupings of statistical procedures. The major distinction between these two groups of procedures lies in the underlying assumptions about the data to be analyzed. *When the data are interval or ratio-scaled and the samples size is large, parametric*

Application	Parametric Test	Non-parametric Test	Efficiency Rating Non-parametric Test with Normal Population
Matched pairs of sample data	T test or Z tests	Sign Test	0.63
		Wilcoxon signed ranks test	0.95
Two independent samples	T test or Z test	Wilcoxon rank sum test	0.95
Several independent samples	ANOVA (F test)	Kruskal-Wallis test	0.95
Correlation	Linear correlation	Rank correlation test	0.91
Randomness	No parametric test	Runs test	-

Exhibit 11.14: Comparison of efficiency of parametric and non-parametric tests

statistical procedures are appropriate. These procedures are based on the assumption that the data in the study are drawn from populations with normal (bell-shaped) distributions and/or normal sampling distribution. *When researchers do not make this assumption of normality, it is appropriate to use non-parametric methods.* When data are either ordinal or nominal, it is generally inappropriate to make the assumption that the sampling distribution is normal (thus non-parametric statistics are referred to as distribution-free).

11.9.1 Non-Parametric Tests

Parametric tests require assumptions about the populations involved (such as normally distributed). Non-parametric or distribution free tests do not make such assumptions.

Advantages of Non-parametric Tests

- Non-parametric tests can be applied to more situations than parametric tests, especially as non- parametric methods do not require the data to be normally distributed.

- Non-parametric tests can be used for categorical data (nominal and ordinal).
- Computations are often easier than the parametric tests.

Disadvantages of Non-parametric Tests

- Non-parametric tests are less sensitive (less powerful) than parametric tests (larger differences are needed before the null hypothesis is rejected).
- Non-parametric tests waste information. Numerical information is often reduced to ranks or signs.
- Non-parametric tests are less efficient IF the assumptions for parametric tests are made.

Research problem	Statistical question to be asked	Possible test of statistical significance
Interval or Ratio Scale Compare actual and hypothetical values of average salary	Is the sample mean significantly different from the hypothesized population mean?	Z - test (if sample large) t -test (if sample is small)
Ordinal Scale Compare actual and expected evaluations	Does the distribution of scores for a scale with the categories excellent, good, fair, and poor differ from the expected distribution?	Chi-square test
Determine ordered preferences for all subjects in a class	Does a set of rank orderings in a sample differ from an expected hypothetical rank ordering?	Kolmogorov-Smirnov test
Nominal Scale Identify sex of key teachers	Is the number of female staff members equal to the number of male staff members?	Chi-square test
Indicate percentage of key teachers who are male	Is the proportion of male teachers the same as the hypothesized proportion?	t-test of a proportion

Exhibit 11.15: Samples of selecting the appropriate univariate statistical method

Data analysis of both nominal and ordinal scales typically uses non-parametric statistical tests. If an investigator has two interval – or ratio-scaled measures, it is appropriate to use parametric tests to make a comparison of the intervals. Among the possible statistical tests is Z-test (or t-test) for a hypothesis about a mean, product-moment correlation analysis, and analysis of variance tests.

Exhibit 11.15 presents some guidelines for selecting the appropriate univariate statistical method. The table is meant to illustrate that there are a number of statistical techniques that vary according to the properties of the scale. Further, similar tables showing examples of the selection of appropriate bivariate and multivariate statistical techniques will be shown in the next section. The appropriate techniques will vary according to both the properties of the scale and the number of variables investigated.

11.10 The t-Distribution

t-distribution: a family of symmetrical, bell-shaped distributions with a mean of zero and a unit standard deviation, used when the population standard deviation is unknown or when testing a hypothesis with a small sample size.

There are a number of situations where researchers wish to test a hypothesis concerning the population mean with a sample size that is not large enough to be approximated by the normal distribution. In situations where the sample size is small ($n \leq 30$) and the population standard deviation is unknown, we use the t-distribution (also called the ***student's t-distribution***). The t-distribution, like the standardized normal distribution, is a symmetrical, bell-shaped distribution with a mean of zero and standard deviation of 1. When sample size (n) is larger than 30, the t-distribution and Z-distribution may be considered to be almost identical. Since the t-distribution is contingent on sample size, there is a family of t-distribution. More specifically, the shape of the t-distribution is influenced by its degrees of freedom (df.). Exhibit 11.16 illustrates t-distributions for 1, 2, 5, and in infinite number of degrees of freedom.

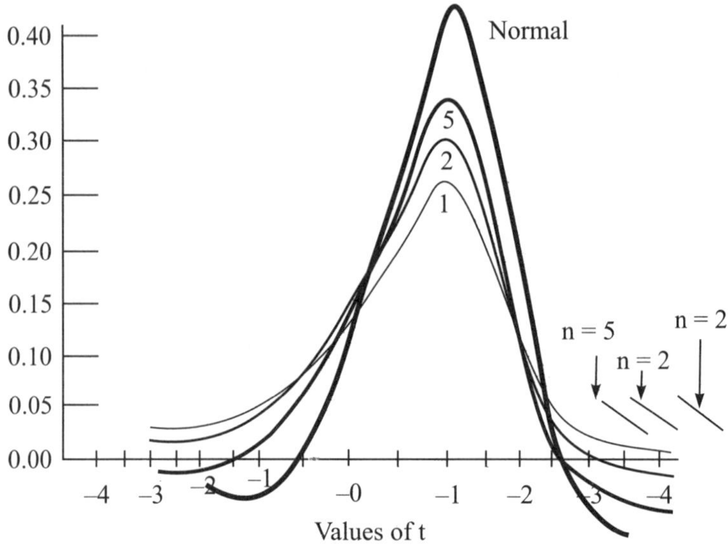

Exhibit 11.16: t-distribution for 1, 2, 5, and infinite number of degrees of freedom

The number of degrees of freedom (df) is equal to the number of observations minus the number of constraints or assumptions needed to calculate a statistical term.

The researcher asked two questions whether the Z-distribution of the t-distribution is the more appropriate for calculating a confidence interval or conducting at test of statistical significance.

- Is the population standard deviation s known?

  If the answer is *yes*, the ***Z-distribution*** is appropriate.

- If σ is unknown is the sample size greater than 30?

  If the answer is ***no***, the ***t-distribution*** should be used.

  If it is *yes*, the ***Z-distribution*** may be used because as sample size increases, the t-distribution becomes increasingly similar to the Z-distribution.

Calculating a confidence Interval Estimate using the t-Distribution

$S_{\overline{X}}$ = standard error of the mean

S = sample standard deviation

n = sample size

The step-by-step procedure for calculating the confidence interval is:

1. Calculate X from the sample
2. Since σ is unknown, estimate the population standard deviation by finding, S, the sample standard deviation.
3. Estimate the standard error of the mean using the following formula:

$$S_{\overline{X}} = \frac{S}{\sqrt{n}}$$

4. Determine the t-values associated with the confidence level desired. To do this, go to Table 3 in the Appendix of Statistical Tables. Although the t-table provides information similar to that in the Z-table, it is somewhat different. The t-table format emphasizes the chance of error or significance level rather than the 95 per cent chance of including the population mean in the estimate.
5. Look under the .05 column for two-tailed tests at the row in which degrees of Freedom (df) equal the appropriate value (n–1).
6. Calculate the confidence interval.

11.11 Chi-Square Test for Goodness of Fit

The chi-square χ^2 test allows us to test for significance in the analysis of frequency distributions. Thus categorical data on variables such as sex, education, or dichotomous answers may be statistically analyzed. Suppose, for example, that we wish to test the null hypothesis that the number of students aware of a certain website equals the number unaware of the website. The logic inherent in the test allows us to compare the observed frequencies (Oi) with the expected frequencies (Ei) based on our theoretical ideas about the population distribution or our presupposed proportions. The technique tests whether the data come from a certain probability distribution. It tests the "goodness of fit" of the observed distribution with the expected distribution.

Table 11.8 shows one-way frequency table to test the null hypothesis H0 that the number of students aware of a certain website equals the number unaware of the website.

Table-11.8: One-way frequency table

Awareness of website	Frequency
Aware	60
Unaware	40
	100

Calculation of the Univariate χ^2

Calculation of the chi-square statistic allows us to determine if the difference between the observed frequency distribution and the expected frequency distribution can be attributed to sampling variation. The steps in this process are:

1. Formulate the null hypothesis and determine the expected frequency of each answer.
2. Determine the appropriate significance level.
3. Calculate the χ^2 value the observed frequencies from the sample and expected frequencies.
4. Make the statistical decision by comparing the calculated χ^2 and value.

To analyze the website awareness data in Table 11.17 we start with the null hypothesis suggesting that the number of students aware of the website will equal the number of students unaware of it. Thus the expected probability of each answer (aware or unaware) is 0.5; in a sample of 100, 50 people would be expected to respond yes, or be aware, and 50 would be expected to respond no, or be unaware. After we have determined that the chi-square test is appropriate at the. 05 level of significance (or some other probability level), the chi-square statistic may be calculated using the formula:

$$\chi^2 = \frac{\Sigma(O_i - E_i)^2}{E_i}$$

where

χ^2 = chi-square statistic

O_i = observed frequency in the i th cell

E_i = expected frequency in the i th cell

The chi-square test of significance is useful as a tool to determine whether or not it is worth the researcher's effort to interpret a contingency table. A significant result of this test means that the cells of a contingency table should be interpreted. A non-significant test means that no effects were discovered and chance could explain the observed differences in the cells.

11.12 Hypothesis Test of a Proportion

The population proportion (π) can be estimated on the basis of the sample proportion (P). Researchers often test univariate statistical hypotheses about population proportions. The procedure for the hypothesis test of a proportion is conceptually similar to hypothesis testing when the mean is the characteristic of interest. However, the formulation of the standard error of the proportion is mathematically different.

11.13 What is the Appropriate Test of Differences?

One of the most frequently tested hypotheses states that two groups are different with respect to a certain behaviour, characteristic, or attitude, For example, in the classical experimental design, researchers conduct tests of differences between subjects assigned to the experimental group and subjects assigned to the control group. Researchers may be interested in determining if males and females perform a task or hold an attitude with the same frequency. ***In statistical terminology the null hypothesis is that the two groups are the same.***

Exhibit 11.17 illustrates that both the type of measurement and the number of groups to be compared influence the type of test of ***bivariate statistics.*** Often researchers are interested in testing differences in mean scores between groups or in comparing how two groups' scores are distributed across possible response categories. Construction of contingency tables and chi-square analysis is a procedure for comparing the distribution of group with the distribution of another group. This is a good starting point for testing of differences.

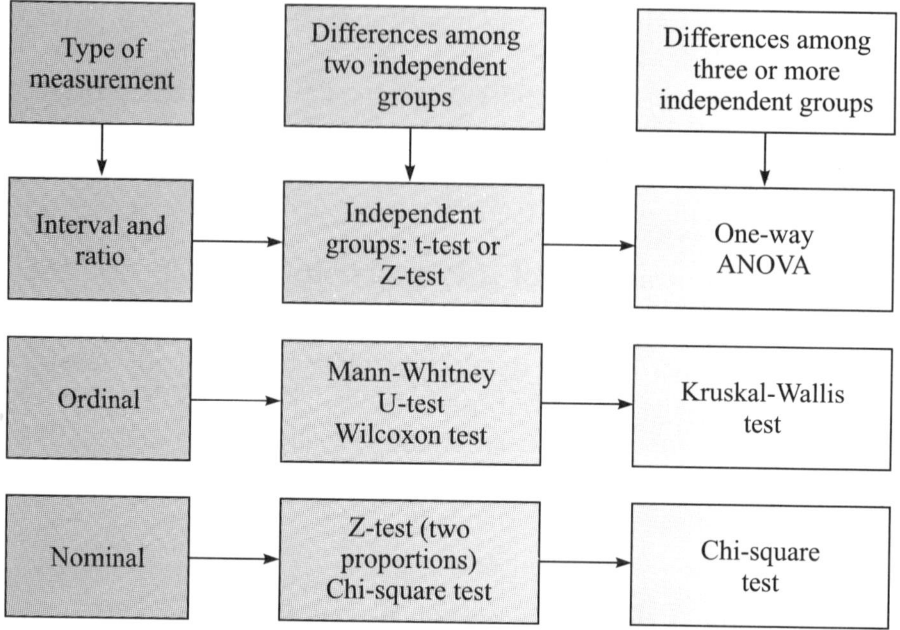

Exhibit 11.17: Common bivariate tests of differences

11.14 Cross-Tabulation Tables: Using the Chi-Square Test for Goodness of Fit

One of the simplest techniques for describing sets of relationships is the cross-tabulation. A cross-tabulation, or contingency table, is a joint frequency distribution of observations on two or more sets of variables. This generally means that tabulation of subgroups will be conducted for purposes of comparison. The chi-square distribution provides a means for testing the statistical significance of contingency tables. This allows us to test differences in two groups' distributions across categories.

Example

Chi-Square Test: Differences among Groups

The Situation:

A survey among BJP Congress and Independents asked: "How often do you contribute money to candidates of an opposition party?"

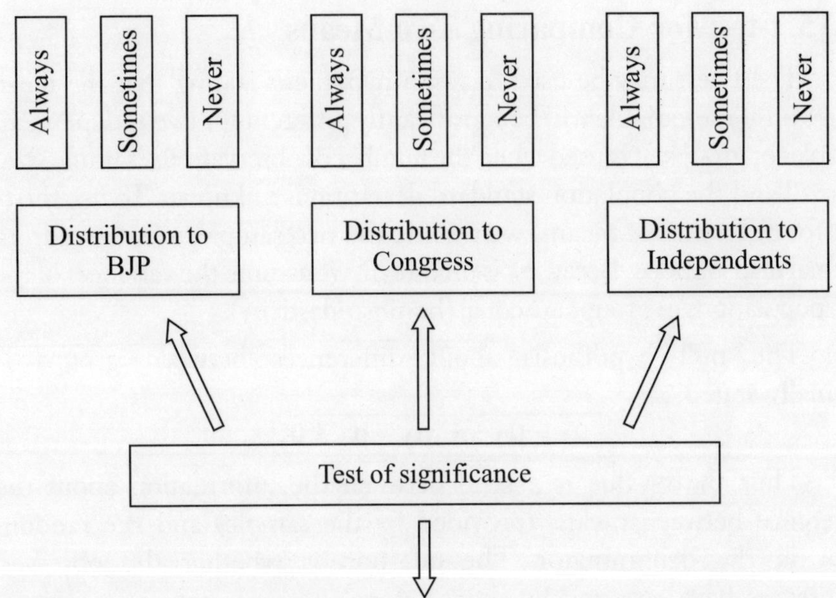

Questions to be answered:

1. Is the difference between the distributions statistically significant?
2. If is statistically significant, is the nature of the difference in distributions of any managerial value?

The logic involved in the chi-square (χ^2) test is that of comparing the observed frequencies (O_i) with the expected frequencies (E_i). It tests the "goodness of fit" of the observed distribution with the expected distribution.

$$\chi^2 = \frac{\Sigma(O_i - E_i)^2}{E_i}$$

where

χ^2 = chi-square statistic

O_i = observed frequency in the ith cell

E_i = expected frequency in the ith cell

Again, as in the univariate chi-square test, a frequency count of data that nominally identify or categorically rank groups is acceptable for the chi-square test for contingency tables. Both variables in the contingency table will be categorical variables rather than interval – or ratio – scaled continuous variables.

11.15 t-test for Comparing Two Means

The t-test may be used to test a hypothesis stating that the mean scores on some variable will be significantly different for two independent samples or groups. It is used when the number of observations (sample size) is small and the population standard deviation is unknown. To use the t-test for difference of means, we assume the two samples are drawn from normal distributions. Because s is unknown, we assume the variances of the two populations or groups are equal (homoscedasticity).

The null hypothesis about differences between groups is normally stated:

$$\mu_1 = \mu_2 \text{ or } \mu_1 - \mu_2 = 0.$$

Thus the t-value is a ratio between the information about the difference between means (provided by the sample) and the random error in the denominator. The question is whether the observed differences have occurred by chance alone.

To calculate t, the following formula is used.

$$t = \frac{X_1 - X_2}{S_{\overline{X}_1 - \overline{X}_2}}$$

where

X_1 = mean for Group 1

X_2 = mean for Group 2

$S_{\overline{X}_1 - \overline{X}_2}$ = the pooled or combined standard error of difference between means

A pooled estimate of the standard error is a better estimate of the standard error than one based on the variance from either sample. This requires the assumption that variances of both groups (populations) are equal.

11.16 Analysis of Variance (ANOVA)

When the means of more than two groups or populations are to be compared, **one-way analysis of variance (ANOVA)** is the appropriate statistical tool. This bivariate statistical technique is referred to as "one-way" because there is only one independent variable (even though there may be several levels of that variable). An example of an ANOVA problem is to compare women students of

Diploma Course in Higher Education of **IGNOU** who are working **full time** outside the home, **part-time** outside the home, and **not employed** outside the home on their willingness to attend the orientation course.. Here there is one independent variable – **working status**. The independent variable, working status, is said to have ***three levels: full-time employment, part-time employment,*** and ***not working outside the home,*** Because there are three groups (levels), a t-test cannot be used for the testing of statistical significance.

If we have three groups or three levels of the independent variable, the null hypothesis is stated as follows:

$$\boxed{\mu_1 = \mu_2 = \mu_3}$$

The null hypothesis is that all the means are equal.

In the above example, we are concerned with the willingness to attend the contact programme of ***three different types of women***. As the name analysis of variance suggests, the problem requires comparing variances to make inferences about the means. The logic of this technique is as follows. The variance of the means of the three groups will be large if these women differ from each other in terms of their intentions. If we calculate this variance within groups and compare it to the variance of the group means about a grand mean, we can determine if the means are significantly different. This will become clearer as we investigate the F-test.

11.17 F-Test

The F-test is a procedure for comparing one sample variance with another sample variance. The F-test determines whether there is more variability in the scores of one sample than in the scores of another sample. The key question is whether the two sample variances are different from each other or are from the same population.

The F-test utilizes measures of sample variance rather than the sample standard deviation because standard deviations cannot be summed. Summation is allowable with the sample variance. To obtain the F-statistic (or F-ratio), the larger sample variance is divided by the smaller sample variance. To test the null hypothesis of no difference between the sample variances, a table of the F-distribution is necessary.

Exhibits 11.18 and **11.19** serve as a guide to the researcher in planning data analysis.

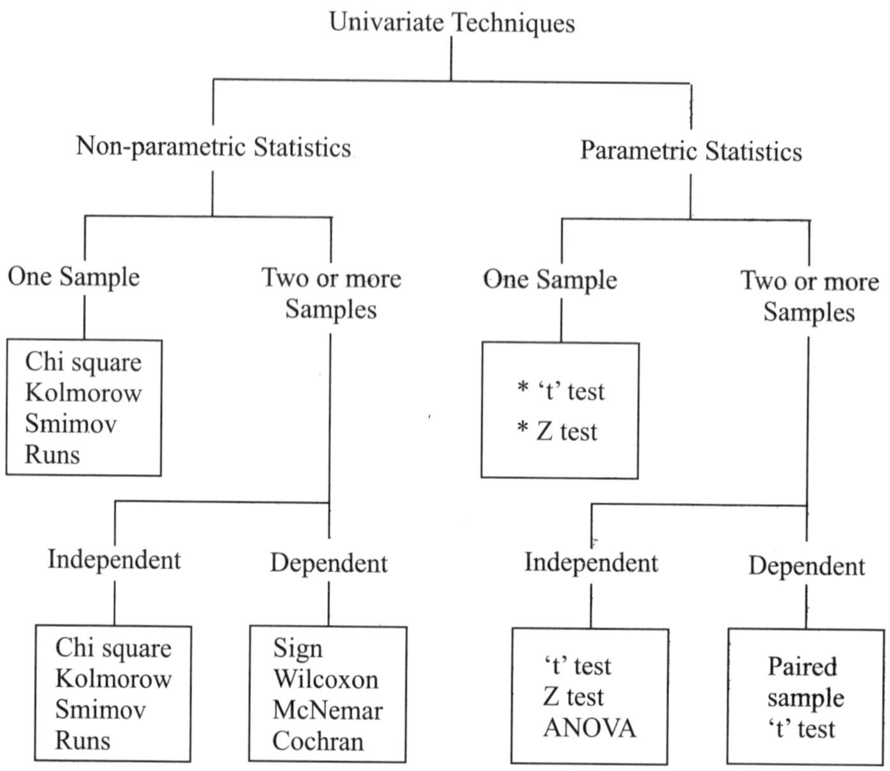

Univariate Techniques
Non-parametric Statistics
Parametric Statistics
One Sample
Two or more Samples
One Sample
Two or more Samples
Chi square
Kolmorow
Smimov
Runs
* 't' test
* Z test
Independent
Dependent
Independent
Dependent
Chi square
Kolmorow
Smimov
Runs
Sign
Wilcoxon
McNemar
Cochran
't' test
Z test
ANOVA
Paired sample 't' test

Exhibit 11.18: Univariate technique

MultivariateTechniques
Dependence Techniques
Interdependence Techniques
One Independent Variable
Multiple Independent Variable
Focus on Variables
Focus on Objects
ANOVA
Multiple Regression
Discriminant Analysis
Conjoint Analysis
• MANOVA
• Canonical Correlation
* Factor Analysis
• Cluster Analysis
• Multidimensional Analysis

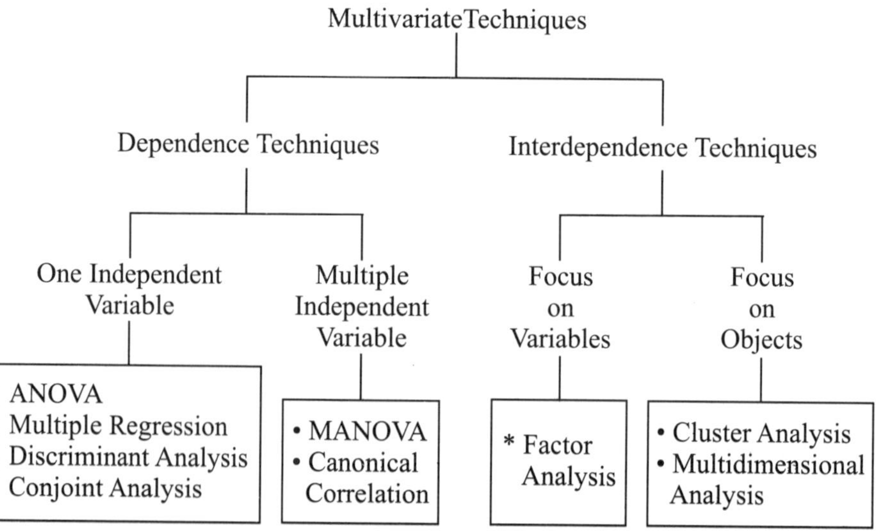

Exhibit 11.19: Multivariate technique

11.18 Bonding Hypothesis, Variables and Statistics

Sl. No.	Statistics Used	Independent Variable	Dependent Variable	Statement of Hypotheses	Test Statistic
I	Pearson Correlation	Quantitative (continuous) that is, interval or ratio scale of measurement	Quantitative (continuous that is, interval or ratio) scale of measurement	*Research hypothesis (non directional)*	r =
				There is a relationship between size of district and average teacher pay (directional)	
		Size of district	*Average teacher pay*	There is a positive relationship between size of district and average teacher pay.	
				Larger district have higher average teacher pay than smaller districts.	
				Null Hypothesis	
				There is no significant relationship between size of district and average teacher pay.	
II	Chi-Square	Categorical that is, nominal or ordinal scale of measurement	Categorical that is, nominal or ordinal scale of measurement	*Research Hypothesis (non directional)*	$\chi^2 =$
				There is a relationship between a person's sex and potential party membership (directional)	
		2 or more groups	*2 or more groups*	More males tend to be in the BJP and CPI (M) while more females tend to be in the Congress.	
		Sex	Potential partners	*Null Hypothesis*	
		Male / Female	BJP, Cong., CPI (M), Telugu Desam, Other	There is no significant relationship between one's sex and one's political party membership.	

Sl. No.	Statistics Used	Independent Variable	Dependent Variable	Statement of Hypotheses	Statistical Used
III	Independent and Dependent t-Test	Categorical that is, nominal or ordinal scale. *2 groups only*	Quantitative (Continuous that is, interval or ratio scale of measurement)	*Research Hypothesis (non-directional)* There is a significant difference in average teacher pay between small and large district (directional).	t =
		Size of district (small < 700 vs Large ≥ 700)	*Average teacher pay*	Large districts have significant higher average teacher pays than small districts. *Null Hypothesis* There is no significant difference in average teacher pays between large and small districts.	
IV	One way Analysis of Variance (ANOVA)	Categorical, that is, nominal or ordinal scale of measurement *2 or more groups*	Quantitative (continuous) that is, interval or ratio scale of measurement.	*Research Hypothesis (non-directional)* There is a difference in average teacher salaries among rural, suburban and urban districts. (directional)	(i) F = (ii) Follow up tests for each pair wise comparison. - LSD - Scheffe - Winer - Newman Keuls - Tukry
		Type of district (rural, suburban, urban)	*Average teacher pay*	Suburban and urban districts have higher teacher salaries among rural, suburban and urban districts. *Null Hypothesis* There is no significant difference in average teacher pays among rural, suburban and urban districts.	

Sl. No.	Statistics Used	Independent Variable	Dependent Variable	Statement of Hypotheses	Statistical Used
V	Two way analysis of Variance (Here there are two independent variables)	1. Categorical–that is, nominal or ordinal scale of measurement – <u>2 or more</u> groups. 2. Categorical–that is, nominal or ordinal scale of measurement <u>2 more</u> groups	Quantitative (continuous) – that is, interval or ratio scale of measurement.	*Research Hypothesis (non-directional)*	F for each hypothesis Follow up tests for each pair wise comparison. - LSD - Scheffe - Duncan - Newman Keuls - Tukey
				There is a difference in average teacher pays among rural, suburban, and urban districts.	
				There is a difference in average teacher pays between small and large districts.	
			Average Teacher Pay	There is a district size and type (rural, suburban, urban) interaction for average teacher pays.	
				Null Hypothesis	
		1. Type of district (rural, sub-urban, urban) 2. Size of district (small < 700; large ≥ 700)		There is no significant difference in average teacher pays among rural, suburban, and urban districts.	
				There is no significant difference in average teacher pays between small and large districts.	
				There is no significant district size and type (rural, suburban, and urban) interaction for average teacher pays.	

11.19 Bivariate Analysis

Measures of Association

In many situations, measures of differences, such as the chi-square test, provide information on whether two or more variables are interrelated or are associated. For example, a chi square test between a measure of computer literacy and a measure of education provides some information about the independence or interrelationship of the two variables. Although measures such as the chi-square are useful sources of information about association, statisticians have developed several techniques to estimate the strength of association.

The mathematical symbol X is commonly used for the independent variable, and Y is typically used for the dependent variable. It is appropriate to label dependent and independent variables only when it is assumed that the independent variable caused the dependent.

Exhibit 11.20 shows that type of measures utilized will influence the choice of statistical measures of association.

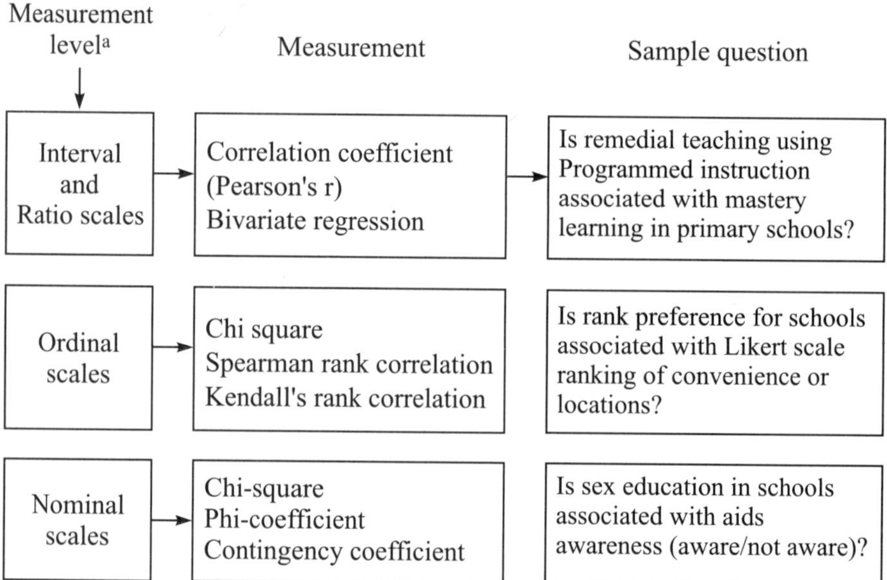

Exhibit 11.20: Bivariate analysis common procedure for testing association

Measures of association Statistical values designed to represent covariation between variables are useful because they can assist the researcher in accomplishing important scientific goals. Measures of association help on tracking causal relationships. They can also be useful for predicting scores from one variable to another. Predicting and causation can be two separate goals. If variables are associated, we can predict from one to the other even if the variables are not causally related. These measures of association perform a number of functions.

11.20 Correlation – Cause-Effect

11.20.1 Simple Correlation Coefficient

The most popular technique that indicates the relationship of one variable with another is simple correlation analysis. The simple correlation coefficient is a statistical measure of the covariation or association between two variables. The correlation coefficient → ranges from +1.0 to 1.0, if the value of r is a perfect linear (straight-line) relationship. If the value of r is –1.0, a perfect negative linear relationship or a perfect inverse relationship is indicated. No correlation is indicated if $r = 0$. Correlation coefficient indicates both the magnitude of the linear relationship and the direction of the relationship. For example, if we find that the value of r = –92, we have a relationship. For example, if we find that the value of r = –92, we know we have a relatively strong inverse relationship. That is, the greater the value measured by variable X, the less the value measured by variable Y.

The formula for calculating the correlation coefficient for two variables X and Y is

$$r_{xy} = r_{yx} = \frac{\Sigma(X_i - \overline{X})(Y_i - \overline{Y})}{\sqrt{\Sigma(X_i - \overline{X})^2 \ \Sigma(Y_i - \overline{Y})^2}}$$

where the symbols X and Y represent the sample means of X and Y, respectively.

An alternative way of expressing the correlation formula is:

$$r_{xy} = r_{yx} = \frac{\sigma_{yx}}{\sqrt{\sigma^2 x \ \sigma^2 y}}$$

where

$\sigma^2{}_x$ = variance of X

$\sigma^2{}_y$ = variance of Y

$\sigma^2{}_{xy}$ = covariance of X and Y.

with

$$r_{xy} = r_{yx} = \frac{\Sigma(X_i - X)(Y_i - Y)}{N}$$

If associated values of Xi and Yi differ from their means in the same direction, then their covariance will be positive. Covariance will be negative if the values of Xi and Yi have a tendency to deviate in opposite directions.

In actuality, the simple correlation coefficient is a standardized measure of covariance. In the formula the numerator represents covariance and the denominator is the square root of the product of the sample variances. Researchers find the correlation coefficient useful because two correlations can be compared without regard to the amount of variation exhibited by each variable separately.

11.20.2 Correlation and Causation

It is important to remember that correlation does not mean causation.

Example

Research reveals that there is a high correlation between teachers salaries and the consumption of liquor over a period of years. The approximate correlation coefficient is r = .9. This high correlation does not indicate that teachers drink, nor does it indicate that the sale of liquor increases teachers' salaries. It is more likely that both teachers salary and liquor sale covary because they are both influenced by a third variable, such a long run growth in national income and/or population.

In this example, relationship between the two variables is apparent but not real. Even though the variables are not causally related, they can be statistically related. This can occur because both are caused by a third (or more) factor(s). When this is so, variables are said to be **spuriously** related

11.20.3 Coefficient of Determination

If we wish to know the proportion of variance in Y explained by X (or vice versa), we can calculate the coefficient of determination by squaring the correlation coefficient (r^2):

$$r^2 = \frac{\text{Explained variance}}{\text{Total variance}}$$

The coefficient of determination, r^2, measures that part of the total variance of Y that is accounted for by knowing the value of X. In the example showing the correlation between unemployment and hours worked, $r = -.635$, then $r^2 = .403$. About 40 per cent of the variance in unemployment can be explained by the variance in hours worked, and vice versa.

11.20.4 Correlation Matrix

The correlation matrix is the standard form of reporting correlation results. Table 11.9 shows a correlation matrix, including some measures of leadership styles (LS) as they relate to school effectiveness.

Table 11.9: Pearson product moment correlation matrix for leadership style LS and its components

Variable & Components	LS	R1	R2	R	R4	R5	R6
Leadership style (LS)	1.00	.94	.89	.93	.93	.77	.84
Assertive Administration (R1)	.94	1.00	.80	.85	.85	.69	.78
Constructional Leadership (R2)	.89	.80	1.00	.80	.79	.67	.71
Assumption of Responsibility (R3)	.93	.85	.80	1.00	.83	.68	.74
Personal Vision (R4)	.93	.85	.79	.83	1.00	.69	.75
Decision Making (R5)	.77	.69	.67	.68	.69	1.00	.65
Standard Relationship Style (R6)	.84	.78	.71	.74	.75	.65	1.00

(All values are significant at .0000 level)

Table 11.10 highlights the appropriate correlational techniques for combinations of different measures.

Another question researchers ask concerns statistical significance. The procedure for determining statistical significance is the t-test of the significance of a correlation coefficient. Typically, it is hypothesized that r = 0 and then a t-test is performed. The logic behind the test is similar to the significance tests already considered.

Table 11.10: Appropriate correlational techniques for combinations of different measurements

Measurement Characteristics		Coefficient and Symbol	Statistical Examples
Continuous (Interval, ratio, or combination)	Continuous	Pearson Product Moment r	Relationship between height (X) and weight (Y) of a set of subjects
Continuous	True dichotomy	Point Biserial $r_p b$	Relationship between history test scores(X)and the answer (true or false) for item no. 1 (Y)
Continuous	Forced dichotomy	Biserial r_b	Relationship between mental ability test scores (X) and above or below the average score on a reading comprehension test (Y)
Forced dichotomy	Forced dichotomy[2]	Tetrachoric r_t	Relationship of position on two tests when subjects are rated as being above or below the median of IQ test (X) and a measure of hand grip (Y)
True dichotomy	True dichotomy	Phi Ø	Relationship of married / unmarried Students (x) and Working / non-working (Y)
Ranks (or capable of being ranked)	Ranks	Spearman rho p	Relationship of ranks (or capable of being ranked) for a set of paintings by art majors (X) and ranks by business majors (Y)

Measurement Characteristics		**Coefficient and Symbol**	**Statistical Examples**
Ranks	Ranks (capable of being ranked)	Kendall's Tau T	Relationship of ranks (or capable of being ranked) for a set of paintings by art majors (X) and ranks by business majors (Y)
Ordinal	Dichotomous	Rank biserial r_{rb}	Relationship between untied ranks of order of Finish of mile race (X) and training with or without weightlifting (Y)
Nominal	Continuous	Nonlinear n^2	Relationship of hair colour (natural) (X) and scores on a test of creativity (Y)
Nominal (or categorized)	Nominal	Contingency Coefficient (C)	Relationship of (or categorized) socioeconomic status background (X or Y) and choice of favourite color (X or Y)
Three or more	sets of ranks	Kendall's Concordance (W)	Relationship among ranks of art major (X), business majors (Y), and philosophy majors (Z) on art objects.

A true dichotomy results from measurement that is made on mere presence or absence of the variable

A forced dichotomy results when an assumed normal distribution is artificially divided into two parts (Test scores above 75; Test scores below 75)

11.21 Regression Analysis

Regression is another technique for measuring the linear association between a dependent and independent variable. Although regression and correlation are mathematically related, regression assumes the dependent (or criterion) variable, Y, is predictively linked to the independent (or predictor) variable, X. Regression analysis attempts to predict the values of a continuous, interval-scaled dependent variable from the specific values of the independent variable.

Bivariate linear form regression investigates a straight line relationship of the type $Y = \alpha + \beta X$, where the Y is the dependent variable and X is the independent variable and a and β are two constants to be estimated. The symbol a represents the Y intercept and β is the slope coefficient. The slope β is the change in Y due to a corresponding change in one unit of X. This slope may also be thought of as "rise over run" (the rise in units on the Y axis divided by the run in units along the X axis.)

Least-Squares Method of Regression Analysis

The task of the researcher is to find the best means for fitting a straight line to the data. The **least-squares method** is a relatively simple mathematical technique that ensures that the straight line will best represent the relationship between X and Y. The logic behind the least-squares technique goes as follows. No straight line can completely represent every dot in the scatter diagram. Unless there is a perfect correlation between two variables, there will be a discrepancy between most of the actual scores (each dot) and the predicted score based on the regression line. Simply stated, any straight line that is drawn will generate errors. The method of least squares uses the criterion of attempting to make the least amount of total error in prediction of Y from X.

The general equation of a straight line equals $Y = \hat{a} + \beta X$, whereas a more appropriate equation includes an allowances for error:

$$\boxed{Y = \hat{a} + \beta X + e}$$

The symbol $\hat{a}$ + β are utilized when the equation is a regression estimate of the line. Thus, to compute the estimated values of $\hat{a}$ and β , we use the following formulas:

$$\beta = \frac{n(\Sigma XY) - (\Sigma X)(\Sigma Y)}{n(\Sigma X^2) - (\Sigma X)^2}$$

and

$$\hat{a} = \overline{Y} - \beta \overline{X}$$

where

β = estimated slope of the line (the "regression coefficient")

$\hat{a}$ = estimated intercept of the y axis

Y = dependent variable
$\overline{Y}$ = mean of the dependent variable
X = independent variable
$\overline{X}$ = mean of the independent variable
n = number of observations

F-test *is a procedure used to determine if there is more variability in the scores of one sample than in the scores of another sample.*

Analysis of variance summary table is a table that presents the results of a regression calculation.

Bivariate linear regression investigates a straight-line relationship between one dependent variable and one independent variable. The regression can be done intuitively by plotting a scatter diagram of the X and Y points and drawing a line to fit the observed relationship. The least-squares method mathematically determines the best-fitting regression line for the observed data. The line determined by this method may be used to forecast values of the dependent variable, given a value for the independent variable. The goodness of the line's fit may be evaluated by a variant of the ANOVA (analysis of variance) technique or by calculating the coefficient of determination.

11.22 Multivariate Techniques

This section presents a description of some multivariate methods which an educational researcher may find useful. Multivariate data analysis is Statistical Methods that allow the simultaneous investigation of more than two variables.

Classifying Multivariate Techniques

A useful classification of most multivariate data analysis techniques is presented in Exhibit 11.21. Two basic groups of multivariate techniques are classified: dependable methods and interdependable methods.

Analysis of Dependence

If the technique attempts to explain or predict the dependent variable(s) on the basis of two or more independent variables, then we are attempting to analyze dependence. An instance where the researcher is interested in specifying a relationship between one dependent variable and several independent variables is illustrated by a common judgement: Is a student a good one or an average one based on age, standard, and IQ? Another example of the analysis of dependence would be forecasting the dependent variable science scores on the basis of numerous independent variables. Multiple regression analysis, multiple discriminate analysis, multivariate analysis of variance, and canonical correlation analysis are all dependence methods.

Analysis of Dependence is a collective term to describe any multivariate statistical technique that attempts to explain or predict the dependent variable on the basis of two or more independent variables.

Analysis of Interdependence

The goal of interdependence methods is to give meaning to a set of variables or to seek to group things together. No one variable or variable subset is to be predicted from the others explained by them. The most common of these methods for analysis of interdependence are factor analysis, cluster analysis, and multidimensional scaling.

Analysis of interdependence is a collective term to describe any multivariate statistical technique that attempts to give meaning to a set of variables or seeks to group things together.

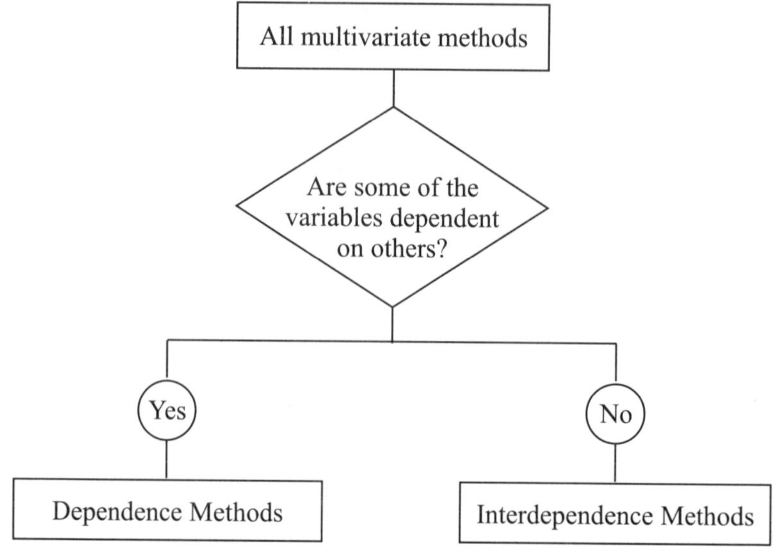

Exhibit 11.21: A classification of multivariate methods

Another example might be to identify and classify similar schools on the basis of student strength, socioeconomic status of students, results on public examination and participation is extracurricular activities at the state level.

Influence of Measurement Scales

As in other forms of data analysis, the nature of the measurement scale will determine which multivariate technique is appropriate for the data. Exhibits 11.22 and 11.23 show that selection of a multivariate technique requires consideration of the types of measures and for both independent and dependent sets of variables.

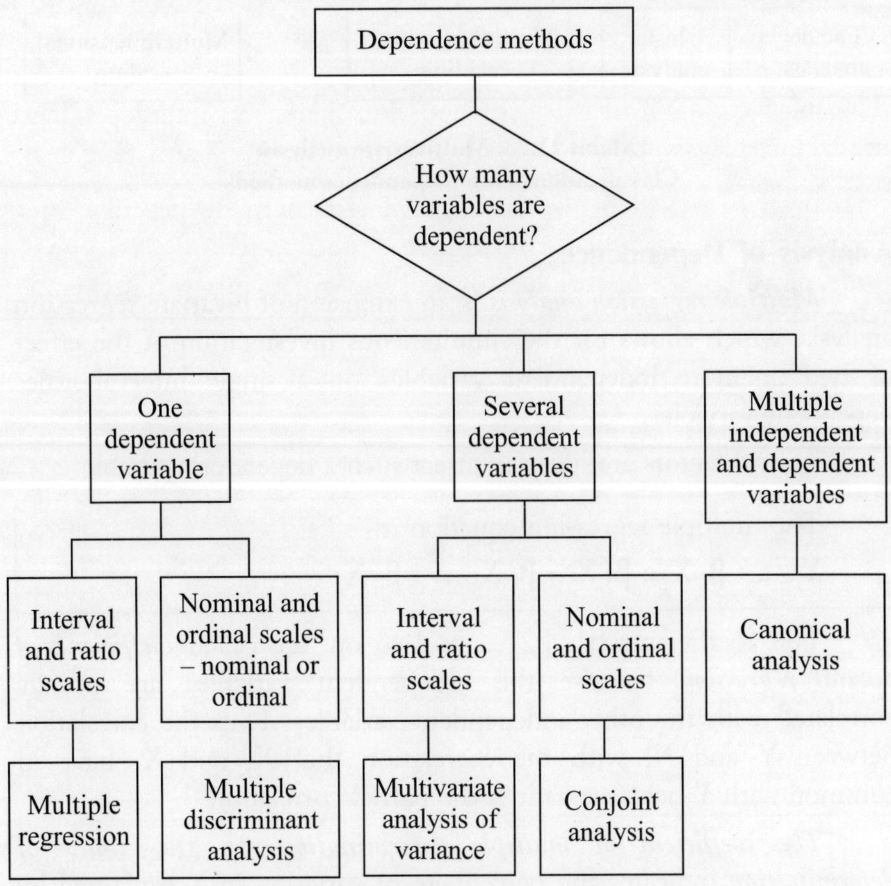

Exhibit 11.22: Classification of dependence methods when using multivariate analysis

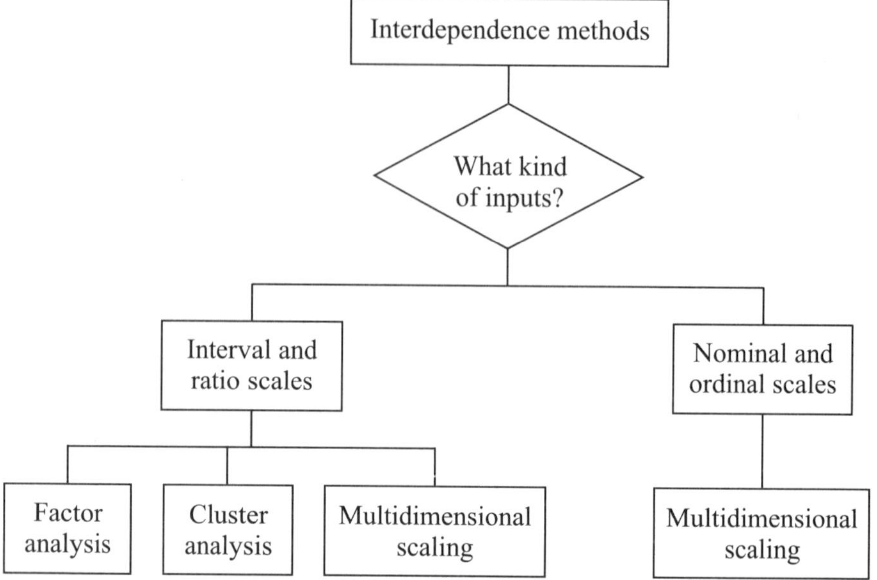

Exhibit 11.23: Multivariate analysis: Classification of interdependence methods

Analysis of Dependence

Multiple regression analysis is an extension of bivariate regression analysis, which allows for the simultaneous investigation of the effect of two or more independent variables on a single interval-scales dependent variable.

Several factors are likely to affect such a dependent variable.

The multiple regression equation is:

$$Y = a + \beta_1 X_1 + \beta_2 X_2 + \beta_3 X_3 \ldots + \beta_n X_n$$

The coefficients β1, β2 ... and so on, are called *coefficients of partial regression* because the independent variables are usually correlated with the other independent variables. Thus the correlation between Y and X_1 with the correlation that X_1 and X_2 have in common with Y held constant is the partial correlation.

The coefficient of multiple determination or the *index of determination* indicates the percentage of variation in Y explained by the variation in the independent variables. The amount of variations explained by two independent variables in the same equation usually explains more variation in Y than either one explains separately. To test for statistical significance, an F test comparing the different sources of variation, is done.

A continuous, interval-scaled dependent variable is required in multiple regressions, as it is in bivariate regression. Interval scaling is also a requirement for the independent variable; however, dummy variables, may be utilized. A dummy variable is a variable that has two (or more) distinct levels, which are coded 0 and 1. There are several other assumptions for multiple regressions (and other multivariate techniques) that require advanced study.

11.23 Discriminant Analysis

Many situations exist where the researcher's purpose is to classify objects, by a set of independent variables, into two or more mutually exclusive categories. An educational consultant may want to distinguish between effective schools and not so effective schools. Researchers may want to group schools as effective and not so effective on the basis of independent variables – location, results, image, student strength.

Multiple discriminant analysis is a statistical technique for predicting the probability of objects belonging in two or more mutually exclusive categories (dependent variable) based on several independent variables.

The challenge is to find the discriminating variables to be utilized in a predictive equation that will produce better than chance assignment of the individuals to the two groups.

The prediction of a categorical variable (rather than a continuous, interval - scaled variable as in multiple regression) is the purpose of *multiple discriminant analysis*. In each of the above problems the researcher must determine which variable is associated with the probability of an item falling into one of several groups or categories. In a statistical sense, the problem of studying the direction of group differences is a problem of finding a linear combination of independent variables, the discriminant function that shows large differences in group means. Discriminant analysis is a statistical tool for determining such linear combinations.. The problem is to find a linear function of the independent variable that shows large differences in group means. The first task is to estimate the coefficients of the individual applicant's discriminate functions. To calculate the individual's discriminant scores, the following linear function is used.

$$Z1 = b_1 X_{1i} + b_2 X_{2i} + \dots + b_n X_{ni}$$

where

X_{ji} = applicant's value on the jth independent variable

B_j = discriminant coefficient for the jth variable

Z_i = ith applicant's discriminant score

Using all the individuals in the sample, a discriminant function is determined based on the criterion that the groups be maximally differentiated on the set off independent variables.

In the computation of the linear discriminant function, weights are assigned to the variables such that the ratio of the difference between the means of the two groups to the standard deviation within groups is maximized. The standardized discriminate coefficients or weights provide information about the relative importance of each of these variables in discriminating between the two groups.

An important purpose of discriminant analysis is to perform a classification function. The object of classification for example, is to predict which applicants will be successful and which will be unsuccessful, and to group them accordingly.

11.24 Canonical Correlation

Canonical correlation, a very complex statistical technique that is not extensively used, is briefly examined here. When the research analyst has two or more criterion variables (dependent variables) and multiple predictor variables (independent variables), canonical correlation analysis is an appropriate statistical technique. Multiple regression analysis investigates the linear relationship between a single dependent or criterion variable and multiple independent variables. Canonical correlation analysis is an extension of multiple regressions. The focus of canonical correlation is upon the relationship between two sets or interval-scales variables.

Canonical correlation analysis is a technique used to determine the degree of linear association between two sets of variables, each consisting of several variables.

11.25 Multivariate Analysis of Variance (MANOVA)

As in canonical correlation, multivariate analysis of variance is used when there are multiple dependent variables that are interval-or - ratio-scales variables. There may be one or more nominally scales independent variables. With MANOVA a significance test of mean difference between groups can be made simultaneously for two or more dependent variables.

A summary of the multivariate techniques for analysis of dependence appears in Exhibit 11.24.

Multivariate Analysis of Variance (MANOVA) is a statistical technique that provides a simultaneous significance test of mean difference between groups made for two or more dependent variables.

Analysis of Interdependence

The analysis of interdependence focuses on understanding the structure of a set of variables, using techniques such as factor analysis, cluster analysis, and multidimensional scaling .

Factor Analysis

Suppose that we measure the height, weight, occupation, education, and source of income for 50 men. The results of a factor analysis might indicate that the underlying dimension of size may summarize height and weight. The variables – occupation, education, and source of income – may be summarized by the underlying concept of social status. In this example two new variables, or factors, explain the five variables at a more generalized level.

The general purpose of factor analysis is to summarize the information contained in a large number of variables into a smaller number of factors. Factor analysis refers to a diverse number of techniques used to discern the underlying dimensions or regularity in phenomena.

If a researcher has a set of variables and suspects that theses variables are interrelated in a complex fashion, then factor analysis

Technique	Purpose	Number of Dependent Variables	Number of Independent Variables	Type of measurement	
				Dependent	Independent
Multiple regression	To simultaneously investigate the effect of several independent variables on a dependent variable	1	2 or more	Interval or Ratio	Interval or Ratio
Discriminant analysis	To predict the probability of items or individuals belonging in two or more mutually exclusive categories based on several independent variables	1	2 or more	Nominal	Interval or Ratio
Canonical correlation	To determine the degree of linear association between two sets of variables, each consisting of several variables	2 or more	2 or more	Interval or Ratio	Interval or Ratio
MANOVA	To determine if statistically significant differences of means of several variables occur simultaneously between two levels of a variable	2 or more	1	Interval or Ratio	Nominal

Exhibit 11.24: Summary of multivariate techniques for the analysis of dependence

may be used to untangle the linear relationships into their separate patterns. The statistical purpose of factor analysis is to determine linear combinations of variables that aid in investigating the interrelationships. For example a researcher may collect a variety of data on teacher trainees attitudes toward their working conditions in the cooperating schools.. Numerous questions about timetable, staff room atmosphere, mentoring by guide teacher, rapport with students and staff and other relevant issues might be asked. The researcher, however, may want to reduce the large number of variables to certain underlying constructs or dimensions that will summarize the important information contained in the variables. Thus the researcher's purpose is to discover the basic structure of a domain and to add substantive interpretation to the underlying dimensions. Factor analysis accomplishes this by combining these questions to create new, more abstract variables called factors. In general, the goal of factor analysis is parsimony: to reduce a large number of variables to as few dimensions or constructs as possible.

Factor Analysis is a type of analysis used to discern the underlying dimensions or regularity in phenomena. Its general purpose is to summarize the information contained in large number of variables into a smaller number of factors. There are a number of factor analytical techniques.

11.26 Cluster Analysis

Cluster analysis is a term given to a body of techniques used to identify objects or individuals that are similar with respect to some criterion. The purpose of cluster analysis is to classify individuals or objects into a small number of mutually exclusive and exhaustive groups. The researcher's focus is to determine how objects or individuals should be assigned to groups to ensure that there will be as much likeness within groups and as much difference among them as possible. The cluster should have high internal (within cluster) homogeneity and high external (between clusters) heterogeneity.

Clusters or subgroups of recreational facilities may be identified on the basis of their similarity of usage and benefits sought from recreational activities. Alternatively, the researcher might use demographic variables or lifestyle variables to group individuals into clusters identified on the basis of recreations.

Cluster analysis is an analysis that classifies individuals or objects into small number of mutually exclusive groups, ensuring that there will be as much likeness within groups and as much difference among groups as possible.

Cluster analysis differs from multiple discriminant analysis in that the groups are not predefined. The purpose of cluster analysis is to determine how many district groups exist and to define their composition. It describes a sample of objects after examining only a sample. It does not predict relationships.

11.27 Multidimensional Scaling

Multidimensional scaling provides a means for measuring objects in multidimensional space on the basis of respondent's similarity of judgements of objects. The perceptual difference between objects is reflected in the relative distance between objects in multi-dimensional space.

Example

An illustration of the ways that B.Ed. students perceive six teacher training colleges also helps to explain multidimensional scaling. The students were asked to provide their perceptions of relative similarities among the set of colleges. Next, the overall similarity scores for all possible pairs of objects were aggregated for all individual respondents and arranged in a matrix. With the aid of the SPSS package, the similarity scores were statistically transformed into distances by placing the six colleges into a specified multidimensional space. The distance between similar objects on the perceptual map is small. Dissimilar objects are not close together.

Exhibit 11.25 is a perceptual map in two-dimensional space. Looking at the map illustrates that College A and College B were perceived to be quite similar to each other, and that College X and College Y were perceived to be very similar. However, X and Z were perceived to be dissimilar. The researchers identified the two axes as "quantitative versus qualitative curriculum" and "less versus more status." The labeling of the dimension axes is a task of interpretation

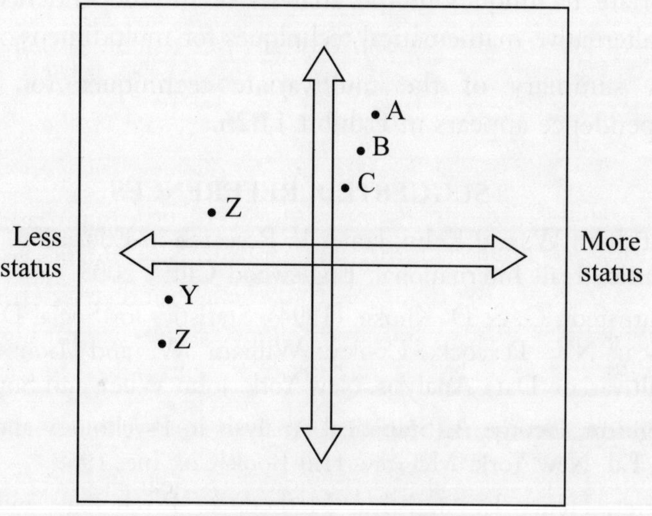

Exhibit 11.25: Perceptual map of six teacher training colleges simple space

Technique	Purpose	Type of Measurement
Factor analysis	To summarize the information contained in a large number of variables into a reduced number of factors	Interval or ratio
Cluster analysis	To classify individuals or objects into a smaller number of mutually and exhaustive groups, ensuring that there will be as much likeness within groups and as much difference between groups as possible	Interval or ratio
Multidimensional scaling	To measure objects in multidimensional space on the basis of respondent's judgements of objects	Varies depending on technique

Exhibit 11.26: Summary of multivariate techniques for analysis of interdependence

for the researcher and is not statically determined. As with other multivariate techniques in the analysis of interdependence, there are several alternative mathematical techniques for multidimensional scaling.

A summary of the multivariate techniques for analysis of interdependence appears in Exhibit 11.26.

SUGGESTED REFERENCES

- Best, John W. and Kahn, James V. Research in Education. 9th Edition. Prentice Hall International. Englewood Cliffs. 2005.
- Bohrnstedt, G. & D. Knoke. (1994). Statistics for Social Data Analysis. Itasca, NY: Peacock. Cooley, William W. and Lohnes, Paul R. Multivariate Data Analysis. New York. John Wiley and Sons. 1971
- Ferguson, George A. Statistical Analysis in Psychology and Education. 4th Ed. New York. McGraw Hill Book Co., Inc. 1959.
- Garret, Henry E. Statistical Methods in Psychology and Education. New York:David McKay Co. 1966.
- Healey, Joseph F. Statistics – A Tool for Social Research.Third edition. Wadsworth Publishing Company. 1993.
- Salkind, N. (2000). Exploring Research. Upper Saddle River, NJ: Prentice Hall.
- Singleton, R. & B. Straits. (1999). Approaches to Social Research. NY: Oxford Univ. Press.
- Sirkin, M. (1995). Statistics for the Social Sciences. Thousand Oaks, CA: Sage.

WEB BASED TEACHING MATERIAL

- http://hsc.uwe.ac.uk/dataanalysis/index.asp A data analysis on-line learning programme.
- STAT 100 Some Experimental Interactive Statistics Pages. The Department of Statistics University of Illinois at Urbana-Champaign, with funding from SCALE (The Sloan Center for Asynchronous Learning Environments), is developing some statistics modules that can be accessed through the web.
- http://www.une.edu.au/WebStat/ This site is designed to provide information, demonstrations, links and quizzes associated with statistics. WebStat is specifically designed with Psychology students in mind. This site is done for the University of New England Australia.

- Teach Modules – Teaching Statistical Concepts to Undergraduate Students
- Multiple Regression with Ren & Stimpy! This overview was constructed by three graduate students at New Mexico State University's Psychology Department as a project for their last statistics course.
- FR 5218 – Regression Refresher We will apply or talk about the application of regression analysis in conjunction with many topics in this course. On-line course in statistics Check out chapter 1 of the on-line course for free !
- Statistics Every Writer Should Know Numbers can't "talk" but they can tell you as much as your human sources can. But just like with human sources, you have to ask!
- Electronic Encyclopedia of Exercises and Examples http://www.whfreeman.com/eesee/eesee.html EESEE is designed to be a resource for educators and an aid for students in the study of statistics. It is intended to serve as a supplement to introductory textbooks written for students with varying degrees of mathematical backgrounds.

Communicating Research

12.1 Communication Process

The process by which one person or source sends a message to an audience or receiver and then receives feedback about the message.

Some insights from the theory of communication help clarify the importance of the research report. Exhibit 12.1 illustrates one view of the of the several elements that enter into successful communication:

1. The ***communicator***, the ***source*** or ***sender*** of the message (the writer of the report).
2. The message, the set of meanings being sent to or received by the ***audience*** (the findings of the research project).
3. The ***medium*** or the means by which the message is carried or delivered to the audience (the oral or written report itself)
4. The ***audience***, the ***receiver*** or ***destination*** of the message (the expert who will make a decision based, we hope, on the report's findings).
5. ***Feedback,*** a reverse flow of communication also involving a message and channel, from the audience to the original

communicator, which may be used to modify subsequent communications (the university's experts response to the report)

This model of communication, though, overstates the case of the communication. It seems that the message flows smoothly along from the writer to the reader, who in turn promptly provides the writer with feedback. Actually, things are more complex, and Exhibit 12.2 emphasizes one of the difficulties.

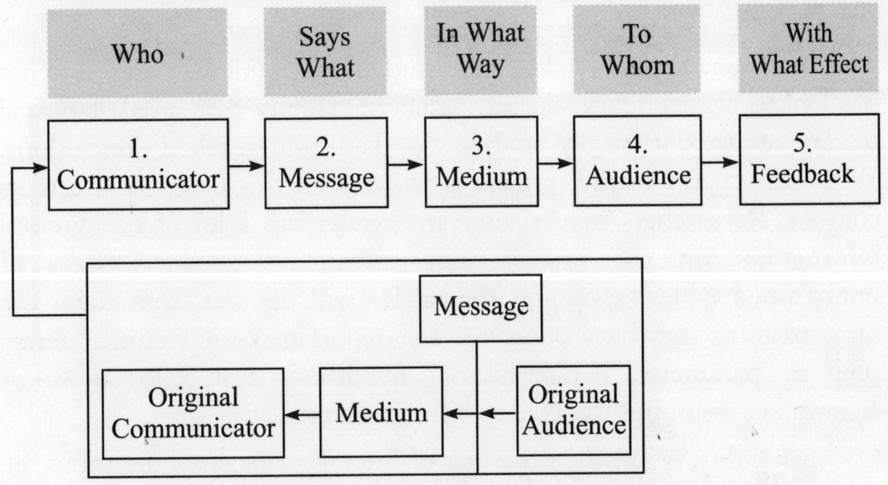

Exhibit 12.1: Communication process

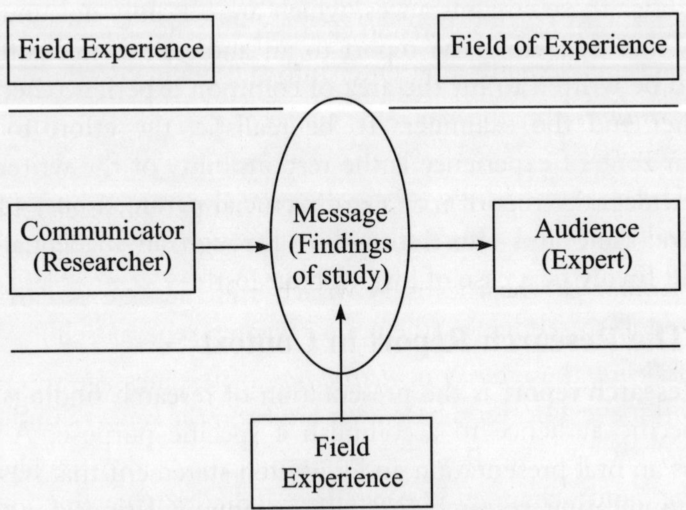

Exhibit 12.2: Field experience and field of experience

The communicator and the audience both have fields of experience. These overlap to some extent; otherwise, no communication would be possible. Nevertheless, there is much experience that is not common to both parties. As the communicators send a message, they code it in terms that make sense to them, based on their fields of experience. As the audience receives the message, individuals decode it, based on their own fields of experience that it may be encoded, transmitted and decoded with roughly the same meaning.

In the research setting we have a communicator (the researcher) who has spent a great deal of time studying a problem. The researcher has looked at secondary sources, gathered primary data, used statistical techniques to statistically analyse the data, and reached conclusions. When the report on the project is written, all this baggage affects its content. Researchers may assume the reader has a lot of background information on the project. The researchers produce pages of unexplained tables, assuming the reader will dig out from them the same patterns they have observed. The report may use technical terms such as parameter, F-distribution, hypothesis test, correlation, or eigenvalue, assuming the reader will understand.

In reality, when the examiner of the report receives the thesis, he or she usually would not have thought much about the project. S/he may or may not know anything about statistics.

Under these circumstances, which are certainly not unusual, it is obvious that delivering the report to an audience is not sufficient. It needs to be written to hit the area of common experience between the researcher and the examiner. To be realistic, the effort to hit that common zone of experience is the responsibility of the writer, not the reader. Unless the report is of a really crucial nature, a busy reader will not spend time and effort struggling through an inadequate report. This will finally be a case of love's labour lost!

12.2 The Research Report in Context

Research report is the presentation of research findings directed to a specific audience to accomplish a specific purpose. A **research report** is an oral presentation and a written statement that has purpose of communicating research findings, recommendations for course of action, and / or other findings to specific audiences. This chapter deals primarily with the final written report, with one section on the oral presentation of the research findings. The chapter emphasizes the sort of written report that is needed in an extensive research project. It is easy to adapt the chapter's suggestions for a shorter, less formal report. It is worth remembering, however, that the final report may not be the only kind prepared. For a small project a short oral or written report on the results may be all that is needed.

The emphasis on the final report in this chapter should not be taken to mean that other communications, such as progress reports, during the project are any less important to its eventual success.

Report Format

Although every research report is custom-made for the project it represents, some conventions of report format are universal. These conventions have developed over a long period of time; and they represent a consensus about what parts are necessary to a good research report and how they should be ordered. . Each report-writing book suggests its own unique format, and every report writer has to pick and choose the parts and the order that work best for the project at hand. Many universities have in-house, suggested report formats, or writing guides that researchers should be aware of. This chapter has a few formats used in Stella Matutina College of Education, Chennai. Thus the suggested format given here is the basis for the discussion in this chapter, and a beginning point from which the writer can shape his or her own appropriate format. The report format is listed here and shown graphically in Exhibits 12.3 and 12.4.

How does the researcher decide on the appropriate level of formality? The general rule is to include all the parts needed for effective communication in the particular circumstances and no more. This factor relates to how far up in research the report is expected to go. The researcher's immediate supervisor needs a one page blueprint on how the investigation is to be done. However, if the study is for a big UNESCO project, the report will have to be structured to suit the requirements.

12.2.1 Major Sections of Research Reports

Research report typically contain four to six major sections. Always included are an introduction, a description of the procedures

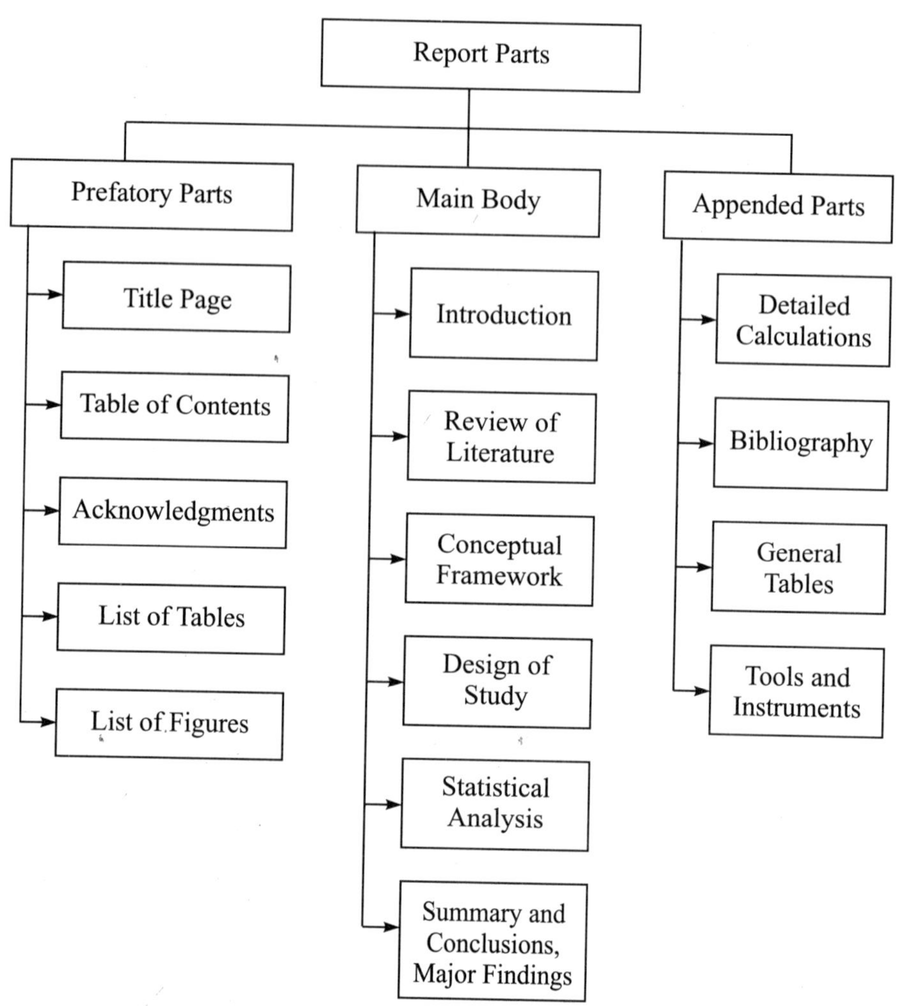

Exhibit 12.3: The make-up of report

used, a presentation of findings, conclusions. Often a review of the related literature is included. You may see an abstract or summary as part of the report, and sometimes an extensive bibliography.

These sections are indicated with headings or given as chapter titles in theses and dissertations. They are always labeled in journal articles and research documents. When you write reports, it is best to label these sections. If you read reports that are not so labeled, you can look for the main sections anyway, because they will be there, in accordance with convention.

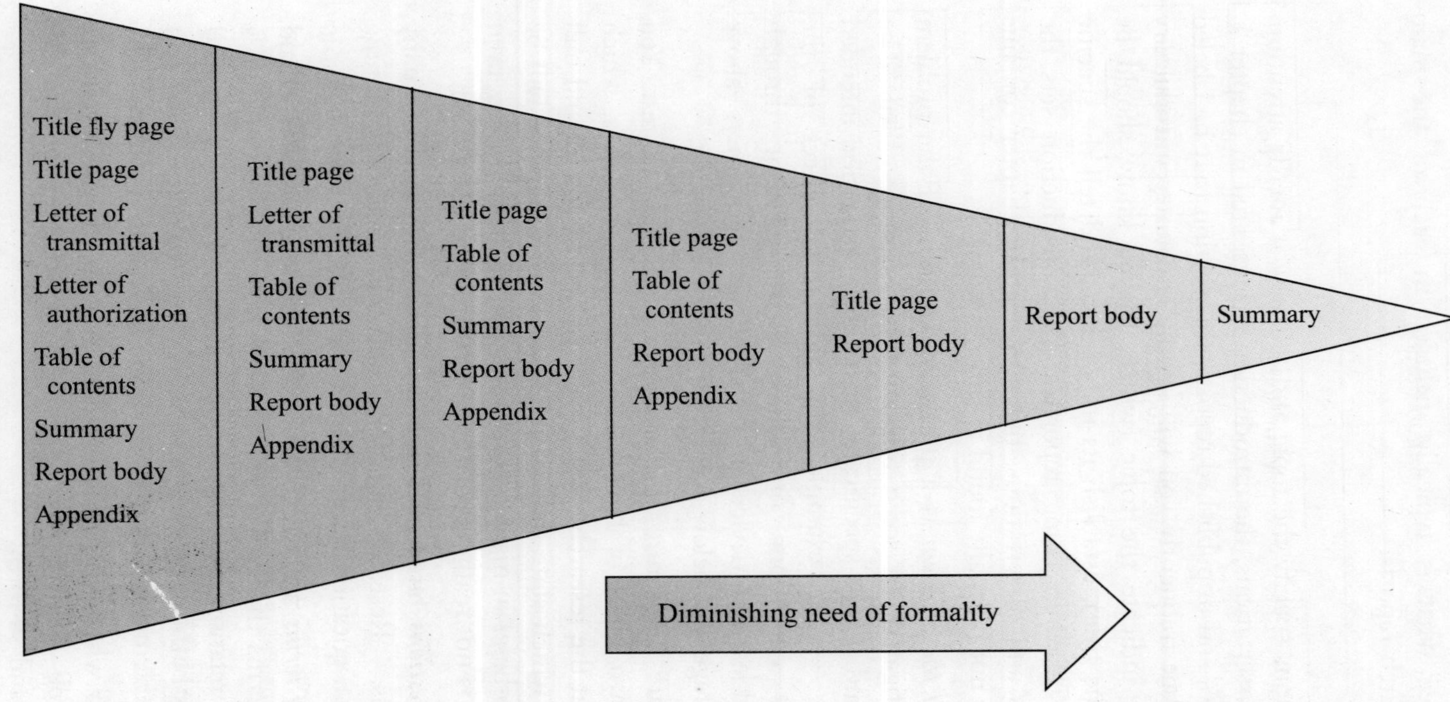

Exhibit 12.4: Adapting format to level of formality

Let us see what is typically included in each of the main sections of research reports.

Introduction

Introductions specify the topic and tell why it merits attention. In theses and dissertations, the introduction is presented in chapter 1. In journal articles and unpublished reports, this section may be labeled "Introduction,' but frequently you will simply encounter introductory paragraphs that indicate the topic (which, as you know, should be made clear in the title), establish its importance, and tell the specific purpose of the research being reported. The introduction sets the scene. In theses and dissertations, the introductory chapter contains additional items not normally found in short reports.

- *Statement of the problem* is a precise description of the problem being investigated. In some formats this is simply called "The Problem," and it tells specifically what the investigation intended to explore — for example, the differential effect of the motivational conditions on scholastic achievement through programmed learning devices on different types of learners -above average, average and below average-in the school setting.
- *Hypotheses* are conjectures the investigator intends to test. You remember two types of hypotheses: research hypotheses, which indicate what the researcher really believes, will be found; and null hypotheses, which state that no relationship or difference will be found. Hypotheses in many reports are stated in the null form, even though that is not really what the investigator expects to find.
- *Research questions* are used instead of hypotheses in many investigations. . Research questions are often organized in tune with the main questions, accompanied by a few sub-questions.
- *Definition of terms* are where you give the meanings you intend for certain terms that are central to your study. For example, in a study of the relationship between body weight and running speed of high school athletes, you would be expected to define what you mean by the terms "running speed" and "high school athletes".
- *Delimitations* where you tell the limits you set on your study, as concerns time span covered, people involved, sources to be investigated and so forth.

Review of Related Literature

You are expected to review literature related to your problem in order to determine three things

— whether studies already exist that are similar to what you propose to undertake

— whether existing research provides guidance or sheds further light on the problem and

— whether existing research provides a point of departure or a platform upon which the new research can build.

This requires that very early in the study you check literature resources. If you find related information, you organize it to bear as directly as possible on your research question or hypotheses.

This review of related literature is presented early in the report. In theses and dissertations, the review is often quite long and is presented in a separate chapter. If the review is short, it may be included in Chapter One.

— Journal articles and unpublished documents sometimes report, in introductory paragraphs, only a few pieces of related literature, as in the following illustration

In the 1990s, educational technology continued to rank high among research concerns. (Solachi, 1991, Srivastava, 1990). Moreover, Solachi (1990) found there existed a significant difference between urban higher secondary schools and rural higher secondary school in their utilizations of mass media devices.

Concern about discipline has several investigators to explore various discipline systems (Childers, 1989), training in discipline (Mc Math and Wilkerson, 1989), and...

There are no hard-and-fast rules for organizing related literature, but the following suggestions add to the persuasiveness of your report.

- Begin with the most general findings and end with the most specific. If you are studying school discipline, you would want to report studies showing that it is a widespread problem.
- Begin with older studies and move toward more recent studies. This shows lines of thought and refinement that have occurred over time.

- Group the literature within the categories you have identified in your research problem. If you are using research questions and sub-questions, a natural organization is to report general findings related to the main question and then specific findings related to each of the sub-questions. If you are conducting a historical study, you might group literature by years or decades; if a descriptive study, you might group by various topics you wish to describe; if research and development, you might group the reports according to processes or products you intend to develop.
- When you report what you consider to be especially significant studies, you should use an adjective that indicates your evaluation- for example, "***In an interesting study, Nagarajan (1985)***"... or "***Singh's(1977) controversial study...***"

Procedures or Method

In this major component of research reports (which may be labeled either "procedures" or "method"), you tell step by step what you did in your investigation. This section is usually Chapter 3 in theses and dissertations. Even if you read a report with no headings, you can find the section because convention requires that researchers outline the steps they followed in collecting and analyzing data.

Again, there is no prescribed method by which this recounting of procedures must be done, but the following are suggested to make your presentation more easily understood.

— In longer reports, and especially in theses and dissertations, begin by repeating the purpose of the study (for example, to explore the relationship between leadership styles and organizational health of effective schools). In short reports and articles this is not necessary.

— Describe the research design of your study. In this portion, you indicate hypotheses or questions; sources of information; people involved, and how they are selected; other important resources necessary to the study; instruments that were used, such as tests and questionnaires; and procedures for analyzing data. In theses and dissertations, the research design should be given in detail. In shorter reports, a brief description is sufficient.

— Divide the procedures into categories-for example, sample, measurement, data organization, data analysis. Then describe, step by step, what you did in each.

It is necessary that readers of your research be able to follow what you did. This allows criticism of your work (it is expected that others will ask questions of, or take exception to, the way you have conducted your investigation). It also permits your study to be replicated by someone.

Results or Findings

The next major section included in research reports is entitled either "results" or "findings". It is usually Chapter 4 in theses and dissertations. Because it is so important, it usually has a heading of some sort even in short reports.

In this section, you summarize and analyze the new information you have discovered. If your report is long, you may want to repeat the hypotheses or research questions, then show the analyses of data related to each.

Results are reported verbally and are usually enhanced with tables and figures. Tables are used to show rows and columns of numerical data, and often include the statistics involved in data analyses. Figures are used to illustrate ideas; and they include graphs, charts, drawings, computer printouts, and the like.

You should use tables and figures whenever they add clarity to what you are describing. Suppose you have investigated the preferences among B.A. (English) students for the writings of Rabindranath Tagore, R.K.Narayan and Amitav Ghosh., You could report verbally that out of a sample of 100 boys and 100 girls, so many of each preferred each of the writers; but by the time you did so, you would have a long paragraph whose information would be difficult for readers to take in as whole. You would do better to present the information in a table, as follows (the data in the table are fictitious):

Table 12. 1: Preferences among 200 B.A.(English Literature) students for the writings of Rabindranath Tagore, R.K.Narayan and Amitav Ghosh

	Tagore	Narayan	Ghosh	Total
Girls	42	38	20	100
Boys	17	34	49	100

You can see how neatly the information stands out when presented in tabular form.

On the other hand, when you wish to make graphic presentation of data that are not organized into rows and columns of numbers, you use figures to clarify the information. Any sort of graphic illustration can be called a figure. Bar and line graphs are among the most frequently used. You could use a bar graph to illustrate the comparative preferences of boys and girls for the writings of Rabindranath Tagore, R.K.Narayan and Amitav Ghosh. (In tables, the title is placed at the top; in figures, it may be placed either above or below the illustration.)

Verbal descriptions accompany charts and figures to ensure that readers understand correctly what is being shown. In your report, you would write:

Table 12.1 shows the preferences of boys and girls for the writings of the three authors. The difference between the two groups can be found using a Chi Square test.

To accompany the figure you might write:

The graph in Exhibit 12.5 illustrates the comparative preferences of boys and girls for the writings of the three authors. One can see the apparent preference among girls for the works of Tagore, and the apparent preference among boys for the works of Ghosh.

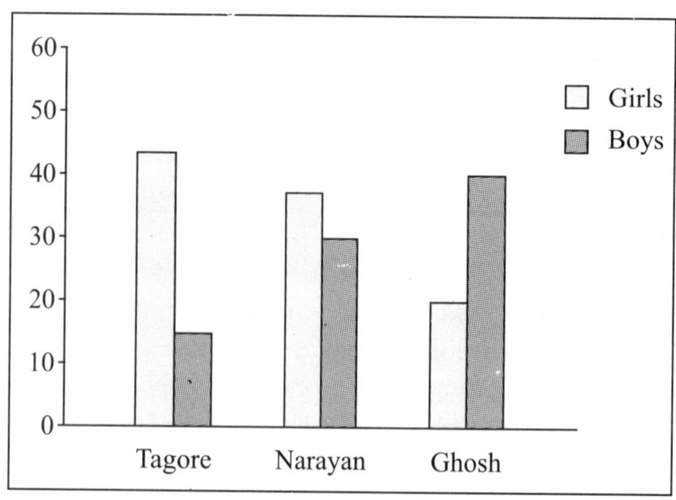

Exhibit 12.5: Preferences of 100 B.A. students for the writings of Tagore, Narayan and Ghosh

The information shown in tables and figures should be related to specific hypotheses or research questions set forth in the study. If hypotheses are used, they may at this point be either retained or rejected, based on data analysis. To retain hypotheses is to accept it as originally stated. To reject a hypothesis is to say it is not as originally stated.

It is also at this point that you decide on the answers to your research questions, if used in your study. In answering the questions you proceed as follows: Take each sub-question separately and select data related to it. Analyze the data logically (there are no formulas for this) and arrive at an answer you believe the data warrant.

In theses and dissertations, you would be obliged to present your data in sufficient detail so that other persons could apply their own logic toward answering the questions. And if you report your work in a short form such as a journal article, others might request sets of your data for further study.

Conclusions or Discussion

The next section of most research reports is that in which you present and discuss your conclusions. Sometimes the section is called "conclusions and recommendations," which is the case of Chapter 5 of most theses and dissertations. Sometimes it is called "findings" and sometimes "findings and implications".

In this final section, you at last have the opportunity to interpret, speculate on, and otherwise discuss the conclusions you have reached. This portion is often quite enlightening because it contains the thoughts of the person most intimately involved in seeking answers and exploring meanings and implications. Here you may discuss errors you inadvertently made, problems you encountered unexpectedly, your surprise at the findings and so forth.

More than anything else, it is the portion of the report that allows you to tell what you believe the findings mean, how they are to be interpreted, what they imply for education, or what they suggest for further research. It is the one place in the report where you are allowed to speculate a bit, to move a little beyond hard evidence and stringent logic.

Front and Back Material

Front and back material refer to materials that come before and after the body of the report. Theses and dissertations contain both. Typical front material includes:

- Title Page
- Certificate from the supervisor to sign with date
- Acknowledgement page
- Table of contents
- List of Tables
- List of Figures
- Abstract (Abstract)

Back material Includes

- Bibliography (complete list of references and other resources)
- Appendix or appendices (materials used or produced in the study, but which occupy too much space to be included in the body of the report)

Journal articles and other short reports typically have no front material (some present a short summary or abstract at the beginning of the article); and the back material consists, at most, of a list of the references cited in the report.

Style Guides

Specific directions have not been provided here for preparing front and back material, citing references, and presenting tables and figures. That is because each journal and each college and university has its own accepted style.

When preparing theses or dissertations, you are expected to follow the style guide approved by the institution through which the work is done. Some colleges and universities have prepared their own. Others have adopted existing stylebooks, of which the following are well known and widely used:

- *American Psychological Association (1983).* Publication manual of the American Psychological Association (3rd ed). Washington, D.C. (This is referred to as the APA style.)

- *Campbell, W., Ballou, S., and Slade, C.* Form and Style 6th ed. Boston: Houghton Mifflin, 1982 (This is referred to as Campbell.)
- *Modern Language Association. MLA Handbook for Writers of Research Papers*. New York:MLA, 1977 (This is referred to as the MLA style.)
- *University of Chicago. A Manual of Style*. 13th ed. Chicago: University of Chicago Press, 1982 (This is referred to as the Chicago Style.)
- Refer *Electronic Reference Formats* Recommended by the American Psychological Association for citing
  - e-mail communication
  - a web site
  - specific documents on a web site
  - articles and abstracts from electronic databases
  - web citations in text.

When submitting articles to journals for publication, the journal expects you to use their style. The journals will inform you of the required style or send you a style sheet on request; or you can examine published articles to determine the style required.

12.3 Summary

Students usually report their research in class papers, journal articles, master's theses, or doctoral dissertations. These reports are done in keeping with conventions concerning style and format. While differences exist among the types of reports-between dissertations and journal articles, for example-certain convention apply to all.

Acceptable style emphasizes descriptive titles, plain language, and use of third person, passive voice, and past tense. Consistency of wording and organization is stressed.

Formats are organized to include an introduction, a statement of the problem, hypotheses or research questions, review of the related literature, proceeding, results, and conclusions.

Reports often include front and back material. Examples of front materials are tables of contents abstracts; examples of back materials are bibliographies and appendices.

Theses and Dissertations	Articles and Papers
Title Page	**Title**
Certificate from Supervisor	
Acknowledgement Page	
Table of Contents	
List of Tables	
List of Figures	
Abstract (one page)	**Abstract paragraph (occasional)**
Introduction (Chapter 1)	**Introductory paragraph(s)**
identify problem	identify problem
discuss importance	discuss importance
present background	present background
state hypotheses/questions	state hypotheses/questions
define terms	
state delimitations	
Review of Literature (Chapter 2)	**Literature** may be reviewed very
general to specific	briefly in introduction
older to newer	
related to hypotheses or	
questions organized into sections	
Procedures (Chapter 3)	**Procedures section**
step-by-step description	summarize what was done, how
describe subjects (sample),	and when
instruments (tests, etc.,)	
research design and procedures	may organize by headings
followed organize report to	such as subjects, instruments,
parallel intent, questions	design and procedures.
Results (Chapter 4)	**Results (findings) section**
show data and analyses,	show data,analyses, and tests
with tests of significance	of significance
present in tables and figures	present in tables and figures
organize by hypotheses or	organize by hypotheses or
research questions	research questions
answer questions; test hypotheses	answer questions; test hypotheses
Summary, Conclusions (Chapter 5)	**Discussion and Summary section**
present writer's conclusions;	present writer's conclusions;
discuss implications	discuss implications
Bibiliography	**References**
list references cited and	list references cited
those used, but not cited	
Appendix or Appendics	
attach important material used or	
produced in the study, but too lengthy	
to be included in the body of the report.	

Exhibit 12.6: An outline of report formats and conventions

12.4 Effective Use of Graphic Aids

The person who first said, "a picture is worth a thousand words" probably had graphic aids in mind. Used properly, graphic (visual) aids can clarify complex points or emphasize a message, but if used improperly or sloppily, graphics can be distracting or misleading. The key to effective use of graphic aids is to make them an integral part of the text. The graphics should always be interpreted in the text. It does mean the key points should be pointed out and related to the discussion in progress in the text.

Several types of graphic aids may be useful in research reports, such as tables, charts, maps and diagrams. The discussion below will briefly cover the most common ones-tables and various sorts of charts. The researcher interested in other types should consult more specialized sources.

12.4.1 Tables

Tables are most useful for presenting numerical information, especially when several pieces of information have been gathered about each item discussed. Using figures allows the writer to point out significant features without getting bogged down in detail. The tables that should be included in the body of the report are relatively short summary tables. Comprehensive tables should be reserved for the appendix.

Each table should include:

- *Table number.* A table number allows for reference from the text to table. If there are many tables, a list of tables should be included just after the table of contents.
- *Title.* The title should indicate the contents of the table and be complete enough to be intelligible without the text. The table number and title are generally placed at the top, since the table is read from top down.
- *Banner head and stub head.* The banner head (or box head) contains the captions for the columns of the table, the stub head those for the rows.
- *Footnotes.* Any explanations or qualifications for particular figures or section should be given in footnotes.

- *Source.* If a table is based on material from a secondary source, not on new data generated by the project, the source should be acknowledged, usually below the table following the footnotes.

Table 12.2 presents a typical table from a survey research report. It shows a cross tabulation of the results of the survey responses.

Table 12.2: Table from a survey research report

Would you say you are enjoying your job more, less or about the same as you were five years ago?

	Overall	Headmasters	P.G.Trs.	Graduate	Secondary
More	52%	60%	55%	51%	44%
Less	19%	14%	18%	22%	24%
About the same	27%	24%	26%	26%	31%
Do not know	2%	2%	1%	1%	1%

Table 12.3 shows how data from a statistical test might be reported in table format.

Table 12.3: Chi-square test for 40 boys and 50 girls on science achievement test

	Below Average	**Above Average**
Boys	17	23
Girls	28	22
Chi Square = 1.62	df=1	
p>0.20		

12.4.2 Charts

Charts translate numerical information into visual form so that relationship may be easily grasped. The accuracy of the numbers is reduced to gain this advantage.

Each chart should include:

- *Figure number.* Charts (and other illustrative material) should be numbered in a series separate from tables. The number allows for easy reference from the text. If there are many figures, a list of them should be included after the table of contents.
- *Title.* The title should include the contents of the chart and be independent of the text explanation. The figure number and title are usually placed at the bottom of the figure.

Changing the visual Image Contracting or expanding vertical (amount) scale or horizontal (time) scale tends to change the visual picture

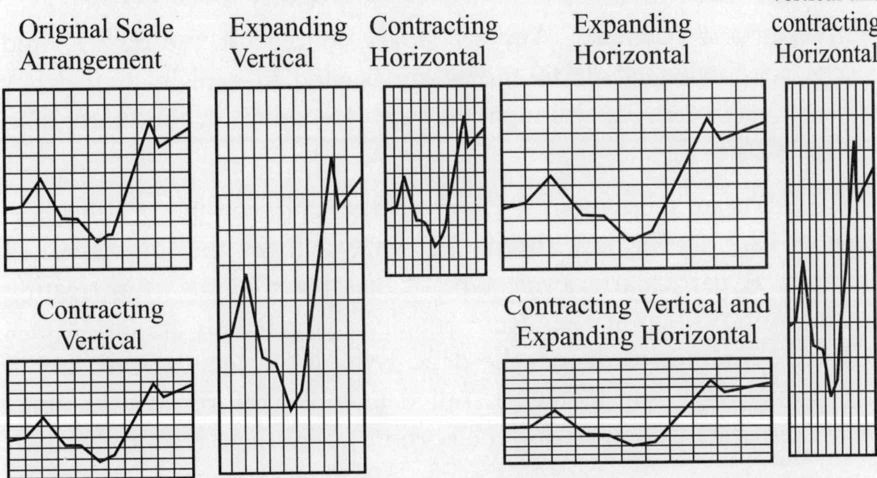

Exhibit 12.7: Distortion by altering scales

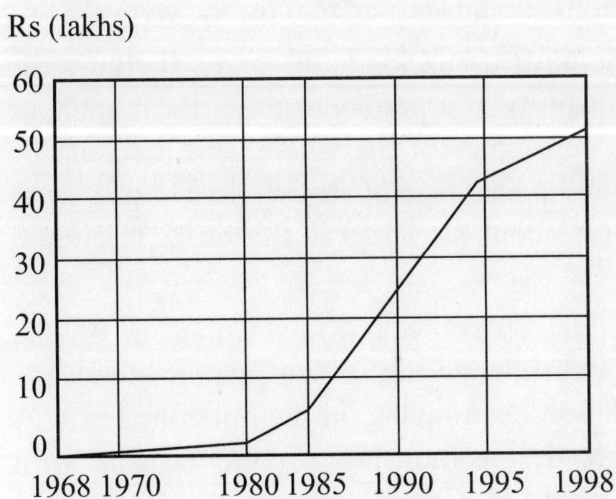

Exhibit 12.8: Distortion in change

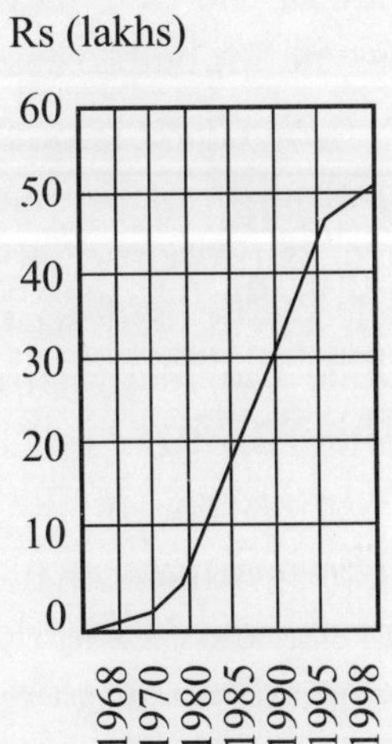

Exhibit 12.9: Distortion from treating unequal time intervals

- *Explanatory legends.* Enough explanation should be put on the chart to guide the reader without reference to the accompanying text. Such explanations would include labels for axes, scale numbers, a key to the different quantities being graphed and so on.
- *Source and Footnotes.* Any secondary source for the data should be acknowledged. If footnotes are needed to explain items, they may also be used, although they are less common for charts than for tables.

Charts are subject to distortion, whether unintentional or deliberate. Exhibit 12.7 shows how alternating scale changes the impression of the data. A particularly severe type of distortion comes from treating unequal intervals as if they were equal. This generally results from a deliberate attempt to distort the data. Exhibit 12.8 shows this sort of distortion, where some one attempted to make the rise on the chart more dramatic by compressing the portion where there is little change.

Another common distortion is to begin the vertical scale at some value larger than zero. Note in Exhibit 12.9 how this exaggerates the amount of change in the period covered. This kind of broken scale is often used in published reports of literacy movements. In this case it is assumed that the readers are mostly interested in the changes and are aware of the exaggeration of a broken scale. For most research reports this will not be the case. Graphs should start at zero on the vertical axis.

Pie Chart is one of the most useful kinds of charts. It shows the composition of some total quantity at a particular time. Each angle or "slice" is proportional to its percentage of the whole, and it should be labeled with its description and percentage of the whole. Do not try to include too many small slices-about six slices is the usual maximum (Exhibit 12.10).

Line Graph is a graphic aid showing the relationship of one variable with another. The dependent variable is generally shown on the vertical axis and the independent variable on the horizontal axis. A line graph is used to show the relationship of one variable with another. The dependent variable is generally shown on the vertical axis, and the independent variable is shown on the horizontal axis. The most common independent variable for such charts is time, but it is by no means the only one. Exhibit 12.11 depicts a simple line graph.

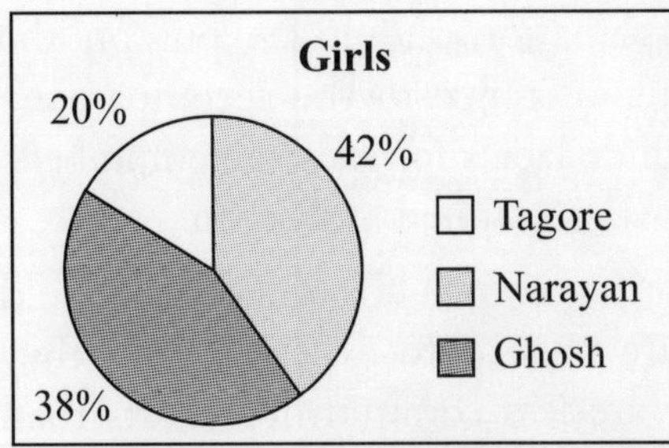

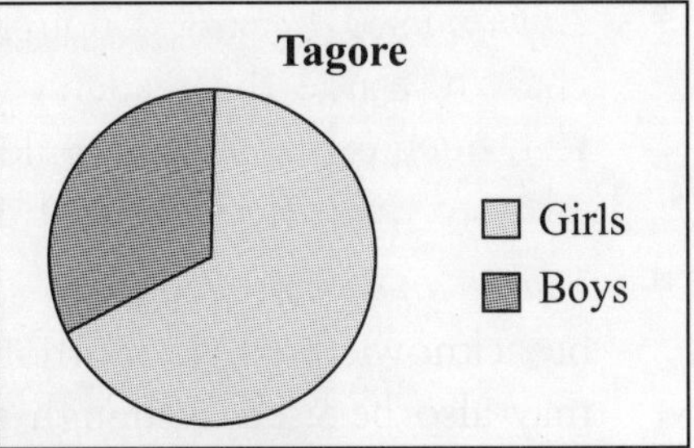

Exhibit 12.10: An author-wise distribution among sample of 100 girls

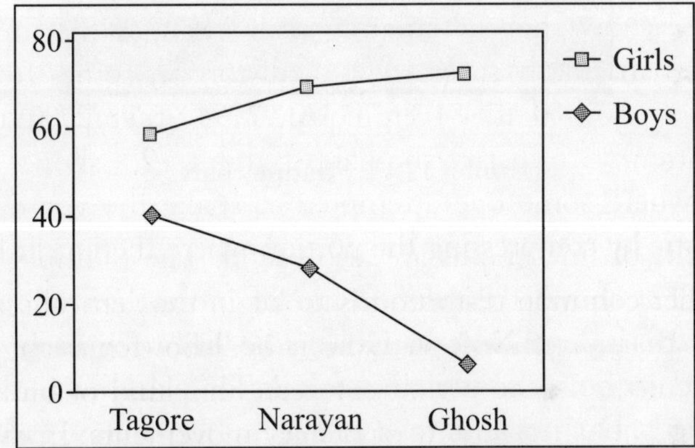

Exhibit 12.11: A simple line graph

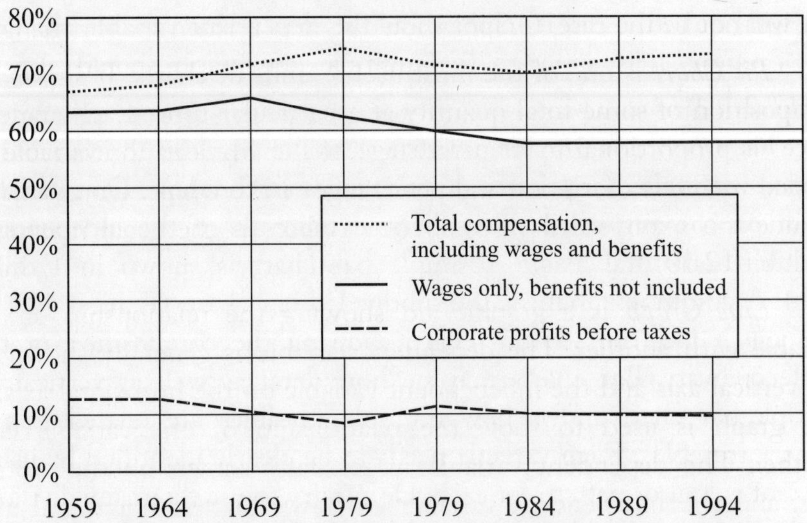

Exhibit 12.12: Compensation, wages, and corporate profits: their shares of national income

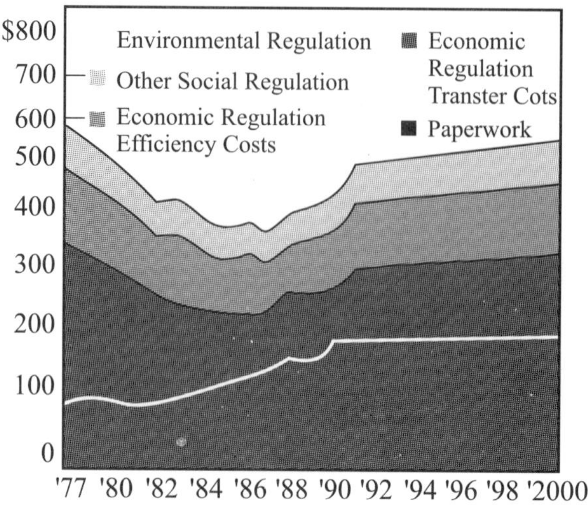

Exhibit 12.13: Stratum chart

Other variants of line graphs are also useful. The multiple line-graph (Exhibit 12.12) shows the relationship of more than one dependent variable to the independent variable. The lines for each dependent variable need to be in contrasting colours or patterns and should be clearly labeled. Do not try to squeeze in too many variables; this can quickly lead to confusion, not clarification. A second variation is the stratum chart (Exhibit 12.13), which shows the composition of a total quantity and its changes as the dependent variable changes. The cautions that apply to the multiple-line graph should also be observed here.

Bar Chart is a graphic aid that shows changes in the variable at discrete intervals. Bar Charts show changes in the dependent variable (again on the vertical axis) at discrete intervals of the independent variable (horizontal axis). A simple bar chart is shown in Exhibit 12.14. A common variant is the subdivided bar chart. (Exhibit 12.15). It is much like the stratum chart, showing the composition of the whole quantity. Bar charts may be horizontal as well as vertical. A multiple-bar chart shows how multiple variables are related to the primary variables. Each variable needs to be clearly identified by using different colour or pattern for each. Do not try to use too many divisions or dependent variables. Too much detail obscures the essential advantage of charts, which is to make relationships easy to visualize.

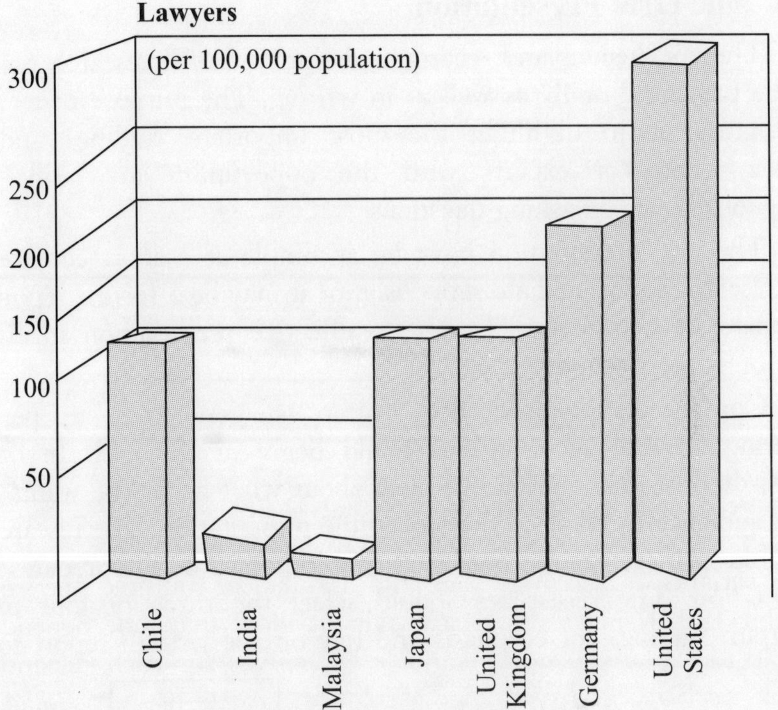

Exhibit 12.14: Sample bar chart

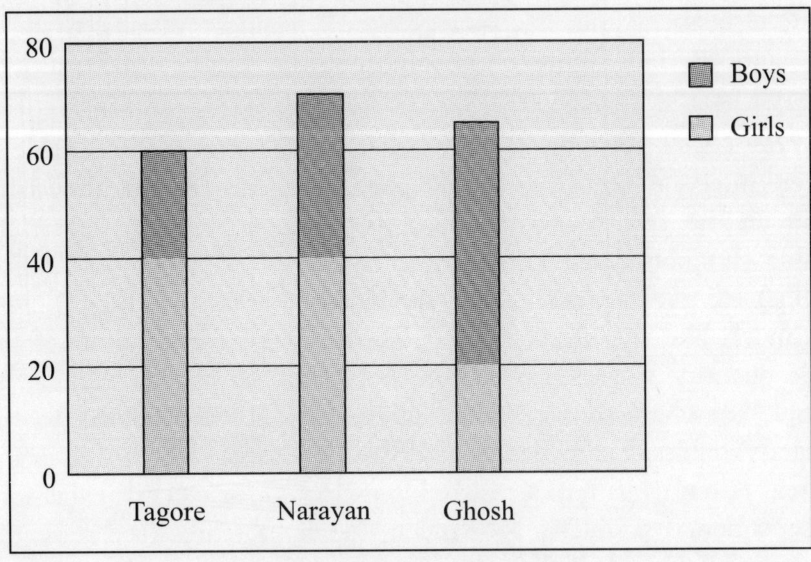

Exhibit 12.15: Subdivided bar chart

12.5 The Oral Presentation

The conclusions and recommendations of most research reports will be presented orally as well as in writing. The purpose of an oral presentation is to highlight the most important findings and to provide clients or experts with the opportunity to clarify any ambiguous issues by asking questions

The oral presentation must be as simple as a short conference with researcher's immediate supervisor, or it may be a formal report to the board of examiners. The key to effective presentation in either situation is preparation.

Communication specialists often suggest that a person preparing an oral presentation should begin at the end. In other words, the researcher should be clear about what he or she wants the target audience to know at the end of the presentation. The researcher should keep these desired outcomes in mind as he or she prepares the presentation. The researcher should select the three or four most important findings for emphasis and rely on the written report for a

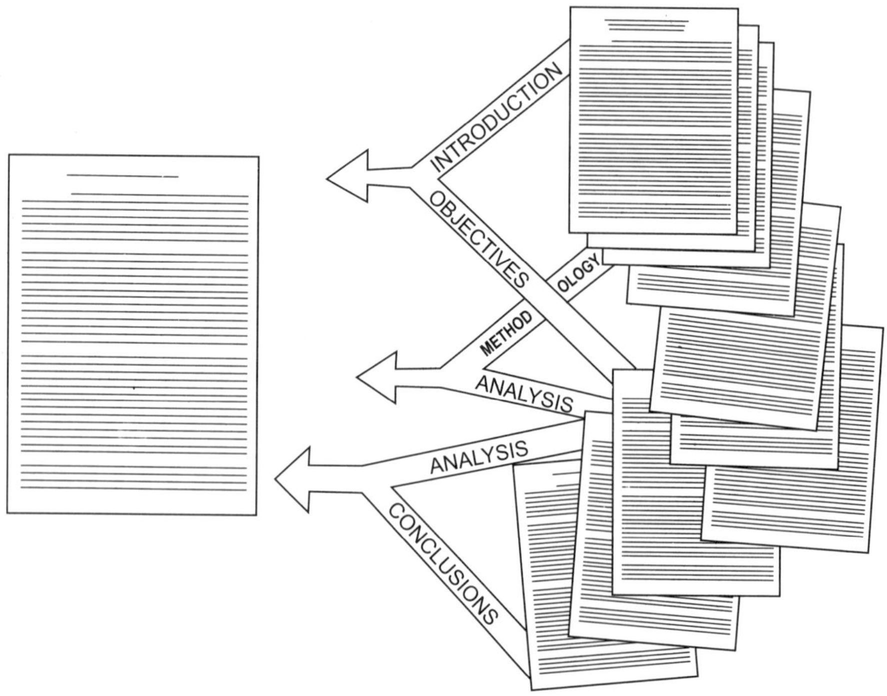

Exhibit 12.16: Condensing full report into summary

full summary. The researcher needs to be ready to defend the results. S/he should be able to defend the thesis in a confident and competent manner without being defensive. Remember that even the most reliable, valid research project is worthless if the audience who must act on its results are not convinced of its importance.

REFERENCES

- Anderson, J., Durston H. Berry and Poole, Millicent. Thesis and Assignment Writing. Wiley Eastern University Press. New Delhi. 1985.
- Gan, E. A practical writing guide. Education Forum. 67, 284-285.
- Gutner, Elliot S.M. and Cordasco, Francesco. Research and Report Writing: New York. Barnes and Noble Inc. 1956.
- Klausmeier, H.J. Research writing in education and psychology – from planning to publication: A practical handbook. Springfield, IL: Charles C. Thomas. 2001.
- Lester, J.D. and Lester, J.D. Jr. Writing research papers: A complete guide. 10th ed. New York: Longman. 2002
- Madson, David. Successful Dissertations and Theses – A Guide to Graduate Student Research from Proposal to Computer. Jossey-Bass Higher and Adult Education Series. Nov. 1991.
- Meloy, J.M. Writing the qualitative dissertation. 2nd ed. Mahwah, NJ-Lawrence Erlbaum. 2001.
- Sternberg, David. How to Complete and Survive a Doctoral Dissertation. New York: St. Martin's Press, 1981.
- Veldman, David J. Writing a Thesis or Dissertation Proposal in the Behavioural Sciences. Fort Worth, Tex. American Publishing Co. 1971.

WEB RESOURCES

- http://www.learnerassociates.net/dissthes/

  This guide has been created to assist graduate students in thinking through the many aspects of crafting, implementing and defending a thesis or dissertation.
- http://web.mit.edu/writing/Writing_Types/writingthesis.html

  MIT Online Writing and Communication Center

❖ ❖ ❖

A

abstract level In theory development, the level of knowledge expressing a concept that exists only as an idea or a quality apart from an object.

alternative hypothesis A statement indicating the opposite of the null hypothesis.

analysis of covariance (ANCOVA) A statistical procedure that improves the precision of a research design by employing a preexisting variable that is correlated with the dependent variable

analysis of dependence A collective term to describe any multivariate statistical technique that attempts to explain or predict the dependent variable on the basis of two or more independent variables.

analysis of interdependence A collective term to describe any multivariate statistical technique that attempts to give meaning to a set of variables or seeks to group things together.

analysis of variance (ANOVA) Analysis of the effects of one treatment variable on an interval scaled or ratio scaled dependent variable; a technique to determine if statistically significant differences in means occur between two or more groups.

area sampling Cluster sampling within a specified area or region; a probability sampling design.

attitude rating scale Measures used to rate attitudes, such as Likert scale, semantic differential and Stapel scale.

average deviation A measure of dispersion that is computed by calculating the deviation score of each observation value, summing up the deviation scores, and dividing by the sample size.

B

backward linkage A term implying that the late stages of the research process will have an influence on the early stages.

bar chart A graphic aid that shows changes in a variable in discrete intervals.

bias Any error that creeps into the data. Biases can be introduced by the researcher, the respondent, the questionnaire, the sample and so on.

bibliography A listing of books, articles, and other relevant materials, alphabetically arranged according to the last name of the authors, referencing the titles of their works, and indicating where they can be located.

biserial r An estimate of the product moment r to be expected for the given data when certain assumptions like (1) continuity in the dichotomized trait (2) normality of distribution (3) a large N and (4) a split that is not too extreme.

bivariate data analysis A type of data analysis and hypothesis used in the testing when the investigation concerns simultaneous investigation of two variables using tests of differences or measures of association between two variables at a time.

bivariate statistics Tests of differences or measures of association between two variables at a time.

box and whisker plot A graphic device that represents central tendencies, percentiles, variability and frequency distributions.

C

canonical correlation analysis A technique used to determine the degree of linear association between two sets of variables, each consisting of several variables.

case study An indepth study of one or a few cases

case study method An exploratory research technique that intensively investigates one or a few situations similar to the researcher's problem situation.

categorical variable Any variable that has a limited number of distinct values.

category scale An attitude scale consisting of several response categories to provide the respondent with alternative ratings

causal research Research conducted to identify cause and effect relationships among variables when the research problem has already been narrowly defined.

chart A graphic aid used to translate numerical information into visual form so that relationships may be easily understood.

chi-square test (χ^2) A non-parametric test of hypothesis for variables organized in a bivariate table.

classification data Personal information or demographic details of the respondents such as age, marital status, and educational level.

cluster analysis A numerical technique for grouping objects or variables on the basis of similarity.

cluster sampling An economically efficient sampling technique in which the primary sampling unit is not the individual element in the population but a large cluster of elements.

coefficient of correlation (r) A statistical measure of the covariation,or association, between two variables.

coefficient of determination (r^2) A measure of that portion of the total variance of a variable that is accounted for by knowing the value of another variable.

coefficient of multiple determination (R^2) In multiple regression, the percentage of the variance in the dependent variable that is explained by the variation in the independent variables.

coefficient of partial regression The percentage of the variance in the dependent variable that is explained by a single independent variable, with the other independent variables held constant.

communality In factor analysis, a measure of the percentage of a variable's variation that is explained by the factors.

concept A generalized idea about a class of objects, attributes, occurrences or processes.

concurrent validity A type of criterion validity whereby a new measure correlates with a criterion measure taken at the same time.

confidence interval estimate A specified range of numbers within which a population mean is expected to lie.

confidence level A percentage or decimal value that tells how reliant a researcher can be about being correct; the usual accepted level of social science research is 95%.

confounded variable A multidimensional variable, a variable embedded

constant error An error that occurs in the same experimental condition every time the basic experiment is repeated.

constant sum rating scale A scale where the respondents distribute a fixed number of points across several items.

construct validity The ability of a measure to confirm a network of related hypotheses generated from a theory based on the concepts.

content analysis A research technique for the objective, systematic and quantitative description of the manifest content of communication.

content validity Establishes the representative sampling of a whole set of items that measures a concept, and reflects how well the dimensions and elements thereof are delineated.

contingency coefficient provides a measure of correlation when each of the two variables under study has been classified into two or more categories.

contingency table The results of a cross tabulation of two variables, such as answers to two survey questions.

continuous variable A variable that has an infinite number of possible values.

control group A group of subjects who are exposed to the control condition in an experiment – that is, they are subjects not exposed to the experimental treatment.

controlled variable Any exogenous or extraneous variable that could contaminate the cause and effect relationship, but the effects of which can be controlled through the process either of matching or randomization.

convenience sampling The sampling procedure used to obtain those units or people most conveniently available.

correlation coefficient (r) same as coefficient of correlation

correlation matrix The standard form for reporting correlational matrix

criterion validity The ability of some measure to correlate with other measures of the same construct.

criterion variable The variable of primary interest to the study, also known as the dependent variable.

critical values The values that lie exactly on the boundary of the region of rejection.

cross-sectional study A study (usually a survey) conducted at a single point in time with a sample thought to be a representative cross-section of the population in terms of relevant variables (age, sex, education etc..) to answer the research question

cross-tabulation A tabulation or table showing the relationship between two or more variables by presenting all combinations of categories of variables (also called contingency table)

cumulative percentage A percentage that has increased by successive additions.

D

data The information gathered and analysed in a study.

data conversion The process of changing the original form of the data to a format suitable to achieve the research objectives.

data entry The process of transferring data from a research project to computers.

data processing error A category of administrative error that occurs because of incorrect data entry, incorrect computer programming and the like.

deductive reasoning The logical process of deriving a conclusion about a specific instance based on a known general premise or something known to be true

degrees of freedom (d.f.) The number of constraints or assumptions needed to calculate a statistical term.

dependence method Any multivariate statistical technique used to explain the behaviour of one or more dependent variables on the basis of two or more independent variables.

dependent variable A variable that is to be predicted or explained

descriptive analysis The transformation of raw data into a form that will make them easy to understand and interpret; rearranging, ordering, manipulating data to provide descriptive information.

descriptive research Research designed to describe characteristics of a population or a phenomenon

descriptive statistics Statistics used to describe or summarise information about a population or sample.

dichotomous scale Scale used to elicit a Yes/No response, or an answer to two different aspects of a concept.

direct observation A straightforward attempt to observe and record what naturally occurs.

direct relationship A positive relationship; a relationship in which an increase in the value of one variable is accompanied by an increase in the value of the other variable, and a decrease by a decrease.

directional hypothesis An educated conjecture as to the direction of the relationship or differences among variables, which could be positive or negative, or more or less respectively.

discrete variable A non-continuous variable containing discrete categories with clear boundaries between categories (for example, male and female)

discriminant analysis A statistical tool for determining linear combinations of independent variables that show large differences in group means. The intent is to predict the probability of objects belonging to two or more mutually exclusive categories based on several independent variables.

discriminant validity The ability of some measure to have a low correlation with measures of dissimilar concepts.

disproportional stratified sample A stratified sample in which the sample size for each stratum is allocated according to analytical considerations.

distorter variable A third variable that distorts the real relationship between two variables so that the observed relationship is not the real one.

double barrelled question A survey question that is really two distinct questions disguised as one.

E

empirical level Level of knowledge that is verifiable by experience or observation.

equivalent form method A method of measuring the correlation between alternative instruments, designed to be as equivalent as possible, administered to the same group of subjects.

error checking The final stage of the coding process, during which codes are verified and corrected as necessary.

ethnography Literally the study of culture; a term traditionally used for anthropological observation of primitive cultures, now applied to observation in general.

ethnomethodology The study of the methods used in everyday, commonplace, routine social activity.

evaluation research Research that seeks to determine how successful applied social programmes have been (for example, literacy programmes)

exogenous variable A variable that exerts an influence on the cause and effect relationship between two variables in some way, and needs to be controlled.

experiment A research method in which conditions are controlled so that one or more variables can be manipulated in order to test a hypothesis.

experimental design A study design in which the researcher might create an artificial setting, control some variables, and manipulate the independent variable to establish cause and effect relationships.

experimental group In an experiment, the group to which the experimental stimulus is given, in contrast to the control group, which is an identical group but receives nothing (or a placebo).

experimental treatment An alternative manipulation of the independent variable being investigated.

experimenter bias An effect on an experimenter's results caused by the experimenter's presence, actions or comments.

exploratory research Initial research conducted to clarify and define the nature of a problem.

ex-post-facto experiment A quasi-experimental design conducted after the experimental stimulus has occurred; thus, the experimenter cannot introduce the test stimulus, but can control (but often only statistically) extraneous factors.

extraneous variable An uncontrolled variable (i.e a variable not manipulated by the experimenter) that may have a significant influence upon the dependent variable.

external criticism Establishes the genuineness and authority of data.

external validity The degree to which a measure is valid when generalized to other populations.

F

F statistic A test statistic that measures the ratio of one sample variance to another sample variance, such as the variance between groups to the variance within groups.

F-test A procedure used to determine if there is more variability in the scores of one sample than in the scores of another sample.

face validity Professional agreement that a scale logically appears to accurately measure what it is intended to measure.

factor analysis A statistical technique for determining the existence of a set of latent dimensions underlying a set of interrelations. Its general purpose is to summarise the information contained in a large number of variables into a smaller number of factors.

factor loading A measure of the importance of a variable in measuring a factor; a means for interpreting and labeling a factor.

factor score A number that represents each observation's calculated value on each factor in a factor analysis.

factorial design An experimental design that investigates the interaction of two or more independent variables.

field study A study conducted in the natural setting with a minimal amount of researcher interference with the flow of events in the situation.

follow up A letter or postcard reminding a respondent to return the questionnaire.

forced choice scale A fixed alternative rating scale that requires respondents to choose one of the fixed alternatives.

forward linkage A term implying that the early stages of the research process will influence the design of the later stages.

frequency distribution A set of data organized by summarizing the number of times a particular value of a variable occurs.

frequency table A simple tabulation that indicates the frequency with which respondents give a particular answer.

G

goodness of measures Attests to the reliability and validity of measures

graphic aid A picture or diagram used to clarify a complex point or to emphasize a message.

graphic rating scale A measure of attitude consisting of a graphic continuum that allows respondents to rate an object by choosing any point on the continuum.

H

halo effect A rating error in which the general impression of the respondent (perhaps as gained from the respondent's answer to a previous question) leads the rater to give a biased rating.

Hawthorne effect An unintended effect on the results of a research experiment caused by the subjects knowing that they are participants.

historical criticism A systematic data evaluation of the evidence required by historical research.

historical research A procedure supplementary to observation in which the researcher seeks to test the authenticity of the reports or observation made by others

history effects A threat to the internal validity of the experimental results, when events unexpectedly occur while the experiment is in progress and contaminate the cause and effect relationship.

hypothesis A testable statement; hypotheses are generally either derived from a theory or from direct observation of data. Hypotheses are often bivariate.

hypothesis testing A means of testing if the if-then statements generated from the theoretical framework hold true when subjected to rigorous examination.

hypothetical construct A variable that is not directly observable but is measured through an indirect indicator, such as verbal expression or overt behaviour.

I

independent variable A variable that is expected to influence the dependent variable. Its value may be changed or altered independent of any other variable.

inductive reasoning The logical process of establishing a general proposition on the basis of observation of particular facts.

inferential statistics Statistical analysis in which sample data is used to make an inference concerning the population from which the sample was drawn.

information A body of facts that are in a format suitable for decision making.

instrument A data collection form such as a questionnaire or other measuring device.

interaction effect The influence on a dependent variable by combinations of two or more independent variables

internal criticism determines if the contents of a document are accurate.

internal validity Validity determined by whether an experimental treatment was the sole cause of changes in a dependent variable.

interpretation The process of making inferences and drawing conclusions concerning the meaning and implications of a research investigation.

interquartile range The part of a data distribution between the 25th and 75th percentiles; also called the midspread.

interval scale A level of measurement that indicates not only rank order, but also the amount of distance between each rank on the variable being measured.

intervening variable A variable intermediate between an independent variable A and a dependent variable C so that A affects C only through B.

interviewer bias Bias in the response of subjects due to the influence of the interviewer.

item A question in an attitude scale

J

judgment sampling A non-probability sampling technique in which an experienced researcher selects the sample based upon some appropriate characteristic of the sample members.

K

Kendall's tau b A measure of association for ordinal variables organized in table format. Especially appropriate for square tables.

Kolmogorov Smirnov Test A non-parametric test of significance for the two sample cases with ordinal level variables.

Kruskal Wallis Test A test of significance of difference between sample means for the two sample cases with (1) ordinal level variables or (2) data based on an interval or ratio scale but for which the underlying distribution may not be normal.

L

ladder of abstraction Organisation of concepts in sequence from the most concrete and individual to the most general.

Latin square design A balanced two way classification scheme that attempts to control or block out the effect of two or more extraneous factors by restricting randomization with respect to row and column effects.

leading question A question that suggests or implies certain answers.

least squares method A mathematical technique for ensuring that the regression line will best represent the linear relationship between X and Y.

level of measurement The mathematical characteristics of a variable as determined by the measurement process. A major criterion for selecting statistical techniques.

Likert scale A measure of attitudes designed to allow respondents to indicate how strongly they agree or disagree with carefully constructed statements that range from very positive to very negative toward an attitudinal object.

line graph A graphic aid showing the relationship of one variable to another. The dependent variable is generally shown on the vertical axis and the independent variable on the horizontal axis.

linear relationship A relationship between variables that when graphed, appears to be a straight line.

literature review The documentation of a comprehensive review of the published work from secondary sources of data in the areas of specific interest to the researcher.

longitudinal study A study conducted over time, in contrast to a cross-sectional study conducted at one point in time, to answer a research question.

M

main effect The influence on a dependent variable by each independent variable (separately)

manipulation How the researcher exposes the subjects to the independent variable to determine cause and effect relationships in experimental designs.

Mann-Whitney U A non-parametric test of significance for the two sample case with ordinal level variables.

matching A procedure for assignment of subjects to groups; it ensures each group of respondents is matched on the basis of pertinent characteristics.

maturation effect An effect on the results of a research experiment caused by changes in the experimental subjects over time.

mean (X) A measure of central tendency; the arithmetic average.

measures of association Statistics that summarise the strength and direction of the relationship between variables.

measure of central tendency Descriptive statistics of a data set such as the mean, median or mode.

measure of dispersion The variability in a set of observations, represented by the range, variance, standard deviation and the interquartile range.

median A measure of central tendency that is the mid point; the value below which half the value of the sample falls.

mode A measure of central tendency the value that occurs most often.

moderator variable A third variable that when introduced into an analysis, alters or has a contingent effect on the relationship between an independent variable and an dependent variable.

monadic rating scale Any measure of attitude that asks respondents about a single concept in isolation.

mortality effect Sample attrition that occurs when some subjects withdraw from an experiment before it is completed, thus affecting the validity of the experiment.

mortality The loss of research subjects during the course of the experiment, which confounds the cause and effect relationship.

multiple correlation A multivariate technique for examining the combined effects of more than one independent variable on a dependent variable.

multidimensional scaling A technique that measures attitudes about objects in multidimension space on the basis of respondents' judgments of similarity of objects.

multiple discriminant analysis A statistical technique for predicting the probability that an object will belong in one or two or more mutually exclusive categories (dependent variable), based on several independent variables.

multiple regression analysis An analysis of association in which the effect of two or more independent variables on a single interval scaled or ratio scaled dependent variable are investigated simultaneously.

multistage area sampling Sampling that involves using a combination of other probability sampling techniques.

multivariate analysis of variance (MANOVA) A statistical technique that provides a simultaneously significance test of mean difference between groups, made for two or more dependent variables.

multivariate data analysis Statistical methods that allow the simultaneous investigation of more than two variables.

N

nominal scale A scale in which the numbers or letters assigned to objects serve as labels for identification or classification; a measurement scale of the simplest type.

non-directional hypothesis An educated conjecture of a relationship between two variables, the directionality of which cannot be guessed.

non-parametric statistics Statistics that do not assume a normal distribution of the variables in the population. Most non-parametric statistics are used in analyzing data presented in the form of contingency tables.

non-probability sampling A sample in which the probability of selection of each case is not known.

non-respondent A person who is not contacted or who refuses to cooperate in a research project.

normal distribution A symmetrical bell shaped distribution that describes the expected probability distribution of many chance occurrences.

null hypothesis (H_0) A statement about a status quo, asserting that any change from what has been thought to be true will be due entirely to random error; a statement of"no difference"

numerical scale An attitude rating scale similar to a semantic differential except that it uses numbers instead of verbal descriptions as response options to identify response positions.

O

objectivity Interpretation of the results on the basis of the results of data analysis, as opposed to subjective or emotional interpretations.

observation The systematic recording of non-verbal as well as verbal behaviour and communication.

observed frequency (f_0) The cell frequencies actually observed in a bivariate table.

observer bias A distortion of measurement resulting from the cognitive behaviour or actions of the witnessing observer.

one group pre-test, post-test design A quasi-experimental design in which the subjects in the experimental group are measured before and after the treatment is administered but in which there is no control group.

one shot design A quasi-experimental design in which a single measure is recorded after the treatment is administered and there is no control group.

one tailed test A type of hypothesis test that can be used when (1) the direction of the difference can be predicted or (2) concern is focused on only one tail of the sampling distribution.

one way analysis of variance An application of ANOVA in which the effect of a single variable on another is observed.

open ended response question A question that poses some problem and asks the respondent to answer in his or her own words.

operational definition A definition that gives meaning to a concept by specifying the activities or operations necessary in order to measure it.; definition of a construct in measurable terms by reducing it from the level of abstraction through the delineation of its dimensions and elements.

oral presentation A spoken summary of the major findings, conclusions, and recommendations, given to the audience to provide them with the opportunity to clarify any ambiguous issues by asking questions.

ordinal scale A scale that arranges objects or alternatives according to their magnitudes.

P

paired comparison A measurement technique that involves presenting the respondent with two objects and asking the respondent to pick the preferred object. More than two objects may be presented, but comparisons are made in pairs.

panel study A longitudinal survey study in which the same respondents are reinterviewed at several points in time.

parallel form reliability That form of reliability which is established when responses to two comparable sets of measures tapping the same construct are highly correlated.

parametric statistical procedures Statistical procedures that use interval scaled or ratio scaled data and assume population or sampling distribution with normal distribution.

partial correlation A multivariate technique for examining a bivariate relationship while controlling other variables.

partial gamma (G_p) A statistic that indicates the strength of the association between two variables after the effects of a third variable has been removed.

path analysis A statistical technique for analyzing the direct and indirect relationships between a number of intervally measured variables, and representing them graphically in a path diagram.

Pearson's r (r) A measure of association for variables that have been measured at the interval ratio level.

percentage (%) A part of a whole expressed in hundredths.

percentile The point in a distribution of scores below which a specific percentage of the cases fall.

phi (ϕ) coefficient A chi-square based measure of association; a measure of strength of relationship for two dichotomized nominal variables presented in a two-by-two contingency table.

percentage distribution A frequency distribution onto a table (or graph) that summarises percentage values associated with particular values of a variable.

pie chart A graphic display device for nominal and ordinal level variables.

pilot study Any small scale exploratory research technique that uses sampling but does not apply rigorous standards.

point estimate An estimate of a population value in which a single value is specified.

point biserial Assumes that the variable which has been classified into two categories can be thought of as concentrated at two distinct points alongh a graduated scale or continuum.

pooled estimate of the standard error An estimate of the standard error based on the assumption that variance of both groups (populations) is equal.

population (universe) The total collection of all cases in which the researcher is interested; a complete group of entities sharing some common set of characteristics.

population distribution A frequency distribution of the elements of a population.

population element An individual member of a specific population.

population frame A listing of all the elements in the population from which the sample is drawn.

population parameter Variables in a population or measured characteristics of the population.

post-test In an experiment, a test to measure the values of the dependent variable after applying the experimental stimulus.

post-test only control group design An after only design in which the experimental group is tested after exposure to the treatment, and the control group is tested at the same time without having been exposed to the treatment, no pre-measure is taken.

predictive validity A type of criterion validity whereby a new measure predicts a future event or correlates with a criterion measure administered at a later time.

pre-test In a survey, preliminary administration of a questionnaire to a small sample in order to identify and correct problematic items. In an experiment, a test to measure the values of the dependent variables before applying the experimental stimulus.

pre-test, post-test control group design A true experimental design in which the experimental group is tested before and after exposure to the treatment, and the control group is tested at the same time twice without being exposed to the experimental treatment.

primary data Data gathered and assembled specifically for the research project on hand.

primary sampling unit (PSU) A unit selected in the first stage of sampling.

probability distribution The organization of probability values associated with particular values of a variable into a table (or graph).

probability sampling A sampling technique in which every member of the population has a known, nonzero probability of selection.

problem definition The crucial first stage in the research process – determining the problem to be solved and the objectives of the research.

proportion The percentage of population elements that successfully meet some criterion.

proportional stratified sample A stratified sample in which the number of sampling units drawn from each stratum is in proportion to the population size of that stratum.

proposition A statement concerned with the relationships among concepts.

purposive sample A non-probability sampling procedure in which the researcher uses his or her judgment to select those respondents that best meet the needs of the study.

Q

qualitative study Research involving analysis of data/information that is descriptive in nature and not readily quantifiable.

qualitative variable Sometimes called 'categorical variables'; is measured on a nominal scale.

quantitative variable is measured on an ordinal, interval or ratio scale.

quartiles The points in a distribution of scores that divide the distribution into quarters.

quasi experimental design An experimental design that fails to control adequately loss of external or internal validity.

questionnaire A preformulated written set of questions to which the respondent records the answers, usually within rather closely delineated alternatives.

quota sampling A non-probability sampling procedure that ensures that certain characteristics of a population sample will be represented to the exact extent that the investigator desires.

R

random assignment The use of a chance procedure to assign subjects to treatments.

random error An error in which repetition of the basic experiment sometimes favours one experimental condition and sometimes the other on a chance basis.

random sampling error The difference between the result of a sample and the result of a census conducted using identical procedures; a statistical fluctuation that occurs because of chance variations in the element selected for a sample.

random selection The use of a chance procedure to select a sample from a population.

randomization A procedure in which the assignment of subjects and treatments of groups is based on chance.

randomized block design (RBD) An extension of the completely randomized design in which a single extraneous variable that may affect test units" response to the treatment has been identified and the effects of this variable are isolated by being blocked out.

range (R) The highest score minus the lowest score

ranking A measurement task that requires that the respondent rank order a small number of activities, events, or objects on the basis of overall preference or some characteristic of the stimulus.

rating A measurement task that requires the respondent to estimate the magnitude of a characteristic or quality that an object possesses.

ratio scale A scale having absolute rather than relative quantities and possessing an absolute zero, where there is an absence of a given attribute.

region of rejection An area under a curve with values that are very unlikely to occur if the null hypothesis is true but relatively probable if the alternative hypothesis is true.

regression (bivariate) analysis A technique that attempts to predict the values of a continuous, interval scaled or ratio scaled dependent variable from the specific values of the independent variable.

reliability The degree to which measures are free from error and therefore yield consistent results.

report format The general plan of organization for the parts of a written or oral research report.

research design A master plan specifying the methods and procedures for collecting and analyzing the needed information.

research follow up Recontacting of decision makers and/or clients after they have had a chance to read a research report.

research hypothesis (H_1) A statement that contradicts the null hypothesis. The specific form varies from test to test.

research methodology A discussion within the body of a research report of the research design, data collection methods, sampling techniques, field work procedures and data analysis efforts.

research objective The purpose of the research, expressed in measureable terms; the definition of what the research should accomplish.

research project A specific research investigation; a study that completes or is planned to follow the stages in the research process.

research proposal A written statement of the research design that includes a statement explaining the purpose of the study and a detailed, systematic outline of a particular research methodology.

research report A presentation of research findings, directed to a specific audience to accomplish a specific purpose.

residual The difference between the actual value of the dependent variable and the estimated value of the dependent variable in the regression equation.

respondent The person who answers questions in a survey.

respondent error A classification of sample biases resulting from some respondent action or inaction such as non-response or response bias.

response bias Survey error that occurs when respondents tend to answer questions in a certain direction. Examples of response biases are acquiescence bias, extremity bias, interviewer's bias, auspices bias, and social desirability bias.

rotation In factor analysis changing of geometric axis that represents the factors so as to contemplate a new problem solution having fewer or more factors.

Runs test A non-parametric test of significance for the two sample cases with ordinal level variables.

S

sample A sub-set or some part of a larger population.

sample bias A persistent tendency for the results of a sample to deviate in one direction from the true value of the population parameter.

sample distribution A frequency distribution of the elements of a sample.

sample selection error An administrative procedural error caused by improper selection of a sample, thus introducing bias.

The size of a sample; the number of observations or cases specified by (1) the estimated variance of the population (2) the magnitude of acceptable error (3) the confidence level.

sample statistics Variables in a sample or measures computed from sample data.

sample survey Formal term for survey; it indicates that the purpose of contacting respondents is to obtain a representative sample of the target population.

sampling The process of using a small number of items or parts of a larger population to make conclusions about the whole population.

sampling distribution A theoretical probability distribution of all possible samples of a certain size drawn from a particular population.

sampling frame The list of elements from which a sample may be drawn; also called working population.

sampling frame error Error that occurs when certain sample elements are not listed or available and are not represented in the sampling frame.

sampling interval The number of population elements between units selected for the sample.

sampling unit A single element or group of element subject to selection in the sample.

scale Any series of items that are progressively arranged according to value or magnitude; a series into which an item can be placed according to its quantification.

Techniques or procedures used to analyse empirical evidence in an attempt to confirm or disprove prior conceptions.

search engine Software programme designed to search and locate information through 'keywords', typically in documents on the World Wide Web

secondary data Data that has been previously collected for some purpose other than the one at hand.

secondary data analysis Preliminary review of data collected for another purpose to clarify issues in the early stages of a research effort.

secondary sampling unit A unit selected in the second stage of sampling.

selection effect A sample bias resulting in differential selection of respondents for the comparison groups.

semantic differential scale An attitude measure consisting of a series of seven hyphen points bipolar rating scales, allowing response to a concept.

sign test A non-parametric technique used when the same people are used in two experiments making for related samples rather than independent ones, wherein a test for the difference between the groups before and after the test; can also be used to determine if there are differences about the median.

significance level The critical probability in choosing between the null and alternative hypotheses; the probability level that is too low to warrant support of the null hypothesis.

simple correlation coefficient A statistical measure of the covariation or association between two variables.

simple random sampling A sampling procedure that assures each element in the population an equal chance of being included in the sample.

slope The inclination of a regression line as compared to a base line, rise (vertical distance) over run (horizontal distance).

snowball sampling A sampling procedure in which initial respondents are selected by probability methods and additional respondents are obtained from information provided by the initial respondent.

software Technology that is capable of designing programmes to meet the different computing needs of individuals and institutions.

Solomon four group design A true experimental design that combines both the pre-test, post-test with control group and the post-test only with control group designs, thereby providing a means for controlling the interactive testing effect and other sources of extraneous variation.

Spearman's rho (p) A measure of association for ordinal variables that are in continuous format.

split half reliability A method of measuring the degree of internal consistency by checking one half of the results of a set of scaled items against the other half; the correlation coefficient between one half of the items measuring a concept and the other half.

spurious relationship An apparent relationship between two variables that is not authentic but appears authentic because an elaboration analysis with a third variable has not yet been conducted.

stability of a measure The ability of the measure to repeat the same results over time with low vulnerability to changes in the situation.

standard deviation (s or σ) The square root of the squared deviations of the scores around the mean divided by N. The most commonly used measure of dispersion, s represents the standard deviation of a sample, and s represents the standard deviation of a population.

standard error of the proportion The standard deviation of the sampling distribution of the mean.

standardized normal distribution A normal curve with a mean of zero and a standard deviation of one. It is a theoretical probability distribution.

Stapel scale A scale that measures both the direction and intensity of the attributes of a concept.

static group design (intact group design) An after only design in which subjects in the experimental group are measured after being exposed to the experimental treatment, and the control group is measured without having been exposed to the experimental treatment; no pre-treatment measure is taken.

stratified sampling A probability sampling procedure in which sub-samples are drawn from simple random within different strata that are more or less equal on some characteristic.

subject A single member of the sample

survey A research technique in which information is gathered from a sample of people by use of a questionnaire or interview; a method of data collection based on communication with a representative sample of individuals.

synopsis A brief summary of the research study

systematic (non-sampling) error Error resulting from some imperfect aspect of the research design that causes response error or from a mistake in the execution of the research, error arising from sample bias, mistakes in recording responses, or non-responses from persons who were not contacted or who refused to participate.

systematic sampling A method of sampling by which the first case from a list of the population is selected by a random process and thereafter every kth case is selected.

T

t-distribution A distribution used to find the critical region for tests of sample means when N is small and s is unknown.

t-test A univariate hypothesis test using the t distribution rather than the z distribution. It is used when the population standard deviation is unknown and the sample size is small.

t-test for difference of means A techniques used to test the hypothesis that the mean scores on some interval scaled variable are significantly different for two independent samples or groups.

table A graphic aid used for presenting numerical information, especially when such information can be arranged in rows and columns.

tabulation The orderly arrangement of data in a frequency table or other summary format

target population The specific complete group relevant to the research project.

test of differences Investigation of a hypothesis that states that two (or more) groups differ with respect to measures on a variable.

test re-test reliability A procedure for assessing the reliability of a measure by comparing results of the measure at two or more points in time.

tetrachoric correlation Assumes that the two variables under study are essentially continuous and would be normally distributed if it were possible to obtain scores or exact measures and thus be able to classify both variables into frequency distribution.

theory A proposition or set of interrelated propositions that purport to explain a given social phenomenon.

Thurstone scaling An attitude scaling procedure in which judges rank proposed scale items in an attempt to construct an interval scale.

total variance In analysis of variance, the sum of within group variance and between group variance

true experimental designs In these designs the control group and the experimental groups are formed, and their equivalence established through randomization

Type I error In hypothesis testing in inferential statistics, the error made by rejecting a true null hypothesis.

Type II error In hypothesis testing in inferential statistics, the error made by failing to reject a false null hypothesis.

U

univariate One variable, as in univariate analysis, a univariate table

univariate data analysis A type of analysis that assesses the statistical significance of a hypothesis about a single variable.

V

validity The ability of a scale or measuring instrument to measure what it is intended to measure.

variable Anything that may assume different numerical or categorical values.

variance A measure of variability or dispersion. The square root is the standard deviation.

W

web site Site accessible on the Internet or Intranet, created by individuals and organizations for the purpose of sharing information

Wilcoxon signed ranks test A non-parametric test of significance which is used to test whether two independent groups have been drawn from the same population. with ordinal level variables.

within group variance Variances of scores within a group due to random error or individual difference.

Y

Y intercept The point where the regression line crosses the Y axis.

Z

Z scores Standard scores; the way scores are expressed after they have been standardized to the theoretical normal curve.

Z test A univariate hypothesis test using the standardized normal distribution, which is the distribution of Z.

Z test for difference of proportion A technique used to test the hypothesis that proportions are significantly different for two independent samples or groups.

Symbols

Symbol	Meaning
a	Point at which the regression line crosses the Y axis
AD	Average deviation
ANCOVA	The analysis of covariance
ANOVA	The analysis of variance
b	Slope of the regression line
df	degrees of freedom
f	Frequency
F	The F ratio
f_e	Expected frequency
f_o	Observed frequency
H_o	Null hypothesis
H_1	Research or alternative hypothesis
M_d	Median
M_o	Mode
N	Number of cases
%	Percentage
P	Proportion
Q	Interquartile range
r	Pearson's correlation coefficient for a sample
r^2	Coefficient of determination
R	Range
ρ	Spearman's rho for a sample
R^2	Multiple correlation coefficient
S	Sample standard deviation
S_x	Standard deviation of the sample distribution of means
SSB	The sum of squares between
SST	The total sum of squares
SSW	The sum of squares within

S^2	Sample variance
t	Student's t score
X	Any independent variable
$\overline{X}$	Mean of a sample
X_i	Any score in a distribution
Y	Any dependent variable
Y'	A predicted score on Y
Z scores	Standard scores

GREEK LETTERS

α	Probability of Type I error
β	Probability of Type II Error
μ	Mean of a population
σ	Population standard deviation
σ^2	Population variance
μ	Mean of the sampling distribution of means
ε	Summation of
x^2	Chi square statistic
ρ	Spearman's rho for a population

❖ ❖ ❖

Index